WASTING TIME
CONSTRUCTIVELY

◆

A GUIDE TO A BALANCED LIFE

PETER J. SOLOMON

ISBN: 978-0-578-20699-8 (hc)
ISBN: 978-0-578-20700-1 (ebook)

Library of Congress Control Number: 2019904429

Pink House, LLC
P. O. Box 4169,
East Hampton, NY 11937
917-399-6789

Rev. date: 04/12/2019

Contents

PART III

PART IV

To Susan Solomon, for inspiring me to write this memoir.

To my robust family, sprouting from my grandparents and parents.

To my loyal friends and colleagues with whom I have
had so much fun. Each has enriched my life.

PREFACE

My mother liked to complain that I remembered too much. She would, nevertheless, encourage me to regale her with tales of our family, our growing up and our present comings and goings.

My stories fill this memoir. The first story originates with my parents, who brought me into a cohesive family with living grandparents, in America and especially in New York. My 1938 birth was also timely, making me too young for the Depression, WWII, and Korea and too married for Vietnam.

My life is a testament to the help my family and many friends have given me, the importance of their support to my personal life and my business career. I thank Susan, in particular, for her help in tending to our large family and in getting this volume published. I thank our children and my brother, Richard, and his wife, Ann, and their families for the robust life we enjoy and the love, not always uncritical, that they shower on me.

This book describes the journey of a nonhistoric life and its influence on people, institutions, and events. It is not intended as a recitation of successes. Rather, it is a chronicle of setbacks, of frustrations, and sometimes of failures. It is meant to point out that one has to persevere to achieve in every aspect of one's life and that family, friends, health, a sense of humor, and luck are powerful allies.

I want to acknowledge my deceased oldest friend, Marty Gross, and my business school roommate, John McCarter, who refreshed my memory, and Joshua Solomon for his usual good judgment. Other friends, such as Ken Schuman, Diane Coffey, Frank Strawbridge, Bob

Shapiro, Dick Beattie, Jerry Stone, Tommy McDaniel, Rich Brail, and Maude Tisch checked facts and added details. Paul Konigsberg supplied a reader's perspective. Binky Urban was kind enough to read the manuscript and recommend Charlie Leerhsen to edit. Andy Blauner used his talents to try to find me a publisher. Eric Rayman made sure I stuck to the facts. My thanks to Judy Vance, my loyal assistant who, among other duties, typed every word multiple times. Finally, over the last five decades, Pete Peterson was a constant pillar of support and encouragement.

I hope you enjoy this commentary and learn something from my stories. Each has a moral or a lesson that I didn't necessarily understand contemporaneously.

Lastly, my thanks to our children, Joshua, Josh (yes, we like the name), Abigail, Kate, and Laura, and their spouses and our grandchildren. Maybe they will get some "nachos" from reading about the joy of life their progenitor enjoyed.

PART I

CHAPTER 1

Wasting Time Constructively

It's not easy to get to Bentonville, Arkansas. It's a schlep, but if you're in any consumer business, it's a must-visit. Bentonville is the headquarters of Walmart, the world's largest retailer. For years, I have flown there to induce successive CEOs to retain me as an investment banker.

I always learned something useful, starting with my meetings with founder Sam Walton. In 1975, Walmart was an average discount retailer seeking new geography. Its sales were $236 million. Mister Sam's idea was simple and more a distribution strategy than a retail formula. He would open stores that could be replenished with goods within 240 miles of a distribution center—the distance a truck could drive in a day. He would enter rural markets, avoiding direct competition with more established chains. He would reduce his warehouse and distribution costs as low as possible so his prices could be lower. There was nothing fancy about his strategy—or about him. We'd drive in his pickup and eat at the local smokehouse, dining on some animal's ribs, and then visit his warehouse. That was an attraction in Bentonville, the Walmart warehouse. It was the first time I had seen a barcode scanner, and I climbed next to the conveyor belt to get the name of the manufacturer.

The retail business excites me—even when I'm not getting paid. It's in my DNA. My meetings with Sam were part of my professional education, designed as sales calls.

I don't mind "wasting time constructively." If a prospective client is receptive, I will pay him a series of calls over the course of months or even years, hopefully inducing him to retain Peter J. Solomon Company, the partnership I founded in 1989. I'll talk about whatever is on his mind at the moment, in terms of business or the wider world. I try to do a lot of listening, though I don't frequently succeed. It's trite but true what Yogi Berra said: "You can observe a lot by watching." Wasting time constructively is something I do consciously, but it's more a way of life than a sales technique. I do it because I enjoy interaction. The lines between a business solicitation and a social visit blur, and I build a friendship from which business may or may not flow.

I enjoyed Sam's enthusiasm, and he liked my curiosity. By the time Sam died in 1992, Walmart had grown to be a $44 billion-a-year business. Today, it has sales of nearly $500 billion annually. The company gets more bad publicity, mostly union inspired, than it deserves, but it has positively affected Americans' standard of living by reducing prices and, in environmental issues, featuring green practices. I have stayed in touch with Sam's successor CEOs—David Glass, Lee Scott, Mike Duke, and Doug McMillon—who seemed happy to meet with me.

On one typical visit to Bentonville, Lee Scott mentioned Walmart needed to improve its home business, meaning housewares, tabletop, sheets, towels, and the like.

"Why don't you start where a 'home' starts?" I suggested to him. "Start with the diamond engagement ring!" Business may be complex, but often the concepts are simple. What's the objective? What does the consumer or client want to achieve? In the case of engagement rings, begin by expanding the selection; through Walmart's buying power, it could lower prices and make the diamond rings more affordable.

Lee liked the idea, but once again, it didn't do me much good. I don't sell diamonds.

On a subsequent visit to Bentonville, I wanted Lee to expand Walmart's health care service by opening "doc in the box" units, otherwise known as urgent care facilities, in its stores. There were a number of companies Walmart might acquire. Lee's initial reaction was to recoil. "You want me to move *sick people* in our stores?" he said.

I countered, "As opposed to the ones already there?" At the end of that hour, Lee said I always gave him a headache. "Okay," I said. "I won't come back."

"No," he rejoined. "Come back in six months."

Fade out, fade into the present. Walmart today sells diamond rings and has urgent care facilities in many of its stores. Each idea has been a success, but in neither case has that success trickled back to me in the form of a fee, which is disappointing but not surprising. Walmart is a tough nut to crack. What I do isn't science. Sometimes you waste time constructively, and sometimes you just waste time.

It can be hard for people to understand what I do for a living. I've often said that I think my business card should say "Master of Nonsense."

When I started my children's book collection, I was immediately drawn to the nonsense of Lewis Carroll and *Alice in Wonderland* and Edward Lear and his limerick and alphabet drawings. Children's books once taught morality. They now conjure fantasy and imagination— states of mind with parallels in finance.

I am an investment banker—but I don't provide financing or trade or recommend securities or other financial products. Advice is my product. I travel light and keep it simple. A few years ago, the *New York Times* included me on a map of "Masters of the Universe." I thank them for the compliment, if that's what it is, but I'm no Sherman McCoy or Gordon Gekko. I don't do hostile takeovers or represent activist shareholders; I don't trade CDSs, RMBSs, or SIVs, which sets our firm, Peter J. Solomon Company, apart from some of the bigger investment banks like Goldman Sachs, Morgan Stanley, and JPMorgan Chase. Sometimes for managements I have to try to encapsulate in a few sentences the reasons to buy or sell a company, do a buyout, or recapitalize a business. Partly because I'm not good at conventional math and I like simplicity, I try to sketch out complex deals on index cards. (I keep a particularly good example framed on a shelf in my office.) Conveying and executing ideas are my livelihood.

My approach may seem too soft and slow for our transactional age, when success depends on the *quantity* of business dealings. I probably compound this impression when I advise younger employees and business students to read Marcel Proust as well as Michael Lewis and Andrew Sorkin. From Proust, you can learn about relationships and attention to detail, important factors in enjoying a satisfying and successful life.

One day not long ago, when I was walking back from lunch, I saw a bright young woman we employ staring at her cell phone and listening to music on headphones like almost everyone else on Madison Avenue. I tapped her on the shoulder and startled her out of her trance. "Hey," I said. "Look up once in a while! You can learn by looking around!" I meant that she should be checking out store windows, watching what people are wearing, what they're carrying, and even eavesdropping on their conversations. The world is a stage and not a place to stand while you check your tablet. Or maybe the world's a classroom. Michael Lewis wrote in his book *Boomerang*, "Walking around Manhattan just before the collapse of Lehman Brothers, you saw empty stores, empty streets, and, even when it was raining, empty taxis; the people had fled before the bomb exploded." But at least my colleague was on the street. People who eat lunch at their desks shouldn't complain if their careers stall or if they feel depressed. Nothing important is ever going to happen there.

But let's get back to whether my approach to business is old-fashioned. It just may be, but it's too late for me to change. It has served me well, allowing me to build an investment banking career, first in media and then to participate in mergers that reshaped the retail industry. I've also managed to structure a balanced life while I made money. In my younger days, I brought in a lot of clients at Lehman Brothers, dealt with the dysfunctional nature of that firm, and somehow rarely missed my three kids' games or school plays. I kept up with my friends from summer camps, schools—including Viola Wolf's dancing school—and never missed family events with my brother, Richard, and our many cousins. I did deals and went fishing for salmon in Canada and Alaska, striped bass in Peconic Bay and off Gay Head, bonefish in the Bahamas, and trout in Montana. I cursed the deals (and the fish) that got away—though without those setbacks, this book and my life would be less interesting. After my first marriage ended, I recovered and made a phenomenal second one. My professional life hasn't been strictly business either. My reputation at Lehman and involvement in not-for-profit work led to my appointment as a deputy mayor of New York City under Edward I. Koch during a time of an unprecedented municipal crisis, and segued into an opportunity to serve in the US Treasury during the Carter administration. When the Reagan era began (as Carter's performance as president assured that it would), I returned with mixed emotions to investment banking—where, as life turned out, I've had an even more satisfying second act, either making events happen (if you believe our friend, the writer Marie Brenner) or being "some kind of Zelig" (as George Sheinberg once called me, a little less generously) who is frequently turning up in the vicinity of important events.

Note that I said, "in the vicinity." One of my talents is that I find myself in interesting places—at the elbows of leaders, behind certain closed doors. As a young man traveling in the Soviet Union between years at Harvard College, I stood a few feet from Richard Nixon and Nikita Khrushchev as they engaged in their famous "Kitchen Debate" in Moscow. Two years later, in Jerusalem, I gazed with revulsion at Adolf Eichmann during his trial. I've seen a lot of history—political, business, baseball—firsthand. In matters of business, I avoid center stage unless there's a reason for me to be there. And there almost always isn't. I know I am usually not the star but the person whose role is to make the star shine. I see my role as helping executives define their goals and take steps to reach them. The first part can be especially tricky. It's a delicate process, teasing out what people who've experienced success want out of particular business dealings. It's not always just more money. Just as often, it is something else, something not material: more status, recognition, or a premonition. That's why I call myself a financial psychiatrist.

The story of my dealings with Gary Comer, the founder of Lands' End, Inc., illustrates how I work with a client—though it is not a perfect example because it lacks my standard lengthy get-to-know-you period. Rather, the process moved quickly after I heard from my business school roommate John McCarter, the president of the Field Museum, that Gary might be looking to do something—although nobody, including Gary, seemed to know exactly what—with his company.

It can be difficult for a founder to view his creation objectively. By any measure, though, Lands' End was something special, an American success story, misplaced apostrophe and all. Gary Comer was the son of a Chicago railroad worker who as a kid discovered the joys of boating on Lake Michigan. In 1963, when he was working in advertising, he and some friends started a mail order business that sold sailboat fittings from a basement office in his hometown. That evolved into a high-end preppy clothing company that, with Comer writing the crisp and breezy catalog copy, became a million-dollar business. Lands' End went public in 1986. During the early internet craze of the late 1990s, the stock had soared—but then cratered. By 2002, when I got to know him, Gary was turning seventy-five, and most of his personal wealth was tied up in that stock. As his wife, Francine, had told John, Gary wasn't sure what his next move would be. Should he cash out? At that time, Lands' End was basically a catalog and (though this was still a new concept) internet operation; it had a single physical store, located in the Minneapolis airport. Should it stick with that plan, or should it open new brick-and-mortar outlets, as Gary's CEO, David Dyer, a veteran department store executive, was urging? How should Gary respond to the interest that Amway, a Michigan-based direct seller, was showing in acquiring his company? He had many questions and few answers at that point.

For founders, the timing of exits depends on the circumstances. One answer does not fit all. I've seen many ungraceful exits. Many founders and CEOs, though brilliant, can't settle on a worthy successor. Gary Comer had a succession problem, but he also had the good sense—and you might even say the courage—to admit that he was stuck and needed outside assistance. When he heard not just from John but also another college friend of mine, Dick Marcus, my college classmate and director of Lands' End, that he should talk to me, he was eager to get together. When I called him, he told me he would send his plane to fly me to his farm in Wisconsin.

I still can't tell you what part of the state I was in. We touched down in the middle of a flat nowhere, punctuated with corn and cows, and then the plane taxied to the side of a huge structure that, when a door opened, turned out to be a hangar with another plane inside. I was directed by the pilot to an elevator, which he said would take me up into the house. I wasn't sure whether I was making a client call or auditioning for a James Bond movie.

It was not your typical business meeting. Gary and I talked for several hours alone in a room lit only by the fading twilight. He told me about being a modern-day explorer who navigated his ship, the Lands' End, throughout the world. He showed me his collection of model ship hulls and other items collected on his voyages. Gradually, we got around to the subject of his business, and Gary confirmed the rumors that the year before he had hired Goldman Sachs to sell Lands' End, but the firm had not produced even one serious buyer. I think that on one level he was glad things had turned out that way, because he hadn't yet been psychologically ready to sell. That didn't surprise me. Every seller feels seller's anxiety at some point in a deal, just as every buyer experiences buyer's remorse. Still, that experience had left a bad taste with Gary—why did no one want his company?—and added to his frustration and confusion.

As the sun started to set, he asked what I thought he should do with Lands' End. Before responding, I noted that he was posing an important question to someone who had known him for a grand total of about 120 minutes. I told him what I heard *him* saying, in the hope that that would bring him clarity. He had told me that he had virtually all of his capital tied up in Lands' End. His children had never showed interest in the business. He had also shared, I reminded him, that he wasn't confident in the direction David Dyer was leading. Gary didn't want to open any more stores.

One factor I *didn't* mention was something I'd observed, not heard: he didn't seem well. The signals were subtle but real, starting with his weak handshake. For a man who had sailed the seven seas and built a company from the ground up, he seemed passive and lacking in energy, though he said nothing about any physical problems. He didn't have to. I've come to rely more on my eyes than my ears when getting a sense of people. Brush up on your Shakespeare, I tell my colleagues: "Yond Cassius has a lean and hungry look." That's all you need to know about Cassius, what you can see from the outside. It wasn't all I needed to know about Gary but a relevant fact in reaching my conclusion that he was not a healthy man.

I left that unsaid, however, and recited the points that he had made to me. The litany seemed to clarify his thoughts. As the last shafts of light faded from the room, he said matter-of-factly, "I guess I should sell the business."

Although he probably couldn't see me, I nodded in agreement.

Once a decision is made, it is wise to execute expeditiously. In Gary's case, his illness was real; he had prostate cancer. We first determined that Amway, despite its initial interest, wasn't prepared to move ahead with an acquisition of Lands' End. But, Gary wondered, was anybody interested? After all, even the renowned Goldman Sachs had been unable to find a single interested party.

"Don't worry about what happened with Goldman," I told him. "It means nothing because it was selling your company the wrong way."

Goldman had offered Lands' End in an auction. For the bigger banks, auctioning companies has been standard operating procedure since Lehman Brothers developed the auction concept in the early 1980s. The idea behind an auction is, of course, to get prospective buyers involved in rounds of competitive bidding that drives up the price. At Lehman, we had a standardized procedure. We'd send out selling memoranda describing the deal; we'd set up a data room where prospective buyers could pore over data; we'd set deadlines for initial and secondary bids. The process has hardly changed over the decades, except that the information is now online. The auction process works best when you are selling a company whose business and status in its industry is clear and comparable. The first auction at Lehman was for the Solar Division of International Harvester. It made turbines. That's all it did. No explanation necessary, no confusion possible. Solar was ideal for the auction system.

But many companies are not. They need to have their strengths highlighted and enthused over by a professional, in a face-to-face conversation; in other words, they need *selling*, the old-fashioned way, not because they're undesirable but because they're unique and the usual business metrics don't apply. Goldman Sachs didn't understand that when they tried to sell Lands' End. Selling a company may take longer than an auction, but it allows each company to get the individual attention that the investment banker, in his sales pitch to represent the company, insists it will. At PJSC, we've blended the two methods. Using a serial sales effort focusing on three to four prospects at a time, with individual meetings supplemented by our detailed data, we combine the advantages of the big bank and bespoke approaches to selling a company.

In the case of Lands' End, we canvassed a mix of domestic and foreign companies. When I call a potential buyer for an appointment, I try never to tell the person the specific purpose of my call. My experience is that if I do, they may casually ask their wife or colleague what they think of the idea and then be influenced by an offhanded remark. ("He's coming to talk to you about *soup*? I *hate* soup!") When I start talking, I want them to be in a neutral place.

One company I thought might be interested in Lands' End was LVMH, a luxury goods conglomerate headquartered in Paris. Antonio Belloni, the acquisition executive, welcomed me to Paris without knowing the reason for my visit. I went to his office on the Avenue Montaigne, but before I could even say the words "Lands' End," he begged my indulgence to take a call. "No need to get up. Stay right there," he told me. "This will be quick." Mr. Belloni must not have known I understand French, because as I sat in front of him, he talked about disappointing financial results at LVMH. That was all I needed to hear. After he hung up, I thanked him for seeing me but said it was clear from his conversation that LVMH was not in the position to make a US $2 billion acquisition. Astounded, he said, "You really aren't going to tell me the name of the company, having flown to Paris to see me?" I replied affirmatively. As he walked me to the elevator, he was shaking his head. I felt I should have emulated the Lone Ranger's famous parting words, "The silver bullet will explain everything."

I thought my best next prospect for Lands' End was Sears Holdings of which Alan Lacy was CEO. For a moment, that meeting looked like it was going to last no longer than my visit to LVMH. As soon as I told him that I wanted to talk about Sears buying Gary's company, he said that he had looked at Lands' End the year before and wasn't interested. "You were wrong!" I shot back—a little too emphatically, I could see from Alan's expression—but I plowed ahead anyway. "You need Lands' End, and I'll tell you why," I said. "When a customer enters a Sears store, on the left she finds some of America's great brand names like Kenmore. On the right is another great brand name, Craftsmen Tools, and in the back is Delco. But in the middle of the store? There the customer finds no brands, only labels." In the retail trade, that term means generic goods.

Alan brightened. He said it was the best explanation he had ever heard for an acquisition and that he'd think about Lands' End. In time, he made an offer. Still, our customized auction went on for several months. Even with our personal approach, it was a challenge to find buyers because of the size and the recent uneven financial results. Toward the end, we had two—Sears and Great Universal Stores of the UK. We had done better than Goldman, but it was still a short list. The day before final offers were due, Great Universal withdrew. Frankly, I was terrified. But my partner Jeff Hornstein showed tremendous nerve by encouraging Lacy to *raise* Sears' bid at the last minute to discourage other buyers. That strategy could have backfired if Lacy had balked. But he didn't, and Sears topped itself with an offer of $1.9 billion.

The price we got for Gary was the highest paid for a specialty retailer, and the sale was publicized widely. As a result, we received a number of referrals, one of which came from Eric Smidt, chairman and CEO of Harbor Freight Tools, a mass distributor of private label tools.

I had never heard of the company—or Smidt—before, but he invited me to his office in Calabasas, California. Over the course of several months, we established a working relationship as we discussed various strategies he might employ to sell his business. Then, at what was supposed to be our final meeting before we were hired, he kicked back and started to chuckle about how rich he was soon going to be relative to certain other people in Los Angeles. Instead of letting the remark pass, I challenged him on the wisdom of making such an important decision on that basis. I may have been correct, but in terms of client relations, it was one of my dumbest comments. He didn't like what I said. The sale never got started, and I lost a considerable fee. I wish I'd kept my thoughts to myself, but the pain is dulled only by the fact that he still hasn't sold the business.

But what about Sears and Lands' End?

The marriage wasn't an outright disaster, but it didn't work out as well as it might have. Sears should have been smarter about the way it integrated Lands' End merchandise. Rather than showcase the line in more prosperous locales, Sears distributed it haphazardly. Whenever Lands' End merchandise was placed in a separate boutique in a more upscale store, it did well, but in poorer areas, as you might expect, it languished.

The acquisition of Sears by the hedge fund investor Eddie Lampert led to the spin-off of Lands' End into a public company. In the subsequent four years, it regained some of its luster. Regrettably, Sears, under Lampert's direction, accelerated its decline, ending in bankruptcy in October 2018. Lampert's financial engineering was not sufficient to overcome his apparent lack of *say'el*, a feel for the cloth.

The most important result for me, though, was that Gary Comer had no qualms about selling his business when he did. He felt he'd made the right move in the right way—and had received a fair price. When he died in 2006, he was at peace with our deal. Because he felt that way, so did I.

CHAPTER 2

"Make a Lot of Money."

(Professor Harry Austryn Wolfson, 1959)

On September 15, 2008, the day Lehman Brothers collapsed and the financial crisis exploded, I was fishing in Lake Clarke, Alaska, about as far from Wall Street, geographically and spiritually, as you can get. Alaska was the present I gave myself for my seventieth birthday, which would be two days later. I love fishing and planned the getaway with my old Collegiate School pal Tom Langman.

I wasn't just in Alaska; I was also in denial—not about the global economy but, in a personal way, about Lehman and the Street. I had seen all of the signs and portents. I had, like a lot of people, watched the debacle take shape over the course of years as the financial markets became more opaque and leveraged. I had noted the dangers ahead in articles and speeches. Yet when "Lehman Day" finally arrived, it was hard to believe that a firm that had been around since 1850, that had weathered wars, depressions, busts, and bubbles—a firm where I'd grown up as an investment banker and worked for twenty-six years, a firm known for its ingenuity—could vanish from the landscape.

Intellectually, I could see the route to Wall Street's decline. But that didn't stop me from wondering—maybe even saying aloud as I sat in my lodge room and stared out at the Alaskan wilderness—*How did it happen?*

For anyone paying attention to Wall Street, the past six months had been intense. In March 2008, Bear Stearns, the fifth-largest investment bank, had gone bankrupt. The federal government had frantically hatched a plan to subsidize its sale to JPMorgan Chase. Treasury Secretary Hank Paulson had made all the wrong moves in the matter. I wrote an article saying as much; I criticized not just Paulson but also the regulatory agencies for not doing their job after the repeal of the Glass-Steagall Act. In response to that piece, I got a call from Dick Fuld, the CEO of Lehman Brothers.

Dick had long been known as one of the most feared men on Wall Street, and in a short time, he would also be, by his own admission, one of the most hated.

The words "Dick Fuld is on the line" did not strike fear into my heart, for two reasons. I had known Dick since the late 1960s, when we first worked together at Lehman. He was a young protégé of Lew Glucksman, who had bullied his way to the position of CEO. Glucksman was an ugly man, both physically and emotionally. He was fat and disheveled with his shirttails flying and a cigar stuck between his stubby fingers. He loved to fish for bluefish and kept a gaff on his office wall—not to remind him of days on the water but to intimidate. Fuld, one of his acolytes, was always socially awkward and communicated with monosyllabic grunts. What a pair. I wasn't fond of either but not because I found them frightening.

In fact, I felt a bit sorry for Fuld. Everyone has patterns of behavior. As I have observed people over decades, I have concluded that they don't change, even if I hope they will. As CEO, Fuld was in over his head. He had neither the breadth of experience nor the intellect to manage a global bank. He didn't coach subordinates; he intimidated them. After a 158-year run, Lehman Brothers was teetering on the brink of insolvency. Except for the fact that it had inordinate exposure to commercial real estate, it had made all the same mistakes as Bear Stearns, allowing itself to become overly leveraged and relying too much on short-term borrowing. The government, I knew, was monitoring its operations closely. Dick was under a lot of pressure.

When he called that day, he got to the point quickly. He strongly disagreed with my remarks on the Bear Stearns situation. I should have refrained from writing anything, he said, but he was most concerned about my criticism of the government's action in arranging a sale of the bank to JPMorgan at a bargain price.

I listened politely, and then said, "I have a question. Does Lehman have enough capital to survive?" He equivocated, preferring to note the broad employee ownership. I let the obvious misdirection hang in the air for a moment.

Lehman's public statements showed leverage at the top end of its peers' ratios, but, as a later outside analysis revealed, Lehman did not point out that its leverage was supported by illiquid commercial and residential real estate. Dick returned to the capital issue, emphasizing viable options. At that moment, maybe he had some, but the fact that he made the call to me at all answered my question.

The winter before, I played golf in Florida with Pete Peterson. As we ambled around the course at Windsor, I listened to Pete bemoan the amount of debt in circulation and the world's indifference to the impending calamity. Finally, I asked him if he had an idea of how all this would end.

"If I knew that," he said, "I'd be a billionaire."

"But, Pete," I said, "you *are* a billionaire!"

I suppose Pete meant that no one could say exactly how things finally would fall apart. But eighteen months later, on September 15, 2008, the doomsday scenario was at hand. I called Dick Beattie, a close friend and chairman of Simpson Thacher, to find out if Lehman would make it through without filing. He darkened my last hopes. I knew it was not going to be an idyllic day on the Alaskan rivers.

I still had a portion of my family's investments at Lehman. I worried that my accounts would be frozen unless I could get them out quickly. Without question, I should have at least set up a custodial account so my securities would be safe. But because of all the history I'd witnessed in my fifty years on Wall Street—all the panics I'd seen come and pass, as well as my personal and in some ways sentimental connections to Lehman—I hadn't taken the prudent precautionary actions.

I got through to Lehman, but all was chaos on the other end of the line. You had to fight with people to help you—people who were uncertain if they even had a job. I sat on hold for long stretches, thinking about a time when phones didn't have hold buttons. When I first arrived on Wall Street in the summer of 1958, it hummed in a different key. Three million shares were traded each day on the New York Stock Exchange, as opposed to the six billion or so traded today. Lehman Brothers, the partnership, had less than $5 million in capital. The partners, who individually were wealthy men, sat in one large room. No one stayed late. There was anxiety, strife, and clashing egos. The reason they sat so close together was so they could overhear one another's conversations, but everything was on a human scale. Now that was no longer the case—and Lehman lay in ruins.

The man who long ago put me on the road to Wall Street was a renowned scholar, one of the greatest living Jewish thinkers: Harry Austryn Wolfson. He was a diminutive man with a shock of white hair and a long list of publications, including *The Philosophy of the Church Fathers, Crescas' Critique of Aristotle,* and *The Philosophy of Spinoza.* He had been born in Belarus in 1887 and had written and thought his way to Harvard, first as a student (he was in the same class as Walter Lippmann and T. S. Eliot) and eventually as a professor of philosophy. But I knew this learned man not just through his writing and teaching. I shared a bathroom with him on the second floor of a three-story house at 22 Francis Avenue in Cambridge, about five blocks from the corner of Harvard Yard.

Wolfson became my mentor and my inspiration. It's strange to think that I would never have met him if I hadn't been such a mediocre high school student.

At the Lawrenceville School, I did well in history and chemistry but poorly in math and just about everything else. I would sit in the library for hours reading novels, enjoying the books but feeling generally unmotivated and out of step. I couldn't believe my older brother Richard, by then at Harvard, had liked the school and advised me to go there. I wasn't ready for prep school and living away from home. My only friends from the city were Robby Froelich, Guy Connelly, and Eric Lasry, who had been expelled.

Senior year was especially awful, starting with the lottery for rooms. I drew number four of 157 and thought that meant I was guaranteed one of the best rooms on campus. Jack Hummer, the senior class proctor, arbitrarily reversed the order, and I ended up living in an off-campus house a half mile from my classes. My grades and SAT scores were lackluster. As a result, I was the only member of the class of 1956 awaiting a college acceptance on graduation day. I had aimed high with my applications—Dartmouth, Cornell, and Harvard College. Having no college in which to enroll made me feel trapped. I had the sickening sense of limited options. The market strategist Byron Wien has written that certain events in your first seventeen years form your identity for your whole life. For me, graduating high school without a letter of acceptance was one of those.

Dartmouth had rejected me. In June, Cornell, which had wait-listed me, wrote to say I'd been admitted. What a relief! Still, I preferred Harvard, where I remained on the waiting list. With my dad, mother, brother, and three uncles having gone there, it was a family tradition. Plus, it didn't require undergrads to take math. Fortunately, in July, Harvard decided to admit a small new group of what it called "forced commuters," students who would have to find their own housing. With Sidney Rabb, my uncle, pleading my case, I got accepted under that condition. Sidney knew Ben Selekman, a professor of labor relations at Harvard Business School who owned the house where Wolfson lived and who happened to have a room for rent. "I just want your nephew to be aware," Ben told Sidney, "that he will be living across the hall from a recluse."

Wolfson wasn't exactly that. When I met him in 1956, he had retired from teaching but retained a key to Widener Library, where he would go to study daily. While he was usually alone (he had never married), he did meet with some fellow philosophers in Selekman's first-floor parlor. He also seemed to brighten when I or certain students approached him with questions.

Wolfson stood about five feet five. He was stocky, and he spoke with an Eastern European accent; he'd say, "An eye for an eye, and a tuth for a tuth!" Stories about him were legendary. Once when a student asked him a question, Wolfson replied, "Come with me!" and led the young man to Widener. They walked through the maze of stacks until Wolfson stopped and climbed up a ladder to a shelf near the top. He withdrew a thick volume covered with dust, climbed down, and started paging through the book. Finally, something occurred to him. "You do read Sanskrit," he asked, "don't you?"

When a large, airy office on the top floor of Widener became available, Wolfson was reluctant to move from the dark, overstuffed cubbyhole he'd inhabited for years. But his friends finally convinced him he'd like the new digs. I helped him settle in between luminaries Reinhold Niebuhr and Paul Tillich.

By then, Wolfson and I were fast friends. Once, he accompanied me to pick up my date at Wellesley College. While I can't recall the coed's name, I vividly remember her astonishment at the gnomelike fellow sitting in the back of my two-toned Chevy Impala (borrowed from Chuck Diker) when I drove up to her dorm.

Wolfson taught me the value of excellence. At one point, he stopped writing for a week until he could express a thought precisely. He guided me through my undergraduate years. In return, I introduced him to the TV series *Gunsmoke*, baseball, and the bouillon cube. The Harvard honorary doctor of philosophy was absolutely astounded by the bouillon cube and praised me often for being able to so easily create such a delicious broth.

At the time, Harvard freshmen were required to see a psychologist. It was the standard Rorschach stuff. When I went back for a second round, the tester left the room for a minute, and I peeked at my results. His conclusion was I was "very personable" but, in essence, not that smart. Between that evaluation and forced commuter status, I felt intimidated by Harvard.

Still, I did okay. Sophomore year, I roomed with my oldest friend, Marty Gross, a man with an immense intellect, curiosity, and memory. Instead of going to Eliot House, the bastion of Harvard preppies and my brother's house, we went to Dunster, the longest walk to the Yard but a more public school environment.

Wolfson had definite ideas about education. He instructed me to seek out great professors no matter what the subject. It was a golden age at Harvard, and I took or audited courses taught by John Kenneth Galbraith, the Asian scholars John Fairbank and Edwin Reischauer, behaviorist B. F. Skinner, Paul Tillich, in the humanities Leon Edel and Louis Kronenberger, and, in government, Arthur Schlesinger, Henry Kissinger, McGeorge Bundy, Zbigniew Brzezinski, Pat Moynihan, and Louis Hartz. I would later advise my own college-bound children to favor great minds over subject matter every time.

To graduate with honors, a student had to write a thesis. I had no idea what to write. My senior tutor, Vincent Starzinger, suggested that I analyze American conservatism, a recurring theme in our republic's history. William F. Buckley Jr. had founded the *National Review* after graduating from Yale. My thesis analyzed the inconsistencies in the editorial policy of the magazine as it reflected the attempts by the conservative movement to champion both strong centralized government in security and military issues as well as less government in issues of social policy and regulation and for the economy. Sixty years later after the conservative movement captured the Republican Party, it still has not been able to reconcile these inconsistencies.

The musical theater always attracted me, but I didn't think I had the time or talent to be in the annual Hasty Pudding Theatricals show, a musical written and performed by Harvard undergraduates. The quality of the Pudding shows was high. In my junior year, Erich Segal, later author of *Love Story*, and Joe Raposo, a gifted composer who later wrote the *Sesame Street* theme song, were the coauthors.

If I was going to be associated with the Hasty Pudding, advertising manager seemed a good spot for me. In this job, I called on the businesses of Boston, such as the carriage trade jewelry companies, Firestone and Parsons located in the Ritz Hotel, and Shreve, Crump and Low across Newberry Street. I made appointments with the brokerage firms of Tucker Anthony and Paine Webber. It was my first exposure to selling, and I loved it. It wasn't exactly a tough assignment. Most of my "customers" were old Crimsons renewing ads they had been placing for decades. Nevertheless, the Pudding experience added measurably to my self-confidence.

Our senior year, Marty become ticket manager, and I became

business manager. The Pudding show was a rather big deal then. We ran for two weeks on Holyoke Street, then toured New York, Philadelphia, and Bermuda. Our Woman of the Year was Katharine Hepburn.

As graduation grew near, it was only natural for me to ask Wolfson for career counseling. Like a lot of young men, I was idealistic and had a vague notion about saving the world. I was thinking about becoming a social worker of some sort, I told him. Wolfson emitted one of his strangely childish giggles and shook his head. "Go to New York," he said. "Be a successful businessman! Make a lot of money! The philanthropy that will result from that will do a lot more good for society than anything you might do as a social worker!"

I liked the way that sounded. I just didn't know where to start.

CHAPTER 3

The Road to Business School

When I was in my twenties, I would envision my obituary. I wasn't depressed. The obituary idea stemmed from the renowned Harvard Business School professor General Georges Doriot. He urged his acolytes to think about the span of their careers. My obituary would acknowledge my accomplishments as CEO of a large corporation, my influence as secretary of the Treasury, and perhaps my musical talents (because I like to sing). Despite Wolfson's life-changing exhortation to go forth and be successful, I was not exactly a young man with a plan.

I did reasonably well at Harvard, graduating cum laude. That wasn't a major accomplishment since we were the first class to have more than 50 percent graduate with honors. Still, Harvard had been a much different experience than Lawrenceville. Leaving was traumatic for me. I remember pulling away from Dunster House feeling that I was being launched out of my comfort zone and into real life. My then girlfriend, Jane Doubilet, with whom I was to spend a romantic summer in Manhattan and at the Ocean Beach Club on the New Jersey Shore, helped pack my few belongings, and off we set to New York City and ...

Well, that was the question.

Retail was certainly one logical option for me. My dad, Sidney L. Solomon, was the chairman of Abraham & Straus, a major New York City department store, based in Brooklyn; and my mother, Jeannette, was the daughter of the founder of the grocery chain Stop&Shop

Companies. I liked retailing and the excitement of stores and had worked at A&S one summer. But I retained the image of my dad collapsing on the couch at nine thirty after work in 1955 and saying, "Don't go into retailing." I didn't think he was kidding.

But if not retail, then what? Many of my classmates, including my pal Marty Gross, were intent on law school. I joined the line to take the law board test. Marty scored as high as you could. I scored somewhere that might qualify me for a Midwestern law school. The result surprised me. I thought I was smarter than my score showed, but I brushed off the disappointment. After all, I had no actual interest in being a lawyer.

I did take the business school test. I scored high on verbal and okay on math but only because I'd memorized formulas, like the way to measure the circumference of a circle, that seemed more relevant to a sixth-grade arithmetic test. I applied to Harvard Business School and was accepted. Dad was thrilled.

I wasn't. I had no interest in further schooling. But with my dad pushing so hard for HBS, how could I avoid it or at least defer going? I had tried to get a job in Japan, a country that had long fascinated me, but there was a slight problem involving my inability to speak Japanese. Even with Professor Edwin Reischauer, the renowned Harvard professor of Japanese and Asian studies, writing a recommendation, my only job offer was from a New York-based foundation that I suspected to be a CIA front. (Perhaps I should have waited a year, by which point President Kennedy had appointed Professor Reischauer the American ambassador to Japan.)

Easing me into the workforce in a way that kept my options open, Dad arranged for me to be on the summer training squad at Bloomingdale's. I was eager to get going.

Maybe too eager. I have always believed in managing my time well, and one thing that means for me is showing up at the appointed hour or being early. On my first day at Bloomingdale's, I outdid myself, arriving not at eight o'clock, as I'd been asked to, but at the stroke of seven o'clock. Bloomingdale's at that hour was eerily quiet and extremely intimidating, like a cathedral at midnight.

My first assignment was selling in "small leather goods," essentially wallets and accessories. The counter was on the east/west passage on the main floor, a location that every shopper passed. It was the ideal location. My friends would come by daily. We'd hang out while I sold wallets and key chains and made mental notes about the customers' dress and behavior.

From small leather goods, I transferred to junior dresses in the northwest corner of the third floor. Dad believed that a retailing executive had to have a fashion sense befitting a true ready-to-wear merchant. Junior dresses was like grad school in this regard.

But that department was no picnic. The buyer was Ida Celino, an old line retailer who brooked little interference even from management. I was put there because she was good.

Dress departments look their best on the day fall styles come in and crisp, colorful goods light up the racks. Leftover summer goods, marked down but not sold, dampen the atmosphere.

One hot August day, Celino and her assistant buyer were out of the store, and I was nominally in charge. We had a number of madras dresses still on the floor, and I decided on my own to mark them down further and place them in the front of the department. Better to get rid of them that way, I felt, than to let them languish. We moved a few but not all.

The next day, Celino returned and hit the roof. She berated me for taking the markdowns and for placing the summer goods so prominently. She clearly would have fired me on the spot had I not been the son of Sidney Solomon.

That night, I sheepishly told Dad the story. I thought he'd take Celino's side since she was the experienced retailer. Amazingly, he backed me. He said she should have taken the markdowns even earlier, and it did no good to keep out-of-season merchandise tucked away. He told me to remember, "Your first markdown is your cheapest!"

That concept has stuck with me. It is true not only in retailing but in every aspect of investing, politics, and business. Take the loss! Confess and own up! Move on!

My next and final posting was in the book department. In terms of traffic, this was the dead zone. Bloomingdale's book department had thousands of titles, did little business, and was not profitable. On my third day on the job, I learned to my surprise that publishers allow retailers to return unsold books for up to twelve months for a full refund. On my fourth day, I returned more than 35 percent of Bloomingdale's book inventory to the outrage of publishers but to the delight of Larry Lachman, the store president.

My summer was idyllic. This was 1960, before Kennedy, drugs, or the pill. We went to cocktail parties, necked but didn't do much else, and, on weekends, went to the Jersey Shore and the Ocean Beach Club, where there was always golf, tennis, swimming, and dances. I met many of my closest friends that summer.

Perhaps the only truly anxious moment I had in those months occurred on a steamy day in August when I lined up for my Selective Service physical at 44 Whitehall Street. America was still a few years away from sending troops to Vietnam, but for young men of that era, the draft was an almost unavoidable reality. Everyone had to serve—unless, of course, you qualified for a deferment. I had always suffered from asthma. It was clearly exacerbated by smoking, which I had begun at Lawrenceville. Playing basketball had become increasingly difficult.

Stress can bring on asthma, too, of course. As I waited at the draft board to be examined, I began wheezing. It was no act, but the army doctors noticed and subjected me to additional testing.

Several hours later, a panel of doctors pored over my charts. One noticed my address, 1095 Park Avenue, and remarked that he lived at 1185 Park. A minute later, he stamped my status 4F—deferred for health reasons. "I am going to give you two years," he said. "Use them well!"

Sometimes you're lucky.

The Kennedy-Nixon campaign was the topic that summer and, of course, into the fall. On election night, thanks to Oscar Schafer, who was a producer on WHRB, Harvard's radio station, I had press credentials for the Kennedy New York campaign headquarters. Schafer called me during the evening and asked me to interview former New

York governor Averill Harriman. I introduced the governor to the audience by saying, "Welcome to Harvard radio!" Harriman then proceeded to talk at length, seeming to focus on Connecticut and its support of JFK. *That's strange*, I thought, but as I sensed him winding down, I jumped in and said, "Thank you from Harvard radio."

"Harvard?" the partially deaf Harriman replied. "I thought you said Hartford!"

By then, I had already deferred admission to Harvard Business School. Dad, through a friend of his named Paul Mazur, had arranged a job for me at Lehman Brothers. It was another temporary position, but it involved training in the firm's offices at One William Street and possibly an internship in France.

Paul Mazur was a good man to know. Well into his sixties by then, he was not just a Lehman partner but also an intellectual force on Wall Street and at the firm. His specialty was economic analysis and the role of the consumer. Paul had authored an important book, *The Standards We Raise*. He had been instrumental in the formation of Federated Department Stores and had served on the board alongside my dad for many years. He established the Lehman Economics Department to publish economic data and analysis before the Commerce Department and other agencies of government took up this task. In terms of personal style, he was stuffy and gruff, and Dad thought him pompous. But Paul was instrumental in my life because it was through him that I came to investment banking.

My arrangement was of finite duration; it was basically a winter job. The deal was that after I spent six months in New York learning how Lehman worked, Marcel Palmero, another partner, would ask Banque Paribas to allow me to intern in Paris. In September 1960, I began a tour of Lehman's departments. The syndicate department, which controlled the firm's participation in underwriting, had the most daily excitement. The industrial department, which provided merger and financing advice to companies, was run by Ed Kapp, an unusual guy but a great teacher. Kapp was the kind of eccentric bachelor who wore a belt *and* suspenders. When you passed him in the hall, he would ask if you were unemployed. He meant "at the moment," but it was an unsettling inquiry for a junior person. Kapp was a stickler for detail who reviewed every number on every table. He taught by example as much as anything else; over the years, he helped Lehman create a score of successful bankers.

My understanding with Mr. Mazur and Marcel Palmero was that they would place me at La Banque de Paris et des Pays-Bas for additional training if I spoke passable French. I was better at French than Japanese, yet despite years of schooling and tutoring, I still wasn't fluent. Marcel called me one day to tell me that Monsieur Raide, the CEO of Paribas, was in his office. My internship would be in jeopardy if he saw how badly I spoke French. My only option, I decided, was to burst into the office spewing English and then get out as quickly as possible. I could see the astonished look on Marcel's face, but it worked.

Life in la belle France started badly. The planned assignation with my former girlfriend didn't work out. Relighting old flames is a good way to get burnt. As far as my job went, I had fooled Palmero into thinking I could speak French, but I couldn't fool my officemates. I hated going in.

It was a strange and tense time to be in Paris. The city was under siege in 1961. President Charles de Gaulle was withdrawing France from Algeria, and the French Foreign Legion, influenced by the Right Wing, was threatening to invade the city. The French Army fortified the Pont Neuf, near the Place Dauphene, where I lived in a small hotel for one dollar per day. Tanks surrounded the Assembly Nationale and other public buildings. Occasionally, cars exploded. War seemed imminent. Eventually, De Gaulle arrested the defiant French Marshalls Salem and Challe. They were convicted of treason and served long jail terms, despite being World War II heroes.

Once the tension eased, I started to enjoy Paris, though for reasons that had nothing to do with international finance. Each morning on the way to work, my colleagues would stop for coffee. I would meet up with them at the café, but on many days, when they continued on to the Bourse, I headed for the racetrack at Auteuil or Longchamps. On other afternoons, I cruised art galleries and museums. While many artists caught my eye, I fell in love with Alberto Giacometti after an exhibition at La Galerie Maeght.

Three months was enough time at Paribas. My college pal Dan Pollack was at Oxford, and we decided to travel for the summer. I was trying both to see the world and avoid entering HBS in the fall.

Dan and I went to Israel by way of Greece. Jerusalem was in the middle of the Adolf Eichmann trial. He had been kidnapped from Argentina a year earlier, when he had been the third most wanted war criminal after Dr. Mengele and Martin Bormann, Hitler's secretary.

Each day, there were a limited number of seats available to the public. The trial was conducted in an auditorium in central Jerusalem that resembled a theater; we watched from the balcony on two consecutive days. Eichmann sat in a glass cage on the left side of the stage. The three judges sat at a raised podium in midstage, facing the audience. The proceedings would have been boring except for an occasional terrifying outburst from a victim or relative seeking revenge. A skinny little man who had once worn a big black Nazi hat with a lot of braid, Eichmann truly seemed to capture the banality of evil, as Hannah Arendt wrote. As a physical specimen, he didn't even rise to the level of accountant. If Eichmann could be the source of so much destruction and misery, anyone could.

After touring around Israel, Dan and I returned to Greece. By this time, it was early July, and I was running out of time if I was going to find some way to avoid HBS. In Greece, the papers reported on the Russian threat to Berlin and the possibility that President Kennedy would call up the Army Reserves. It was another scary Cold War moment, but I wanted to see it for myself. Dan went to the Italian Riviera to visit friends.

What was I thinking? To this day, I can't believe I went to the Olympic Airlines office in Athens and booked passage to Berlin. There was no problem getting a seat. In fact, on the last leg of the journey, from Frankfurt to Berlin, I was the only passenger on the plane. I had booked a room at the Felix Kempinski on the Kurfürstendamm. If there was trouble, I wanted to be in the best hotel.

The eye of the storm was calm. Berlin didn't seem agitated. After war and the blockade, perhaps a big power confrontation was just another testy situation. I spent the days walking around Berlin and stopping at military checkpoints. One afternoon, I took a tour of the Communist side. I couldn't believe I was using East Germany to stave off Harvard Business School. But a week or so later, after a brief trip to Scotland to play golf at the Royal and Ancient St. Andrews and then on to Shannon, I boarded Air Lingus to return to New York City and face the inevitable.

~

"Peter, can I drive with you to Cambridge?" my mother sweetly asked.

Dad was a renowned merchant who had risen from modest beginnings in Salem, Massachusetts, to graduate from Harvard College and the same Harvard Business School. He was a successful executive, accustomed to giving instructions and having them carried out. He ran the country's most profitable department store, Abraham & Straus, where he didn't miss a discarded paper on the floor, or a dress hung out of order on a rack. Dad liked opera, Dewar's White Label, gin rummy, fishing, and golf.

Mother deferred to him, as women did in the 1950s, but she was no one's handmaiden. Mother had been sent to live with a cousin in Portland, Maine, for three years at age nine because of her mother's mental illness. She was a tribute to nature over nurture. She graduated from Radcliffe in 1930 and earned a master's degree at Simmons College Retailing Program. She never had a paying job until Dad died, although during WWII, she worked at the secret Interceptor Command. Mother chose the schools my brother, Richard, and I attended, took us to doctors and orthodontist appointments, and taught us to drive. She dragged us to art galleries on Saturdays, and it was Mother who used her own money to build an art collection. She played golf with me and tennis with Richard and me and later with our children. It was she who got us out of trouble by charming whomever we offended, meanwhile lecturing me over lunch at La Grenouille when I had failed to live up to Dad's expectations.

Mother would remain a force in my life and those of our children and my brother's until her death in 2006 at age ninety-seven. Cousin Betty Rabb called her Auntie Mame, the flamboyant character in the Patrick Dennis play. She had a list of sayings that framed her attitudes, such as "water seeks its own level," "a prophet is not honored in his own country," and "if you laugh before breakfast, you'll cry before dinner."

She was an eccentric mixture of snobbery and populism, commenting that poor people were lucky to have Central Park while preferring public busses to limos. She loved and studied art, even taking painting with an eccentric teacher, Norman Raeburn. One day when we were no older than ten, Mother returned home hysterical because Raeburn had criticized her painting. She said she "had been all sweetness and light before he yelled at her." The phrase became a shibboleth in our family.

Clearly, Mother had been instructed to deliver me to HBS by Dad, who did not trust that I would actually enroll.

Over the years, many young people have asked me whether they should go to business school. It's impossible to give a general answer. It depends on a student's goals and backgrounds.

For me, business school wasn't a good use of two years. I would have been better off working at a job I liked in a foreign country and being exposed to other cultures and languages.

Two of my children, Joshua and Kate, did go to business school. Joshua combined HBS with Harvard's School of Education. He used the experience to enter public education and started three public noncharter schools in New York City, each based on a theme and under the auspices of New Visions founded by Dick Beattie. Joshua's Business of Sports School combines his love of sports with his education.

Kate probably got more from Kellogg School of Management at Northwestern. Kate knew she wanted to be in marketing, and the marketing network and specific marketing skills gave her entry to better opportunities. Kate says business school did help her organize presentations better.

My advice on attending business school is:

1. If you have a good job and can keep it, keep it.
2. Business school will expand your contacts, as would any large group activity. It will enhance your social network. It will improve your verbal presentation skills.
3. If you know exactly what you want to do in your career, evaluate whether business school will allow you to accelerate your progress or get you hired.
4. Do not go to a business school in the same vicinity as your undergrad college or where you grew up. One of the principal values of business school is learning about, and adapting to, a different environment.
5. If you have had good academic training at college and only want to learn the tools of business, such as accounting, they are available cheaper from online courses.
6. Do not go to business school just because you don't want to go to law school or become a doctor.

HBS started slowly. On day one, we were asked how to make and market a man's shirt. Considering I'd grown up in a retail business and worked for a summer in Hempstead A&S in men's accessories, the shirt case struck me as rudimentary. With my study group, I developed a plan to manufacture shirts, price them, and distribute them through department stores.

The next day, we spent ninety minutes on how to think about this issue of making and marketing a shirt. I hadn't made it to Wednesday of the first week, and my interest was fading.

Outside the classroom, I wasn't doing well either. I found eating in Kresge, the HBS dining hall, depressing. For less money, I could eat dinner at Boston's most famous restaurant, Locke-Ober's off Washington Street, if I didn't order too many side dishes. A part-time job at Stop&Shop allowed me to avoid Kresge entirely.

In January, my roommate, with whom I had nothing in common, moved out. In moved Howard Sylvester Jr., a six-foot-four gawky guy who claimed he had been married to Miss New Jersey when he was at Princeton. He was fun, and at least we had some common background. Ward graduated at the top of our class and later went on to Hollywood, where he discovered David Jones and the Monkees. He subsequently popped in and out of my life.

I found I could do well enough at HBS if I took control. There was a tradition of the professors cold-calling students to present a case at the start of a class. Rather than being caught off guard, I volunteered to present a case in each course, such as finance, control, human relations, marketing, and production. I got better grades than I would have otherwise and avoided anxiety.

All things considered, though, I was wasting time at HBS. I alerted my parents that at the end of the year, I would leave the school. I still wanted to work in Asia and had qualified for a competitive program with the US State Department in Thailand for the summer of 1962.

Dad was apoplectic. Bad enough I had deferred HBS for a year. Now I was quitting. Mother, always the more practical, advised staying and finishing the second year. If I didn't, she argued, I would spend my life explaining why I had left. She advised doing whatever I wanted during the second year—golf, skiing, or whatever amused me—as long as I remained enrolled. Was that good advice? Forty years later, I mentioned to Marion Heiskell—the widow of Andrew Heiskell, who had attended HBS and later became an important member of the exclusive Harvard Corporation—what Mother had said. Marion gasped and replied that Andrew had spent his whole life explaining why he had left HBS before graduating. "Your mother was absolutely right!"

The summer job with the State Department fell through, and I wound up taking another summer job in San Francisco with Draper Real Estate. I didn't set any sales records, but I did get my first exposure to the West Coast state of mind, something you were not likely to encounter in the 1950s at Harvard. I traveled from Eureka, Oregon, to Anaheim, California, saw the Monterey Peninsula, and went to

Disneyland. In retail terms, California was breeding new formats. White Front Stores was a groundbreaking discount chain, and California clothing designers were coming into their own. For many years after, California concepts moved east rather than vice versa.

My biggest mistake that summer was investing in Draper's holding company, buying a preferred stock. My dad's close friend, Elias Pinto, then running an auto parts distributor, Chanslor & Lyon, in San Francisco, told me I'd made a mistake. He was right. Draper went bust in the late 1960s. I lost much more money than I made that summer.

On my way back east at summer's end, I drove with a Draper colleague and two girls to Las Vegas. We paid fourteen dollars a night for rooms at the Flamingo Hotel. It was pure honky-tonk, not the Vegas of today—and the girls weren't the girls of today either. We had separate rooms.

The most memorable event in my second year at HBS occurred outside the classroom. On an early spring afternoon in 1963, when I should have been in class, instead, as I often did, I took five or six golf clubs and hit practice balls in an open space along Storrow Drive. Before long, a motorcade sped west on the Drive. I remembered that President Kennedy was speaking at Boston College and figured it must be he.

About an hour later, I was still hitting balls when I once again heard the motorcade's sirens. A moment or two later, I sensed someone watching me as I hit a lofting wedge. On my follow-through, I saw a man slightly slouched, thin, and laughing, standing about five feet behind me. It was the president of the United States, John F. Kennedy.

This was not how I imagined meeting a president—amidst a scattering of golf clubs and balls, while I simultaneously trespassed and played hooky. I started to tidy up the area while he broke into a laugh and said, "Hello." Strange to think now that it was just me and him. There was no security around the president. He had stopped because he was early for his next appointment. My makeshift practice range was a proposed site for the Kennedy Presidential Library, and he was coming by to look at it.

That was actually my third encounter with JFK. I had seen him at Harvard where he had been an Overseer and had a brush with him late one night in 1961 in New York City when our shoulders grazed as he scurried into the Carlyle Hotel.

My second year at HBS, John McCarter was my roommate. He was a natural leader, and I wondered how long he would stay in business until he went into politics. Handsome and athletic, he had won the Pyne Prize at Princeton as outstanding graduate. Mac and I came up with a sweet gig, becoming movie reviewers for the *Harbus*, the HBS newspaper. We had passes for all the movie theaters and used them frequently.

I consider my second year at HBS a waste, but not because I should have studied more. Rather, I should have interviewed with businesses in fields other than finance and thought about firms other than Lehman, and I should have enrolled myself in an intensive foreign language course.

Dad had always told me, "You'll enjoy life more if you are a good golfer, a good public speaker, and fluent in French." At that point, I was still working on two.

CHAPTER 4

First Steps on Wall Street

It was laziness that brought me back to Lehman Brothers in 1963. My first experience at the firm had been, on the whole, neither good nor bad. Three years later, I had graduated from business school and was kicking myself for not having explored other options. I guess I'd been too busy having fun. The week before I started at Lehman, I was in Pamplona with my fiancée, Linda, her brother, and my friend Bob Glauber, drinking rioja and running with the bulls. On the way out of town, our minivan broke down, and we pushed it three hours into San Sebastian. It was one of those terrible/wonderful experiences you always remember. I flew home from Spain on a Friday, and on Monday showed up at One William Street in my best blue suit.

In outward appearances, little had changed in the years I'd been gone. The imposing iron gates were still there. The elevators still had uniformed operators, and beneath the elegant marble lobby, down in the rodent-infested basement, purchases and sales of securities were still entered in large ledger books by hand. But I soon discovered something was different. Two sons of senior partners and contenders to succeed Bobbie Lehman had joined the industrial department, the firm's corporate finance area. In retrospect, those hirings marked the start of political turmoil that, years later, would devastate and nearly destroy the firm.

In a number of ways, Lehman—indeed, Wall Street in general— was an odd choice for me. I wasn't good at anything to do with academic mathematics, but I had a knack that was not measurable in the classroom: I could look at a series of numbers in a financial analysis and see the one that didn't make sense, either because it was wrong or because there was a change in the patterns. Algebra was beyond me, but I could do six-horse parlays in my head, just like Al Capone.

My chief strength, though, was that I liked to sell, and I knew how to communicate. I was able to get to the core issue of a problem and explain it in simple declarative sentences like the ones my seventh-grade teacher at Collegiate, Eugene Swan, taught me to write. I'm a stickler for clarity and the sworn enemy of superfluous words. I edit a lot of adverbs out of my company's reports and memorandums. To this day, my friend Jamie Niven, former vice chairman of Sotheby's, greets me by saying, "The purpose of this memorandum"—the way I, later in my career, insisted he and others at Lehman begin all investment banking memoranda. My point was to get to the point.

In 1963, Lehman Brothers was a partnership of just twenty-five with fewer than two hundred employees. Underwritings were small and required little permanent capital. If the firm needed capital, it took out day loans.

Lehman was among the top "Jewish firms," ranked somewhere below Morgan Stanley, Eastman Dillon, and First Boston Corporation but more prestigious than its smaller rival, Goldman Sachs, which was still a trading company. It was a clubbier time in the financial business, though not as clubby as it once had been. Years later, I would discover in the files a 1938 letter signed by Goldman's Sidney Weinberg and a Lehman partner with the unlikely name of John Hancock. They had crafted what was essentially an illegal agreement to divide banking clients and to share other client revenues. I wish I'd saved that letter, which showed how the times—and crimes—have changed.

Lehman was one of the few firms to have its own building, a stone structure eleven stories high. The second floor housed the small brokerage unit led by Marvin Levy, a well-known tennis player. His most illustrious salesmen were Mickey Tarnopol and Dick Savitt, the first Jewish man to win Wimbledon (in 1951). Both would become my lifelong friends.

The trading desk, about sixty feet long, was in the annex, which you reached via an industrial stairway. The top traders were Artie Wagner, a tough character who chomped cigars and frequently took off for Las Vegas, and James Leipner, who handled Mr. Lehman's trades. Jimmy wore a coat and tie and always wore a hat, a man of high style in a low-tech time. The over-the-counter market in those days was conducted via the pink sheets where brokerage firms listed their bids and asks. The derivative market, which now has a notional amount outstanding of $630 trillion, didn't exist except through limited puts and calls.

The large partners' room occupied most of the third floor. Each partner theoretically had a desk. In fact, most also had a working office in the annex. Any partner could commit and risk his partners' capital, but to make a commitment without the blessing of Mr. Lehman would be a capital offense in more ways than one. (It wasn't until 1971 that Lehman incorporated and experienced the benefits of limited liability.)

If the layout sounds difficult to maneuver through, it was; the firm had lousy feng shui. Nothing was convenient. Lesser partners had offices on the fourth, fifth, and tenth floors. The library—run by Miss Johnson and Miss Sanford, bunned and powdered figures out of an English miniseries—was for no particular reason on floor six. The seventh floor contained the municipal department, and the eighth had a large partners' dining room and five smaller dining rooms. The corporate finance department, which Lehman called the industrial department, was on the ninth floor.

I worked on that floor, sharing a cramped office with an older associate and a secretary. It was dingy in the way that offices of that day often were. The walls hadn't been painted for decades. We had no computers, and our calculators were black Monroe machines with long chassis that literally cranked out calculations. We did all our charts in pencil so we could erase.

The industrial department had some talented people, but it was mostly littered with friends of the partners and senior nonpartners who either lived like partners or were abused by them. One of the associates there was Barry van Gerbig, for many years the major domo of the famous Seminole Golf Club. Barry had gone to Princeton and played goalie on the ice hockey team. He had little interest in banking but was a distant cousin of Mr. Lehman.

A few desks away was Billy Hitchcock, the son of "Ten Goals" Tommy Hitchcock, the famed polo player who died in a bombing run in World War II. Billy would later gain fame as the host to Timothy Leary, who perfected LSD on Billy's Millbrook, New York, estate. Farther down the hall was Nat Sherman, age forty-five or so. Nat was senior partner Herman Kahn's brains. We admired him for his abilities and the way he endured Herman's harassment.

Gordon Calder was a polished Texan, also in his forties, who never seemed troubled by work but was kind to younger associates. Doug Anderson had played hockey at Harvard. Len Richman, the oldest of the senior people, often talked about how he'd built his own harpsichord. Jimmy Leonard, the brother of well-known CBS TV reporter Bill Leonard, always had some angle.

The best of the bunch was the laconic Robert S. Rubin, not the former secretary of the Treasury but arguably the smartest banker in the firm. Rubin spent his days reading the newspaper and answering complex questions posed by the partners. Everyone relied on him. I felt close to him through mutual friends in Boston, particularly Bernard Bunny Solomon, his cousin (but no relation to me), who had been a vice president of Stop&Shop. For reasons I'll describe ahead, Rubin and I later became distant. I have to say, though, he and his wife, Marty, made significant contributions to New York City and particularly Brooklyn, where he helped found St. Ann's School and the Brooklyn Children's Museum and was president of the Brooklyn Museum.

In a tiny office just beyond the elevators on the third floor sat Robert Owen Lehman Sr., the chairman. Mr. Lehman had moved from a larger space that he worried might intimidate people to a smaller one that certainly did. The hundred-square-foot room was barely big enough for a couch, a desk, and two or three paintings—not original works of art but copies he had painted himself from original Renoirs, El Grecos, and Picassos that hung in his apartment on East Fifty-Fourth Street or that he had lent to his partners, such as General Lucius Clay, for their larger offices. The sheer oddness of it all somehow contributed to the idea that Mr. Lehman, at seventy-something, was truly a man apart from mere mortals. When he called you in and you sat on his couch, you were directly across from him, the Sun King, with no room to maneuver. For a newcomer like me, it was terrifying.

Not that I spoke to Bobbie Lehman much in those days. My first contact with him was on November 22, 1963, the day President Kennedy died. At that point, I had worked at the firm for just over four months. Like most people, I had gone home almost immediately after the announcement of the assassination at 1:15 p.m. When I got back to my four-and-a-half-room apartment on East Sixty-Ninth Street, Linda was crying hysterically. We were watching coverage when the phone rang. It was Mary Jane Marshall, one of Mr. Lehman's two secretaries. "Mr. Lehman would like to speak with you," she said.

Immediately I assumed I shouldn't have gone home and I was going to be chastised.

"Mr. Lehman," I said, "isn't this awful?"

"Well," he replied, "it is too bad, but these things happen."

I was just learning that if you are Robert Lehman, the world turned around you and beneath you, and major events that involved others didn't matter. He continued with the purpose of the call.

"Last night, I saw your dad," he said. "He reminded me that you are at the firm. I'm sorry I didn't realize that and hope everything is going well."

"Oh, everything's just fine," I said, resisting the temptation to add, "except that somebody has just killed the president."

Fifty-three years later, I finally understood Mr. Lehman's perspective. Friends and family were appalled when Trump was elected. He seemed so intemperate, inexperienced in governing, and intolerant. While not as fatal as an assassination, his election to the presidency is a shock because of the nature of the man and not his policies.

By age eighty, I, like Mr. Lehman, have seen a lot. I have realized that the sun comes up daily, and no event beyond those affecting my family and friends throws me into a loop.

If it's true that timing is everything, Mr. Lehman was the exception that proved the rule.

A month after my first conversation with the boss, Frank Manheim, the most literate of the Lehman partners, composed a poem that captures the spirit of the firm in 1963 and the reverence in which Bobbie Lehman was held.

A Poem Dedicated to Robert Lehman and Composed on Christmas Day 1963

Twas the night before Christmas, and all through the
    firm no debenture vas 'cruing, not even short-term.
Bobbie was phoning - alas, it is true -
    If only to partners, enquiring "What's new?"

The building was quiet that star-studded night, No sign
    of distemper, no hint of a fight.
Not even with Laza d, let alone others!
    Christmas was here, at olde Lehman Brothers.

Paul Mazur B forebodings of our country' s decay
    Wilted not Thomas, nor caused Gudemen dismay.
Szold stayed judicious, while Kahn chortled vith glee,
    As he counted again the split Pan Am fee.

A venturesome jockey set to mount a wild horse,
    Lucius vas strategically charting his course,

While cheerful Monroe went early to bed, Assured our
    results were not writ in red.

The Manheims were suffering, as if plagued with the
    boils, But it was only Great Western, and vegetable
    oils.
Ehrman seemed dour, Morris N. seemed sad,
    'Tis merely the way they look when they're glad.

Both Osborn and Schulte, as each slumber sought,
  Were grateful for changes the Excom had wrought,
Palmaro relaxed, restored to good health,
  As Ed K. toiled on, towards glory and wealth.

Then a mild Voice was heard in the night cold and
  clear,
    Twas Bobbie's, of course, as the Cadillac changed
    gear, "On Sage! On Hellman!" it was heard to say,
    "On Levy! On Black!, oh, On Lehman JI".

"On Hunter! On Eddie! (who helps LBJ rule)
  "On Glanville! On Oakley! Forvard, Stephen
  DuBrul! "On RusmiseU", and after "On Bobbie Bl"

The Voice trailed off in the Cadillac 's lea,

Christmas Day dawned, in the morn's early light One
  William was silent, gleaming and bright,
But Bobbie was 'phoning - alas 'tis true -
  If only to partners, to enquire "What's new?"

My next contact with Mr. Lehman came in 1964 when he decided
that the firm should buy a motor yacht to take clients up the East
River to the World's Fair held in 1964 and 1965 in Flushing Meadows
in Queens. It was a quaint notion. What I've never understood is why
he decided I should help buy the boat and manage it for the firm.

I had signed up to be an investment banker. I was now a cruise
director. Everything went wrong. The captain was a perpetual drunk.
Mr. Lehman would stop on his way to One William Street to inspect
the vessel, which was never up to his standard of tidiness. One day
around this time, I was making a new business call on a low-end retailer
called John's Bargain Stores in the South Bronx. In the middle of my
pitch, Mr. Lehman called and demanded to speak to me immediately.
Not surprisingly, something about the yacht was upsetting him. The

client was treated to the sight of me giving a stream of "yes, sirs." At the same time, he was impressed that this young banker was important enough for the famous Robert Lehman to be so eager to speak to him. Ultimately, we didn't get the Johns Bargain Store business. The best outcome of our period as boat owners was that none of our clients drowned.

Bobbie Lehman was hardly what you'd call an affable sort, but he did have a sense of noblesse oblige. In April 1964, I took a trip to solicit new business, calling on supermarket chains from Northern California to Albuquerque, New Mexico. As a result, the following year, I instigated the merger of Red Owls Stores, a dominant grocery chain owned by Floyd Bell in Minneapolis, with an up-and-coming Bay Area–based chain called Lucky Stores. This was exciting for me because second-year associates generally didn't produce business.

Mr. Lehman called me to the third floor and congratulated me on the deal. He praised my initiative. I thanked him but remarked that the deal was still not closed. "Peter," he said. "You have done your job. The rest is up to the partners!"

Regrettably, my comment was prescient. Floyd and Red Owl were icons in Minnesota. In the end, he couldn't face selling to upstarts and sold instead to Bert Gamble, a local Minneapolis businessman who controlled the retail conglomerate Gamble-Skogmo. The deal worked out badly for the Bell family; Bert Gamble, not long thereafter, bankrupted his company.

This was one of my first lessons in the fact that owners make decisions based on more than money or any other quantitative factor. Psychological issues are frequently decisive. A client's standing in his own hometown after a sale can be critical in a decision to sell.

The most substantive interaction I ever had with Mr. Lehman occurred one day in 1966, when he called me to his office to introduce me to Enrico Braggiotti, a senior officer of Banca Commerciale Italiana, one of the most well-connected commercial banks in Rome. Braggiotti explained that BCI had lent the filmmaker Dino De Laurentiis, the producer of *War and Peace* and, later, *Barbarella*, $15 million and did not know what had happened to the loan. Mr. Lehman told me I should fly to Italy, visit De Laurentiis at his famous studio south of Rome, and find the money. All I had to go on was BCI's suspicion that De Laurentiis had moved the money out of Italy to another country.

This was a big step up from my usual assignments. At the time, I was working under a group of four or five men ranked below the partner level. They were the NCOs of the firm, guys in their fifties who had been at Lehman about twenty years and were never going to become partners, but everyone realized that, and it was fine. Today we'd call them senior vice presidents. They were probably smarter than most of the partners, but they also tended to be lazy. I got a lot of assignments simply because I worked late on Fridays and all the NCOs went home early. When a partner would call looking for someone to do something, I'd be the only one around to say, "Okay, sir, I'll come right down!"

Most of what I got to do wasn't terribly glamorous though. When Mr. Lehman called about sending me to find De Laurentiis, for example, I had just come back from a quick trip to Houston. We were doing an underwriting with an oil company down there, and there had been a problem with the accounting. "I want you to fly to Houston," Bob Rubin had said, "and I want you to read the accounting documents and tell us if they're all right and if we'll go ahead with the underwriting." I was the human equivalent of FedEx and fax, which didn't exist in those days, and I didn't know much about the oil business, but I took the assignment as a compliment, a sign that they thought I was reliable.

My mission in Rome was to find the missing $15 million; when I did, I was to report to a banker named Dr. Dente at BCI's home office on the Via Veneto. Since I knew as much about film production as I did about oil, I asked Mr. Lehman who could help me understand the movie business. He advised me to call a man named Martin Davis, then a PR guy at Paramount in New York. I met with Davis, who gave me some rudimentary information but was not that helpful.

Linda and I went to Rome and checked into the Hassler on the Spanish Steps. Before long, an American fellow slightly older than I, a Wharton grad named Fred Sidewater, showed up. He worked for Dino and, for the remainder of our trip, attached himself to me like a pilot fish to a shark.

Dino's studio was going full throttle. In one area, he was filming his epic *The Bible*; in another, Jane Fonda was shooting *Barbarella*; and all this while a war movie called *Anzio* was being shot. On my first day there, I almost bumped into Marcello Mastroianni.

Dino knew I was coming to look at the books, but I don't think he knew why. The studio accountant spoke English as poorly as I spoke Italian, but he was forthcoming. He immediately showed me the income statement, balance sheet, and cash flows; though foreign in format, they were clear and showed the equivalent in lira of BCI's $15 million loan. I studied these for the morning and saw that despite all the activity, each year showed little profit.

After lunch, the accountant proposed showing me the "tax books," which not surprisingly showed large losses, though these also reflected the "missing" loan. Dino was hardly put off by my audit. That night, Dino invited us to his villa near Rome, which appeared to be a castle. We dined at a long table by candlelight with his wife, the actress Silvana Mangano, whose fame at one time rivaled that of Sophia Loren, the wife of Dino's rival filmmaker, Carlo Ponti.

The next morning, Sidewater, who had not been invited to the dinner, picked us up but once again left me alone with the bookkeeper. I asked some perfunctory follow-up questions, which he answered without hesitation. He then asked whether I would like to see the "real" set of books. Startled, I said yes. He then showed me a third set of books, which recorded a series of transfers clearly moving the cash equivalent of the BCI loan to an unconsolidated company based in Geneva. I didn't confront Dino; I just thanked the accountant and went back to the hotel.

Well, I thought, *that didn't take long!* As instructed, I called Dente and scheduled an appointment for the next day.

BCI's headquarters was a block-size building with blackened walls. It looked like it could survive anything (although not, as it later turned out, the Vatican Bank scandal). I found Dr. Dente sitting behind a desk at the far end of a large room lit only by a small lamp. I told him I had located the missing money in a Geneva bank. Would he like any other information? By this time, he still hadn't looked up; nor had he asked me to sit down. I asked again if he had need of further details. "No," he said. I waited a few long moments, during which he never looked up, and then I left.

Upon returning to the Hassler, I called Mr. Lehman. "Good job," he said. "Come home." So, I booked a flight and went off with Linda to dinner.

Lehman Brothers had done what it had been asked to do—find the money. But, weirdly, no one from BCI ever followed up with me. As a postscript, Braggiotti was later convicted of bribery in a major Italian scandal, the Enimont affair. Dino soon after closed his Rome studio and moved his operation to North Carolina, probably using the BCI money. And he took Fred Sidewater with him.

As for me, I got hepatitis from eating clams on our one night out in Rome and was in bed off and on for six months. The Lehman partners treated me very well during my illness, but for me, it was extraordinarily traumatic. I could not move; when I took a bath, Linda had to lift me. I could tolerate nothing but ginger ale for weeks. When I asked my doctor, Henry Erle, when I would be better, he said I would know I was cured when one day I felt better. I loved Henry Erle for his common sense.

Moral of the story? Who knows? I continued to see Dino socially in New York. Marty Davis, the unhelpful publicist, became head of Paramount and Gulf & Western. Fifty years later, I have no idea what that little adventure was all about.

CHAPTER 5

Lehman Brothers Chaos: 1960–1969

The 1960s moved along, and I saw less and less of Mr. Lehman, who would die in 1969. As he faded from the lives of his employees, Ed Weisel, the senior partner of the firm's general counsel, Simpson, Thacher & Bartlett, became increasingly present. Almost every morning when he was in New York City, he began his day at One William Street. The partners treated Mr. Weisel as Mr. Lehman's surrogate, which no doubt he was. The two were of a similar temperament and philosophy. Mr. Lehman, at the time, was chairman of the Democratic Party's finance committee. Lyndon Johnson was president, and Ed Weisel was one of his closest advisers, often taking calls from the Oval Office when he was in the Lehman offices. Mr. Weisel would occasionally offer me rides home in his chauffeured car, and he encouraged me to meet his younger partners, Dick Beattie and Matt Nimetz. As generous as these gestures were, the message I took from them was that Lehman Brothers was Simpson's largest client, and he was doing what he could to assure continuity.

But who would serve as chairman? Mr. Lehman had steered the firm through the Great Depression and managed the sometimes difficult partners brilliantly, in his fashion—he was a better Svengali than he was a banker—but had created no clear plan of succession. That was a mistake I would see in the years ahead that a lot of successful people make. As Manny Chirico, then CEO of Phillips-Van Heusen, remarked when discussing his need for a successor, "Its timing is only one biopsy away."

The next senior partners at Lehman by age and tenure were Monroe Gutman, then in his eighties, and Paul Mazur in his seventies. They both became partners in the mid-1920s after John Hancock, the first non-Lehman family partner. I have already written about Mr. Mazur's intellectual prowess and his exalted status on Wall Street. Gutman had led the closed-end mutual fund Lehman Corporation since its founding in the 1920s. While it had not prospered, it had stayed solvent, something Goldman Sachs couldn't say about its 1930s trading company under Waddill Catchings. Monroe was respected but no longer active in the firm. The Lehman Corporation and newer One William Street Fund were run by his deputy, Al Pearson, a buttoned-up gentleman who ate enormous bowls of raspberries at partners' luncheons and had probably been the only student in a three-piece suit at hippie-ish Reed College in Oregon.

Al and Monroe were important to me in terms of their not-for-profit activities. In his early years, Monroe had been aided by the Hudson Guild Settlement House, of which I, in 1970, became president and then chairman. His was one of the classic American success stories. In gratitude, he gave $1 million to the Guild so we could expand our educational program, a meaningful gift for us both.

Mr. Mazur was generous to me in other ways. One day in 1965, he asked me to write a memorandum to the top management of Federated Department Stores proposing an acquisition strategy. As a second-year associate, I felt daunted by the task but prepared a lengthy memorandum. In it, I argued that the rise of discount stores and the general availability of credit through the credit card would continue to erode the market share of department stores, something I had learned from my dad. I proposed that Federated expand in fields where its geographic dominance and superior financial strength would create a competitive advantage. Two fields I proposed were the rental car business and the television, radio, and cable television broadcasting businesses. Many original broadcasting licenses had been owned by local department stores because the stores viewed television as an extension of their geographic dominance. In fact, in the 1960s, many stock security analysts covered companies in retailing and broadcasting.

I have no idea whether Mr. Mazur ever showed my ideas to Federated's top management, but he did tell my dad it was a most brilliant memo. Dad, whose admiration had seemed limited to my long drives in golf, was duly impressed.

Small favors mean a lot to a new associate. Mr. Mazur was on the board of RCA. He invited me and my wife to a black-tie dinner at their apartment at 10 Gracie Square. Among the dinner guests were the famed coanchor of the NBC nightly news, Chet Huntley, who appeared in a kilt, and RCA's CEO Robert Sarnoff, General Sarnoff's son and successor.

Such courtesies and connections were not naturally extended at Lehman Brothers, where the partners were lords, and the associates, vassals. That was a shame, because binding young partners and associates to the firm requires more than pay. Including them in social events and encouraging them beyond the office provides an example of the style of living and working you want them to adopt, while, at the same time, giving them the social ease to pull things off in what one might have called "the Lehman way."

Lehman by then had a tradition of welcoming former government officials into the partnership. In the mid-1960s, the most important such person was General Lucius Clay. Wiry, rather short, with a craggy nose and a southern twang, Clay resembled what I imagine General Robert E. Lee must have been like. He had been Dwight Eisenhower's indispensable logistics general in the European Theatre of Operations. Clay got the gas to Patton and the rifles to Bradley, and Ike couldn't do without him. After the war, he was military governor of Germany from 1947 to 1949. But Clay resented the fact that he never was as famous as Clark, Hodges, Patton, or Bradley because he never received a field command. Nevertheless, he was loyal to Ike and helped him defeat Taft for the Republican nomination and win the presidency in 1952.

General Clay took an interest in me and gave me a lot of support.

When in 1964 I wrote a new business memorandum laying out an area I wanted to call on—group owners of radio and television—he, as the chairman of the firm's underwriting committee, took my side when some of the partners, not wanting to upset our clients NBC and ABC, argued that we should do nothing until we got the green light from the networks. Later in my career, when I won a hotly contested initial public offering of the Block Drug Company, beating out Goldman Sachs' Gus Levy and Sy Lewis of Bear Stearns—both friends of Leonard Block, the CEO of the company—it was those competitors and General Clay who congratulated me, not the other senior partners of Lehman.

But Clay was tough. The steely nerve he showed while breaking the Russian blockade of Berlin in 1949 was never far from the surface.

The general's command presence was illustrated by his standing in 1965 as not only a Lehman partner but also an advisory board member of the Chase Bank, something inconceivable today, when his dual positions would be recognized as a conflict of interest. This turned out to be more than a theoretical conflict. In one instance, Lehman had been chosen to manage a debt underwriting for Chase. Lehman priced the bond offering at 3:30 p.m., basing it on the prime rate, as was done in those days before LIBOR, and sent confirming wires to its syndicate. But immediately after the pricing at 4:30 p.m., Chase raised the prime rate a quarter of a percentage point, meaning the value of the bond would go down, and Lehman would take a hit. Even now, almost fifty years later, this seems bizarre.

The partners of Lehman were understandably shocked and yelped to Clay that this was some sort of double cross and the bond had to be repriced. Clay refused. He said a deal was a deal even though Chase had done something inappropriate.

As a young associate, I thought it a great privilege to be exposed to a man like Clay and to learn how he thought about different situations in and out of the financial business. I especially enjoyed the forum that daily lunches provided, with all the available partners sitting around an enormous oval table on the eighth floor, dining on food prepared by the former chef at Pavilion. General Clay was a frequent attendee of these lunches. Much to the chagrin of other older partners, I would ask him, and later George Ball, for their thoughts on various topics. They answered fully and frankly. Clay was unfashionably easy on Richard Nixon during the Watergate crisis. He saw no problem with the type of break-in, he said, and revealed that he and others had organized the same kind of dirty tricks for Ike. What bothered him, he said, was the stupidity of Nixon's soldiers. He also was upset—to an odd degree, I thought—by Nixon's spending more than $300,000 of government money to improve his San Clemente "Casa Pacifica." His partners, who personified Wall Street Republicans, were particularly shocked at his admission of dirty tricks for Ike.

At one lunch, Clay said something I have never forgotten. Fred Ehrman, a senior partner, asked Clay why he had taken a position as chairman of the New York City Public Development Corporation, the city's agency responsible for the development of its industrial parks. It wasn't a prestige assignment, and Mayor John Lindsay, who had appointed him, was by that time on the decline. Clay stared at Ehrman across the table. In a voice firm and tinged with indignation, he said, "This country has been very good to me. And whenever I am asked to serve, in whatever capacity, I do so!"

Not all of the senior partners were so admirable.

Joe Thomas—then in his sixties and for a while thought to have been a serious contender for the chairman's job—was a tough guy wannabe who sounded like he was from West Texas but was basically a well-connected bigot who had gone to Exeter, Yale, and HBS. A former naval officer, he had made his mark investing with Tex Thornton and Roy Ash, two former Department of Defense whiz kids who founded the first conglomerate, Litton Industries. By the time I encountered him, Joe had a chronic case of emphysema and carried an oxygen bottle while he puffed—and constantly relit—his cigars. He scared the hell out of everyone around him who thought he would blow up the room. At various points during the working day, Joe would repair to the eleventh-floor gym for a massage from Don, the in-house trainer. He would talk on the phone to clients and in person to junior associates like me while he smoked and swilled vodka.

For some inexplicable reason, I worked with Joe Thomas on two of his major accounts. Black & Decker was in its heyday of growth under Al Decker and Bob Black, and Associated Dry Goods was the owner of Lord and Taylor, LS Ayers, and a number of upscale department stores.

On one of my first business trips, I sat next to Joe as we flew on a US Airways prop plane to Baltimore to visit Black & Decker. With a cigar in his mouth and the *Morning Telegraph* in his hand, he said, "Kid, stocks go up and down. But every year, the yearlings at Keeneland sell for more than they did the year before." Unlike Joe (and Bobbie Lehman), I never invested in thoroughbreds. But after our conversation, I followed the horse auctions in the newspaper. Joe was right for about thirty years.

At the other end of the spectrum from Joe Thomas in terms of education, social background, and demeanor was Herman Kahn. Herman had worked his way up from a runner, a young man who would physically cart stock and bond certificates between firms. Beneath the image he tried to project—that of an opera-loving sophisticate in tailored suits—he was a City College graduate with an aggressive personality, a booming voice, and a pronounced talent for making money. Herman had come up with the idea for the private placement of corporate long-term debt with insurance companies, such as Met Life and New York Life. As one of the most aggressive partners, he dealt with many of the firm's toughest CEOs, such as Tom Macioce of Allied Stores and Nat Cummings of Consolidated Foods in Chicago. When Stop&Shop Companies went public in 1961, Paul Mazur had brought in Herman to deal with my uncle Sidney and to handle the offering. Sidney thought Kahn screwed our family in the pricing of the stock. Sidney was wrong, as he often was on the facts, but probably right on Herman's intent.

Both Thomas and Kahn didn't just have obvious flaws that made them difficult to be around at times. They also had problematic sons whom they brought into Lehman and who caused serious divisiveness.

Joe's son Michael M. Thomas—a.k.a. the Chipmunk—came to Lehman in 1962. He had hoped for a career at the Metropolitan Museum, and had in fact worked there for a while, but Thomas Hoving, who would become the Met's director, forced him out. Even

Mr. Lehman, who was on the museum's board, couldn't keep Michael Thomas at the Met.

Sidney Kahn, Herman's son, who was in the same class as Michael at Yale, was tall, somewhat elegant, and spoke with a stilted upper-crust accent. He did not want to be identified with his father, yet he worked only with his father's clients. He treated his peers like inferiors.

Sidney and the Chipmunk had more in common than Yale. Smart though they were, both were undisciplined in their personal lives and spoiled by their fathers. Over the next ten years, until both left, they created tensions along religious and cultural lines within the partnership. Neither deserved to become a partner, but both did within five years of joining the firm. Michael's life was chaotic, and its effects sometimes had unintended repercussions.

A truly farcical incident occurred once during a hiring period. George Riordan, an associate who was the same age as Michael, was responsible for recruiting. By then, Michael had been appointed head of the industrial department. George screened possible hires and then brought each to see Michael, whose job it was to tell the candidates whether or not they were going to be hired.

One day, he was seeing several recruits from University of Chicago Business School. The group included a young man we thought had superior potential, and the firm was eager to offer him a job. But Michael got confused, sent the prized recruit packing, and hired a guy to whom he was supposed to have said, "Sorry, we have nothing for you." The beneficiary of Michael's ineptitude was Roger C. Altman, who would in time become the youngest partner the firm.

Years later, Gerry Gallagher, the former CFO of Dayton Company and the founder of Oak, a top venture capital firm, asked me how Altman happened to be hired by Lehman. He said he wasn't that good a student at Chicago, and his classmates had been shocked. As Ken Auletta said in the 1985 book *Greed and Glory on Wall Street: The Fall of the House of Lehman*, Roger was known primarily as a pleasant fellow who didn't make waves. When I told Gerry about how Michael Thomas had mixed things up, he laughed hard and immediately telephoned his former classmates to explain the riddle of Altman's hiring.

50

But back to the senior partners.

Somewhere between the polar opposites of Joe Thomas and Herman Kahn, and combining the worst qualities of both, was Fred Ehrman. Also in his sixties when I joined the firm, Fred was a genuine misanthrope, a man who made others miserable, no doubt because he was so miserable himself. Fred had once punched the bartender at a dinner party given by his partner Arthur Schulte at the Century Club in Purchase, New York, a bastion for "Our Crowd" German Jews. On another occasion, he leapt across a dinner table at a New York restaurant to strike Philip Graham, the publisher of the *Washington Post*, accusing him—perhaps correctly—of causing the suicide of Fred's daughter due to a love affair gone wrong. (Graham later committed suicide himself.)

My own experience with Ehrman had been even more bizarre. Fred was playing golf one day at the Century as part of his usual foursome that included Gus Levy, Teddy Low of Bear Stearns, and Tubby Burnham of Burnham and Company. I found myself stuck behind that slow-moving bunch. (Although I descend from Russian, not German, Jews, I joined Century because I had a lot of friends there.) When they had moved just beyond my range on the par-five eleventh hole, I drilled a drive that struck a dove that was minding its own business. The poor bird spiraled from the sky. A few minutes later, I saw Fred Ehrman walking toward me. As he got closer, I realized he was holding the dove. "These are good eating," he said as he handed it to me. I doubt that I parred the hole.

Two other senior partners were less important in the management and structure of Lehman, but they gave the firm a sense of humanity and humor.

Frank Manheim was a former English teacher who was brought into the firm by his older brother Paul. Frank was a poseur of the first rank, affecting long, combed-back hair, bespoke English suits and purple shirts. He had an enormous nose. Frank could cope with such eccentric clients as Charlie Revson of Revlon. To this day, when I wear a lavender shirt, I think of Frank Manheim, and if I run into former

Lehman colleagues, they will kid me about my supposed homage to him.

Paul Manheim was a joy and made my life at Lehman tolerable when the *mishegas* of the firm went beyond manageable. Educated at the University of Virginia when no one north of Richmond went there, he maintained a circle of friends that included J. Harvie Wilkinson, chairman of United Virginia Bankshares, and the Tennant Bryan family of Media General, the owners of the *Richmond Dispatch*. He played golf with Alistair Cooke of the BBC. Whenever we traveled, we went to the airport so early we often caught an earlier plane. Paul was a renowned collector, particularly of Asian art. At every stop on our travels together, we would visit a museum.

Paul had grown up in asset management, and he didn't know much about mergers; still, he was trusted by all and did a lot of business. To the extent that anyone was a mentor to me at Lehman, it was Paul. His success was a lesson that taking an interest in your clients' lives will not only help your business but enrich your life. He couldn't match Herman Kahn or Fred Ehrman in a deal sense, and he never wielded power within the firm, but of all the bankers at Lehman, I believe he was the most personally fulfilled.

Paul and I had a lot of fun together, and we accomplished a great deal. In 1967, we sold KOA-TV, the NBC affiliate in Denver, to General Electric. That same year, we also sold the Water Pic, which was invented by a Ft. Collins, Colorado, dentist, to Teledyne. That was a hard sell. All the buyers thought the Water Pic was a fad like the electric toothbrush. Warner Lambert, which owned Listerine, the dominant mouthwash, should have been interested. The marketing manager was desperate to buy it and told the CEO that he could envision the Water Pic spewing Listerine everywhere. But the CEO couldn't be convinced. Finally, Dr. Henry Singleton, CEO of Teledyne, offered a contingent deal that the seller earned within two years.

A fad it was not. Forty-six years later, Jay Eastman, the son of my close friend John Eastman, sold Water Pic, which he had bought in a leveraged buyout and sold for a substantial profit.

There was always excitement in Paul's life. His collection of jade and Eastern sculpture was once stolen from his maisonette at 2 1/2 East Sixty-Seventh Street. (No item was ever recovered.) Another time, he asked me to stay at his house on West Lane in East Hampton for the weekend. He had worried his estranged wife might take the furniture. I got to the house, opened the door, and saw there wasn't a stick of furniture to be found, just a black telephone on the floor of the entry hall. Its dial tone worked. I called Paul at Lehman (Bowling Green 9-3700) and said, "Broom clean!"

Each of these partners taught me something about banking or about style—even if it was sometimes how *not* to be.

Still, as much as I was learning, there were fundamental problems at the firm, and disaster loomed.

CHAPTER 6

1960s
Turmoil on William Street and in Chelsea

Lehman Brothers gradually ceased to be dynamic. From 1963 to 1967, there were no additions to the corporate finance group, where I worked. Of the twenty-five professionals in that department, except for the two sons, only five bankers—Bob Rubin, Bob McCabe, Bill Morris, Alan Sternlieb, and I—became partners of the firm, in my case, in 1971. The asset management business surrounding the open-end mutual fund One William Street and the closed-end Lehman Corporation traded on the NYSE was underperforming. The one area of growth was in trading, particularly fixed income and commercial paper. But even that limited success was tainted by its association with a man who would ultimately do a lot more harm than good.

Lew Glucksman's arrival at Lehman was like something out of a spy novel. The partners had envied the increasing prominence of the firm's rival, Goldman Sachs, and its commercial paper business—essentially the purchase and sale of short-term corporate debt. Companies finance working capital composed of inventories and accounts receivable on a daily basis, giving bankers a reason to talk to a prospect or a client daily. And those conversations often led to additional business.

Looking to jump-start its involvement in that area, Mr. Lehman asked partner Eddie Gudeman, who was from Chicago and had been deputy secretary of commerce in President Kennedy's administration, to hire away the commercial paper team at the Chicago-based firm of A. G. Becker: John Friedman, Jerry Stone, and Glucksman. After highly complicated and secretive negotiations, the three, along with three subordinates, agreed at a meeting at Newark Airport to defect to Lehman.

What a bad move for Lehman that turned out to be. Glucksman did build the commercial paper business, but because of his rampaging ego and understandable insecurities, it was never integrated into the firm's overall new business effort the way it had been at Goldman. He kept it a separate fiefdom, demanding loyalty to himself first. When the firm installed Arthur Schulte, a man as elegant as Glucksman was slovenly, as the chairman of the commercial paper department, Lew contrived successfully to undermine his oversight. Given his paranoid management style, it is no wonder that no successful leader ever emerged from the Glucksman operation. The closest he ever came to producing a leader was Dick Fuld, the CEO who in 2008 led Lehman into bankruptcy.

Blatantly ambitious, Glucksman soon established himself as a candidate for the chairman's job. But he was one in a crowded field that, in addition to all the partners I've already mentioned, included five bankers in their thirties and forties who were, for a time at least, acknowledged to have the inside track.

One of the brightest of those young stars was Warren Hellman, who had become a partner in 1960 when he was just twenty-six. Smart, competitive, and impulsive, Hellman was the scion of a great San Francisco banking family. He had been sent by his father, Mickey, to train at Lehman after HBS. Warren didn't return to San Francisco for twenty years, and his father fell out with Mr. Lehman over Warren's defection to the East Coast.

Hellman was married to Chris Sander, an English former ballerina whose father was an active member of the British Communist Party. Warren, definitely not a Communist, lived in a townhouse on East Seventy-Ninth Street befitting a Lehman partner and, as a fanatical skier, hired a bus to drive the couple and their four children four hours to Stratton Mountain, Vermont, every winter weekend. In 1972, he founded the Stratton Mountain School so skiers could train for competitive racing while receiving a superior education.

Another "star of the future" was Andrew G. C. Sage. If you met him outside of his professional context, though, you might be surprised. A congenial roly-poly fellow about six feet in height, Andy gave the appearance of being neither very bright, educated, nor ambitious. He was nominally in charge of the syndicate department but didn't seem to work hard, leaving most of his duties there to the usually inebriated Bob Thayer. Andy never graduated from anywhere. He had joined the firm in 1948 and had previously been the lifeguard at Mr. Lehman's Sands Point estate. The secret of Andy's stature—and the only reason he was ever mentioned as even a long shot candidate for the chairman's job—was that the C in his name stood for Carnegie. As in Andrew. He was also a Mellon. Andy had good human instincts. When he concentrated, he succeeded, but seldom did he apply himself. Nevertheless, he belonged to all the right clubs.

Bob Shapiro, a talented and affable 1956 Yale graduate, was responsible for the equity activities of the firm. Brought to Lehman through the then traditional route, via a connection with partner Johnny Fell, he became a partner in 1967 and a member of the executive committee in 1971. Bob was identified with Andy Sage, whom Fell had asked to watch over Bob when he joined Lehman.

Then there was Stephen DuBrul, the oldest of the young cadre, a product of the Midwest who had gone to HBS. He'd married into the family of Walter Paepcke, who was an executive with the Container Corporation of America but, more notably, in the early 1950s founded the Aspen Skiing Company and the Aspen Institute. DuBrul was the ultimate in managing upward. Mr. Lehman, it was rumored, bought him his townhouse on East Seventy-Third Street. He succeeded Mr. Lehman and another senior partner, H. "Jim" Szold, on the boards of the May Company, the Jewel Companies, and other establishment companies. At just thirty, he was Lehman's smoothest operator.

The final member of the closely watched next generation was slightly older but also the son of a former banker. Bill Osborn was interested in technology and flew in daily on a seaplane from the North

Shore of Long Island with Andy Sage. His wife drank too much, and he acted like a man who was afraid of something, but he was smart and a good banker.

I should note, for the sake of historical accuracy, that there was one other person in the firm to whom the partners might have turned for leadership, but he died suddenly of a heart attack. Ray Rusmisel, in his mid-fifties, was general counsel. A Canadian, a bit chubby with a good sense of humor, he had the respect of both the older and younger generations of Lehman bankers. One story demonstrates Ray's modesty as well as his tenacity.

In 1966, Ray and I met in our offices with Roy Ash and Tex Thornton, the heads of Litton Industries, to discuss the acquisition of NuTone, a Cincinnati-based manufacturer of door chimes. They expressed interest, which, for Litton, was surprising.

Litton was never the easiest client to deal with. Ash liked to boast that he knew every company. By that, he meant that he owned the Standard and Poor's compendium that contained the *names* of every company. In his usual imperious way, Ash said he and Thornton wanted to meet with us that afternoon in Cincinnati on their return trip to Los Angeles. This might have been inconvenient under any circumstances, but the country was in the midst of a prolonged 1966 air traffic controller strike. Ray Rusmisel, playing the situation just right, didn't ask Ash for a ride on Litton's private plane. Instead, as soon as they left the office, he hired a twin-engine prop, and three hours later, we arrived in Ohio. Not only hadn't we risked imposing on a client, but we had a way to get back home when our business was done.

The meeting went well, and Litton later concluded the acquisition of NuTone. By three in the morning, we had landed back at LaGuardia. I had plans to visit our close family friends Gretchen and Donald Glickman in Mill River, Massachusetts, so after dropping Ray at LaGuardia, the plane flew on and landed at five o'clock on a gorgeous summer morning at the Berkshire County airport. I walked to town feeling good about the deal we'd done.

The issue at Lehman was governance. I am a longtime beekeeper and tend to see things in terms of the hive. When the queen—Mr.

Lehman—died in 1969, the worker bees who had hovered around him were lost. They frantically tried one candidate (Joe Thomas) for the CEO job, then another (Lucius Clay) before settling on a third (Fred Ehrman), who was more a sign of their desperation than anything else.

Ehrman didn't so much rise to the position of CEO as he was sucked into the vacuum at the top. I tried to avoid contact with him. You can tell a lot about a man by the way he behaves on the golf course, and I've already recounted one instance of Ehrman's odd behavior there. On another occasion in the late 1960s, when my game was as good as it would ever be, I was in the semifinals of the Century Club Championship, playing Julian Frankel, a well-known floor trader. It was a very competitive matchup. I had managed to lose the lead I'd established, and we were all even after eighteen. Ehrman saw fit to join us as we drove off the nineteenth. My drive landed in a sand trap on the right side of the first fairway, and I went into the trap to address it. As I took my stance, I noticed Ehrman standing about ten feet behind me in the bunker itself, watching me. What was he thinking? He knew enough about golf to understand that what he was doing was just plain weird. Though scared to miss while standing in front of my boss, I hit a good shot and halved the hole only to lose on the twentieth.

☙

History doesn't remember great bankers; it remembers great philanthropists. A woman named Susan Wimpfheimer taught me that.

When I met Susan in 1965, she was, at age fifty-two, the director of the New Leadership Division of the Federation of Jewish Philanthropies, an umbrella organization for 130 social agencies, including major hospitals and settlement houses. The Federation wasn't a Zionist organization; it attracted Jews like my parents who wanted to stay connected to their heritage but also to assimilate. As its name suggests, the NLD focused on donors in their twenties and thirties.

Over a three-year period, I worked my way onto Susan's board. The NLD was an active group holding social events around the theme of philanthropy. The lessons I learned from my involvement I have repeated to my colleagues wherever I've worked. No one remembers Sidney Weinberg, who, with Gus Levy, laid the foundation for the modern Goldman Sachs. And Gus is remembered because of his leadership of Mt. Sinai Hospital. The same is true of J. P. Morgan. He is remembered because of his library. Except for the name on the bank, only a history buff could remember his bravado in halting the 1907 panic and bailing out banks in New York City.

In the spirit of giving back, I volunteered in the study den run by Alan Cohen at the Hudson Guild Neighborhood House on West Twenty-Sixth Street. The Guild was one of America's largest and oldest settlement houses, organizations that originally helped integrate immigrants into the fabric of New York.

Getting involved with the Guild, I realized, would be good in more ways than one. While life at Lehman was intellectually challenging and politically intriguing, it soon became obvious that it would not augment my administrative skills; I wanted experience in managing people and supervising organizations. Why? I'm not sure, but my dad and uncles had managed businesses, and I had gone to HBS, so maybe order and administration were ingrained in me. Volunteerism was also a value in our family. Dad and Mom were both involved in Jewish organizations like the Federation and civic groups. Dad was chairman of the Better Business Bureau. In Boston, my mother's family, the Rabbs, were involved in virtually every charity. The Hudson Guild felt like a natural fit for me.

The organization's founder was John Lovejoy Elliot, one of the pioneers of the ethical culture movement. In 1964, Dan Carpenter, Lovejoy's son-in-law, was the executive director. After a year of tutoring black and Puerto Rican elementary school kids in arithmetic and English as part of the study den, I met Dan, who asked me if I would like to join the Guild's board of trustees. It was an eclectic group. The doyen of the board was Arthur Strasser, eighty-eight, the senior partner of the Wall Street firm Strasser Spiegelberg; Ruth Uris, the wife of the real estate developer Harold Uris, was chairman. The board also included Plummer Whitehead, a neighbor in Chelsea who drove a cab and ran a soul food business, and Ron Freeman, a small, outspoken black man who worked in the storeroom at Gimbels. I was the only board member under thirty.

Chelsea in the 1960s was undergoing a transition from a neighborhood of older, low-income immigrant Jews, many of whom lived in a housing project built by the International Ladies Garment Industry under David Dubinsky, to a community of mostly blacks and Hispanics. The longtime residents weren't happy with the change.

The Guild operated a seniors' facility on Nineteenth Street and a nursery school adjacent to its main building; within that building, it offered cultural and educational activities for adults. It had a theatre used by Off-Broadway producers and a sports program too. At one time, the original Boston Celtics and famed college coach Nat Holman coached at the Guild.

It would be hard to overstate the positive impact that settlement houses such as the Hudson Guild, Henry Street, Educational Alliance, and Grand Street Settlement House had on New York City. Over the course of the century, they were on the front line welcoming waves of immigrants and providing social services. Their work on the streets reduced the tensions inherent in the city's melting pot.

In the 1960s, the Guild Board reflected those tensions. On one hand, there were the richer and older liberals, mostly but not all Jewish, who had financially supported the Guild for decades. On the other hand were the local residents, poorer by a lot, less educated, both whites and minorities who wanted more say. The neighborhood was getting younger, creating generational issues of language, drug use, and social activism.

Before long, Ruth Uris asked me to be an officer of the board. I urged my friends—such as Stephen Schulte, who later founded the law firm of Schulte, Roth and Zabel, and Gretchen Glickman, a leader at the Community Service Society—to join the board. Dan Carpenter recruited José Cabranes, the son of a fellow settlement house head and a young lawyer of Puerto Rican descent who later became counsel to Yale University and now sits on the United States Court of Appeals for the Second Circuit. Jose was reputed to have been a possible nominee for the Supreme Court. Associate Supreme Court Justice Sonia Sotomayor refers to Jose as her mentor.

I felt Dan needed a younger, more business-oriented assistant. Luckily, I found Ken Schuman, a graduate of Columbia Business School, who was willing to work for a not-for-profit. Ken brought discipline to the raucous Guild. He subsequently became my assistant in City Hall, and after I left the office of commissioner of economic development, he joined me at Lehman Brothers.

The Guild was in the middle of the street turmoil. As the Young Lords gained more influence among Puerto Ricans and the Black Panthers began to infiltrate the Chelsea neighborhood, tensions and tempers flared. Steeped as he was in the tradition of ethical culture and the reasonable discussion of differences, Dan Carpenter decided in the fall of 1967 to have a conference on the racial and generational issues facing the Guild, the city, and the country.

The Hudson Guild Farm, donated by George J. Hecht, the owner of *Parents Magazine,* was located in bucolic Hopatcong, New Jersey, about an hour from the George Washington Bridge. Dan organized an outing where the rainbow of Chelsea residents would meet for a picnic and a conference. The issues were not solely racial. It was a tumultuous time. Women members of the Guild had grievances, as did the young people and the seniors.

It was a bright and beautiful fall day, and the turnout was large. José Cabranes was the perfect moderator for a conference that could easily morph into a confrontation. At least he would have been, if he hadn't canceled at the last moment. As calm as Dan sounded, I could tell he was agitated when he called and asked if I could chair the conference instead.

Fifty years later the details are unclear to me, but the outcome isn't. We met, argued, debated, attacked, and laughed. Those meetings, lasting all day, exposed the rawness of the issues. Dan was perceptive in holding the sessions that at times I could barely control. Though every group felt victimized or betrayed, by late afternoon they had exhausted themselves into moderation.

It was the first time I realized that I had a talent for getting people to move toward a common goal. I also saw that humor could relieve a tense situation. At one point, a young black man made an impassioned speech about racial equality. A middle-aged white woman interrupted to disagree, complaining about the denigration of women and arguing that equality between the sexes was more important. The tension created by the opposing views stunned the audience into silence, until I remarked that I would be back as soon as I took the men's and women's signs down from the restrooms. Many, including the angry woman, had to laugh at that. Though Harvard undergrads now share bathrooms, in 1967 it was a radical—even comical—notion.

Often it's the things you don't see coming that wind up making the most difference. As a result of that day, the old guard gave up, I think, with an audible sigh of relief. At thirty, I became the youngest president of a major settlement house.

My adventures at the Guild during this volatile time had only begun. At one community meeting dealing with the sharing of the Guild's facilities among a neighborhood group—to which I'd brought my Lehman Brothers colleague Henry Breck, who had been a covert CIA agent in Rhodesia—a teenager named Lloyd threatened to kill me as Henry and I departed. In case that remark wasn't sufficiently confrontational, he added that his pals would burn down the Guild's building. Breck told me he had dealt with dangerous people in the line of duty, and these guys weren't to be taken lightly. (He had that right; Lloyd and several pals later served time for violent crime.) Still, I wasn't much older than those angry young men, and I had no guilt about their circumstances, a condition they were accustomed to exploiting. So, instead of acting intimidated by their threats, I told them that I didn't live in Chelsea and if they burnt down the Guild, they were dumber than I thought because they would be destroying their own resources. The Guild is still standing.

Some of the young women in Lloyd's group were as rowdy as the guys. Caryn Johnson had an especially loud mouth. Dan Carpenter, an elegant, old-fashioned man, was appalled that a girl of about fifteen could and did tell him to go fuck himself. It was the age of *Hair*. Cursing, unruly hair, and sloppy clothes flew in the face of convention, and the Guild was a conventional institution. They were weapons against the establishment. Caryn Johnson understood that and knew that in such an environment, her curses had an extra sting.

Flash forward thirty years. Dan was praising Whoopi Goldberg for her attachment to the Guild, saying she always sent extra tickets for her shows and remembered the Guild in other generous ways. "You remember Whoopi," Dan said. I had no idea what he was talking about.

"I know a lot of people," I said, "but I assure you I have never met Whoopi Goldberg."

"Oh yes you have!" Dan said. "Don't you remember Caryn Johnson, the girl with the loudest mouth on Twenty-Sixth Street?"

"Oh my God," I said. "That tough kid is Whoopi Goldberg!"

Whoopi and I delivered Dan's eulogy several years later.

One of the toughest characters who hung around the Guild was Angel Lugo, or as he was known within the Young Lords, Angel X. I had no idea if he actually had a criminal record, but he certainly carried himself with the swagger of a felon. One day, he called me at Lehman. He and the Young Lords had real beefs they wanted to discuss with me. I suggested meeting at the Guild, but he refused, proposing a spot just off Tenth Avenue and Twenty-Seventh Street. "Be there at six o'clock," he said. It was winter, and it would be dark by then, but I agreed to meet him. I don't know why I wasn't scared, but I wasn't.

Angel was waiting in a hallway of a dingy tenement building. (It's hard to imagine that street today, as it is now under the High Line and in the midst of Chelsea art galleries.) As I opened the door, he launched into a tirade about everything in the world that was bothering him and the Lords, except maybe Vietnam. The bottom line was that his gang, together with the Black Panthers, wanted to occupy the Guild physically and throw out the executive director and board.

Angel was not making an idle threat. The Guild operated a city-owned building with only modest security, and these were dangerous times when people did violent things in the name of social progress. "Angel," I said, "this is ridiculous. The Guild is one of the few forces for good in your world. They are trying to educate and assimilate the

Puerto Rican influx into Chelsea. You will infuriate whites, the aged, and Puerto Rican and minority mothers who send their kids to Head Start and the nursery schools.

"It's the Great Society," I went on. "President Johnson has made it possible for everybody to have their own programs. Forget trashing the Guild. Get your own agency. Run it and do whatever the hell you want."

Angel seemed to disappear after that night. Relative calm prevailed. On my way to a Guild board meeting about nine months later, I was walking up Eighth Avenue and walked past a storefront. I turned around and peered in. Sitting at a desk was Angel Lugo, no longer exuding Angel X. I threw open the door. "Angel," I said, "what's going on?"

Without missing a beat, he answered, "I took your advice. I went to the city and got a grant to start a Puerto Rican social agency. I like what I am doing and want to thank you."

America is a great country. Anyone can be an entrepreneur.

CHAPTER 7

Branching Out

As my career progressed, I decided to focus on two areas: retailing (a natural fit for me and for Lehman) and broadcasting. At HBS, I had begun to read about Metropolitan Broadcasting, run by John Kluge, and Capital Cities Broadcasting. These groups owned radio and TV stations; seven was then the maximum allowed according to the FCC. Being naturally interested in new business, I proposed that I call on group broadcasters throughout the United States. In each region, there were families or individuals who had built nice media companies. A number of them, such as the Outlet Company in Providence and Hubbard Broadcasting in St. Paul, would become clients.

I was especially interested in the possibilities surrounding CAT-V, as it was called. Although cable was primarily a rural phenomenon at that time, I argued to the Lehman partners that it would find acceptance from subscribers, who might eventually use it not just for entertainment but also for shopping. I used the vivid metaphor of a heroin needle in the arm of an addict. "Once subscribers were connected, it would be hard to remove." My bosses had no idea what I was talking about. I realized immediately I might have used a better example. What I didn't know then, despite my confidence, was how right I would be.

Within the sometimes hidebound firm, my talk about broadcasting conglomerates was controversial. The older partners were worried that doing business with these new groups and cable companies would offend the networks ABC, CBS, NBC, which were all Lehman clients. It was odd that the partners knew so little because the networks depended on their affiliates, and cable was too new to be a threat.

Not long after, Tom Unterberg called Warren Hellman to discuss the possibility of Lehman joining Unterberg Towbin in investing in LIN Broadcasting Corp., a collection of AM radio stations in Louisville, Nashville, Little Rock, and Shreveport, then expanding into broadcast TV and cable.

In October 1964, the Lehman partners and Unterberg each invested $500,000 to buy a minority position in LIN. The founder and principal of LIN, Fred Gregg, had also begun to acquire cable franchises in a number of towns. My colleagues and I were impressed by Gregg and the success he was having with his diverse group of stations, but my penultimate wife, Linda, whispered to me at the closing dinner that Gregg didn't seem trustworthy. A native of St. Louis, she felt that northerners like me were always overly impressed by smooth-talking southerners, of which Gregg was a prime example. Boy, was she right on both counts.

LIN was headquartered next to Printers Alley in Nashville, a hot town at the time where Grand Ole Opry stars like Minnie Pearl seemed to open restaurant chains every week. And Gregg, for all his slickness, was associated with Nashville's true movers and shakers. The company lawyer and one of the investors was Henry Hooker, whose brother John had been Bobby Kennedy's UVA law school roommate and was later governor of Tennessee.

For two or three years, all went well with LIN, as we acquired TV stations like Wand-TV in Decatur, Illinois, from Metromedia, and cable properties in places like Hobbs, New Mexico. Gregg filed for and received cable franchises along Piedmont Airlines' routes from Paducah, Kentucky, to Galesburg, Illinois. His clever technique was to give 10 or 20 percent of each franchise to the town coroner, who almost always had useful connections to the local city hall and could smooth the way for LIN's entrance into the community.

As time went on, Tom and I began to worry about how Gregg was operating. He seemed to be branching out in strange and scattered directions, making us wonder if he was a little crazy or a little crooked. Many of his new ventures had nothing to do with radio and television. He took over a contract with the Office of Economic Opportunity to train people in St. Louis. He acquired an outdoor advertising company. For a while, LIN owned the contract of the singer James Brown. I was concerned enough to have a talk with Warren Hellman, who oversaw my work even though I was the LIN director. When I went into his office, I didn't mince words. "Warren," I said, "I am worried that Fred Gregg might be up to something illegal!"

To my complete surprise, Warren exploded. "The problem with you Harvard Business School types," he said, "is that if someone does something differently than you think he should, you call them a crook!" Then he added, "I have had enough—you don't have a career here! There isn't a place at Lehman Brothers for you!"

I didn't know how to respond. I had come seeking advice. Now it sounded as if I was fired.

Nominally, I worked for Bob Rubin, whose office was one floor down from Warren's, not far from mine, so I went to him and explained what had happened. Rubin heard me out, then took me by the hand and escorted me back to Hellman's office. "Warren," Bob said, "you have no authority to fire Solomon. He doesn't work for you. He works for me!" With that, we turned and left.

My relationship with both men would change. Although I was always grateful to Bob for defending me when I was defenseless, fifteen years later, when he served as Glucksman's aide and apologist, he and I had a serious falling out. Meanwhile, Warren and I became close friends and remained so until his death in 2011.

But back to Fred Gregg.

Perhaps realizing we were on to him, Fred called me one day and said he had arranged to sell his stock to Martin Ackerman, the high-flying CEO of Perfect Film and Photo. One of the terms of the sale was for Ackerman to become CEO of LIN. Tom and I went to meet with Ackerman at his office, a brownstone on Thirty-Eighth and Park. We were skeptical of him and Perfect Film, which seemed not the healthiest company. In response to our questions, Ackerman pointed with aplomb to a pile of IBM computer printouts on his desk and said that if we read through them, we would see how profitable Perfect Film was. At the time, Tom was only thirty-seven, and I had not yet turned thirty. I'm sure Ackerman thought he could bully or con us.

We had a brief meeting and made a date to meet again at his other office on the Miracle Mile in Manhasset, Long Island, the next evening. To prepare for the meeting, Warren and I talked with Fred Ehrman, who by then had become Lehman's CEO. Ehrman gave me a stern lecture about the firm's reputation and bad investments but told me to use my best judgment. From Ehrman, this was a ringing endorsement. I must have said something that amused him, because at one point he smiled, or so I thought. As we left his third-floor office, Warren said, "I guess you're proud of yourself because you made Fred Ehrman smile."

"Well, maybe a little," I conceded.

Warren snorted ruefully. "Don't kid yourself. Fred wasn't smiling," he said. "He was just passing gas."

The meeting Tom and I had with Ackerman had been scheduled, at his request, for 8:30 p.m. At that odd postdinner hour, the suburban office building was silent and dark, but the lobby door was unlocked. It was a weird scene, and we were both nervous about the inevitable confrontation ahead, but I at least had the advantage of feeling like I was on familiar turf, having spent summers in the area as a kid. On the otherwise uninhabited second floor, we found Ackerman sitting alone in the dark at a desk with a single light. I got to the point quickly, telling him that despite what Gregg had told him about becoming the CEO of LIN and getting two other board seats, we were against his deal and would not be voting for it. The meeting was tense and short, lasting no longer than fifteen minutes.

The next day at the LIN board meeting at Perfect Film's office in New York City, Ackerman was represented by Milton Gould, the bombastic head of the law firm Shea, Gallop, Climenko & Gould. He, former governor Driscoll of New Jersey, and Ackerman were the three potential new directors. Unterberg and I were joined by Bob Roseman, Tom's Deerfield roommate and a young partner of Cravath, Swaine and Moore. I made a motion to reject the deal and not seat the directors. Unterberg seconded, at which point Milton Gould rose and shouted, "I am too rich and famous to deal with the likes of you!" He then stalked from the room, and Driscoll went with him.

In the same way that Russia walking out of the Security Council in 1950 had allowed the UN to defend Korea, Gould and Driscoll leaving let Tom and me carry the vote not to elect them to the board or Ackerman as CEO.

The company now had no CEO. The stock, which had shot up to forty-four dollars on the basis of the Perfect Film deal, began a precipitous decline. It was a situation that needed fixing. At Lehman, if you got a firm into a mess, you had better get it out. I commuted to Nashville during the rest of 1968, while Unterberg and I oversaw the former sales manager, Joel Thorpe, running LIN on an interim basis.

One upshot of the Gregg debacle was that Warren never doubted me again. Not long before his death, he told me a story about having a shouting match with one of his grown daughters on a street corner in San Francisco. In the midst of the argument, he said, he had a flashback and suddenly gave in. "Oh my God," he said to his daughter. "What happens if you are right like Peter Solomon was right?"

Finding the right person to succeed Gregg wouldn't be easy, but I had an idea up my sleeve. While calling on group broadcasting companies, I had become familiar with Donald A. Pels, then third in command at Capital Cities. I approached him about becoming CEO of LIN, and on February 17, 1969, we hired Pels for that position.

One day about a month later, Warren's secretary—they weren't called assistants then—summoned me to his office. As I rushed in, I heard him on the phone with Joe Gruss, a fabled Jewish oil man (of which there were few). "Yes, yes, Mr. Gruss," Warren was saying. "I know, it is terrible about LIN. We are so sorry." Then, Warren added, "Peter Solomon has just come into my office. He has hired terrific new management—a CEO named Don Pels. Would you like Peter to introduce you to Donald Pels?"

Although I was standing about ten feet from Warren, I could hear Gruss's voice on the phone saying, "I don't *vant* to meet the management! I *vant* to meet my money!" The ultimate investor lament!

Pels—whose background at Capital Cities was in over-the-air TV and whose first major LIN acquisition was the NBC KXAS Ft. Worth affiliate (from Capital Cities)—eventually made the mistake of giving up all of the company's cable franchises. By 1973, the stock traded at one dollar. But having realized his mistake, Pels grasped the emerging cellular telephone technology and built significant cellular assets, which were sold to AT&T in 1986 for $5 billion. Although I had hired Pels, he later acted badly toward me in ways that I will describe ahead.

LIN was not the only investment I sponsored with Tom Unterberg. In 1965, I convinced some Lehman partners to join a Dallas group led by Ted and Bob Strauss in starting Trini's, a Mexican food restaurant chain, under Trini Lopez, then a famous singer.

Timing and footwork are important in business as in sports. We were too early for the Mexican food wave that lifted Taco Bell and others, but we were fast on our feet. We managed to sell Trini's in 1967 to Riviana Foods for the value of our investment. It was my best sale that year.

Ted and Bob became friends of mine. Bob—who later rose to prominence as a major Democrat, ambassador to China, and adviser to presidents—was the world's best storyteller. When he came to New York to meet with Ed Koch, I would sometimes join them for a meal. The conversation was always hilarious, as they gossiped about almost everyone.

∾

I still cannot understand my compulsion to reach the level of partner at a well-respected firm by age thirty. In retrospect, it seems absurd. This self-imposed pressure, plus the political instability of Lehman as Robert Lehman faded from the scene, compelled me to consider other employment prospects. One firm I talked to was A. G. Becker. I had meetings with Bill Cockrum and Barry Friedberg, later president of Merrill Lynch, but concluded that Becker would not soon be able to crack the top bracket of investment banking.

One day in 1967, Ben Sonnenberg called me. I knew him as the father of modern public relations—and a man whom my own dad thought was a poseur and always avoided. Sonnenberg sported a black bowler, a cane, and a carnation in his lapel. His son, several years my junior, was driven to the Collegiate School in a limo while we both were in lower school. My friend Isadore Barmash wrote a biography of Ben after his death, noting he liked to live better than his clients.

Ben's immediate question was whether I could give him an update on some investments he had made as a "friend" of the firm. Lehman partners frequently bought positions in public and private companies with their own money and invited clients and hangers-on to co-invest. Unfortunately, usually no one kept clients informed of how these investments were doing because they weren't officially connected to the firm. My own experience was that for every LIN Broadcasting success, there were dozens of investments that languished, like most of Ben's.

In the course of checking on things for him, I learned from Lehman partners that Ben had an unusual relationship with the firm: he was not only Mr. Lehman's public relations man but also his "beard." Mr. Lehman apparently had a number of female romantic liaisons, a revelation not altogether surprising.

I also soon realized that Ben had an ulterior motive for reaching out to me. Clearly, he knew that Robert Lehman and his contemporaries were not the future of the firm, and he wanted to befriend people who would be, to assure he'd continue to be employed by us. For similar reasons, he had, I learned, concurrently begun to cultivate Bob Greenhill, the partner of Morgan Stanley responsible for mergers and acquisitions, and Jim Wolfensohn, a star in the corporate finance area at Salomon Brothers. Putting aside how smart he was with regard to me, Ben proved to have superb judgment about the future prominence of Wolfensohn, who became chairman of the World Bank, and Greenhill, who became president of Morgan Stanley and achieved prominence in his own business.

Ben lived in a large stone townhouse at 19 Gramercy Park South that was the site of continuous teas, receptions, soirees, salons, and, I suspect, assignations. The rooms were large and furnished elaborately with shiny brass accessories. Hanging over the winding staircase in the front hall was the famous portrait of Millicent Leveson-Gower, duchess of Sutherland, painted by John Singer Sargent.

Ben invited me to a number of soirees there. The guests were the elite of New York business, Wall Street, media, and entertainment. My wife and I were too young to socialize with these characters, but Ben introduced us around and always made us feel comfortable. I usually fled early, not feeling at all as if it was my milieu.

One day, Ben invited me to tea. I didn't normally leave the office in the late afternoon, but I accepted, assuming Ben had someone important for me to meet.

A single guest was waiting with Ben. I recognized him immediately, having seen him at the Century and because a number of my friends worked at Loeb, Rhoades.

John L. Loeb was one of Wall Street's giants. He had built Carl M. Loeb & Co. into a major brokerage firm. He was the center of German Jewish society, otherwise known as "Our Crowd." He was married to Frances "Peter" Lehman, the daughter of Arthur Lehman, solidifying his position. A gaunt man with chiseled features, he reminded me of Abraham Lincoln.

Ben didn't waste time getting to the point, and neither did Mr. Loeb, who asked me to join Loeb, Rhoades' investment banking division and become a partner. It was an enticing offer. I wasn't sure of my future at Lehman or of the leadership of the firm itself.

I considered the offer seriously. Ultimately, though, I made the same decision about Mr. Loeb's proposition that I had made about A. G. Becker. I thanked him and turned him down. Loeb, Rhoades seemed to have the same succession problems as Lehman, and I didn't think they had a strong commitment to banking; the ethos and tradition of the firm was in brokerage and securities trading.

Mr. Loeb saw my dad sometime later. He told Dad that he had always liked me, but he gained added respect for me after I turned him down.

From then on, I didn't see Ben much. I guess he didn't think he needed me. He died in 1978. Loeb, Rhoades did run out of blood and was acquired by Shearson Hayden Stone in 1979. Mr. Loeb died in 1996 at the age of ninety-four.

Like a lot of people, I went through some philosophical and attitudinal changes in the sixties, particularly about Vietnam. I had originally supported the war, buying into the domino theory. By 1966, though, I had turned against our policies, realizing we were sending young men to die in a conflict we couldn't win. By 1968, the anti-Vietnam protests were a common occurrence. I supported them and once inadvertently participated in one.

One day in the spring of that year, I was in the office of Bobby Bernhard when we heard about a large noontime antiwar rally on the steps of the sub-Treasury building at the corner of Broad and Wall Streets. Bobby, a Lehman partner, was Mr. Lehman's nephew and a cousin of the Loebs, an easygoing guy who sat at the nexus of two formidable Jewish banking families. Since both of us shared the same political views, we went out together and joined the well-behaved, modest-size crowd. It was democracy in action. But a short time later, we were set upon by an unruly brigade of construction workers from the future Salomon Brothers headquarters—led by Peter Brennan, a future secretary of labor under President Nixon—wearing hard hats and wielding construction tools, charging toward the crowd. One of them struck Bobby with a pipe, splitting his head open. I helped him back to the office, where he received first aid.

Bobby Bernhard may have been progressive in some ways. As a banker, though, he embodied the conservative attitude that often hobbled Lehman's efforts and caused me to wonder if I was at the right firm. I'll give you an example of what I mean.

John Eastman, a friend of mine from Viola Woolf's dancing school days and a partner in the entertainment law firm of Eastman & Eastman, was the brother-in-law of Paul McCartney. John represented Apple, the Beatles' music company. He asked me if Lehman would be interested in taking it on as a client.

You'd have to be crazy to say no to such a proposition, and I didn't. But I didn't have the confidence or the standing to commit the firm. Only a partner could do that. When I brought in John Eastman to meet with Bernhard, Bobby turned him away, saying the Beatles and their music publishing company were too "speculative" for the esteemed House of Lehman. John said I rolled my eyes. I couldn't believe it. I pushed Bobby, then and later, but unfortunately, it was not my call. John and I are the closest of friends, and we still both regret that relationship that never was.

As the sixties drew to a close, my fellow partner and friend Paul Manheim urged me to leave the firm. Investment banking is a business with no shortage of egoists and other difficult personalities. But with all the political machinations and leadership instability at Lehman, he said, there were less dysfunctional places for me to have a career.

Coincidentally, at around the same time, John Gutfreund had reached out to me about joining Salomon Brothers, the firm of which he was the nominal head. He wanted me to run the banking division as a successor to Dan Sargent. Dan was more of a traditional commercial banker, and apparently, he felt the firm needed whatever I had to offer. John offered me a partnership.

I agreed to join Salomon Brothers. John and I shook hands, and I felt good about the move. As I was leaving his office, he said that Billy Salomon, the man with his name on the door, wanted to greet me. Mr. Salomon was the father of my Harvard classmate and longtime friend Peter F. Salomon. (Because we were the same age, both grew up in New York City, and both belonged to the Century Country Club, we were often taken for each other.) Billy was cordial enough but asked me what deal John had offered me. I told him the terms: 1.25 percent of the profits, 1.00 percent of the losses, and I had to invest $1 million in the partnership. Billy mulled this for a moment, then frowned and said, "That sounds like too good a deal!" That startled me, because I had seriously wondered if it was fair to ask me to invest $1 million for such a small percentage of the profits.

I practically ran back to Lehman and told Paul Manheim what had happened. He was outraged. "What?" he said. "You can't go to a firm where the senior partner renegotiates with you before you've even started!"

I agreed. I was, after all, trying to find a saner and more civil work environment than I had at Lehman, not to move from one dysfunctional place to another. I called John and told him what had happened and said that under the circumstances, I could no longer come to Salomon Brothers. He was furious, not with me but with Billy. He couldn't believe the old man had criticized the deal he made with me.

Did I make the right move? Until his death in 1999, Paul rued the advice he gave me about not going to Salomon, because they went public in 1981, and the partners became richer than ever. Even so, and despite how rough it got at Lehman in the years ahead, because of the way my personal and professional life has worked out, I never regretted reneging on the offer from John, as I assured Paul repeatedly.

These were the principal partners of Lehman Brothers in the 1960s, and these were the personalities and situations with which we had to cope. Not many of us prospered in that environment. To survive, one had to enjoy the excitement of the unexpected and have the stamina to work through problems, so many of which needn't ever have occurred.

CHAPTER 8

Good Deals ... Bad Deals

When the firm incorporated in 1971, the partners had more capital to work with and limited personal liability. The not-good news was that they also had limited leadership. I still have trouble believing that Fred Ehrman—a deeply troubled man who treated people rudely when he was not ignoring them—was running Lehman Brothers. The general lack of faith in him was evidenced by the fact that when he became chairman and CEO, the partners, in an attempt to balance the ethnicity and the personality of the firm, elevated the pleasant but ineffectual Andy Sage to the position of president.

A worrisome changing of the guard had been going on at Lehman since early 1969. Paul Mazur, Marvin Levy, Paul Manheim, and Arthur Schulte became limited partners, and Frank Manheim retired and moved to Ireland. The tension among the remaining bosses was palpable—and visible in the sometimes contradictory memoranda we received. In December 1968, Bobbie Lehman and Joe Thomas jointly sent a letter to the employees, expressing what a "difficult year" it had been for Lehman. About a week later, Thomas alone issued a much more upbeat memo regarding a "special bonus distribution" the firm would be paying.

I became a managing director on January 1, 1971, in a class that included Alan Sternlieb, a banker about ten years older than I, Bill Welsh Jr., a top retail stock salesman, Jonathan Smith from the syndicate department, and Jean-Francois Malle, who ran our Paris office and was

Louis Malle's brother. Jerry Stone from Commercial Paper was added shortly thereafter. The quality of my colleagues and the fact that they represented various prominent areas of the firm was encouraging, a sign that there was perhaps some hope for Lehman yet. But thanks to a miserable cast of characters, including Ehrman, Glucksman, and another snake in the Lehman garden named Jim Glanville, whom I'll get to in the pages ahead, the center did not hold.

From the moment I became a managing director, my life seemed more difficult. Dad had retired from A&S in 1969 as chairman and moved to the Federated Department Stores office on Seventh Avenue, which he shared with Federated's president Harold Krensky. After having walked through the Fulton Street Brooklyn store to get to his office for forty years, he found the adjustment difficult; he was a natural-born merchant who loved the selling floor. Shortly after he started working in Manhattan, we noticed a change in his behavior. My senior partner Jim Szold told me that he had seen Dad walking somewhat aimlessly along Fifth Avenue. More tellingly, when I had dinner with my parents one night at the Madison Avenue Deli on Eighty-Sixth Street, Dad, a whiz at arithmetic, couldn't make change. In the 1970s, people were aware that older men tended to get what was then called arterial sclerosis, a clogging of the arteries that lessened the flow of blood to the brain and diminished intellectual capacity. Today, we're more likely to recognize what my father was going through as the early stages of Alzheimer's.

Dad had always taken good care of himself, going to the Proger Clinic in Brooklyn annually for a checkup, but once he started to lose his mental powers, his condition steadily worsened. Mother did her best to keep up appearances and made excuses for him, but in 1973, his doctor decided he needed more aggressive treatment: in his case, an angiogram. The procedure involved injecting liquid into an artery and tracing it as it went toward the brain. It was dangerous, and Dad was warned that it could precipitate a stroke.

Dr. Vitalli, a noted surgeon, performed the procedure at Columbia Presbyterian Hospital. I drove Mother and Dad to the hospital. I had a sense of dread. Afterward, Vitalli met with Mother and me and told us that following the injection, Dad had thrashed around violently, but the nurses had restrained him. Vitalli thought Dad had come out of it okay. I asked when Dad might return to work, knowing how important that was to him. Dr. Vitalli said that full-time work wasn't in the immediate future, but he assured us that Dad would soon be back to leading a fairly normal life. Standing before us, the doctor exuded confidence about his medical opinions, but nothing he said came to pass. Instead of getting better, Dad remained badly incapacitated. He never said another word and died two years later, in September 1975, at age seventy-three.

Subsequent advances in medicine, like CAT scans and MRIs, came along just a few years later and rendered many invasive treatments unnecessary. Dad was unlucky in his timing. Still, I think his life could have been prolonged if he'd been in the hands of a more skilled physician.

With our two children—Joshua, age three, and Abigail, age one—and planning to have a third—Kate, born in 1972—Linda and I bought an apartment on East Seventy-Ninth Street. We paid $125,000 for four bedrooms on the second floor. It was the cheapest apartment in a prestigious building housing John McCloy (former US high commissioner for Germany after WWII and titular head of the American Establishment), Roswell Gilpatric (whose son had been a Collegiate classmate), and Thomas Dewey Jr. (my brother's HBS classmate). We moved in in March 1971, the day of the funeral of Dewey's father, the former governor of New York and two-time presidential candidate. The family had a reception at home, and all I could think about were the extra charges that might be caused by the limos being double-parked in the way of our moving van.

The assignments Warren Hellman initially gave me as a managing director were to resuscitate Lehman's retail banking franchise and improve our professional hiring of investment bankers. Lehman's recruiting at business schools had been, like a lot of things at the firm, disorganized and not especially productive.

When I took over, I decided we would concentrate on Harvard and Stanford. The HBS class of 1972 was our first target. We interviewed in alcoves at Allston Burr Lecture Hall on campus and invited five prospects to One William Street. I personally met with three students: Tom Hays, Steve Schwarzman, and Bill Shutzer.

Hays impressed me because he had graduated from West Point, served in Vietnam, and showed leadership. Schwarzman was the most interesting. I noticed he was president of the Yale Ballet Club. I asked how this came about. Without missing a beat, he replied, "Well, I had to be president of something, and it was a good way to meet women!" *Wow*, I thought, *a perfect investment banker!*

Bill Shutzer was also memorable. His resume was almost identical to mine: Harvard College and HBS. At Harvard, he had run the Combined Charities Drive, as I had as a junior. He had even gone to Camp Kennebec, as I had. I asked him if this was really his resume. He was taken aback, thinking I was accusing him of plagiarism, until I said, "Because it could also be mine!"

One of the problems of recruiting was that there was no fact-checking during the interviewing process, nor was there at that time any way to see the candidates interact with anyone other than the interviewers. The usual way was for two Lehman bankers to interview a candidate at the same time. I reversed the process: now each Lehman banker interviewed two candidates at once, to see how they played off the interviewer and each other.

Including prospects from other business schools, we offered seven jobs and got seven acceptances, including the three above and such future partners as Betty Eveillard and Theodore Roosevelt IV. Only Hays and our top prospect, Bob Bodkin from Stanford, didn't work out. Over the next four years, we recruited other stars such as Jim Stern, Fred Seegal, Ken Crews, Ron Moore, and Dennis Kelly, each of whom had successful careers on Wall Street.

Beyond recruiting and retail banking, one of my first partner-level assignments was directing the initial public offering of Booz Allen & Hamilton, the prominent management consulting firm. Warren Hellman had led the sales effort to get this trophy underwriting prize. It was an indication of the change in our relationship that he asked me to navigate the process.

To insulate itself from a possible downturn in its corporate consulting business, Booz Allen had diversified, from an emphasis on strategic advice to senior corporate management, to a number of services such as logistical support and construction and design. My analysis of its client list and revenue streams confirmed the wisdom of diversification. While revenues would decline in a recession, I felt that the slope of the decline would be flattened by Booz Allen's new plan.

The stock offering was successful and highly valued. The price rose from twenty-four dollars to thirty dollars. The problem was that Booz Allen's revamped strategy—and my conclusions about it—were dead wrong. When the 1973 recession hit, Booz Allen paid the price for not realizing something fundamental: when corporations cut costs, they cut them everywhere. Booz Allen's business collapsed. The stock fell to one dollar, at which point Booz Allen repurchased its outstanding shares and became private once again.

I learned several lessons from this debacle. First, trophy underwritings are frequently overpriced. Second, the smartest may not be that smart. And third, a phenomenon repeated in the 2008 Great Recession: when the tide goes out, all the boats are stranded. Diversification is not a guarantee against loss.

By 1971, I had established my media credentials. In 1970, the Federal Communications Commission (FCC) proposed rules (so-called fin-syn) to prevent the three networks from owning programming they aired in prime time. The networks also would not be allowed to have a financial interest in any programs. As a result, CBS would have to divest its syndication division if it was going to continue to produce television programming. George Castell, who was in the class ahead of me at Collegiate, was the treasurer of that CBS division and the man responsible for recommending how to divest. He asked me to meet with Ralph Baruch, whom CBS had designated as the CEO of the soon-to-be divested entity, Viacom.

Despite my great "in," it was not an easy situation. Baruch had no experience with public companies and tended to be cantankerous. Nor was he the only person I, as the future financial adviser, had to please. Frank Stanton was the president of CBS and its point person. He had labored long in the shadow of network founder William S. Paley, who had ultimately spurned him as a successor. At age sixty-three, Stanton was disaffected.

As part of the negotiations between Viacom and CBS, I met with Stanton. By chance, it was August 16, 1971, the day after President Nixon, in a major economic address, outlined "A New Economic Policy," which, among other actions, suspended the convertibility of the dollar into gold, froze wages and prices, and proposed a series of tax credits, tax reductions, and a spending freeze. It was quite a mouthful!

Stanton had a cavernous office and a large desk, which was bare. He didn't rise to greet me but sat immobile, not because he was rude but because he seemed stunned. Almost as soon as I sat down, he told me that he had been in the news business for forty years, most of them at CBS. "Today is the first time I have not been consulted by the White House on a major policy shift by the incumbent administration," he said. Rejected by his boss and now ignored by President Nixon, he had suddenly realized his marginalization. I sympathized with him, but the candor with which this distinguished man expressed himself to me, a person he barely knew, was embarrassing.

Soon afterward, Viacom was spun off into a successful public company.

By coincidence, Dr. Stanton and I, in the early 1980s, served on the Harvard Overseers together, striking up a friendship that lasted for the rest of his life. I never reminded him of our first meeting, I don't believe he ever associated me with the Viacom conversations.

After the spinoff, CEO Ralph Baruch was always under pressure. Competing companies wanted to acquire the company. Viacom was vulnerable. Management owned little stock, and there was no concentration of stock ownership. Baruch was a moody client. He had fled Nazi Europe and worked his way up at CBS. He reminded me of Henry Kissinger's line, "Even paranoids have real enemies." George Castell and his general counsel Terry Elkes were helpful, but overall, I had a tough time getting along with Ralph.

Matters came to a head one day in 1976, when Storer Broadcasting expressed interest in Viacom. Storer, a group owner, was represented by my Lehman partner George Wiegers. George, whose office was adjacent to mine on the fifth floor of One William Street, urged me to arrange a meeting for George Storer with Ralph and Terry. I told George that the Viacom folks wouldn't be open to the idea and would wonder about Lehman's loyalties. Wiegers kept badgering me, though, and I finally relented and arranged the meeting. Explaining the circumstances to Elkes, I said, "Just say no, and that will be the end of it."

The meeting at Viacom's offices turned out to be a disaster for me and for Lehman. Despite Wiegers and George Storer's protests, Ralph and Terry did indeed feel threatened by Storer's interest. As a result, they told me, they could no longer trust Lehman to protect them and to represent their interests. They fired me and the firm.

I take the blame for what happened; it was a terrible error in judgment. Never again did I let anyone convince me he knew what was better for my client than I did. And never again did I put a client in a position where even a "no interest" answer sounded too equivocal.

Lehman suffered from our stupidity. During the 1980s, Viacom was Wall Street's largest-paying client. George Wiegers left Lehman in 1983. Ralph and Terry had a falling out. Terry became CEO in 1978 and left the company after Sumner Redstone gained control. He had an office next to our firm in the early 1990s, and we were friendly until his death in 2008.

I had established my reputation and become a partner principally by focusing on media. In addition to the LIN investment and the Viacom spinoff, I was working with the Outlet Company and doing banking in the emerging cable television business, so I was far from delighted when Warren Hellman told me he wanted me to reorganize Lehman's retail efforts. If I had wanted to have a career in retailing, I told Warren, I would have become a retailer. Warren—who was about thirty-six at the time, and whom Bob Shapiro and I called "Hurricane Hellman" for his activities—said that was nice but he needed my help, and pronto.

Reorganizing Lehman's retail effort was a complicated task.

Through death, retirement, and resignation, virtually all the retail legends of the 1960s had left the firm.

My main goal was to reinvigorate our new business effort. With the consent of my colleagues, I reassigned our clients, such as Federated Department Stores—where Pete Peterson replaced Paul Mazur on its board—Allied Stores, Gimbels, R. H. Macy, Zayres, May Company, and Kresges (later Kmart), to new managing directors. I replaced Joe Thomas on the Associated Dry Goods board, where I was fortunate to work first with Dick Pivirotto—the blocking back on the undefeated Princeton football team of 1950, which had featured All-American triple threat tailback Dick Kazmaier—and later with Bill Arnold. Fortunately, we retained all our clients during the transition.

Dick Pivirotto was not only a football star but a top retail prospect when he graduated Harvard Business School. Dad would have liked to have him at A&S, but he returned to Pittsburgh, his hometown, joined the Joseph Horne Company, the dominant Pittsburgh department store, and married the boss's daughter. Dick had also been supportive of me. At one time, Lew Seiler, the then chairman of the White Shoe Board of ADG, complained that I hadn't handled a financing well. Dick told us that Seiler was wrong.

A decade later, Bill Arnold became frustrated with Dick's hesitant responses to ADG's declining profitability. He organized a corporate coup replacing Dick but asked him to remain on the board. When I left government in 1981 and returned to ADG's board at Bill's invitation, I always felt that Dick was hurt by my friendship and close working relationship with Bill. Regrettably, I wasn't able to repair our relationship prior to his death.

I also brought in the potential underwriting of a formerly bankrupt company, Miller Wohl Company. We sold stock on behalf of Bankers Trust and Chemical Bank, which had converted their debt into equity. It was one of the first instances of a creditor's successful recovery. I joined Miller Wohl's board, and Heinz Eppler and his cousin Klaus became lifelong friends. We sold Miller Wohl to its competitor, Petrie Stores, in 1983.

In a development with personal implications, Sidney Rabb asked me to succeed my father on the Stop&Shop board, an invitation I accepted after discussing the matter with Mother and my brother, Richard.

One of the most interesting clients I had at Lehman was the Outlet Company (a department store in Providence, Rhode Island), a rare combination of retail and media (TV station WPRO). My relationship with the CEO, Bruce Sundlun, later governor of Rhode Island, started with a cold call. One day in 1967, I took the New Haven Railroad from our weekend house in North Stamford, Connecticut, to Providence. On that hot summer's day, my uncomfortable three-hour train ride was followed by a walk up Providence's main street. In the late sixties, Providence wasn't the hip college town it is today. I was introduced to Bruce through Brown, Lisle & Marshall, the top Rhode Island brokerage firm. Until the 1970s, every state had a local firm that participated in the underwriting syndicates of New York–based "major" firms. Bruce and I became friends, and the Outlet Company became a client. With our help, over the years he built a major broadcasting company while selling the Outlet department stores and specialty stores such as Cherry & Webb.

In 1971, Bruce had his eye on a Columbus, Ohio, TV station, the NBC affiliate WCMH, but did not have enough cash or debt capacity. He wanted to make the acquisition without issuing common stock. I told him I was heading to Jamaica for a week's vacation and would mull it over.

I have always valued vacations, not only for the obvious benefits of being with family and friends and for visiting new places but also for the time to think. It is hard to reflect when you are running hard. Somewhat bored in Jamaica, I struck upon the idea of "kickers."

Kickers were a form of additional payments often requested by insurance companies and pension fund lenders such as US Steel Pension Fund, Mass Mutual Insurance Company, and All-State Insurance, major private lenders. Usually, these kickers were in the form of warrants, the only form of derivative in the 1960s and 1970s. The use of interest rate swaps, puts/calls, and derivatives flooded the markets twenty years later.

I reasoned that since most television stations sold as multiples of net broadcast revenues—in those days, usually two to three times—why not give potential lenders the opportunity to acquire a kicker, a payment in addition to annual interest, based on the revenues and this multiple. The lender would have the option for a defined period during the term of the loan.

We proposed this novel idea to New York Life Insurance and to Teachers Insurance, which liked the idea and financed 100 percent of the purchase price of WCMH-TV.

Another call on Bruce Sundlun's behalf led me to meet a legend.

Bruce was, among other accomplishments, a former marine pilot. He sent me to Columbus to meet the CEO of Executive Jet Aviation, then owned by the bankrupt Penn Central Railroad. Retired Colonel Paul Tibbets greeted me in his plain, 1960s-style, cheap, wood-paneled office. The name struck a distant chord, but I couldn't connect until a few minutes into the meeting, I noticed behind his right shoulder on his credenza a black-and-white photo of a plane. Distracted, I stared at it for a moment—the same moment it took for Tibbets to read my thoughts. The photo was of the *Enola Gay*, the B-29 that dropped the bomb on Hiroshima. "Did you hesitate at all?" I asked.

"Not for a moment," he said. "My only thought was not getting myself blown out of the sky!"

Bruce bought Executive Jet. It is now NetJets, owned by Warren Buffet. Bruce was an exciting client, and he always trusted me, which made me a better banker.

CHAPTER 9

Old Lehman Crumbles

In 1971 and 1972, Lehman enjoyed good years, thanks in part to the successes of commercial paper and fixed income trading. Glucksman was emboldened and in 1973 undertook a series of trades designed to create profits large enough to dwarf banking and to propel Glucksman to the top of the firm.

At the same time, he began a frontal assault on the top bankers. Jerry Stone was asked by Glucksman to set up a lunch for him with Warren Goeltz, then Gluckman's closest colleague, and Warren Hellman. Hellman arrived late, and by that time, Goeltz had several scotches. According to Jerry, Goeltz shouted at Hellman, "We have both barrels loaded. One for your uncle (Ehrman) and the other for you!" The lunch ended abruptly.

On the trading floor, Glucksman had hired two economists from Schroeder Bank and had followed their predictions of a decline in interest rates. To capitalize on this forecast, Lehman Commercial Paper bought $1 billion of certificates of deposit from various banks. Rates, in fact, did not fall but began to rise. From the fall of 1972 until August 1973, CD rates rose from 4.55 percent to 7.1 percent, causing what Lehman later said was an $8 million loss but, according to Stone and Tommy McDaniel, was closer to $18 million.

In another case, Glucksman bought New York State Housing Authority notes and was unable to resell them. Unbeknownst to the firm, he entered into a REPO agreement with IBM. Glucksman agreed to repurchase the notes periodically at a fixed price. REPO or repurchase agreements, fully disclosed, are not unusual in trading. Unwritten and undisclosed, they are illegal. Lehman took a large loss on this transaction, especially when the firm's equity capital was barely $20 million.

Ironically, thirty-five years later, Dick Fuld, Glucksman's junior colleague in 1973, used a technique called REPO 105 to hide Lehman's lack of equity capital and outsized leverage.

Although Glucksman joined the partnership in 1967, his resentment of Lehman's investment banking partners grew.

Arthur Schulte's patrician oversight of Glucksman's operation was not sufficient. After the discovery of these losses, the partners replaced Schulte with Bob Rubin, the most admired and trusted banker in the firm. Regrettably, over time, Glucksman coopted Rubin and made him his consigliere and apologist.

Lehman was faced with almost catastrophic losses. I had been a shareholder for fewer than three years, and I was losing money.

Both Jerry Stone and Tommy McDaniels became my neighbors when Susan and I bought a home in John's Island in 1998. I asked them what, back then, had been going through Glucksman's mind. They affirmed that Lew wanted to "fuck" Hellman and the bankers and show them how much money he could make. Tommy told me that Glucksman routinely lied to the rest of his partners and that his colleagues knew that. As cynical as I was about Glucksman, I was taken aback by some of the things Jerry and Tom told me.

Why didn't the partners immediately fire Glucksman when they discovered his fraudulent acts? One reason was that no one at the firm knew nearly as much as he did about commercial paper, by then a vital part of Lehman's business. But beyond that, there was no unity of purpose or philosophy of the firm. Those in high positions couldn't speak to any issue with one voice. For an investment bank to succeed, partners have to be partners of and with one another. At Lehman, there was no relationship between Hellman and DuBrul or between DuBrul and Jim Glanville, who worked for Ed Kennedy in the oil department. Glucksman was on his own, occasionally conspiring with

Jim Glanville against Hellman. But even that was a strategic alliance, not a friendship. Cowardice also played a part. Ehrman and the other weak-willed senior partners simply lacked the courage to confront Glucksman.

Still, after Glucksman's disastrous illegal dealings came to light, Warren Hellman and some of the other partners decided they'd had enough. Glucksman wasn't the sole or even the main reason for the partners' dissatisfaction; he was the last straw. The firm was floundering in 1973. The economy was weak. Nixon was on the ropes. Ehrman had to go, and Andy Sage was no longer a viable successor. As a first step, Warren became president, and Sage became vice chairman, a title with no responsibilities.

Warren was in an awkward position. Fred Ehrman wasn't just Warren's boss; he was also his uncle. Yet once Warren decided to move, he didn't hesitate. A tip-off that something was about to happen came in July 1973, at Lehman's industrial department's annual summer outing. That year, it was held at the Creek Club in Glen Cove, Long Island—rather than the Century in Westchester—but the more significant difference was that none of the managing directors above my pay grade attended. Instead, most of the partners were headed toward the last of a series of clandestine meetings to plan a coup: Ehrman would be replaced by Peter Peterson, a former CEO of Bell & Howell who had also served as secretary of commerce under Richard Nixon and had just joined the firm.

Why didn't Warren take over the leadership of the firm? He was certainly smart enough and a skilled banker. He was also self-aware. Warren believed that since he played the role of Brutus in the conspiracy, he couldn't be seen as acting to satisfy his own ambitions. But the truth is he didn't have such ambitions. He had too many other interests to want to be burdened with the job of CEO, and he was too impulsive, too aggressive—Hurricane Hellman—to be a good manager. He was comfortable with who he was and wasn't.

Another good question, though, is, Why Peterson? Despite his success, Pete didn't possess the obvious credentials. He had never worked in New York, didn't know any of his prospective colleagues, and—here's something of a drawback to being chairman of Lehman Brothers—he didn't know anything about investment banking. Like a lot of other distinguished former government officials, such as General Clay and George W. Ball, he had come to Wall Street for money. He was the kind of person firms employed as a door opener, not manager. Ultimately, though, Warren liked him *because* he had no track record. He came to the firm with clean hands. He was the Wendell Willkie of Lehman, the least objectionable candidate, and he got the nomination. And the way Pete tells the story, he reluctantly accepted.

The day after the Creek Club outing, Pete, Warren, and George Ball went to Ehrman's office in the third-floor annex to tell him that the board had decided to replace him. They offered him softening words and gestures of respect, to which Ehrman replied, "Fuck you! No way."

When Warren told the story, I said, "At least you fired the right guy this time."

Four months later, Fred Ehrman died in his sleep of a heart attack at the age of sixty-seven. Meanwhile, Glucksman raged on.

CHAPTER 10

Collecting

It was around this time of turmoil at Lehman that I began harvesting honey. Linda and I would invite friends to our weekend place and then enlist them in the process of honey production.

Let me tell you how all this started.

In 1964, we visited our friends Gretchen and Donald Glickman in Mill River, Massachusetts, at their eighteenth-century farmhouse. I was immediately attracted to the simplicity of the structure and the connection of the building to American history. It felt comfortable evoking our family's New England roots.

Soon afterward, we began a search for our own authentic colonial country house. After looking from the Berkshires south, in July 1965 we bought an eighteenth-century farmhouse in North Stamford, Connecticut, on the stagecoach route from Danbury. Legend had it that the three-story house was built by August Weed in 1780. The house was called Woodpecker Ridge Farm, although by 1965, its plot had been reduced to 1.9 acres. We paid $55,000, a lot of money then.

The house was built into the side of a hill facing southeast, away from the wind. It had a stone floor, American chestnut beams, and a beehive oven on the first floor. The second-floor living room had wide pine floorboards and a parlor with oak floors, an indication of the room's importance. The house had been divided between two families, with one family using the so-called coffin door, which led from the parlor to the front porch. Originally, the coffin door's only use was for funerals. The wooden-shingled roof was topped by a beehive chimney of the type generally associated with the Hartford area.

The house and my interest in American history melded, and we began hunting for eighteenth-century furniture, art, and accessories. One of Mother's axioms was that one of the joys of collecting was remembering when and where you purchased an item. This was certainly true.

We bought a 1915 Leonard player piano with four hundred rolls we saw advertised in the *Newtown Bee* and put it in the parlor. Many days and nights, the kids pumped out early twentieth-century songs.

There were wonderful "pickers" and dealers in the 1960s, such as Florence Maine on Route 7 in Wilton, Marguerite and Arthur Riordan in Stonington, Peter Tillou in Litchfield, and America Hurrah and Schoelkopf Gallery in New York City. From Jim Kronen, a picker with an extraordinary eye, I bought a carved wooden Indian statue from a barn in Oswego, New York, a wooden pig from the Pig & Whistle pub in Western Pennsylvania, and a Chambers lookalike of Washington crossing the Delaware.

Among the best pickers were Avis and Rock Gardiner, who lived near us in North Stamford. The Gardiners owned two barns filled with letters, magazines, engravings, and other ephemera from the American past. I could spend hours rummaging through the barns, one of which later exploded due to spontaneous combustion. I wish I had bought everything I saw in those barns and their modest farmhouse.

In time, we bought American folk art at auction, using one dealer in particular, Stuart Feld at Hirschl & Adler. A great collection is a collaboration between a dealer or adviser and a collector. I had originally gone to Israel Sack, the leading dealer in American antiques, but had been rebuffed, probably because of my age and casual attire. Had he taken some time and interest in me, I might have owned a collection of Salem, Boston, and Philadelphia colonial furniture.

Ted Stebbins of Boston's Museum of Fine Art became my guide. My focus was Connecticut Valley artists, including Ralph Earl, Ammi Phillips, Erastus Field, Chambers, Brewster, Jennys, Kennedy, et al. We also periodically bought highlights from other parts of the colonies, principally Pennsylvania. We bought three Edward Hicks paintings, one as it was decommissioned from the State Department. In 2015, the three paintings hung together in an exhibition of our folk art at the Metropolitan Museum in New York. One of my favorite paintings is a view of a Van Reed's Farm by Hoffman, a Pennsylvania alms house artist, so known because he was an alcoholic who would leave the alms house and venture forth to paint.

Another copy of Van Reed's Farm is in the Abby Aldrich Rockefeller Folk Art Museum in Williamsburg, Virginia. The famous curator of the Abby Aldrich was Mary Black. She and I developed a writing and telephone relationship for many years. It was a sort of Victorian thing. Fifteen years after our relationship began, I was at an opening of a folk art show at the Clark Museum and heard a voice I recognized. I turned to the speaker and said, "Aren't you Mary Black? I am Peter Solomon." Mary apparently needed money at the time, and I reluctantly bought an Ammi Phillips that I later resold.

From 1965, when we bought a Kennedy portrait of brothers, until the purchase of the Earls in the mid-1980s, we filled the walls with portraits, a fireboard from Maine, whirligigs, weathervanes, utensils. Each purchase taught me something about American history and complemented the 1780 house.

We became friendly with neighbors a mile down Cascade Road. Monique Shay, a French divorcee with seven children, lived with a police officer, Chris Kanel. Our first encounter with Chris occurred with a loud knock on our front door around nine o'clock at night. Apprehensive, I opened it to find a rather imposing man in uniform. He thrust a book—Hans Holzer's volume entitled *The Ghosts of Stamford Hill*—at me. One chapter described the murder of a woman who had lived in our new house and how, after being strangled, she was stuffed down the well adjacent to our front steps.

The book was to cause us some inconvenience. For many years, on Halloween, neighborhood kids would come around the house seeking the ghost. Every October 31, we would drive to the house to assure there would be no vandalism. One night, my friend Stephen Schulte was convinced he heard ghosts and saw lights when he came for dinner. Regrettably, we never did, and the legend of the house faded.

But I was talking about honey.

Bugs and critters had always interested me. I remember catching an orange salamander at camp in 1945 and knowing the date because no one but me was interested. It was VJ Day when WWII ended. In the lower school at Collegiate, we walked each afternoon to the Seventy-Ninth Street playground. In early spring, I remember seeing cocoons on the cherry trees and watching butterflies emerge just before school ended for the summer. Besides scrounging for golf balls in the woods along the North Shore Golf Course, I caught praying mantises. Nights were filled with fireflies that we put in jars with holes punched in the lids in a vain attempt to help them survive.

The Stamford Museum is on the site of the former Henri Bendel estate in North Stamford on High Ridge Road. My son Joshua was six years old when I thought it would be fun to take a course in beekeeping at the museum. Within an hour or two, I was hooked.

To make a bad pun, bees have given my life more buzz. When I was asked to run for Overseer at Harvard in 1981, I submitted a short autobiographical sketch. I had to mention beekeeping and noted that there is nothing like forty thousand angry bees to focus one's mind. Without doubt, my ability to focus intensely and to listen as well as see—both important qualities in an investment banker—were honed by beekeeping.

The most important decision for a novice beekeeper is to find a sympathetic bee equipment supplier. Ed Weiss and his wife, Nina, lived in Weston, Connecticut. Ed's book, *The Queen and I,* contains all the information a beekeeper needs. Ed was a tough taskmaster, insisting that we follow the procedures for a model hive. He delivered bees by truck each spring from Georgia. The pickup day was chaotic, with eager hobbyists like me lined up to receive their boxes of bees. Ed remained a friend and bee mentor until his death in 2016 at age ninety-six.

Much has been written about bees for the simple reason that there is a lot to say about these fascinating creatures. Bees create their civil society dominated by the queen. All the other bees in the hive are devoted to servicing her. The workers, unfertilized female bees, gather honey and pollen, tend to the needs of the queen, and protect the hive. The male drones do nothing except fertilize the queen. There is no record of drones mating with the queen. It occurs in midair, and multiple drones may fertilize a single queen. Drones are otherwise so worthless to the bee society that in the fall, the worker bees drive the drones from the hive so they don't have to feed them during the winter.

Tending bees requires constant care and a rigid schedule. Bees are ordered from breeders usually located in the Southeast. Sometimes they arrive through the US mail at the local post office. Each hive contains ten thousand bees plus one queen. The most panicky call you will ever hear is one from the local post office pleading with a beekeeper to pick up his bees. Spring is a busy season, but summer also requires caring for the bees to be sure they are reproducing and making honey, as well as taking honey at the optimum time. In the fall, the bees must be fed again, medicated, and provided shelter from the freezing winds.

In a strong hive, the bee population may grow to thirty thousand bees, who each year produce up to 120 pounds of honey. The most hives I ever had at one time was nine, and the most honey collected in one season was 300 hundred pounds. One of the great characteristics of honey is that it lasts forever. When it solidifies, you just heat it, and it liquefies.

I started harvesting honey in 1974. We would invite our friends for the weekend and, like Tom Sawyer, entice them to help. The process takes an entire day. First, it is necessary to drive the bees from the small boxes called shallow supers where they have stored the honey on the top of the deep hive bodies. You clear the honey-holding supers of bees so they won't sting when you begin to empty the frames of honey. We use a fume board soaked with a foul-smelling liquid. One year, as my brother and I drove hives he tended for me from his house in Bedford, New York, some ten miles away, the liquid spilled. His truck still stinks.

Once the bees abandon the shallow supers holding honey, we remove the ten frames in each super, use an electric knife to decap the cells holding the honey, and spin the frames in a large stainless steel centrifuge. The honey flows to the bottom of the steel tub, and we strain and bottle in gallon containers.

Beekeeping is hard work. A shallow super filled with honey can weigh thirty pounds. A large, deep super can weigh twice that. I was never comfortable working my bees without a bee suit, bonnet, veil, and gloves. Expert beekeepers, such as my daughter Kate Solomon, frequently work their bees with only a bonnet. It is cooler and less cumbersome but not for me. Since we chose to remove honey the last week of July before we went to Martha's Vineyard, removing honey happened on one of the hottest days of the summer. By day's end, it was clear our friends would not return the next year.

We also kept bees on Martha's Vineyard. In 1978, as we arrived at our newly purchased house—mother called it a "shack"—the gardener was in the process of removing a feral hive from the shingled side of a woodshed. We stopped the extraction and, using a funnel technique, were able to insert the colony into wood hive boxes.

After I left the Vineyard in the early 1990s, the colony seemed to disappear. In 2013 when Joshua, Abigail, and Kate decided to remodel the shack, the builder found a colony in the same place I had extracted one thirty-six years earlier.

People frequently ask me if I've ever been stung. I have been stung frequently. There is nothing as terrifying as having a "bee in your bonnet." And there are other hazards. When bees get too crowded or they feel the queen is getting too old and needs to be replaced, they swarm. Swarming involves leaving the hive en masse and heading to the branch of a tree or somewhere they can gather until they find a new permanent home in the hollow of a tree. Swarming in the Northeast frequently occurs toward the end of May.

One Memorial Day, I heard the telltale buzzing of thousands of bees. I looked up and saw them swarm from the hive and fly into the branch of a tree, twenty feet above the ground. I cut a limb off another nearby tree, attached a cardboard box to the top of it, and jabbed the box up to the hanging swarm. Unfortunately, I hit the swarm so hard that the hanging branch broke and crashed onto my head, cutting my eyelid and ripping my left tear duct. A doctor at Stamford Hospital's emergency room sewed it up. It still waters a little.

I learned from that experience. The next year, another swarm went into a tree. This time, I was smart enough to wear glasses and a hat. Once again, I hit the branch with an open box. The swarm scattered, and I was furious. The box fell off my stick and tumbled to the ground with not more than a handful of bees in it. I walked away frustrated. But turning back, I noticed a bizarre performance. A line of bees had formed overhead and had begun to make, yes, a beeline to the box lying open on the ground. Soon the entire swarm settled in the box. I had knocked only a few bees off the limb, but one was the queen. I installed that swarm into a new hive.

On a summer's day in about 1980, I was working in my yard. Joshua, twelve at the time, was helping me when my neighbor ran into our driveway.

"Your bees are all over my house!" he screamed. "Get them out of there!"

I was surprised, since my bees seemed calm, but I hastened to his house, hauling Joshua along with me.

Once there, it was clear to me that they weren't my bees but yellow jackets. Yellow jackets are dangerous. Unlike bees, which sting in self-defense and die from the experience, yellow jackets sting aggressively.

"Not my bees," I said.

Immediately, my neighbor went from accusing me to begging me for help. I told him to call the fire department. There was a lesson in this for him: Don't panic. Find the facts. Be nice. And someone may help you.

Bees, oddly, make me relax. Watching the bees enter and leave a hive loaded with nectar and some with red or yellow pollen is a spectator sport. You can begin to sense a rhythm to your hives and can almost identify the individual characteristics of each hive. In fact, hives are different. Not only does each queen have different genetics, but the drones do as well. As the queen interacts sequentially with the different drones' sperm, the resulting worker bees will have different characteristics. Some months, the hive will be quiet and unaggressive. Weeks later, the hive might become more skittish. Such a change may signal a new crop of workers.

A parent has little idea what might influence his children. It is pretty clear that nature plays at least as large a role as nurture. I can tell you that the personalities of my three children haven't changed since they were four years old.

As Kate was nearing graduation from Harvard, I gently inquired what she planned to do come June. Without hesitation, she replied that she planned to go into the Peace Corps. Susan and I had known each other for over two years by that time. Kate liked Susan and was intrigued by her service in the Peace Corps, helping deliver babies in the bush in Sierra Leone in 1965. Unlike in the early days of the Peace Corps, by 1995, a volunteer needed a skill.

"What will be your skill?" I asked Kate.

"Beekeeping," she replied without hesitation. Since Kate had rarely shown any interest in bees, I was shocked.

"How will you learn?" I naively asked.

"You'll teach me," she said.

Kate became a superb beekeeper, tackling the task of teaching beekeeping to Paraguayan women so they could have a cash crop. Beekeeping in South America is complicated by the presence of the Africanized bee, which stings without provocation. These bees stung to death Kate's pet rabbit and other smaller animals during her two-year tour of duty. At one point, Kate, wearing a beard of bees, was pictured in *Beekeeping for Dummies*.[1]

When we sold our house in North Stamford in 1998, I moved our bees to my dear friend Edgar Cullman's hundred-acre farm two miles from our house. As a sign of his affection and unselfishness, Edgar accepted our hives even though he was allergic to bee stings.

---

[1] Kate's interest in beekeeping developed into a career in organic products. She founded Babo Botanicals, a skin-care company, which she sold in 2018.

Eventually, after Edgar's death, the hives died too, from disease and invading mice.

Resuming beekeeping in 2013 after I moved to East Hampton was not easy. Pesticides and the advent of some form of epidemic is destroying the bee population. And East Hampton might not be the most conducive environment, with its combination of ocean moisture and winds. But UPS added to the difficulty.

Bees may be shipped by UPS or the US Postal Service. Fed Ex doesn't ship bees. One would think UPS Priority would be the reliable choice. Well, not exactly.

In April 2013, I ordered two packages of two pounds (ten thousand bees) and a queen from the Pigeon Mountain Bee Company in Georgia, to be shipped UPS Priority. UPS emailed me that the bees would arrive before noon on a certain date. On the appointed day, UPS emailed me again to say that my bees had arrived at 10:31 a.m. I rushed home, but there were no bees.

A number of urgent calls to UPS finally found an agent who asked if I lived in Kentucky.

"No!" I exclaimed, perturbed. "I live in East Hampton, New York."

"Well," he said. "Your bees have been delivered to a warehouse in Louisville." Then he asked the corker, "Would we know if the bees were alive?"

Not only were my two packages of twenty thousand bees dead, but Pigeon Mountain's entire shipment—456 packages of ten thousand bees each, plus 456 queens—was dead. In an era of scarce bees, UPS had managed to kill 4,560,456 bees in one fell swoop.

I then called the assistant of Scott Davis, UPS's CEO, and asked her to look into the situation. I pointed out that it wasn't good public relations for UPS: big Atlanta-based company kills over 4.5 million bees of a small Georgia company.

My replacement bees arrived safely through the US Postal Service in June, too late in the summer to make honey. Apparently, UPS no longer ships bees. In 2014, I directed my bee suppliers to always ship my bees through the US Postal Service.

UPS never reimbursed me. As far as I have been able to determine, the Pigeon Mountain Bee Company has also had a hard time getting reimbursed by UPS. I subsequently heard from a UPS representative who didn't seem all that concerned with the situation or the potential for bad press. When you have a near monopoly, providing customer satisfaction seems to become less important.

৵

Beyond collecting honey, for almost forty years I have bought children's books and illustrations. My interest started benignly as a fortieth birthday present for Linda. The Collegiate School, which Joshua attended, asked her to develop a middle school book list, including Mark Twain's classics, *The Red Pony* by Steinbeck, *The Black Stallion* by Walter Farley, and *The Scarlet Letter* by Hawthorne.

Justin Schiller, then in his late thirties, was and still is the preeminent dealer in children's literature. As with Israel Sack, Justin initially relegated me to a young assistant who sold me a copy of *The Red Pony* at an exorbitant price. On my next visit, Justin realized I might be worthy of his attention.

A bibliography, *Peter Parley to Penrod*, novels from colonial times to the 1930s, contained most of the titles on the reading list. Linda was astonished when I presented my purchases on her birthday but showed little interest in adding more volumes. I, however, was hooked.

Soon, collecting first editions became less appealing, and my interest shifted to two more creative and artistic categories: illustrations of children's books and particularly works highlighting nonsense and fantasy. My collection focused on the illustrations of Edward Lear, Frank Baum, Beatrix Potter, Maurice Sendak, and Lewis Carroll.

Lewis Carroll (Charles Dodgson) combined nonsense with fantasy to create the surreal then unknown in children's literature. Over decades, I acquired letters, first editions, including the "suppressed" 1865 edition of *Alice's Adventures in Wonderland*, Carroll's (and the White Rabbit's) silver pocket watch, and Carroll's mathematical games. Illustrator John Tenniel was Carroll's collaborator on the Alice books.

One of our most unusual purchases occurred in London at

a Sotheby's auction. The catalog offered eight original Tenniel illustrations for *Alice*. Justin determined that these were, in fact, not drawings by Tenniel but by Dodgson himself.

There were two clues. First, the drawings were done in the exact purple ink issued to Dons by Oxford University starting in 1872. Second, while Dodgson could not draw himself, he was a superb copyist. Schiller concluded that the offered drawings were Dodgson's copies of Tenniel's original drawings. As additional proof, he cited other examples of Dodgson's copies residing in the Christopher Wren Library at Christ Church at Oxford.

Justin bid successfully in London while we cowered nearby at the Connaught Hotel. Television news publicized the sale throughout England.

The next day, as we passed through Oxford on our way to the Cotswolds, Linda and I decided to see the proof for ourselves.

We approached the library at five thirty that evening. Being winter, it was dark and rainy. The library was obviously closed. Nevertheless, I knocked. No answer. I knocked again. A middle-aged man peeked out. Before he could say the library was closed, I blurted out that I was the person who had bought the Tenniel drawing the day before. Before he could correct me, I corrected myself and said, "I mean the Dodgson drawings." I asked whether I could see Christ Church's Dodgson drawings.

Astonished, he motioned for us to follow him and led us to a kiosk in the library. He then disappeared.

We sat there for about fifteen minutes. At one point, not altogether kidding, I thought he might be calling the cops. Finally, he returned with a modest-size manila envelope. Without ceremony, he spilled the contents onto the small table.

The envelope held seven or eight tiny drawings, each in purple ink, depicting a parrot and other animals. The envelope was clearly labelled "Dodgson." The ink and the hand confirmed Schiller's conclusion. I thanked the librarian as we disappeared into the stormy night.

Book auctions can engender odd behavior. A most bizarre auction experience occurred after I was the high bidder for a manuscript book created by Hans Christian Andersen in 1869 for the three-year-old daughter of a friend. Bidding by phone in kroner, I waged a battle against a bidder in Copenhagen, each of us bumping amounts by 100,000 kroners. My auction house agent properly refused to identify my competitor.

Shortly after the gavel announced that I won, the auction house informed me that Denmark had exercised its rights of patrimony and would seek to ban export of the manuscript. The result is that I won the battle and might lose the war.

The state-owned Hans Christian Andersen House and Museum, knowing that it would exercise patrimony, had bid against me alone for over 1 million kroner, potentially forcing itself to pay the higher hammer price.

I decided my best chance of obtaining the manuscript was to pledge it to the Houghton Library and enlist Sarah Thomas, Tom Hyry, and Hope Mayo, Harvard's library leadership, to write in support of export, offering to digitize the manuscript and make it available to scholars everywhere. Alas, our appeal failed. Steven Murphy, formerly CEO of Christie's, reminded me that there is no more competitive bidder than someone who had previously been outbid. The museum had indeed underbid on a Hans Christian Andersen picture book at Sotheby's in London twenty years earlier, when Lloyd Cotsen prevailed.

On another occasion, one late afternoon, Susan and I were in our Paris apartment on Rue Francois Premier during a London children's illustration and book auction of Beatrix Potter's two watercolors of "The Rabbits' Christmas Party: The Arrival." Sipping wine, we suddenly had an epiphany: I was bidding in English pounds and not US dollars. Fortunately, we have enjoyed owning the "The Rabbits' Christmas Party: The Arrival," but the Rabbits left their Christmas party with another collector.

We lend from our collection frequently because they deserve to be seen by a wider audience. The stories and illustrations provide context for what society valued and passed on to its children.

Susan and I have labored over the decision of what to do with our volumes. Certainly, our children will be interested in certain items, but the core should be available to scholars and the public.

We looked at possibilities such as the Morgan Library, the Cotsen Children's Library at Princeton, and Houghton's rare book library at Harvard. Rare book libraries, of which Houghton is no exception, were built to protect material from damage and tend to be precious and off-putting.

Energized by the promise of our collection, Harvard commissioned an architectural plan to renovate Houghton and its surroundings to make the library more inviting and its collections more accessible. After reviewing the plans, Susan and I decided to underwrite the renovation, allowing Harvard to move ahead expeditiously.

In return, Houghton will elevate the exposure of children's literature and illustrations, combining our collection with its holdings. We anticipate more exhibitions, seminars and lectures and, hopefully, a future curator whose purview will include the now expanded children's material.

I told Harvard that we did not intend to name any of the renovated rooms, nor did we think it appropriate to impose our names on the Houghton name. Houghton was free to "sell" naming rights to new donors.

We noted, however, that the opening to Harvard Yard from Quincy Street leading to Houghton and Lamont libraries did not have the same stature as the other twenty-four "gates" to the Yard. We suggested that in recognition of our gifts to Houghton and sixty years of support, Harvard construct a new gate named Peter J. Solomon Class of 1960. Somewhat to our surprise, the dean of the college and the president of the university graciously and enthusiastically supported this idea.

CHAPTER 11

Conflict—Foreign and Domestic

The Yom Kippur War in October 1973 set the tone for the early 1970s. The Israel Defense Force never thought the Arabs, whom they so easily dispatched in 1967, would employ the daring strategy of a surprise attack on the Israeli-occupied territories on the holiest day of the Jewish calendar. Fear over the ascendancy of the Arab world and OPEC cast a pall over the West.

Three days after the start of the Yom Kippur War, I was at a cocktail party at Don Glickman's on Park Avenue. My fellow guest Tom Unterberg told me he was going to join an Israel Bond Mission the next day. With just a moment's hesitation, I decided to join him. Once again, a chance encounter and an impulsive decision added immeasurably to my life.

The Bond Mission group was composed of about forty Jews from Chicago and New York. The New York contingent included Harvey Krueger, the senior partner of our competitor Kuhn, Loeb & Co., Larry Leeds Jr., the second in command at the Manhattan Shirt Company, and Larry Phillips, the CEO of Phillips-Van Heusen, another garment manufacturer.

The four-day trip was an adventure. The evening we arrived on El-Al in Tel Aviv's Ben Gurion Airport, we motored to Jerusalem. I joined Larry Leeds at a dinner with two friends of his, Ezer Weizman, former commander in chief of the Israeli Air Force and later seventh president of Israel, and another Israeli general whose name I didn't catch. They discussed the dire straits of Israel and how just thirty-six hours earlier, they had been sure the country was going to be overrun by the Syrians and Egyptians. As jet-lagged as I was, I perked up when I heard them explain to Larry that they had vowed to repel the invaders and decided to get Israel's atomic bomb and drop it on Moscow. That sounded absurd to me at first, mostly because I doubted the Israelis could fly as far as Moscow. On the way back to the King David Hotel, I asked Larry who the other dinner guest was. "Mordechai Gur," he said, "the general who led the paratroopers in the Six-Day War and later was the tenth IDF chief of staff." That got me thinking, as did the large map of the Middle East in the hotel lobby. Passing it on the way to my room, I noticed with some alarm that Moscow was due north of Jerusalem and not as far away as I had imagined it. Years later, I asked Larry what he thought of the conversation about employing the nuclear option. He told me he hadn't taken it seriously. But once I saw the map, I certainly had!

The first day of our mission, we flew to the Golan Heights and then drove close to the Syrian town of Quneitra. It was not a pretty sight: bodies, of both Israelis and Syrians, were still smoldering among the remains of a major tank battle. At the Israeli forward position, I tried to take a picture of a single soldier returning exhausted from a night of patrol but was so mesmerized by him that I never snapped the shutter. It didn't matter; the image is indelible, as if I were looking at him today.

The next day, we crossed the Suez Canal on a land bridge the Israeli Army had constructed to the west side of the canal. The Egyptian Fifth Army had been trapped by the Israelis on the east side. We passed enormous SAM missile sites built by the Russians for the Egyptians. The world situation was tense as nations waited to see what the Israelis would do with the entrapped twenty thousand Egyptian soldiers. Occasionally, machine-gun fire erupted from the Egyptians—a suicidal move on their part, it seemed—but the Israelis did not respond. An armistice was in place. We were scheduled to witness its signing at kilometer 101 on the highway to Cairo, but Israeli tanks made travel impossible.

While the war situation was unique, the conversations with Leeds,

Phillips, and Krueger in Israel more lastingly affected my life. Being there together during those historic days bonded us forever.

I encouraged Leeds to replace his cousin Bob, who was not competently managing the Manhattan Shirt Company. Several months later, he fired Bob and for a number of years ran the company. Larry Phillips and I became close friends during the course of the trip, and I later joined the Phillips-Van Heusen Board of Directors. Lehman, and then Peter J. Solomon Company, have represented PVH for the ensuing forty years as the company has grown into an international apparel company.

Over the course of three years, Harvey Krueger and I negotiated for me to leave Lehman and join Kuhn, Loeb. One day in 1976, over breakfast in my office, I proposed that we reverse roles. "Rather than me joining KL," I said, "why don't Lehman and KL merge?" I was aware that KL's business was not growing, but it was still a prestige firm, with smart bankers and an impressive list of industrial and international clients. What I did not know was that KL was in merger discussions with Shearson and that its partners were balking because of Shearson's lower status.

Discussions between Lehman and KL started soon afterward but then ceased. I knew I had to do something. Harvey lived in our building as a result of my suggestion that he buy an apartment. I wrote a note saying, "Hope we can sweet-talk you back to the table?" I attached it to a bottle of honey and had six-year-old Abigail Solomon take it by elevator to Harvey.

The merger was supported by all the partners of Lehman, each for their own reasons. I continued on the merged company board and, with a KL counterpart, Mario D'Urso, produced an extravaganza to celebrate the merger of the two most important Jewish firms on Wall Street. The new entity was called Lehman Brothers, Kuhn, Loeb in the US and Kuhn, Loeb, Lehman abroad, in recognition of its superior international reputation. Four years later, the name was changed back to simply Lehman Brothers.

The firm—by any name—under Pete was not measurably better. As previously noted, his strength was not finance. As someone who had never lived or worked in New York City and had never aspired to be a Lehman partner, he was still oriented toward Washington and the titles and social folderol of the political scene, all of which has little to do with Wall Street. (As Pete himself later told me, the secretary of commerce's principal job is running the National Aquarium.)

Lehman Brothers was a dysfunctional organization. It needed structure. It also needed a leader who could reduce mistrust among partners, encourage cooperation, and inspire younger colleagues. The crucial facts that Pete didn't grasp were that he could not impose a new order and that accomplishing the goals was a political challenge perhaps beyond meeting. Pete lost several years before he understood how to exert positive leadership.

An amusing incident in a Boston cab early in his tenure was illuminating. I was supporting Pete on a new business call. With us was a younger associate, Jack Lentz, who had gained renown as the quarterback for Holy Cross. The most watched football game in Massachusetts in those days was the Holy Cross–Boston College game, a showdown between two leading Catholic colleges. In 1966, Jack, with what the *Boston Globe* described as a "miracle pass," had led Holy Cross to a 32–26 win over BC. Jack also had a brief professional career as a defensive back with the Denver Broncos before he arrived at Lehman.

In the taxi, I was in the front passenger seat, while Pete and Jack shared the back. I asked the driver whether he recognized anyone, and Pete, naturally, puffed up a bit. After a moment or so of studying the rearview mirror, the driver said, "Yes, isn't that Jack Lentz?"

Glucksman's disasters and the generally poor state of the financial industry in the mid-1970s put Pete in a tough position as Lehman's CEO. After the firm incorporated in 1970, it had taken out a $25 million loan from the Mass Mutual Insurance Company, basically to redeem the senior partners and to supplement its balance sheet. One of Peterson's first acts after joining Lehman was to visit Mass Mutual in Springfield, hat in hand, to ask its forbearance because the firm had violated the debt covenants. In need of still more capital, Lehman sold equity to two European banks and also started selling Lehman stock to younger partners such as Jerry Stone and me. The stock I bought at that time would result in my having a violent confrontation with Glucksman in the early 1980s.

Some of the veteran bankers, steeped in the Lehman way, were not ready to embrace Peterson's austerity measures. At one of Pete's first meetings with the partners in early 1974, he spoke of difficult times, predicted personnel cuts, and added that it would seem inappropriate for senior members of the firm to be seen arriving and leaving in limos and flying first class. At one point, he gestured toward Joe Thomas, seated at the other end of the conference table, and said, "Joe, as a senior member of the firm, you must surely agree with these steps."

Joe didn't miss a beat. "Whoever thinks that any partner of this firm is going to fly in the back of an airplane is out of his fucking mind!"

Thus spake Zarathustra.

Having fired his uncle, Warren Hellman began to withdraw from the firm, eventually relocating to Boston; he would leave Lehman in 1984. With some encouragement from the partners, Andy Sage stepped aside. Regrettably, this new leadership vacuum left an opening for Lew Glucksman and an equally bad character, Jim Glanville.

Glanville was the protégé of Ed Kennedy, a gentleman and an authority in the oil business. Ed had been on Kerr McGee's board for years and was widely respected at the firm and in oil circles. He had hired Glanville, a short, stocky Texan who, while smart, aggressive, and a moneymaker, had none of Kennedy's admirable qualities and was never considered a contender to run the firm. Glanville openly expressed his dislike of all minorities, including Jews and Greeks, which was, to say the least, curious at Lehman Brothers, where a Greek American, Peterson, was CEO of a traditionally Jewish firm. Glanville was also a conniver. "Poison," Pete would call him one day. I foresaw that despite Pete's intentions, the toxic combination of Glucksman and Glanville would prevent Lehman from ever evolving into a well-managed firm.

One of the bankers Glanville tried to co-op as a possible fellow anti-Semite was George W. Ball. George, a Chicago lawyer, had joined the firm in 1968 after a notable career in the State Department, rising to the second highest position, undersecretary for Economic and Agricultural Affairs, during the Kennedy and Johnson years. This title amused me, because he hadn't the foggiest idea of economic or agricultural affairs.

George was not an anti-Semite. He told me once how much he admired Golda Meir and thought she was the toughest "pol" he had ever met. Yet he was insensitive to the realities of the Jewish experience and the appropriate paranoia. After the Yom Kippur War, he seemed to take an anti-Israel stance.

Personally, he was a nice bear of a man, gentle in his demeanor but possessing a sharp mind. He often wove tales of encounters with the most powerful people in the world. He was always on the move, flitting around the globe. He drank to distraction—meaning yours, not his. He traveled with a bottle tucked in his carry-on. The security measures enforced today would have ruined his career.

George and I met up in Copenhagen once in 1976 to visit a successful pharmaceutical company, Novo Nordisk A/S. He had already been in at least three countries that day, and when he arrived at nine o'clock that night, he immediately wanted to get a drink. Copenhagen was closed tight, and we wandered the streets for an hour looking for an open pub before admitting defeat.

Knud Hallas-Møller, the elegant chairman of Novo, was thrilled to meet George, and the meeting went well. Novo would have been a significant client for Lehman at that time. As a follow-up to the meeting, Hallas-Møller had arranged a dinner at his home with members of the board. But George begged off, pleading some pressing engagement elsewhere. He just had to keep moving—or drinking, I'm still not sure which. In any case, I was left to apologize for him during an awkward evening.

Needless to say, Novo did not become a Lehman client. Today, it thrives, as it has since that time. Mads Øvlisen, the just-retired CEO and Hallas-Møller's son-in-law, was at the dinner. Despite my efforts, which included taking him to Yankee Stadium for the 1976 World Series, we never overcame the insult.

George was famously known for having thrived in the Johnson administration despite being a dove on Vietnam. His stance had made him a hero to many Americans. Once I asked him how he had ever managed to express those views.

Perhaps he was being too modest, but he told me that once a week he met with LBJ and Secretary of State Dean Rusk for lunch. On one such occasion early in the Vietnam buildup, the president asked Ball to state the case against increased involvement. George said he was reluctant to comply because he knew that Rusk and LBJ favored a stronger presence, but after prodding by them, he stated the case. They responded thoughtfully and asked him to make his argument again at a subsequent lunch.

JFK said the ship of state is the only ship that leaks from the top. Somehow George's comments became known, and he was branded as a dissenter. He was lucky; the label enhanced his reputation.

He was not as prescient on Middle East matters. In 1974, he and Pete advocated that Lehman open an office in Beirut to tap the emerging OPEC-created oil wealth. We didn't, which turned out to be fortunate because soon Beirut was engulfed in war.

❧

As a result of selling Water Pik, I had begun to call on a number of small appliance companies. One of the most intriguing was Mr. Coffee. I had first met Vince Marotta and partner Sam Glazer in 1972 at their factory outside Cleveland. The two owners sat side by side in a small office behind a large assembly plant staffed by hundreds of immigrant workers.

Vince and Sam started out as real estate developers who liked to drink coffee. They had bought a number of drip coffee machines for their homes and office, but none made coffee to their taste. After looking into the situation, they concluded that the problem with coffee machines was the inconsistency of the water temperature while brewing. Their solution was to create a thin metal disc that would bend, depending on how hot it became. They called this innovation a "bio metal activator," but their master stroke was to call the appliance Mr. Coffee.

Vince was even smarter when he hired the Yankee Clipper, Joe DiMaggio, to be their television spokesman. With DiMaggio's unquestioned integrity and fame, Mr. Coffee became a hot household item. By 1974, consumers had bought more than one million of the machines.

In 1976, I convinced Vince to think about selling the business. It had a value over $100 million at that point, which was good money for a product created mostly through brilliant marketing. Mr. Coffee probably wasn't as efficacious as the Water Pik, but it had broader appeal at the time.

A logical buyer was the fast-growing Black & Decker Company, which I serviced under the guidance of Joe Thomas. Its quarter-inch drill was the basis of the company's growth, but it wanted to move from the workshop to the interior of the home. A coffee machine was a natural fit. With B&D's manufacturing knowhow, they could drive down the costs and, with the elasticity of demand, create more volume and greater profits.

B&D had been built with the expertise of the Boston Consulting Group and Bill Bain. Management naturally asked Bain its opinion of the coffee market and the potential demand, not just for this product but in macro trends. BCG concluded that demand for coffee would decline.

Management turned down the opportunity. In the subsequent decades, as I have watched the global growth of coffee consumption, I think of the genius of Bill Bain and how his team could nevertheless be so wrong.

Other possible acquirers of Mr. Coffee reached different conclusions. American Home Products was one of the world's great companies. I felt it would be a fitting acquirer. In fact, this management was interested in entering the home device market and made an offer to Vince Marotta. The offer was $125 million in American Home Products stock. Vince turned it down. It wasn't enough.

I never sold Mr. Coffee. It went through the normal decline associated with companies that have nothing unusual to offer besides a great marketing concept. The luster even faded from Joe DiMaggio. In 1987, Mr. Coffee was sold for $82 million.

I last saw Vince as we walked into a dinner at the White House, the day in 1980 that I went to Washington. He seemed happy, but for me, Mr. Coffee will always rank as one of the Ones That Got Away.

Most of my deals didn't get away, though, and I'm proud to say that I was among the young partners who helped the firm return to profitability in 1974 and 1975. In 1976, when I was elected to the board, Lehman had the second-best year in its history.

CHAPTER 12

Meeting a Best Friend

While Pete wrestled with his partners and the firm hired a lot of young associates and merged with the brokerage firm of Abraham and Company, I forged ahead, bringing in new clients and honing my skills.

In 1972, shortly after I had become a managing director, I was invited to lunch with two Lehman colleagues and a client. The lunch turned out to be an audition. Edgar M. Cullman, the CEO of the General Cigar Corporation, wanted another Lehman partner on his board to replace retired director Jim Szold. Apparently, after the meal, Edgar would decide which of the three of us would replace Szold.

I knew Edgar in passing. I was, however, close to his daughter Lucy and her husband, Mike Danziger. Our house on Cascade Road in North Stamford was minutes from Hickory Farm, where Mike and Lucy lived on Edgar and Louise's property. We'd spent many hours there playing tennis or just visiting. Our children were friendly. We had also fished on the Restigouche River in New Brunswick, Canada, together, but I had no memory of having had a conversation with Edgar or Louise. My colleagues at the lunch, Bob Shapiro and John Herrmann, knew Edgar much better. But somehow he selected me. It was the start of a wonderful romance.

What are the characteristics that cement the bond between two grown men twenty years apart? And how did our relationship affect my choices? What did I learn from his experience? Edgar played such an important role in my life over almost fifty years as friend and confidant, critic, mentor, and client that my memories of him could fill this book.

Let me say first that Edgar loved his cigars, particularly Macanudo and Partagas, both manufactured by General Cigar Holdings, a company he acquired in 1963. Seeing Edgar walk through a cigar factory in the Dominican Republic in his white linen shirt, reminiscent of Sidney Greenstreet, was to behold an owner in all his glory. Accompanied by the plant manager and watched by the legion of "tobacco women" who rolled the cigars by hand, he would take a leaf and hold it to the light to see its texture and the pattern of the veins. He would caress it between his thumb and forefinger, then press it to his nose and take a slow, deep breath. Then he would tear it slightly— for what purpose I never determined—and, finally, replace the leaf in the bundle. As he did this, everyone leaned forward, and the plant manager's anxiety was palpable.

Then Edgar would nod. "Good," he said. One hundred workers exhaled as the plant manager beamed. At that point, I always felt like shouting, "El Exigente, the demanding one!"

This was Edgar. Demanding but reinforcing. Even when critical, he didn't put you down. I and the coterie of Edgar's friends sought refuge in his unique ability to listen, ponder, probe—and then either question or applaud. But he never made you worry that he was judging you as a person and that a negative opinion would have an effect on your relationship. He held negative thoughts about people but rarely revealed them—a trait, as the reader knows well, I never mastered.

Edgar was born into wealth, the son of a tobacco seller and owner of Benson & Hedges cigarettes. The Cullmans lived at Tryall in Jamaica, on the Restigouche and Upsalquitch Rivers in Canada, around the Century Country Club in Westchester, Hickory Farm, and New York City. He was a preppie and then a Yalie, as were his older brothers, Joe, later the fabled CEO of Philip Morris, and Arthur, who became a professor of retailing at Ohio State, and his younger brother, Lewis, one of the first leveraged buyout investors, generous philanthropist, and avid skier into his nineties. The boys had a sister, Nan, who was always *un peu parte*, as the French gently say.

The siblings were competitive until death did them part but shared a fierce family connection. They were worldly but traveled little beyond their various far-flung homes. They were Jewish but never went to temple and didn't know a bagel from a baguette.

Edgar met Louise Bloomingdale when he was an adolescent and married her when he was at Yale. Louise and Edgar were matched perfectly. She liked golf, painting, taking walks to collect wildflowers, playing backgammon, and being with Edgar. When Edgar talked, Louise frequently interjected, "Oh, Edgar!"

In some ways, Edgar led a sheltered life. He was often surprised by the prosaic or the commonplace. He had never tasted a tuna fish sandwich when General Cigar acquired Helme Products, Inc., manufacturer of potato chips and snacks. He'd eaten in restaurants, of course, but mostly he dined in his own home, on turkeys and chickens that had been raised on his property and on produce from Louise's garden. He was startled that most people ate canned tuna fish. He had just never experienced it.

Edgar was an enthusiast. The world was exciting to him, and his excitement and optimism were contagious. He professed interest in the days' events but, except for a tenure in the Office of the Alien Property Custodian during WWII, he did no government service. He was committed to three institutions: Hotchkiss School, where into his nineties he attended board meetings, Yale, and Mt. Sinai Hospital, where he and Louise were generous and committed trustees.

Former Major League Baseball commissioner (and former partner at Peter J. Solomon Company) Fay Vincent, in a tribute to Edgar written after his death at ninety-three in 2011, said that he was a snob, and Edgar's three children objected vociferously. It was true, but he was never haughty when it came to the social classes. He was generous and affectionate to his employees—Lorne Irving, who ran his fishing camp, the household staff at Tryall and in Stamford, and his friend Nelson Long, the long-serving golf pro at Tryall and Century, and his wife, Terry. But a snob Edgar definitely was in the sense that the "best" was all that mattered to him: in education, in the conduct of one's life, in friendships, and in business.

Perhaps it was Edgar's optimism that buoyed my spirits through a divorce and the inevitable tribulations of my career. There was never a doubt that I was his banker, and when I started PJSC in 1989, General Cigar was my first and, for a while, only client.

With me, and all of his friends, he was never too busy for lunch or a conversation. When I was thinking of divorcing in 1990, I took a number of walks with Edgar through the gardens and fields of his Stamford place. He listened and asked questions. I knew how much he hated the idea of divorce and knew he liked Linda, yet if this was my decision and I had thought about it, it was fine with him. I needed that assurance and needed to know, when asked, that he would respond evenly and not blame me for some impulsive, destructive act.

Humor and trust were two leitmotifs in our relationship. We both believed that there are no modifying words for integrity. You either had it or you didn't. We trusted each other to the extent that nothing we said would ever be used to harm the other person, no confidences revealed, and no advantage taken. We were both committed to quality; for him, that meant there was no sacrificing the ingredients in his beloved cigars, and for me that there was never any compromising when dealing with my clients. We both loved people and gathered friends of all ages to ourselves. Edgar embraced Fay Vincent, Dan Lufkin, Tommy Israel, and John Angelo, among others. Only one time did Edgar show his disappointment in someone, but in doing so, he demonstrated the qualities I adored.

Judd Pollack was his Yale classmate, and they had remained close: he served on Edgar's board, and Edgar gave his advertising firm business. Their wives were friendly, they golfed together, played bridge as a foursome, and fished at Edgar and Joe's luxurious Runnemede Lodge. Pollack was a superb athlete and by all outward appearances a gentleman.

Judd Pollack and his wife, Jane, wintered on John's Island, a gated community in Vero Beach, Florida, and spent the rest of the year in Darien, Connecticut. By coincidence, in 1998, Susan and I were interested in a winter home at John's Island. We knew the Pollacks lived there and called them. Jane Pollack showed Susan around but, in the course of their tour, took her to a lesser community, Orchid

Island, and suggested we might be happier there. Susan was worried by the comment, but we had other good friends and contemporaries at John's Island so went forward with an application. When asked, Judd would neither propose us nor write a letter of recommendation. He didn't explain his nonactions to us, but he confided to Edgar that he was uncomfortable supporting us because we were Jewish.

Edgar was thunderstruck. For fifty years, Judd Pollack had been one of his closest friends and had taken advantage of all the hospitality the Cullmans could offer—and they could offer an immense and varied amount.

Edgar wrote Pollack an excoriating letter, and he and Louise never spoke to him again. Disloyalty and anti-Semitism—even for a German Jew who wasn't observant—were traits not to be tolerated.

Edgar loved throwing his own birthday parties. They were always elegant affairs with friends from across the years: no flashy people, no show biz types or glitterati. I was always comfortable at his parties, surrounded by people he and Louise truly liked. At his eightieth, I quoted John Angelo, who observed that Edgar continued traditions that had ceased to exist before his birth. At his ninetieth, I toasted him by observing that while he had spent a lifetime working to save the Atlantic salmon from extinction, and the few that we had caught over the last twenty-five years were always released, we must have mistaken his purpose. For that night, we were eating those same wonderful fish—smoked.

Though he owned a plane, Edgar did not like to fly. He berated me constantly for my asocial habit of falling asleep as soon as the jet engines engaged. In 1998, I began a tradition of taking him fishing as a birthday present; after all, I had mooched off him for so many years. On his eightieth birthday, we flew to Helsinki and then Murmansk, Russia, and the Kola Peninsula. On our way to the Ponoi River, we flew in a former Russian military helicopter with bullet-hole patches in the tail, a reminder of Russia's Afghan folly. Edgar was not particularly pleased by that or by the rustic camp, where the accommodations were two cots in a tent with the shower and toilets one hundred yards away. The weather was chilly, even though it was August.

Edgar was the oldest fisherman in our group by fifteen years, but he never hesitated. And, as always, he became the favorite of the twenty fellow travelers. I can still see him on his way to the shower in the early morning in his cashmere bathrobe and fedora.

On his eighty-fifth birthday, I took him, Mike and Dick Danziger, and Edgar Cullman Jr. to Montana, where we fished with Rock Ringling, my longtime friend, guide and head of the Montana Land Reliance, a wonderful group dedicated to "cattle not condos." Edgar had never gone west to fish. On his ninetieth, we fished a morning in New York Harbor for bluefish and striped bass. Ever the game person, he smiled though the catching was slim and the seas were rough.

The first time Susan met him was at a lunch in Stamford in 1993. My children, particularly Abigail, loved a Cullman meal. The corn, brussels sprouts, tomatoes, and lettuce were all straight from their garden. Louise's flowers were everywhere. If it was spring, there were soft-shelled crabs or shad roe; in summer, white peaches and pears from their orchards. And often there was steak, which he favored with tons of butter and Lipitor-negating creams and sauces. In the fall, Edgar delivered a huge turkey—so large that our oven couldn't accommodate it—and apples of all varieties.

At this particular lunch, Susan got a chance to see Edgar in action. He was probably ragging on me about something, as he always did, but I don't remember what. It could have been baseball—for he had never gotten over the fact that the Giants had left New York—or that I hadn't found General Cigar a good business to buy, though it hadn't made a good acquisition since Ex-Lax thirty years before. He always liked to sound gruff, which I and his other friends ignored and responded to with the occasional, "Oh, Edgar!"

As we drove away, Susan said that he was the most awful man she'd ever met and added, "I never want to see him again!"

"Really? What did he say?" I said.

"Oh, my God, didn't you hear him?"

"Frankly, no. I love him, but I never listen to what he says."

Before long, Susan grew to love him too.

CHAPTER 13

My Own President: 1974–1976

I was walking along Stonewall Beach in Chilmark on Martha's Vineyard over Labor Day weekend in 1974, thinking about the recent resignation of Richard Nixon, when an idea occurred to me: why shouldn't I try to influence the process of picking a president? Why be a bystander? Why not have a positive effect on the process, even influence the outcome of the next election somehow? Until then, I had focused on New York political candidates. But with the nation still reeling from Watergate and its aftermath, I felt it was time to try to make a more meaningful contribution.

After analyzing the possible Democratic candidates, I concluded that two had reasonable shots at winning the nomination and the election: Birch Bayh, the senator from Indiana, who had survived a plane crash ten years earlier that almost killed him and his pal Ted Kennedy, and Jimmy Carter, the former governor of Georgia. I wasn't so sure about Bayh, who seemed too close to organized labor for my taste. Carter seemed to be the sort of middle-of-the-road Democrat with a southern base that could win.

I had never met Carter, but I knew that all Democratic candidates had to pass through New Hampshire. Marty Gross, my oldest friend and college roommate, was an important figure in New Hampshire politics: the general counsel of the New Hampshire Democratic Party and mayor of Concord. Every four years, he was particularly important in Democratic circles because of the New Hampshire primary. Marty told me Jimmy Carter was going to stay at his house. I drafted a letter to Carter, saying that I was interested in supporting his candidacy, and sent it to Marty. He left it on Jimmy's pillow.

About a week later, I got a call from Carter's chief policy aide. When I called back, I wound up speaking with deputy policy director Stuart Eizenstat. We eventually became friends and remain close. I was also introduced to another campaign aide, Jack Watson, by attorney Griffin Bell of King & Spalding in Atlanta (and later attorney general), whom I had met when we both spoke at a conference at Disneyland. Still, I found national politics frustrating. Outsiders rarely penetrate the inner workings of a campaign. Although I wrote papers on various economic and financial issues, I was naïve: most of Carter's associates were not interested in my thoughts, only in how much money I could contribute and raise.

I wasn't the only person at Lehman involved in the coming election. My colleague Roger Altman—who became a partner in 1975, when Pete Peterson found it necessary to create a passel of new ones—was always more interested in politics than banking. Roger, who had worked for Bobby Kennedy, wasted no time ingratiating himself with Carter's chief strategist, Hamilton Jordan. He asked me to join him and Howard Samuels ("Howie the Horse," former undersecretary of commerce and head of New York City's Off-Track Betting Corporation) to lead the fundraising effort in New York City.

We raised a lot of money for the Carter campaign. Howie was skilled at getting our group credit, so it was not a coincidence that we got to spend time with the candidate. Carter came to New York City frequently, but because of his populist bent, he stayed away from the Financial District, never going south of Fourteenth Street. That aspect of his personality annoyed me, particularly since his credibility on economic issues was related to the Trilateral Commission, a creation of David Rockefeller, the ultimate financier. Despite his sometimes holier-than-thou demeanor, Carter tried to have things both ways.

Jimmy Carter as a person was difficult to fathom. He could put sincerity into overdrive at any moment. Once when I was sitting next to him at a small fundraising breakfast in Washington, he asked me what issues I was really concerned about. "The stability and prosperity of New York City and the existence of the State of Israel," I said. With that, he grabbed my right forearm and, squeezing it hard, said that he, too, was committed to Israel because it is "the natural fulfillment of God's prophesy!" A couple of years later, when I was walking into a fundraising event in New York City with him, he turned to Linda and said, to both of our astonishment, "I wouldn't be president if it wasn't for Peter!" That was both very kind and, we knew, very untrue.

It was amusing to watch supporters maneuver for postelection positions. The Secret Service supposedly never worried about Carter in New York because attorney Bill vanden Heuvel clung so close to him that he would take the first bullet. Howie the Horse played up to Carter, as well. Still, I admired the dashing Samuels. If he hadn't seen it all, he had seen enough.

The general election campaign contained a few disquieting moments, such as when Carter told a *Playboy* reporter that he occasionally had "lust in his heart" when he looked at women. At such times, I thought, *Peter, you have picked a candidate of your own, and, by God, he may be just as bad as all the others!*

I still believed Carter could win, but by September 1976, I was sufficiently concerned about his candidacy that I decided to get the perspective of Lehman's outside counsel at Simpson Thacher and Bartlett: Cyrus Vance, a former secretary of the army under John Kennedy and, under LBJ, deputy secretary of defense. When I entered Cy's office, he was wary. I realized later that it was so unusual for a Lehman partner to ask to come see him that he suspected my visit involved something bad. But I just wanted the opinion of an experienced Washington hand.

"Cy," I said, "I have known Jimmy Carter for almost two years, and I have worked hard to get him elected. There is something really odd about him. I can't quite put my finger on it, but he isn't normal. You've known Presidents Truman, Eisenhower, Nixon, JFK, LBJ, and Ford. How would you rank Carter alongside them?"

Cy—who would later become secretary of state, only to resign after the failed Iranian hostage debacle—was a cautious man. After thinking it over for a moment, he said he would rank Carter "about in the middle." He said Truman, Ford, and Ike were "normal people." LBJ and Nixon were not. "They were very difficult to deal with," he said. But Carter and JFK, he said, fell somewhere in between. He spoke with such authority that I was much relieved.

Two weeks after the election, the Friday before Thanksgiving, Stuart Eizenstat called. He said that the outgoing President Ford's advisers, including Treasury Secretary William E. Simon, had recommended that the incoming administration not support an International Monetary Fund loan for the UK. Stuart and the president-elect both thought this was odd, but they needed someone to look into it. Stuart knew I had a number of friends in the UK and asked me to go to London and give the president-elect an answer ASAP. Of course, I agreed.

By coincidence, Sir Antony Burney—the chairman of Debenhams, a major UK department store—was a Lehman client and a good friend. Tony was an accountant by training and knew little about retail. He had asked me to come to London and look at his stores there, as well as in Nottingham and Birmingham. He wanted my views on their merchandising. I had scheduled to go over Thanksgiving weekend. Stuart was thrilled to hear that I was bound for London already and could report back to him shortly.

I then called Tony Burney and explained the situation. I said I would still do everything I'd promised, including meeting with his senior people to give them my conclusions, but told him I needed him to help me set up meetings with everybody relevant to the IMF loan and Britain's budget and balance of payments. It was a productive trip. For four straight days, I met with senior members of the Treasury and Harold Wilson's cabinet, as well as senior Tories and academics, while I worked in visits to stores around London. What I found in them was appalling; Debenhams stores were badly merchandised with, for example, enough coats to outfit all of England.

The IMF loan problem turned out to be much simpler to solve. North Sea oil was about to pour into England, turning its sterling outflow around. Under those conditions, it made perfect sense for the US to support the loan. I wrote a brief memo to Stuart for the president-elect saying as much.

I knew that Stuart and Jack Watson were promoting me for a position such as deputy secretary of the Treasury. I waited for a call through December—but nothing. In the meantime, Treasury Secretary Michael Blumenthal appointed attorney Robert Carswell, a Sherman & Sterling partner, deputy secretary of the Treasury, and Roger Altman became an assistant secretary. But I was left out.

What went wrong for me? Two things. First, Hamilton Jordan fired Jack as head of the transition team, a position that was evolving into the president's chief of staff. Apparently, Hamilton had trouble seeing Jack or anyone else as the gatekeeper; he wanted that job for himself. By chance, I was visiting Jack at the transition offices in Washington the day Hamilton gave him the news. When I walked into Jack's office, Hamilton had actually just left. Jack was in shock. He told me that Hamilton had said, "I haven't worked all these years for Carter just to be relegated to some secondary position!" Jack didn't know whether the president-elect had sent Hamilton or not, but he knew he was through.[2] He eventually moved to an office on the second floor of the West Wing across from Stuart but with the secondary job of being the liaison with governors and mayors. For me, that meant one of my most forceful and prominent sponsors was gone.

My opportunity to be appointed to the Treasury was also hurt by Altman's appointment. After President-Elect Carter chose Blumenthal, Roger worked assiduously to become an assistant secretary. I suspected correctly that Carter would never appoint two people from the same Wall Street firm. (The time was distant when a prerequisite for a federal appointment was employment at Goldman Sachs.)

---

[2] In 2017, Chris Whipple, in his chronicle of White House chiefs of staff, *The Gatekeepers*, cites the historic significance of Jordan's confrontation with Jack. He writes that Jordan was such a terrible chief of staff that Carter eventually fired him and replaced him with Watson. According to Whipple, Watson was a "first-class choice." Whipple wrote that at a reception before his inauguration in 1981, Ronald Reagan told the outgoing chief, "You know, Jack, my people tell me that if you'd been chief of staff from the beginning, I wouldn't be here." Like President Reagan, it's hard not to think of what the effect might have been on my life.

During the campaign, I had worked with John Bowles, an early Carter supporter and a partner of Kidder, Peabody. Bowles' area was appointments affecting financial markets, including the SEC. On the day after Carter's inauguration, January 21, 1977, Bowles and I met with Hamilton Jordan in the chief of staff's office in the West Wing.

It is hard to describe the disorder of Jordan's office. There were no carpets, and the walls were bare. Across from the blazing fireplace—extra logs were scattered around the floor—stood a large mahogany table covered with and surrounded by papers, binders, briefing books, and all sorts of memos. It was not the office of someone in charge of the US government in the twentieth century. (One could envision the White House of Andrew Jackson.) It made me think about how different this same room must have looked under Nixon's buttoned-up H. R. Haldeman.

When Hamilton asked how many appointments the president could make at each regulatory agency, Bowles got on his hands and knees and dug through the pile of material on the floor for the "plum book," which is named not only for its color but also because it lists every appointive job in the federal government. Whatever the number was, Jordan was surprised that Carter had so many positions to fill. I was even more surprised that he knew so little about the workings of government.

On a Friday a couple of months later, I got a telephone call from Stuart. He told me that the next day's *New York Times* would be reporting that Stanford Business School Dean Harold Williams and I were the leading candidates for chairmanship of the SEC. Sure enough, when the paper arrived at my apartment the next morning, there on page one, column one, was the story.

I asked Stuart what I should do about the job. "Try to get it," he said. I had no experience in this area and so began to grope my way through a new chapter in my life, which I might call, "How to run for appointive office."

My first call was to my friend (but not relative) Bunny Solomon, who worked for Stop&Shop in government relations. Bunny had been in Massachusetts Governor Foster Furcolo's administration as a purchasing agent and gained a measure of fame as the only member of the cabinet who didn't go to jail. Now he was my uncle Sidney Rabb's political adviser and was close to Senator Teddy Kennedy and Speaker Tip O'Neill.

Bunny arranged for me to meet with Teddy; through Teddy, I met with Senator Harrison Williams, "Pete," of New Jersey, the chair of the Banking Committee. Pete told me that though he was committed to Harold Williams as head of the SEC, he would meet with any friend of Ted Kennedy. I later found out that while I made the rounds, talking to relevant senators, Senator Alan Cranston, the Californian Democratic whip, had told Carter that Williams' appointment was the one and only favor he wanted.

The reaction of Wall Street to the possibility of my appointment was decidedly mixed. Tubby Burnham of Burnham & Company, the predecessor to Drexel Burnham, was supportive, but many Wall Streeters didn't want to be regulated by one of their own. Mostly it was a fear of the unknown, as I would be the first financial person in the job since Joe Kennedy. Senator Pat Moynihan, who would figure again in my life three years later, wrote Carter, saying, "Once in every generation" someone who knows an industry from the inside should regulate it.

During this process, a long-forgotten classmate reentered my life. Salim Lewis, "Sandy," had left Collegiate in the fourth grade. My last memory of him was at his ninth birthday party, when we played pin the tail on the donkey. Sandy had been an adviser to Rod Hills, chairman of the SEC. He arranged for me to meet with Rod and gain his support.

This was another time when I learned an enormous amount from a failure. In this case, the lessons centered on the workings of Congress and the appointment process. But the experience also taught me that I had no interest in being a regulator. In fact, it made me wonder whether I wanted any appointment in the federal government other than the White House. Chairman of a federal commission is a prestigious position. But when I asked for the chairman at the SEC reception desk, the civil servant there didn't recognize Rod Hill's name.

Later, Stuart told me that when Carter appointed Williams, he was apologetic, explaining he felt he just couldn't have someone from within the securities industry regulate the SEC. Nevertheless, in 1981, President Reagan would appoint John Shad, the former CEO of EF Hutton, to head the SEC, and President Clinton would choose Arthur Leavitt, who had spent his career in the financial industry. Carter was a man of limited imagination.

Bowles and I, meanwhile, had kept our hand in by creating the Policy Forum with my assistant Patti Holiday. The group held monthly lunches attended by prominent New Yorkers, where cabinet officers and other senior Carter officials spoke.

As emissaries for the president, the Carter cabinet as a whole was not particularly impressive on these occasions, but the least impressive was the budget director, Jim McIntyre. McIntyre was Carter's second budget director, replacing Bert Lance. The loss of Lance, forced to resign over questions about dubious banking practices at his rural Georgia bank, was a significant setback for Carter. Lance had the worldliness and "good ole boy" warmth Carter and his campaign associates lacked. McIntyre, in answering one question about financing the budget at one of our luncheons, displayed a shocking lack of knowledge about the state of the debt markets. Several years later, when the newly appointed comptroller of New York State, Ned Reagan, paid a courtesy call on Mayor Koch, he asked me for some advice. I told him that the least he should always know is the level of interest rates.

PART II

CHAPTER 14

City Government

> "I hear you work alone and get things done."
> (Mayor Edward I. Koch, 1978)

It is a steamy July day in 1978 in the Board of Estimate Chamber on the second floor of City Hall. I have just been sworn in by Mayor Edward I. Koch as New York City's deputy mayor for economic development and policy. But before I can enjoy the moment, I hurry to LaGuardia for a flight to Washington, where I negotiate for economic development funds and financial support for the city from the federal government. It's a dire time in New York, as the city needs increased credit and capital from the feds to finance its operations and rebuild its crumpling roads and bridges. The South Bronx is literally burning, as shown on national television during the 1976 World Series. Unemployment is about 9 percent, and major employers are relocating to the South and New Jersey and Westchester. Dirty streets and crime have sapped New Yorkers' morale. One million New Yorkers have fled the city since 1950. As I'm hurrying to LaGuardia, wondering if things can possibly get any worse, my city-owned car catches fire. Mike Patrone, my driver, pulls over on the busy Brooklyn-Queens Expressway, and, without thinking twice, I hop out and hail a yellow taxi. Got to keep going—but I can't help thinking, *Is this some kind of prophesy?*

My Ed Koch years began with a call from City Hall. David Brown, the acting first deputy mayor, whom I hardly knew, called me in early March 1978, asking me to meet the new mayor.

The internal situation at Lehman had continued to deteriorate. Glucksman and Glanville were gaining power at the expense of Peterson, and it felt like Glucksman would eventually triumph. He had somehow co-opted the still highly regarded Bob Rubin and Bill Morris, my rival in the banking group. Business was picking up, but I was concerned about my future.

The campaign for mayor in 1977 had finished with the left-leaning Congressman Ed Koch winning the Democratic primary by ten thousand votes. He had come from nowhere in a crowded field against former state senator Basil Patterson, former congressman and Bronx congressman Herman Badillo, and New York Secretary of State Mario Cuomo. Koch had started with only 7 percent recognition, according to the polls, but had won on one issue: the death penalty. That year, the city was recovering from the Son of Sam terror. Koch's pro–death penalty stance contrasted with the liberal views of his primary competition and had visceral appeal to large segments of the voting public.

I knew Koch slightly, having shared a few meals with him over the years. He was my congressman from the Silk Stocking District, an area that runs from Greenwich Village to the Upper East Side. What little I saw of Koch I didn't like. He struck me as a loudmouth, shoot-from-the-hip left-winger whose sole positive accomplishment was confounding the Tammany Hall machine.

After much cajoling from Brown and his offer to walk with me from William Street to City Hall, I met with Koch, Brown, and Phil Aarons, a Koch assistant. After a few minutes of small talk, the mayor abruptly asked me to become deputy mayor. I was shocked. I had no experience with government or politics on the city level and had no idea what a deputy mayor did. In fact, although I was a native New Yorker, this was my first time inside City Hall.

I told the mayor I'd consider his offer, but when Brown escorted me from the office, I asked him, "What the hell was that?" He was caught off guard himself, saying that the mayor had told him he wanted me to go on the Municipal Assistance Board. About a year later, I asked Koch why he'd offered me the job. He said, "I'd heard you traveled alone and got things done!" His answer surprised me, because that was exactly how I viewed myself.

Pete Peterson had urged me to meet with Koch and was eager to hear what had transpired. Pete and I had a wary relationship. He tended to treat me as a Lehman legacy banker, which, to his Midwestern and DC-centric eye, wasn't good.

When I told Pete about Koch's offer, he enthusiastically urged me to accept it. He argued that New York was still on the brink of insolvency and that I was being offered what amounted to "the second most important economic job in the US!" I was somewhat skeptical of the importance, wondered about his enthusiasm for my departure, and asked if he was trying to get rid of me. He said that he was thinking of the bigger picture: "The country cannot afford to have New York City collapse!" To get a second opinion, I spoke to my politically connected friends Stu Eizenstat and Ed Costikyan, who had directed Koch's campaign but quit because he was not appointed first deputy mayor. Both encouraged me to accept. My family was worried that Koch had shown his volatility by firing Robert Milano, the previous deputy mayor for economic development, after seventy-four days. But in the end, they were supportive.

The next day, I called Brown and outlined the job that I would take. I realized that dictating conditions to a newly elected mayor might seem arrogant, but Pete cautioned me to "get the job description in writing." My title, I told Brown, had to be broadened to deputy mayor for economic development and policy. (I would have preferred deputy mayor of finance, but Koch had already appointed Phil Toia to that title.) In federal terms, I outlined the responsibilities of the commerce, energy, and treasury secretaries and the special trade representative. My office had to be in City Hall, physically near the mayor. Years before, George Ball had advised me, "Nothing propinks like propinquity."

Brown listened without comment, and two hours later, a messenger delivered a letter signed by the mayor, delineating the responsibilities I'd asked for and adding oversight of New York City's ports and terminals. I showed it to Pete, whose only comment was, What did "oversight" mean? Even I knew that. When I put the question to Brown, he, exasperated, said it meant "in charge." Pete congratulated me. Few of my fellow managing directors seemed to care I was leaving. In late summer, they tossed me a perfunctory little going-away party at which I received the gift of a popcorn machine. I never opened the box.

When I arrived at City Hall for my first full day, before I was sworn in later, the mayor was in the midst of creating his first budget. New York City was in terrible financial shape.

President Gerald Ford stood against a bailout of the city, which was characterized by the *Daily News* as "Ford to City: Drop Dead." The rebuke energized Governor Hugh Carey to put the state on the line and to drive the municipal unions and bankers holding municipal bonds together to create financing vehicles to sustain the city's access to the credit markets. With intensive lobbying led by one of the heroes of the period, real estate developer Lew Rudin, Congress had agreed in December 1979 to backstop the city's seasonal borrowings.

At a June meeting, Budget Director Jim Brigham laid out the facts. The budget of $13 billion had a deficit of about $2 billion. Koch had some perfunctory questions. He then asked Brigham why he couldn't be more precise. Brigham reminded him that the systems left behind by Koch's predecessor, Abe Beame, were not computerized. The mayor then pushed Brigham about the number of city employees. Again, Brigham reported that he thought the city had about 220,000 employees, but the number was not exact. After a few more exchanges, the mayor asked whether the budget could be balanced, and Jim mumbled, "By law, it has to be."

Koch had not been elected because of his fiscal acumen. He was a congressman who had never shown much interest in money—his own or anyone else's. Suddenly, and to his great discomfort, he was confronted by the realities of a complicated and unstable financial situation. I could see his exasperation as he turned to his corporation counsel Allen Schwartz, seated to his left. "Allen," he whined in a tone that was to become famous, "what happens if I don't balance the budget?"

Schwartz, in an off-handed manner I later grew to dislike and distrust, quipped, "You go to jail!"

Everyone in the room witnessed Edward I. Koch having an epiphany. An hour earlier, he had been a classic liberal from a Democratic clubhouse on the Lower East Side. Before our eyes, he started morphing into a fiscal conservative.

Although my office was in City Hall, as I'd requested, I was in charge of the Office for Economic Development located across Broadway. A typical pol in some ways, Koch had filled it with campaign pals, most of whom didn't have the foggiest idea of proper business principles or how to complete a project. It became clear immediately that I had to build my own staff. It is a fact of political life, whether you are in City Hall or at 1600 Pennsylvania Avenue, that it is only your staff that you control completely. I assembled a first-class group. Eli Ginzberg, a friend who had served at senior levels in the Eisenhower administration, gave me wise counsel. "Political employees are not like business associates," he said. "They know they are relatively short-term and acknowledge the brutality of the system. Therefore, pay them as much as you can, be sure they are totally loyal, and if they don't work out, fire them!"

My secretary from Lehman, Helen Burlew, joined me at City Hall. I took Phil Aarons and Judith Friedlander from the mayor's staff. Judith was a Harvard graduate and brooked no guff from the bureaucracy. She also swore and didn't wear a bra, which was almost more than city workers could endure. My friend Ben Sonnenberg, the famous public relations guru, pointed me toward Ellen Weissman. She was a lawyer and, serendipitously, the daughter of Philip Morris CEO George Weissman. Paul Watterson, a quiet recent law graduate, applied randomly. He later became an important figure at my friend Stephen Schulte's law firm. Ken Schuman, who had so ably run the Hudson Guild, also joined our staff, as did Fritz Favorule, a Koch campaign staffer who was later a liaison to the 1980 Democratic National Convention. (Our office organized the New York bid and coordinated the city's participation.)

I appointed Tom Langman, one of my oldest friends from Collegiate, who had been in the New Communities program at HUD, to the position of "schnorer in chief," his job being to scour the federal government for money. Partially through his ingenuity in the city's Washington office, we received EDA funds from Commerce and Urban Development Action Grants (UDAG) from HUD and developed a New York City procurement program for federal contracts to smaller New York City companies. This program involving the DOD was facilitated by Eizenstat and Bruce Kirschenbaum in the White House and encouraged by Congressman Joe Addabbo of Queens, chair of the House Armed Services Committee.

Robert Herzog was my energy adviser. City government faced a myriad of issues in dealing with Con Edison, the Power Authority of the State of New York, which, among other proposals, wanted to build an unnecessary coal-fired plant on Staten Island, and the placement of innovative resource recovery plants.

In 1978, the mayor held the common view that New York City energy prices were high—they were, in fact, 50 percent higher than in Boston, the second most expensive in the nation—because Con Edison was incompetently managed. There was little understanding that New York City used Con Ed and other utilities as tax collection vehicles. Thirty-five percent of their charges to customers represented property taxes and other city- and state-imposed fees. Additionally, electrical usage in the city peaked for about one hundred hours during hot summer months. Con Ed had to maintain sufficient capacity for this peak load, and customers carried the resulting capital costs throughout the year.

We needed to work with Con Ed and PASNY to assure the continuity of electricity, so that there would be no sequel to the blackouts of 1965 and 1977. We needed to find suitable technology to recycle waste into electricity and then find acceptable locations to store it. The latter task was challenging, not only because of the technology. A favored site at the underdeveloped Brooklyn Navy Yard, for example, was blocked by the Orthodox Jewish community because the necessary smoke stacks reminded them of death camps.

My team was as competent as any I have known. They worked endless hours, but more importantly, I could count on their judgment and loyalty. In government, your own staff can be your only true friends; everyone beyond them is loyal to someone else.

Shortly after my appointment in 1978, Marty Bregman, a movie producer operating from New York City, demanded that I come to his office. One of the least attractive aspects of being in city government is that many citizens treat you as though you really are a public servant. Bregman, then known best as the producer of *Serpico* and *Dog Day Afternoon*, berated me about the office of film, theatre, and broadcasting that was established under Mayor John Lindsay in 1966 to promote filmmaking and production in New York City. It was poorly managed, Bregman said. The head position in the office was vacant, and he ordered me to fill it.

The unions had a candidate for the spot: Steve D'Inzillo, a pistol-toting, politically connected, and perfectly pleasant member of Local 306 of the Projectionists Union. Rejecting his immediate appointment, I told Fritz to run a search. Koch agreed to delay an appointment until we found someone more acceptable to us. We eventually selected Nancy Littlefield from a list of qualified candidates. She had no connection to Koch or politics but had been a successful director in television and documentary films. When the unions heard that, they demanded a meeting with me. And so it was that fifteen members of the principal film production unions faced off against me and Fritz at the Office of Economic Development at 225 Broadway on the fifteenth floor. The meeting started badly, with them insisting on D'Inzillo and me saying no way. The mood was tense, and after a while, I started to worry that I might not make it out in one piece, when the door opened and one of the secretaries asked by name for the chief Teamster representative. He left the room. Now, I thought, I was really toast. Then the door opened again, and the Teamster rep returned. After some hushed words on the other side of the table, all fifteen union members stood up and left. On his way out, the Teamster turned and said, "Okay, you can go with Littlefield." I later heard that the caller had told him that D'Inzillo had crossed a Teamster picket line. I couldn't believe my luck.

Nancy Littlefield served five years with distinction as head of the Mayor's Office of Film, Theater, and Broadcasting. In 1977, before she arrived, forty-two films had been made in New York. Thanks to her efforts, in 1979, ninety-seven films, including *Kramer vs. Kramer*, *All That Jazz*, and *Fame* helped create $500 million of business in New York City. And, incidentally, we found that the primary issues of concern to the industry were labor rules and police regulations. Tax credits were a benefit but not decisive.

People told me that I'd have a hard time adjusting to life in City Hall, but I didn't. Investment banking had taught me how to interact with clients and operate independently. In my new job, I had to identify constituencies and then figure out how to deal with each, which was basically what I'd been doing at Lehman Brothers. My first constituent and by far the most important—and the trickiest to deal with at times—was the mayor himself. My position had been created in 1975 by the Charter Revision Commission to promote jobs and to raise the importance of economic activity in the city. Koch and I, however, came from vastly different backgrounds, and he was not naturally interested in jobs or economic development.

One of the most striking aspects of Ed Koch was how alone he was. Bess Myerson, a friend of Mother's and the former Miss America whom political consultant David Garth had stuck by Koch's side during his mayoral campaign to make him look more "normal," told me, "Koch is so alone he never even walks a dog!" That was a hallmark of his administration: a number of the people in Koch's City Hall then were loners. After Koch fired a number of deputy mayors, I was the only deputy mayor who was married and had a family to go home to.

My office in the basement connected directly to the mayor's office by a flight of stairs. The mayor's office had a small kitchen at the top of the stairs. Koch tended to spend late afternoons in his office—alone—reading reports. Often I would walk up the stairs at around four in the afternoon and rustle around in the always-full refrigerator. If he wasn't too absorbed, he would motion me into his office and ask me what I was up to, and we would talk for a few minutes. In this way, we began to know each other better and break down the formality between us—but never beyond a certain point.

Running the city isn't glamorous. It's not the White House. Citizens could get to City Hall for less than a buck by mass transit, and they aren't shy. Running a city is not like running the country. It is basically a business of picking up garbage, controlling crime, and lessening tensions among constituencies. It is hard work. Koch knew that. He knew his job was to be the cheerleader while we filled potholes. He understood the citizens didn't like stepping in and over dog shit.

Since the mayor's deputies are supposed to get things done and not just talk about them, being effective counts. Regrettably, particularly my job required cooperation from other agencies, not commanding legions. That's the rub.

Whenever an appointed official tries to do something, every other agency will decide how it is affected by what he or she wants to do and demand to be part of an interagency task force. If you acquiesce and invite them to your meetings, they will send low-level personnel in an effort to demean you and muck up the project. Invariably, memos get lost, the members of the task force are called off to more important matters, and six months later, nothing has been accomplished. And it's your fault. This form of open government doesn't lead to much progress. But then, as you can see from its design, in the federal government, progress isn't really what government is about. In city government, progress is essential.

But let's say you do, against the odds, manage to get something accomplished. In that case, one of two events will occur: either the news will be leaked, and everyone will be in an uproar, or other appointees and their superiors will jump on the news and try to take credit for it by leaking their alleged involvement to the press. There is no point at any level of government to try to avoid leaks.

There is no way to change this phenomenon. Treasury Secretary G. William Miller used to rant about all the leaks. Kissinger famously hired the plumbers to stop them. Trump calls leaks "fake news." Koch had the most sophisticated approach. He assumed that anything said in a room with more than two people would become public immediately and that anything written down was liable to appear—probably out of context—in the next day's *New York Times*.

For me, working under Koch was easy because he never gave me an order. I asked Jay Goldin, the former controller of the city, why he didn't give me more direction. He said on the good side, the mayor had confidence in me. On the bad, he wanted "ultimate deniability." Both of these traits were apparent in his approach to controlling decisions and the direction of his administration.

Koch had a unique way of being simultaneously right and wrong on the same issue. One example concerns the city government's attempt to control the proliferation of street peddlers selling food, handbags, hats, clothing, and almost every conceivable object on street corners. The retail merchants paying rent and taxes were furious. The cops didn't like the congestion and the probability that many of the goods were stolen. The citizens loved them because the products were cheaper, even though many were counterfeit and second-rate.

After much work with the relevant constituencies, under my supervision the police department and consumer affairs developed a plan for dealing with street vendors, which was presented by Commissioners Bob McGuire and Bruce Ratner and me in the mayor's office. As always, the mayor was sitting in his chair, with interested parties from the public across from him. After I had introduced the plan, the mayor interrupted to exclaim, "What do you have against peddlers?"

Thrown by his remark, I asked, "What?"

"You heard me," he said. "What do you have against peddlers?"

At this moment, I turned to the others in the office and asked them to talk amongst themselves for a minute. Turning back to the mayor, I said, "You know, Mayor, I have nothing against peddlers. But we have a condition here that must be addressed, and we have worked out a plan to everyone's satisfaction, and that's why we are here."

"You rich German Jews," Koch said. "I don't know what you have against peddlers."

"Mayor," I said, accused and exasperated simultaneously, "you know I am Russian."

"I don't care if you say you are poor and Polish," he said. "To me, you will always be rich and German."

We put the plan into effect, until Judge Robert Sweet, a former deputy mayor under Lindsay, ruled that there is a constitutional right to peddle!

You learn a lot of things quickly in government, such as never to get between a photographer and the elected official. You try to be independent, but unlike the social contracts in business, you serve at the sole discretion of the elected official. You, the appointee, better acknowledge that he or she got elected and you didn't.

Despite its pressures, you can have fun. I made sure that my family took advantage of the opportunities. Abigail had her third-grade classmates to a party in the Blue Room at City Hall with Koch presiding. Joshua and I got front-row seats at the World Series. He, Kate, and Abigail went to Gracie Mansion for dinner with the cast of *Annie*. There were parades with the Yankees, meetings with Olympics athletes like Suzy Chapstick—I mean, Chaffee—Broadway openings, and trips to China. Koch and I had a lot of laughs together, as you can see from newspaper photos of the day. Of course, whether you're elected or appointed, it is always good to put on a smile for photographers. But it wasn't acting. To survive the bathos of City Hall, it is better to laugh, and Koch had a sense of irony.

Over the period, the distance between Koch and me narrowed considerably. I could cajole him into going to the World Series—he didn't care about sports in the slightest—knowing that Joshua and I would be left on our own with good seats.

The 1978 Yankees were a formidable team, with Ron Guidry's twenty-eight wins and a cast of characters—including Catfish Hunter, Reggie Jackson, and Mickey River—hitting, but they still had to beat the Red Sox in a one-game playoff and Kansas City in the ALCS to get into the World Series, where they once again played the Dodgers.

I had used my connections to get tickets for the playoffs against the Royals. Even though I, as deputy mayor, was the nominal lessor of the stadium, I ended up with seats in the upper deck. I decided I could do much better with the mayor as my beard.

"How about we go to Game Four?" I said to Koch. He unenthusiastically agreed to ask for two tickets, and I brought along Joshua, who would sit on my lap.

On the way to the Bronx, Ed, between his signature nod-offs, asked me some perfunctory questions about the game. I told him that Guidry was pitching and mentioned a few other tidbits to give him some context.

When we pulled up to Gate 2, the mayor bounced out of the back seat to meet the fans, who spotted him immediately. "Mayor … we gonna win tonight?" one fan yelled. Without missing a beat, he hollered back, "With Guidry going, how can we lose?"

The three of us settled into our box adjacent to the home team dugout along first base. By the third inning, the mayor's patience was exhausted, and he groused that he was leaving. I advised him to stay put for a few more innings.

Ignoring me, he began to leave. At that precise moment, we looked up at the centerfield screen and saw a huge image of the mayor rising from his seat. As soon as he noticed it, he broke into a smile and a wave, looking totally in his favorite element.

He snuck out successfully an inning later—much to my relief, as I got Joshua off my lap. Guidry pitched the Yankees to a 5–1 victory.

It was always easy to talk Koch into going to a restaurant. Eating was one of our favorite activities. Peking Duck restaurant on Mott Street in Chinatown and the Second Avenue Deli on Fourth Street were the centers of our culinary experience for lunch. Shelia Lukins, wife of Koch's pal Dick Lukins, had opened the gourmet Silver Palate. The mayor's office pantry was always stocked.

One June night, I took the mayor to the Century Country Club in Purchase, New York, which is reputed to have the best food in Westchester.

After dinner, as we sat on the veranda on that mild evening, he looked across the golf course and exclaimed, inexplicably, "Everyone deserves to live like this, or they should get two chickens!"

Of course, the mayor almost met his maker at Peking Duck. In the middle of lunch, he began choking and had to be rescued by the Heimlich maneuver. The press reported that an egg roll had caught in his throat. In fact, a barbequed pork sparerib was the culprit, but it would have been hard to explain to the Hassidim.

About every other week, we would ride home together, and he would come for dinner with our family. The demands of the job were enormous, and he would always be tired. During the thirty-minute drive—we never used the red roof light or siren—he would fall asleep as we listened to the songs from *Evita*. Once during dinner, Abigail, then ten, asked the mayor why he never seemed to know her name or those of her brother, Joshua, and sister, Kate. Koch at last was at a loss for words. He came for Thanksgiving dinner in Stamford in 1979 and gave my mother a ride home to the Upper East Side. She was insulted that he didn't seem at all interested in talking to her and dozed the full sixty minutes.

Because Koch got bored so easily and was not terribly interested in people who, he sensed, were not interested in him, he often invited me to come along with him on forays that had nothing to do with my City Hall job, figuring that I could perhaps revive a flagging conversation. As a result, I got to meet some interesting, or at least well-known, people.

In early 1980, Jerry Brown of California was a two-term governor with not enough to do, so he thought he'd run for president. Governor Brown visited New York to raise money for his campaign, and the mayor invited him to dinner at Gracie Mansion, along with his two close associates, Tom Quinn and Dick Silverman. Koch brought along Dan Wolf, his éminence grise, and Maureen Connolly, his press secretary, as well as yours truly.

It was a chilly evening in January, and the staff lit a fire in the mansion's dining room. Suddenly, smoke engulfed us, bells sounded, and moments later, helmeted firemen swung open the kitchen doors. We had already begun remedial action—with the kind of speed shown by government officials only when their own comfort is involved—by opening the damper. In short order, the evening continued.

The conversation did not go well. Brown quickly revealed himself to have all the worst aspects of a politician; he was smart, yes, but also cynical, self-absorbed, arrogant, and utterly lacking in humor.

"So," said the mayor, after we'd chatted awhile, "what brings you to New York?"

"Jews," said Brown. "I have to meet Jewish leaders."

Both the mayor and I were taken aback, because we thought we were Jewish leaders.

"Which Jewish leaders?" I asked. "In New York, everyone on the IRT is a Jewish leader!"

"Silverman," Brown ordered, "get the list of Jewish leaders."

Silverman disappeared into the kitchen for a good twenty minutes, during which the governor explained that while he was conservative in some ways, he was also most liberal candidate in the race for the presidency. For instance, he explained, he vetted all his appointments with Farm Worker Unionist Caesar Chavez. When Koch heard this, one of his eyes rolled upward, and the other drooped. He was done with Jerry Brown.

Silverman finally reappeared with a list of Jewish names, which Brown read aloud. Koch churlishly said he recognized only a few. I recognized practically all of them, but most were not New Yorkers. After that, the mood grew even more uncomfortable, especially when my after-dinner cigar once again set off the mansion's fire alarm.

"Why are you running for the presidency?" the mayor asked. His point was that mounting a campaign was ridiculously expensive and that Jimmy Carter, while not a great president, was a sitting Democrat who would be difficult to defeat for the nomination.

The governor didn't have a great answer for this. "Well," he said, "I'm bored. I've done what I wanted to in California, and I want to do other things."

The next day, when someone on his staff asked Koch about his reaction to Governor Brown, he replied, "He's fat! His clothes don't fit him!"

As Koch gained renown, he was always good for a photo op. Not only politicians but movie stars and other celebrities would also flock to City Hall. The most notable of these stars was Sophia Loren, who filled the mayor's office as no one before or since. Koch could have cared less. On another day, I returned to my basement office to find Sally Field sitting on my couch. She had hoped to meet the mayor, but he wasn't available, so the deputy mayor had to do.

CHAPTER 15

"Plans Are Worthless. Planning Is Essential."

(Military Maxim)

In government, you've got to have a plan. If you don't have a plan, they—meaning legislators, press, and public—will eat your lunch. The plan can get changed on the fly or fail altogether, and it probably will; it doesn't matter as long as you have one. And yet, as tried and true as this advice is, some government officials ignore it. Carter's Secretary of the Treasury Bill Miller kept repeating his "six points to control inflation," but he never had a plan. In New York, my fellow Deputy Mayor Bobby Wagner once criticized Koch for not having an overall strategy for the city. Koch was nonplussed. "You come up with a plan," he said with a shrug, "and I'll announce it."

Initially, I myself resisted stating an overall plan for the economic development of New York City in 1978. The idea seemed absurd and presumptuous; after all, we had almost two hundred thousand businesses covering 2.8 million workers in hundreds of industries. Nevertheless, I soon came to realize that without a plan, I would be considered a lightweight or—within the city government—a threat. Rick Rosan, the head of development and a seasoned bureaucrat, told me to stop going around saying that having a plan was ridiculous, even if on a rational level it was. "You can't tell all these bureaucrats, many of whom are paid to create plans, that planning is silly," he said. "You say that, you threaten their jobs."

Ultimately, I became a man with a plan, and the plan I came up with was simple:

1. Cheerlead the business community through the period of decline.
2. Improve responsiveness of bureaucracy and halt the decline in confidence in city government.
3. Promote development of commercial real estate and smaller industrial sites. Avoid large-scale projects that are beyond the competence of City Hall.
4. Focus on revitalizing retail business districts in all boroughs.
5. Promote tourism and marketing of the city.

It was a simple plan, targeted to my constituencies, but in itself it wasn't a valuable contribution to New York City's economic development. That came early in my tenure, when I decided economic development needed its own funding source, one that could make loans directly to businesses operating in the city and rely less on the city's annual operating budget. In present terms, the concept was somewhere between private equity, venture capital, and a nonbank lending facility. Today the concept seems tame. In the context of city government in 1979, it was revolutionary. My funding sources would be the repayment of federal economic development funds to the city by the Department of Commerce. The other source would be from repayments of UDAG given to city projects from HUD. I named the fund the Economic Capital Corporation (ECC). The mayor liked the sound of the concept but doubted I could get it done without state legislation.

I went ahead anyway and asked Don Regan, the chairman of Merrill Lynch, and later secretary of the treasury under President Reagan, to become chairman. He agreed. I then went to Bill Spencer, the president of Citibank, and asked him to be president. Spencer operated in the shadow of Walter Wriston, the chairman, and was glad to get some visibility. With these two senior executives, we formed a board and instituted the ECC. Koch said it was a miracle I could get it done without approval from Albany. The ECC became key to our efforts, a model for how the private sector can work with and for government. Mayor Bloomberg's Deputy Mayor Dan Doctoroff used this vehicle three decades later.

While in the service of the government, it's important to keep your plan in one hip pocket and your sense of realpolitik in the other. When I joined the Koch administration in 1978, development in the city had stagnated, along with the rest of the economy. I wasn't exaggerating much when I said in those days that you could have a picnic in the inbound lane of the Triborough Bridge, and you wouldn't be run over; there were so few people coming into New York City. When Continental Insurance proposed to build an office tower at the foot of Wall Street in the late 1970s, it was the first major construction project planned below Fourteenth Street in ten years.

As deputy mayor, I had the power to do something about that. Two of the positions I held by law were chairman of the Industrial and Commercial Incentive Board (ICIB) and the Industrial Development Agency (IDA). Additionally, I was chairman of the Public Development Corporation (PDC), which managed two large industrial sites. These boards had the authority to bestow tax breaks on developers and enable real estate projects. It was through these boards that I hoped to exercise my influence on development and manage my relationship with the other elected officials, such as the five borough presidents, the comptroller, and city council president, all of whom had seats on these boards.

At the start of my tenure in 1978, New York City desperately needed any form of development, so we granted tax abatements to most proposed commercial developments. By 1979, though, the city began to come back to life. The Rudins built on Lexington and Fifty-First Street. IBM and AT&T planned new headquarters on Madison Avenue and Fifty-Sixth and Fifty-Seventh Streets. We granted abatements to IBM and AT&T with a provision that if they moved their headquarters from these buildings, they would be required to repay the abatements. (This provision became especially relevant in the late 1980s, when AT&T proposed to sell the site.)

With the city's economy strengthening, I decided that we needed to tighten the abatements and be more sophisticated and selective about projects. At this time, the Fisher brothers had arranged to buy the air rights of the Racquet and Tennis Club at Fifty-Second and Park and planned to build an office building above it. To the surprise of many, I recommended that the board deny the Fisher brothers abatement. Giving them a tax abatement would, in essence, have reimbursed them for what they'd paid for the air rights. Meanwhile, the Racquet and Tennis Club restricted its membership—no Jews or other minorities allowed—and I didn't want the city to reward the club even indirectly.

I still can't believe that I lost the vote at the ICIB on this issue. I was furious because I believed that at least one member of the board had an ulterior motive. Proof was impossible, but revenge wasn't; I got mine by proposing legislation to eliminate abatements in Manhattan's central business district. Charles Goldstein, then a partner of the Schulte Roth & Zabel law firm and a major real estate lawyer, assured me that I had wound up with the best of all worlds: I got the Fisher building built, shed light on the club's membership restrictions, and used the project as an example of how to achieve my long-term policy goal of limiting abatements. I hoped he was right.

The IDA faced similar pressures. At one point, Andy Stein, the Manhattan borough president, came to me with a request that we approve a particular project. I told him I would do it only on the condition that it achieve certain goals in terms of employment. He agreed, but at the board meeting, his representative startled me by refusing to agree with the conditions.

I adjourned the meeting and called Stein. "Your representative voted against the proposal," I said. "What's going on?"

"Peter," he said, "I told him not to agree unless you accept the following"—at which point he started to list several additional demands.

"Borough President!" I yelled. "We already had an agreement on some other items, and now you can forget that agreement too! I won the vote on the proposal without you."

Over time, we reformed the IDA to limit tax-exempt financing, excluding all retail stores, restaurants, and consumer-driven projects, on the basis that they were not adding to the economy or creating new employment. Consumption is a zero-sum game. When a new location opens, it does not increase overall consumption. It merely replaces consumption at a competitive location, and the government should not be using tax expenditures to promote one business over another.

The Public Development Corporation was a different matter. Under the Lindsay master plan, the city had established two large industrial parks, one in the wilds of Staten Island and the other in the swamps of College Point, Queens, at the edge of LaGuardia Airport and Long Island Sound. The only activity in the Staten Island Park was the dumping of bodies. College Point was slightly more active, housing a small airport and a gypsy-operated brothel. After looking at this inactivity for a year, I appointed Phil Aarons, my able assistant, as executive director. Koch initially objected, arguing that Aarons had no real estate experience, which was true. But appealing to the mayor's ego, I suggested that Aarons must be talented; after all, I had recruited him from the mayor's own staff.

Today, College Point has a number of lessees, including the *New York Times* and a movie theatre complex. Staten Island is still undeveloped. Phil Aarons, after City Hall, became a principal in Millennium Partners, a major New York City real estate developer.

Even in the 1970s, Donald Trump was a savvy, aggressive New York real estate developer, who exploded on the Manhattan scene in 1976 by proposing to convert the Commodore Hotel on East Forty-Second Street into a new Hyatt.

One of Donald's real estate gambles in the 1970s was to option the Penn Central railroad yards running between Thirty-Fifth and Thirty-Ninth Streets along Twelfth Avenue. Donald had spent considerable sums promoting this site for the proposed New York Convention Center.

In July 1978, Deputy Mayor David Brown, City Planning Chairman Wagner, and I agreed the city did not have the competence to build the center. The price of over $400 million was beyond the city's financial capabilities, and, more important, the project was beyond our ability to oversee and control. Seeking assistance, we approached the state through Richard Kahan, president of the Urban Development Corporation. Kahan and the UDC were always eager to help me and the city. He was agreeable to overseeing the center, and the state would provide the funding, assuming the city legislative leaders could work out an equitable deal with the upstate legislators. I was authorized to negotiate the price with the (Victor) Palmieri Company, agents for the Penn Central. Palmieri and the city, after many meetings, agreed on a value of $23 million for the site.

Because of Donald Trump's option on the property, it was necessary to deal with him as part of my negotiation. As an experienced investment banker, I understood the value of having my own witness while I was negotiating. Another person can listen while you talk and talk while you think. He can put forth ideas that you can modify, repudiate, or underscore. When a government agency is involved, he can, if necessary, attest in a hearing or investigation to the fact that, despite what the other side may be saying, no deals were actually made. Phil Aarons accompanied me when I first met Donald Trump.

One thing we wanted to know was whether Donald would surrender his option to the city without compensation. While that may seem like a brazen request, in cases like the one we were discussing, the city holds most of the cards. If Trump was obstinate, we could as a last resort invoke eminent domain and take the property. Besides, a developer like Trump depends on the cooperation of city officials. Without a variance here, a street closing there, development is more difficult.

Trump was agreeable to surrendering his option. But, he explained, he was owed a commission of over $4 million. He would need to be paid the full amount.

Startled, I asked what he was talking about. When Penn Central was in bankruptcy, he explained, he had negotiated a deal with the trustees granting him a commission of $500,000 based on a sales price for the yards of $15 million. The commission would increase with the sales price over a base of $15 million, adjusted for interest at the prime rate between 1975 and the sales date. Based on Donald's calculations, a

$23 million price yielded a $4 million commission. He told us to "look it up." It was in public court records.

Before we could digest his claim, he magnanimously said he would surrender his whole fee if we would name the center after his father. Donald is bold, brash, and amusing. He is also cynical and devious. Like a lot of private sector people, Donald doesn't think government officials can read the fine print.

When we returned to City Hall, I asked Phil to check the court records, as Trump had challenged us to do. Sure enough, a careful reading showed "The Donald" was entitled to a commission of $650,000, not $4 million.

We laid out the facts to the mayor, including the offer to forego the commission if the center was named for Fred Trump. The mayor smiled and told us to simply pay the $650,000 commission. I don't think Trump expected us to verify his claim.

UDC acquired the land. We then had to convince the state legislature to authorize the acquisition and provide nearly $400 million. We also had to provide a satisfactory Environmental Impact Statement (EIS). On the EIS, we made two decisions. We reduced the size of the hall slightly, eliminating part of the north end, and we also eliminated parking. The parking issue was a particular challenge since no public transportation serviced the site at that time. We felt we could make compromises, hoping that eventually good sense would prevail, and it would become apparent that the center needed to be expanded and parking added. So much for our faith in good judgment; it is now more than thirty years later, there is still no parking, and the Javits Center is only now being expanded.

As we were putting together the 1979 city budget, it was clear that the meaningful way to reduce spending was to lower government-worker headcount, probably by consolidating agencies. Decades later, Deputy Mayor Dan Doctoroff asked me how we balanced the budget in the early Koch years. It isn't a mystery. I said, "You have to reduce headcount; there is no other way." The idea of "increased productivity" in the public sector is an illusion.

Still, eliminating government employees is never easy. As Henry

Gavan, my office's chief counsel, liked to say, "If you want to make the effort to fire a civil servant, you probably shouldn't be in your job!"

One day, the mayor told me I had to reduce the headcount in my Office of Economic Development and ports and terminals by fifty. He delivered the news rather sheepishly, and I knew why. Combined, there were fewer than three hundred employees who weren't managing line operations in my department. Fifty layoffs all at once seemed too much.

At times like that, I realized the value of having my own smart budget director, steeped in the ways of city government. At the OED, Sy Birken was the holder of that all-important title. Quiet, like most budget guys, he had gone to City College and had been at OED since its creation. While nominally responsible for just OED, I actually ran most important programs from City Hall. But, like most appointees, I didn't want to cede any territory. Sy Birken understood, and when I talked to him about what seemed like a devastating situation, he was calm. "Don't worry," he said. "Tell Koch you will do it."

I was startled. "How is this possible?" I said. "We've already eliminated a bunch of Koch's political cronies that he dumped in OED after the campaign."

Birken smiled and said our OED budget had a number of what were called "open lines." These appeared to be employees but weren't really because the "lines" had never been filled with actual workers.

I recalled Gogol's novel *Dead Souls*, which I had read for a Russian literature course at Harvard. In it, a village counted names in cemeteries to increase its census numbers, long before this became fashionable in Chicago and Boston.

Several days later, with Oscar-worthy anguish, I reported to Koch that as painful as the process was, we would be able to reach the goal.

Soon after, I promoted Sy Birken to deputy commissioner.

Before going further, I should underscore that, though civil servants often get a bad rap, most are, as a group, no less competent than the political appointees who sometimes manage them. Civil servants are a mix of ordinary folks, some brilliant and relatively hardworking, some unbelievably obtuse and disinterested. The smart ones do not usually make it a career unless some personal event such as their own health or the sickness of a family member has made them dependent on the government health plans that come with their jobs. Some have told themselves that they will just stay until they're pensioned after twenty years, and forget that by that time business may find them less attractive, and so they may never escape. Within the city bureaucracy, however, there are civil servants who are neither civil nor servants in any sense. These people lower the standards of their peers, provoke their superiors, and abuse the public. What do you do about them?

If you are the elected official and want to improve the system, you may try civil service reform through legislation. Jimmy Carter's major success was such reform, giving the executive branch more power over its own bureaucracy. Koch mounted a program to achieve the same goal within New York City, but his legislation went nowhere in the Albany legislature. An example of a single meeting in 1978 will illustrate the difficulty of making progress in this area. Addressing the leaders of the municipal unions, the mayor detailed his civil service reform legislation, saying he wanted to hire more by merit than by civil service procedures. After several minutes, Albert Shanker, president of the United Federation of Teachers, leaned across the table and said, "Mayor, my union helps elect 90 percent of the state legislature, and your proposals aren't going anywhere."

Not one to be intimidated, Koch coolly responded, "Al, who are the 10 percent you missed?" But he was in an impossible position. Despite extensive campaigning throughout the state and support from most city and county executives, there was no civil service reform.

Against this background, political appointees do as well as they can. The only way you can remove a bad civil servant, except for criminal acts, is if you can eliminate their line. For example, if they are an "assistant project manager," you might get rid of them by not having any assistant project managers. But this doesn't mean the whole government can get rid of any one particular person. Take away an incompetent's line, and they'll catch on somewhere in another department, say City Planning, if it still has a line for an assistant project manager. The person you removed, if they have seniority, will bump the current assistant project manager, who will bump the next one down the line, and so on until the youngest and probably brightest assistant project manager is pushed out. The system was designed to work this way, and it is the only system in government that works perfectly.

The independent truckers rampaged across the country in the summer of 1979. Agitated by gas price increases, they blockaded highways, shot out the tires of truckers not participating in their protests, and generally wreaked havoc. In Suffolk County, a group of truckers announced their intention to come down the Long Island Expressway at rush hour and, on successive days, stop at the Suffolk-Nassau County and then the Nassau-New York City lines, snarling traffic. If they weren't met at these lines by county or city officials, they intended to keep going until they blocked the Queens Midtown Tunnel and the Fifty-Ninth Street Bridge.

We didn't pay too much attention to the truckers on day one. When they reached the Suffolk-Nassau line, they demanded to see the Suffolk County executive, and he shot back, "I will not be intimidated!" That is what politicians say when they see a problem they can't solve but think they have a decent chance of weaseling out of it. On day two, more traffic was blocked by the moving blockade. The trucks remained out of the major media's sight range, but with New York City as the eventual target, the Nassau County executive felt safe proclaiming that he would not be intimidated.

City Hall is a cool place on a steamy June morning, and day three started calmly in Manhattan. But at 10:35 a.m., the atmosphere changed suddenly when Police Commissioner Bob McGuire called Maureen Connelly, the mayor's press secretary, and advised her of a dangerous situation building on the Nassau–New York City border in Douglaston, Queens. The truckers had pulled off the expressway and were demanding to see the mayor.

That wasn't going to happen; Koch was testifying in Washington that day. So Maureen asked me to meet with the truckers at the city line. My first reaction was, "It's not my job! I run the office of economic development!"

"Well," she argued, "these are business people, and they are blocking other people trying to go to work, so it's your job."

I still wasn't convinced, but the alternative was facing down a group of angry Queens merchants, so I agreed to go, providing I got a police chopper and was accompanied by the mayor's political assistant, John LoCicero. If I wound up striking some agreement with the truckers that was later repudiated, I wanted the political guy to share in the embarrassment. When you work in government, you always have to think of who might get the blame.

The chopper got to the spot on the LIE in ten minutes. We circled for five minutes so I could see the extent of the trucks along the expressway and the truckers could see me. Finally we landed, but I still didn't know what the hell to say or do. There were about twenty large trucks on the grassy bank of the parkway and in the left lane. They had signs asking passing motorists to honk if they agreed with the truckers. Judging by the cacophony, many apparently did. Three police cars were on the scene, as were numbers of TV camera crews, still photographers, and a few random citizens. The heat and the din from the car and truck horns increased the tension. Meanwhile, the truckers' demands for lower gas prices and better rates were beyond the city's capacity, just as the police on the scene were beyond my domain. There seemed to be no way to resolve the situation; the potential for disaster was as great as any situation I've ever been in.

When all else fails, try acting as if—or, as we called it as kids—make believe. In this case, I pretended to be That Guy Who Knows What He's Doing. I leaped from the chopper, looking tough, decisive, aggressive. It was an act but, I must admit, a pretty good one. Ripping off my suit jacket and rolling up my shirt sleeves à la Bobby Kennedy, I strode purposefully toward the leader. "What the fuck do you think you are doing?" I said, without introducing myself (a CBS guy standing nearby leaned in and told him who I was). There are only a few times in life when you swing for the fences and connect. Fortunately, this was one of them.

The leader, Val Janik, an independent trucker from Suffolk, said he knew who I was—because he was the trucker for my boyhood friend

Peter Strasser, an owner of a paint and chemical company. He said that the truckers had started a protest that he could no longer control. The chaos, the confrontational mood, the cops, the cars whizzing by—all made him as nervous as it made me. What extraordinary luck!

I acknowledged his demands but pointed out the city government couldn't do anything about them. We didn't control fuel prices. He understood that but asked for us to arrange a meeting immediately with Governor Carey. I said we would try, then and there. I thought the police could reach a communications center with their car radios and that we could be patched in to Albany and speak to the governor. But the technology didn't allow for that, and we had to drive Janik to the nearest precinct house to see if we could arrange a meeting. This meant leaving the volatile group of trucks on the highway with no leader, but that seemed our only choice.

When we finally got through to Carey's office, his people didn't want to have a meeting. I could sense Janik becoming anxious and agitated because he was separated from his troops, so I stayed on the phone. After about an hour, the governor's office relented and agreed to send Lt. Governor Mario Cuomo to a meeting the next day.

We returned to the scene of the protest with a triumphant Janik. The truckers had achieved their goal: a sit-down in Queens with a high official and broad media coverage. The press hailed the decisiveness of the Koch administration and the deputy mayor. The entire front page of *Newsday* featured a picture of LoCicero and me negotiating with the truckers. Jim Jensen on CBS Channel 2 News started, "Well, finally someone has shown some leadership." Silently, I thanked Peter Strasser—and Bobby Kennedy.

The postscript says something about the symbolic uses of government. Lt. Governor Cuomo didn't show up for the hard-won meeting the next day, but neither I nor the truckers made a big deal about it. In the end, the so-called issues weren't really what mattered. It was all about the show of force—and the reaction to it. As often happens in the political arena, the process was more important than the product.

CHAPTER 16

"Government Is Like Combat."

(Joseph F. Cullman III)

If I wasn't dealing with gas or truckers, I was negotiating with politicians and businessmen. Everybody had an agenda, there were no dull days, and disaster was always a possibility. And that is good in a way because government is mostly fun in crisis. Joe Cullman, the former chairman of Philip Morris, told me, "Government is like combat. If you survive it, it's terrific!"

The key to enjoyment in a crisis is to be involved but not to declare that you are in charge. Who can forget Al Haig's ridiculous statements in the White House after President Reagan was shot. Better to show yourself in action, be calm, thoughtful, and resolved, to bring the crisis to a close. Be able to supply facts to the elected official, making him or her look in command. Brief the press on a regular basis with the kind of colorful details that liven up stories so that they don't get duller as the crisis drags on. For example, how many employees get to work in which industries, or the number of restaurants closed in Manhattan, are appreciated fun facts during a transit strike.

The press has always been an ally. My banking career was propelled by the favorable coverage I received from Isadore Barmash, the *New York Times* chief retail reporter, and Sidney Rutberg and Sam Feinberg, *Women's Wear Daily* top retail editor and columnist, respectively. Barmash quoted me weekly, sometimes with a picture. Sid and I held an annual lunch with my Lehman partners for over a decade, which he always turned into a feature article for WWD. Sam twice ran a seven-part series on me. I trusted them all so implicitly that I let them complete my quotes.

The political media was something else. I valued my relationship with the men and women who worked in Room 9, the press room, and was usually available to print and broadcast reporters. But the constant scrutiny government officials are subjected to is intense. During my tenure as deputy mayor, the *New York Times* alone had nine reporters assigned to City Hall, more than any other location besides the White House.

My first experience with the *Times* as deputy mayor was trying. Three days before my appointment was announced in May 1978, James P. Sterba, an excellent reporter, broke a story about a minority businessman in the South Bronx who could not get help from the city to enlarge his chicken-processing plant and was going to move to Maryland. It was a tale that played into all the well-known predispositions about the city, the perfect example of an incompetent bureaucracy thwarting the ambitions of a minority entrepreneur, so was beloved by *Times* readers. Worse, the Federal Economic Development Administration had stepped in to advance funds to the company.

The *Times* welcomed me with an editorial, "Chickens Roosting in the Bronx." Noting my "meteoric" career, the editorial challenged me "to make a quick, favorable decision." I was suspicious from the start—for one thing, the story sounded too pat—but dealing with this situation and the outrage it stirred took most of my first months in office. Eventually, thanks to the due diligence skills I'd developed at Lehman, I was able to get the truth. The company had labor issues and would later be charged by the National Labor Relations Board for unlawful activities, and even with city and federal assistance, it didn't have sufficient cash flow. Once I discovered the real story, the media coverage disappeared, albeit without the slightest apology. Shortly thereafter, the company was acquired.

Life was simpler then, in the days before the internet and cable, when a city government official only had to worry about the daily papers, TV, and radio. I learned quickly that when it came to negative news, a breaking story is tough but not as bad as the follow-up—and the third day's story can kill you. (For some reason, nice stories never last more than a day.) Obviously, your best bet was to kill a negative story before it was written, but you rarely had more than a few hours to act. Barring that, all you could do is get up early, buy the first edition of the *New York Times* on Seventh Avenue and Fourth Street, and start to plan your rebuttal. I also learned to smile on television no matter what the question, because the audience is focused on your appearance, not your words. On radio, if you didn't like the way the interview was going, you'd just swear a little, and the piece wouldn't get on the air.

For the most part, the political press was friendly, but I had a number of close calls. In 1979, the city faced a shortage of gasoline. Lines appeared at service stations, and eventually we rationed by methods such as alternate-days gassing. Wondering how we could alleviate the problem before the summer driving season set in, I asked for a meeting with members of the federal Department of Energy. During our discussion of the problem on a hot Friday afternoon in June, a DOE representative mentioned in passing that the department had changed its method of allocating gas and was diverting gas to California. My able aide, Robert Herzog, and I were brought up short by the remark; neither of us had known that the federal government allocated gas. From that point on, though, we knew we had to focus on changing the DOE's allocation methods.

The meeting ended about six o'clock that night, and I left my office feeling tired and perplexed. On the way out, I passed Steve Weisman, the chief *New York Times* correspondent in City Hall, who greeted me with a "How's it going?" Without thinking, I said, "Not so well—I just learned we are going to have a major gas shortage." Steve continued on toward the press room, but before I reached the street, I realized that I had inadvertently given him a major story, one that could cause panic. Even though we were on friendly terms, I couldn't go back and ask Steve to forget what I told him.

I worried the whole night but was glad I didn't hear from him, and even happier that the morning papers had nothing about a worsening gas shortage. Several days later, in response to the mayor's protests, the Department of Energy changed its method of allocating gas, and the shortage in the city abated. I saw Steve about a week later and kidded him about how I'd gone sleepless after our brief encounter. He replied that he later realized that I had given him a potentially big story, and he had not immediately understood the ramifications of my remark.

Nothing happened in City Hall without some degree of press involvement. During the energy crisis of 1979, we asked business leaders to cut down on electricity usage. The Empire State Building dimmed its lights, and Times Square reduced the wattage of its billboards. My children knew that I was responsible for implementing and policing this voluntary program. On a Sunday night in November, we were driving home past Yankee Stadium. Joshua, then eleven, pointed out that the stadium's full complement of lights was blazing although there was no game in progress.

The next morning, I called my counsel, Hank Gavan, asking him to check the city's lease with the stadium. Mayor Lindsay had made a sweetheart deal with the Yankees: not only did the club pay the city little rent, it had the right to offset the rent for any capital expenditure. The city had retained few rights, but the eagle-eyed Gavan found a clause that, oddly, allowed the city to designate the language on the two large electric signs on the stadium's façade.

I instructed Gavan to send a letter to George Steinbrenner asking him to put the following in the signs: "There will be public executions in the stadium for those who waste electricity."

Gavan sent me a copy, and I sent it up to the mayor with a note, saying that Joshua Solomon had started this and "who says government can't be fun!" About two hours later, my office door burst open, and in barged three networks and all the dailies, waving the letter and demanding to meet Joshua Solomon, who, at the time, was safely ensconced in his sixth-grade classroom at Collegiate. In this instance, I admired the media's enthusiasm but not its accuracy. The next day, the *Daily News* ran a story about my precocious son, Josh Logan.

In June 1979, the health commissioner, Reinaldo Ferrer, alerted us to the presence of Legionnaires' disease in Manhattan. Like most crises in New York City, it occurred on a Friday. The commissioner informed the mayor that the likely locus of the disease was the northeast corner of Thirty-Fifth Street and Eighth Avenue, right by Macy's department store. Everyone in those days remembered what happened in Philadelphia in 1976. When Legionnaires' disease was traced to the Bellevue-Stratford, the hotel went out of business. I didn't want a premature panic to cause similar damage at Macy's. It was a New York landmark, billed as the world's largest department store. Many thousands of people passed through it every day. I had personal connections there too. I had known many people in Macy's management, including Jack Straus and Don Smiley, the CEO. They were also Lehman clients. In 1970, when Macy's was having difficulties, I had been instrumental in Moody's rating agency sustaining its credit rating. At my urging, the mayor instructed everyone to identify the source as being on Thirty-Fifth and Seventh but to avoid mentioning Macy's.

With Smiley's permission, I arranged for our health officials to enter the store and do a top-to-bottom inspection, trying to locate the precise source of the airborne virus. The department took hundreds of samples, which they sent to its Randall's Island facility.

By noon on Saturday, I had heard nothing, so I called the health commissioner, who explained that the all of specimens had somehow been "misplaced" somewhere between Thirty-Fifth Street and the lab. I surprised myself by how calm I remained as I asked the commissioner to repeat the entire process immediately.

By Sunday morning, the city had identified an unused water tower in the northwest corner of the store as the source of the disease. I called Don Smiley and gave him the good news/bad news alert. The good news was that we found the source and were already cleaning the tower. The bad news was that Macy's had dozens of health violations, including waste water going into the drinking water of its main cafeteria. Smiley was simultaneously relieved and appalled. I told him that if he rectified the situation completely by the following Friday, the city wouldn't issue any violations.

We kept the press informed throughout the process, except for details about Macy's. We ordered other tests and found that the Legionnaires' virus had infected residents throughout the city and particularly many who worked near the Hunts Point Market in the South Bronx. But no new cases were reported.

The Legionnaires' disease caper taught me another useful lesson in government crisis management: the value of not turning on your car siren. As we were swinging down lower Broadway delivering information to an anxious mayor, a driver in a new Mercury became transfixed by our siren. She broadsided us, but we escaped with minor scratches. The moral of the story: don't panic the citizens.

Six months later, Ron Sullivan, the *Times* reporter covering health issues, alerted me to a story the *Times* was about to run on the cover-up of the Legionnaires' disease. He said that the article would report that I had ordered no mention be made of Macy's to protect its business.

A cover-up is no small thing in government, particularly in matters relating to health. The mayor and I discussed our position. He had been fully in accord with my wish to keep Macy's out of the Legionnaires' news. We agreed that I would talk to Sullivan and tell him exactly what we had done and why. I believed I had taken the correct action and that my constituency, the business community, would applaud my discretion. We had acted promptly and taken the necessary precautions and never obstructed the health commissioner's work.

When I talked to Sullivan, he said that all he wanted was confirmation, not an explanation. I replied, "Ron, what do you want me to confirm?"

He said, "I want you to confirm that you did not identify Macy's to avoid undue panic."

"Ron, is this the precise question?"

"Yes."

"The answer is I did make the decision not to identify Macy's to avoid undue panic."

The story ran as written. It was one of my better days.

My primary constituency, the business community, happened to be in despair. Mobil Oil had announced plans to leave its headquarters on Forty-Second Street. Other companies, such as American Airlines and J. C. Penney, would follow. The financial industry, while rallying to support New York's financing needs, was not committed to the city. Arthur Levitt, son of the longtime New York State comptroller, was threatening to move the American Stock Exchange to New Jersey. The Port Authority of New York and New Jersey had built a beautiful industrial park and container port in New Jersey but in New York City had only carved out small parks and created the marginally useful Red Hook Container Port. The Port Authority had built the World Trade Center, it was true, but those huge towers had a depressing effect on downtown rents. The situation was grim.

I was relatively well known on Wall Street, but I had no connections with either the business establishment or organized labor. Realizing that I needed to forge relationships with these groups, I asked the two former economic development commissioners and the head of the New York Chamber of Commerce to meet with me. I also asked David Rockefeller, chairman of Chase Bank, Howard Clark, CEO of American Express, and Don Platten, chairman of the Chemical Bank, to help me. I, of course, offered to go to Mr. Rockefeller's office, but he insisted on coming to City Hall. When he got there, he said he had not been in City Hall since he had been Mayor LaGuardia's secretary. Along with Howard and Don, David became a trusted adviser.

I had tangential relationships with the Rockefellers. In college, Nelson Rockefeller's son Michael was an acquaintance. He lived in Eliot House at Harvard, where the preppies resided, and seemed unusually pleasant despite a certain noblesse oblige. Michael's death while on an anthropological expedition in New Guinea two years after we graduated, besides being a tragedy in itself, was for me and my friends the first shocking proof that someone our age could die.

The same generosity of spirit that Michael exhibited was shown by Laurence Rockefeller to my parents in 1970, when my mother wanted to buy an apartment at 834 Fifth Avenue. My father, in particular, was apprehensive and not just about spending the then princely sum of

$200,000: the building was a much more exclusive address than it is today, and it housed few Jews.

Mr. Rockefeller was president of the cooperative board. He told my parents they had been admitted to the building even though they never had the supposedly mandatory meeting with the co-op board. Later, he put Mother on the board. (I used to kid her about how that was a dubious distinction. Eight thirty-four subsequently housed a number of convicted felons, including Ed Downe, John DeLorean, and Al Taubman. "Mother, your building has almost as many white-collar criminals as Riker's Island," I said.)

When I needed to convince Levitt to keep the American Stock Exchange in New York, it was David Rockefeller who persuaded him to remain. (That Levitt's members didn't have the capital to move also helped.) David later asked me to become the first head of what is now the New York Partnership and did me the honor of asking me to address the board of directors of the Chase Manhattan Bank.

George Weissman, the chief executive of Philip Morris, was also an important figure to me and the city. At a time when many Fortune 500 companies were fleeing, Philip Morris completed a new headquarters on Forty-First Street and Park Avenue. The company was a cornerstone of our attempt to revitalize Forty-Second Street, as well as a major contributor to the arts; George was later chairman of Lincoln Center.

But George didn't know the mayor and wanted to meet him. I usually discouraged such encounters—not because I wanted to impose myself between business executives and the mayor for reasons of self-aggrandizement, as some thought, but because Koch could be mercurial and undiplomatic. This time, though, I arranged a meeting, and George began by saying how committed Philip Morris was to the city. I was just beginning to think things were going well when Koch interrupted him and began castigating George for selling cigarettes. The meeting was brief, and when George left, he was furious. It took me months to calm him down and regain his support.

Koch had many fine qualities, but he could also be boorish and unnecessarily combative. One day, I was particularly upset with him. We had had a constituent meeting, and the mayor had been just plain rude. Late in the afternoon, I appeared in his office doorway. As usual, he was reading, a single light illuminating the memo. He looked up after a minute. "What?"

"Mayor," I said quietly, "the citizens have confidence in you. They admire you. You are their leader." I deliberately used the word "citizens" occasionally to invoke the spirit of the French revolution. "But if you act out, if you rant and are nasty, they will lose confidence in you. It will make all our jobs more difficult." We had become closer, so I could say such things when I was alone with him.

He listened, his right leg crossed at a sharp angle across his left. Then, with a characteristically ambiguous acknowledgment, he turned his left palm to the ceiling and uttered, "Uh!"

Because everyone comes to City Hall to get something, and no one comes to do you a favor, sometimes being cantankerous and treating everyone like the enemy isn't such a bad tactic. One day, I was striding into the mayor's office when I bumped into Congressman Charlie Rangel leaving in a huff. "That damn mayor of yours," he fumed, "he hates black people."

"Congressman," I said, "you are right. But I have Bob Tisch in my office downstairs, and I can assure you that the mayor hates rich Jews and poor blacks and everyone in between."

Tisch was in my office because the city was then trying to attract the 1980 Democratic National Convention. The most likely possible host was the New York City Convention and Visitors Bureau, under Tisch's chairmanship. Bob and the president, Charles Gillett, did valuable work for the city, promoting tourism at a time when Americans, in particular, were afraid to travel to the Big Apple because of crime. The bureau asked the city for a contribution to help finance the convention, but Koch was giving me a difficult time on what should have been a simple request. "I'm not doing anything for Bob Tisch!" the mayor said to me. "He said he would support me in the election, and he did nothing at all, and I'm not doing anything for him." If Koch held his position, it would be a monumental problem for me.

As often happened, other people were mulling around the mayor's office. A mayoral confidant, the restauranteur Peter Aschkenasy, said,

"Ed, what are you talking about? We never approached Bob Tisch. We talked to Bob Tishman."

Koch said, "Oh my god!" and approved the contribution. We won the bid, and the convention was a huge success for the city.

Some months later, Bob Tisch pulled me aside after a meeting. He was confused. He said lately the mayor, who always had been quite cold to him, was suddenly very friendly. I told him the story.

My duties required me to interact continually with the offices of the five borough presidents. They were a diverse lot with power through their votes on the Board of Estimate, then the governing board of the city. The three citywide elected officials—mayor, comptroller, and city council president—had three votes each. Each borough president had one vote; majority ruled. The meetings of the Board of Estimate and the negotiations preceding the meetings on every single issue assured tumult. It was important for the mayor and for me to have good relations with them.

My principal relationship with the boroughs was to determine tax abatements for commercial and industrial projects. I also found federal, state, and city economic development funds for projects such as Urban Development Action Grants (UDAG) and the revitalization of main streets such as Pelham Parkway and the Hub in the Bronx, Fifth Avenue in Bay Ridge, Fulton Street in Brooklyn, and Queens Boulevard.

Manhattan, while doing better economically, was not thriving. Traditional retail areas such as Nassau Street and Thirty-Fourth Street needed revitalization. Even Madison Avenue looked dumpy. No area was worse than Third Avenue from 103rd to 120th Streets in the neighborhood known as El Barrio. The 1977 Con Ed blackout had provoked looting and fires, destroying many stores. The federal, state, and city governments had promised help, but it was two years later, and the street still had blackened stores. Support did not arrive until 1980, by which time the small shopkeepers were out of business. I mused that in future emergencies, potential aid recipients should be invited to Yankee Stadium, where bags of cash would be dropped from planes. By circumventing the bureaucracy, the cash had a chance of getting to its target audience in a timely fashion.

Upon examining the pattern of Con Ed's restoration of power after the blackout, we suggested that it redo its grid so that lights would come on in the highest crime rate areas first. The utility's management agreed, and I told the mayor that he and I would get our electricity last.

One of my toughest challenges as deputy mayor was dealing with the Port Authority of New York and New Jersey, an agency created in 1921 by the two states to coordinate construction and operations of the port. Under Robert Moses, it became a force, financing bridges and tunnels and circumventing local laws and regulations. It was a novel approach at the time, described brilliantly in Robert Caro's book, *The Power Broker*. By the time Koch was elected, the Port Authority's primary mission appeared to be the protection of its AAA credit rating. It operated all three metropolitan airports and had built the Twin Towers. It had built the massive container port in New Jersey.

The Port Authority's governance reflected its bistate mission. Its chairman was appointed by one state—in my time, it was New Jersey—and the executive director by the other, with responsibilities switching every four years. At the time, the executive director was Peter Goldmark, a bright man who had been New York State's budget director but who, regrettably, reflected the widely held view that New York City was a nonfunctioning entity and that everyone working for it was incompetent. Worse, the Port Authority bureaucracy had a distinct New Jersey bias. Even after working with Peter for more than two years, I felt that the PA was an enemy and that the only thing worse than dealing with one government was being a city that had to deal with an agency controlled by two state governments.

Prior to my appointment, the city foolishly authorized the Port Authority to build large-scale industrial parks in New York City and New Jersey. While it sounded like equal treatment, from my point of view it meant that the Port Authority had another way to induce New York companies to relocate to New Jersey, which also had large container ports and superior rail connections. New York City had no way to offer similar facilities.

In response, I began a two-part program. First, we began to clear lots in the other boroughs, creating a form of vest pocket industrial park that would attract small manufacturers that populated the city. Second, we asked the Port Authority to build warehouses and manufacturing plants on spec—in other words, before there was a specific buyer for them. The idea originated with the consul general of Great Britain. While visiting the mayor and Jay Goldin, he mentioned that in Wales, where there was little employment, the government built spec buildings that companies would see, like, and move into. In a rare show of unanimity, Koch and Goldin agreed to support such a program. The Port Authority agreed to experiment with buildings in Bathgate Industrial Park, located south of the Cross Bronx Expressway. Today, Bathgate is thriving.

While my relationship with the state's agencies was uneven at best, my relationship with New York Governor Hugh Carey was excellent. Carey was hardly a model leader. He drank too much, and his behavior was sometimes erratic. He was, nevertheless, one of the best elected officials I have ever observed. Carey had a quality difficult to find in the private sector and almost unknown in the public world: he could find the best possible person for a job, hire them, and then follow their advice. Look at the people Hugh Carey appointed to jobs or incorporated into his circle: Felix Rohatyn at the Municipal Assistance Corporation, Steve Berger at Budget, Dick Ravitch at UDC and then the Metropolitan Transit Authority, Richard Kahan at UDC, Jim Larocca at Energy, Peter Goldmark at the Port Authority and Mike Del Giudice. (The one exception in the governor's cabinet was John Dyson, a rich man's son and commissioner of commerce. Dyson demeaned the city repeatedly by telling everyone how incompetent the city was. Ironically, he later served under Mayor Giuliani as deputy mayor.)

My own experiences with Hugh Carey showed his impulsive nature and his good intuition. President Carter was meeting with the governor and the mayor in the mayor's office, just above mine. This was not a daily happening—nor was the unannounced appearance of the governor in my basement office, just prior to the meeting, to tell me that he and I were going to go upstairs and explain to President

Carter that the 1984 Olympics just had to be held in New York. It was all about politics, as he saw it: if the Olympics were held in Los Angeles in 1984, as seemed likely, the right wing of the Republican Party would use it to its advantage and promote the presidential aspirations of Ronald Reagan. As good Democrats, we couldn't sit back and let that happen! New York City had an earlier plan for the Olympics prepared by Ravitch, he noted; we should use that. And not incidentally, said Governor Carey, I, Peter Solomon, would run the Olympics. His vision of it all was so clear—and at the same time so nutty—that I was flabbergasted. I also explained that while I knew President Carter well, I could not burst uninvited into the meeting.

My demurral was in vain; the governor ordered me to accompany him. We joined the president and the mayor in his office, much to their surprise, although the president greeted me warmly. Carey rolled out his idea with the same intensity; when he stopped, I excused myself from the meeting. I never heard another word on the subject. Carey's vision wasn't wrong. Los Angeles did host the 1984 Olympics, but by then, Reagan was already president.

My second telling experience with Hugh Carey happened during the gas shortage of 1980. I had already made something of a mark in this area, having anticipated the gas shortage. On the mayor's behalf, I had initiated a number of conservation measures. Jim Larocca was an able state energy commissioner, but the governor felt that someone should be focusing on gas alone. I looked up one day at my desk in City Hall, and Carey was once again standing before me. "Peter," he began; before I could say, "Governor," he said, "I am appointing you gas czar for the state of New York with broad powers to decide on gas consumption!"

Having some experience with him by that point, I was slightly more prepared. "Governor," I said, "you have a terrific commissioner in Jim Larocca, and I work for the mayor. I don't think I can work for you and the mayor at the same time." This reply simply carried no weight, and I became gas czar of the state of New York.

The city was at that time consuming about twenty-two million gallons of gas annually. Upon the mayor's orders, about fifteen million gallons were set aside for the Sanitation Department, which had little leeway to cut its consumption. To waste less gas, my energy assistant, Robert Herzog, suggested we try to reduce the number of city-owned cars by 10 percent. Thus began an intricate game whereby I tried to bend the bureaucracy to my will.

We designated Jim Capalino, a twenty-nine-year-old wunderkind and commissioner of General Services, to list the 2,200 cars owned by the city, noting which were essential for the Police and Fire Departments. We met with Capalino and the relevant commissioners to give them quotas on the number of cars each department must surrender and, hopefully, to arrange a quota for gallons consumed in the remaining cars. Of course, immediately the Police and Fire Departments argued that the squad cars and chiefs' cars should be exempted. We now had 1,100 cars to regulate. Then, the Sanitation Department, Highway Department and others with extensive workforces complained that a "massive reduction" (remember, it was just 10 percent) would result in materially less supervision, and, of course, they could not be responsible for open potholes or dirty streets. The Commission for the Handicapped pleaded necessity, too, and so it went. Clearly, this exercise was not going to achieve the reduction in gas we needed.

After several weeks of tedious meetings, which I had to attend to demonstrate the seriousness with which City Hall approached gas reduction, we arrived at quotas for each department. It came down to one car in this department, another two here, maybe ten in sanitation, a dozen in police. In all, about 120 cars—not what we targeted, but at least we felt the bureaucracy had gotten the message about reducing cars and gas consumption.

The agencies were instructed to turn their vehicles in to GSA at the Brooklyn Army Terminal. About a month later, I asked Commissioner Capalino how many cars we'd received and whether he thought I had to follow up with the various departments. Well, Capalino replied, there was good and bad news. Yes, we had received the requisite 120 cars at the Army Terminal. But unfortunately, about forty didn't belong to the city. They were clunkers, some not running at all, that agencies bought explicitly for the purpose of turning them in to us and meeting their quotas. We had gotten our cars, but they had also kept almost all of theirs. In the bureaucracy, two minus two doesn't always equal zero.

The moral of this illustrative tale is that it's almost impossible and not worth the effort to try to rein in the bureaucracy. The people who populate it are too clever and entrenched.

The public unions were in constant battle with Koch on every issue; Victor Gotbaum, the president of the American Federation of State, County and Municipal Employees, District Council 37, who happened to be married to my childhood friend Betsy Flowers, was a stalwart adversary. A low point for the citizens, however, was the eleven-day transit strike of April 1980, the first work stoppage in the city in fourteen years. Koch rallied the citizens against the Transit Workers Union. My role was to report daily on how businesses were coping. My objective was to keep the city's morale upbeat so we could beat the union. Unfortunately, Governor Carey pressured Ravitch into settling with the union. We all felt betrayed. A postsettlement meeting between Koch and Ravitch in City Hall was embarrassing, as Ravitch tried to explain the agreement's benefits.

My bailiwick was the private employer unions. In this endeavor, I had considerable success. Harry Van Arsdale, head of the Electrical Workers Union, joined with David Rockefeller to lead a council promoting labor and business cooperation. My union confidant was Sam Meyers, head of the United Auto Workers local. I developed working relationships with Vinnie Pitta, the head of the Hotel and Restaurant Workers, and Chick Chaikin, head of the International Ladies Garment Workers. (After I left government, his successor asked me to chair the Garment Center Development Corporation, which managed the orderly conversion of manufacturing lofts.)

My relationship with Anthony Scotto, the head of the Longshoreman's Union, was more distant. The city's ports and terminals were under my aegis. I tried to convert the Brooklyn Navy Yard into an industrial site and warehouse facilities, and to lease the Brooklyn Army Terminal, where rents were ninety cents per square foot. The union, meanwhile, had a long history of illegal activity.

One of the worst situations was the Bronx Terminal Market, near Yankee Stadium. The lessees, the Buntzmans, had contributed to John Lindsay's abortive presidential bid in 1968. The lease needed redoing, but the BTM was a pit of corruption that no one wanted to engage. Some who knew me felt that, with my reputation, I had a chance to resolve the disputes between the city and the Buntzmans, but the situation was too messy even for me.

One day, Tony Scotto invited me to lunch at Windows on the World. When I arrived, he began talking about a number of projects on the docks. I mostly listened. He was in the midst of his trial for tax evasion, and as far as I could tell, he was going away for a while. What was his agenda? As lunch went on, I got the uneasy feeling he was wearing a wire. On the way out of the restaurant, he turned to me and said pointedly, "You know, you never have to worry when you are on the docks. We watch you all the time." Until that moment, I hadn't been worried about anything.

After Tony got convicted, his successor invited me to lunch, and we sat in the same booth at Windows on the World and had a similar conversation. Plus ça change. That guy may have also been wearing a wire.

There were times when I didn't know if I was in city government or another sequel to *The Godfather*. Meade Esposito was the legendary head of the Brooklyn Democratic organization. He was a boss in the old-fashioned political sense. Everyone deferred to Meade.

John LoCicero, the mayor's chief political aide, told me that Meade wanted to see me. He wanted to meet with me at eight o'clock the next morning at Junior's, the famed deli on Fulton Street in Brooklyn.

"Why me?" I asked. "I don't even know him and have nothing to do with him."

John looked at me. "Just go see him!"

I got dropped off in front of Junior's at 7:45 a.m. The glass door was locked with a steel gate across it. Inside, I could see a guy mopping the floor. I rattled the gate, and he opened the door. Through the gloom, I could see Meade sitting in the back of the dining area on a raised platform, smoking a cigar. With some apprehension, I approached him, half-expecting to hear Francis Ford Coppola yell, "Cut!"

"Sit down," Meade growled in a raspy voice. I did as instructed. He pushed a coffee cup toward me, and the guy previously mopping filled it. "Look," he growled without any foreplay. "I asked you to come here because I need some respect from the mayor. I know you guys in City Hall don't give a shit what I think. And you can do whatever the hell you want. But I want you to tell people you have talked to me. Then do whatever the hell you want."

I still had no idea why he had asked for me. I had little to do with the political decisions the mayor made or with the appointments that would concern a Democratic boss. Maybe it was because I was not political. Maybe it was because I had built a good relationship with Howard Golden, the Brooklyn borough president. Or maybe Meade knew that my father had run Abraham & Straus just a few blocks down Fulton Street. Whatever the reason, he had chosen me as his conduit. I told him that I would convey his message to the mayor, which I did. Koch just shrugged. Esposito was convicted in 1987 for giving an illegal gratuity to Bronx politician Mario Biaggi. In the end, a once powerful man had become an embarrassment.

CHAPTER 17

From City Hall to the Great Wall

Power in city government often comes down to such mundane things as getting a street paved, a task that is not as straightforward as you may think. Not too long into my term as an appointed official, I was home watching Steve Jones, the "Action Reporter" on Channel 5 at 10:00 p.m. He was reporting live from Broadway, a major thoroughfare in the Bushwick section of Brooklyn. "Broadway has been torn up for years waiting for the city to repave it, and nothing has happened," he told his viewers. Jones then went on to castigate the incompetence of the city and its neglect of Brooklyn. It was odd, I thought, that the usually vocal borough president hadn't been screaming about this Broadway situation. The next morning, I called Ken Schuman into my office. I told him to call Transportation Commissioner Anthony Ameruso and instruct him to pave the area immediately. Ken, who knew that I would usually make such a demand myself, asked what was going on. I explained the rules that I was now playing by. "Ken, if I make that call and nothing happens, then everyone will know I have no authority and no power. If you make the call and it doesn't happen, it's just one more bureaucratic failure."

An hour later, Ken reported that Ameruso had been shocked to get a call from City Hall. A week later on Channel 5 News, Steve Jones was again reporting live from Broadway in Bushwick. Everywhere the camera panned, gleaming new asphalt could be seen. Jones expressed amazement at the city's response. I never told him how it happened.

Government, particularly city government, is actually as incompetent as it seems. There are many obvious reasons, such as lack of schooling, training, and incentives.

Within the Police Department's homicide bureau, however, there is competence. New York cops aren't interested in crimes against property; there are too many in the metropolitan area, and they view most as insurance issues or maybe even scams. But show them a homicide, and they really know what they are doing.

A triple murder in Beverly Hills in 1979 is an illustration. One day in July 1979, Bob McCabe, a partner of mine from Lehman, called for help. Joanne Cotsen, wife of Lloyd (founder of Neutrogena), her son Noah, and a friend had been murdered by an intruder in the family's Beverly Hills home. Bob told me that the Beverly Hills cops didn't seem competent, and Bob asked if it was possible for NYC cops to help. It certainly was an odd request, and my initial reaction was to be polite and say no.

My relationship with Bob McGuire, the police commissioner, was good, so I called the PC and asked if he could help. After further discussions, he allowed two off-duty homicide detectives to fly to Los Angeles, not at the city's expense, to see what they could find out. Within several days, the detectives concluded that the intruder knew Mr. Cotsen. They speculated that his brother was the murderer.

They were right on about a relationship, but the murderer was, in fact, Cotsen's competitor, Erich Tali, a Belgium businessman. Tali killed himself in October 1979 days before being interviewed by the Beverly Hills police in Brussels.

City Hall has its own coterie of fixers, lawyers and lobbyists who prey on city officials and represent special interests. One of the most successful of these lobbyists was the law firm of Abe Lindenbaum, "Bunny." Bunny had been Mayor Abe Beame's Brooklyn crony and the top zoning lawyer in the city. Under New York's complicated zoning laws, a developer couldn't put a hole in the ground without retaining such a lawyer. Bunny's son Sandy had inherited the mantle. Sandy was a competent enough lawyer, but the Koch administration was determined to break his hold on zoning representation. We let developers know that the times were changing and that they didn't absolutely have to have a Lindenbaum representing them.

As it happened, one of the law firms that aspired to share in the zoning business was Shea, Gallop, Climenko & Gould. A partner, Bernie Ruggeri, a fiftyish lawyer known around City Hall, called one day to book an appointment.

Bernie waxed poetic about his law firm, and after a few minutes, I asked if the Gould in the title was Milton Gould. "Oh yes!" he assured me. He then began an enthusiastic description of Gould and his active involvement in every aspect of the firm. What he didn't know, of course, was that Gould was the lawyer who, ten years before, during the LIN Broadcasting incident I described earlier, had insulted and dismissed me as too insignificant for him to address.

I asked Bernie to pull his chair closer to my desk. He brightened, thinking he had made such a good impression that I was about to favor him with some confidential info. I leaned forward to narrow the distance between us even more. "Mr. Ruggeri," I said, "please go back to your firm and tell that fat fuck Milton Gould that you have just met the new deputy mayor and that he is Peter Solomon, the same Peter Solomon that he was once 'too rich and too famous' to deal with!" Bernie blanched. I felt like Joseph of biblical fame when he confronted his brothers who had sold him into slavery.

The Health and Hospitals Corporation was the mayor's bête noir. From my experience as vice chairman of Mt. Sinai and chairman of the planning committee, I knew how complicated managing a hospital was, and the city ran seventeen of them. Koch had made a bad decision in 1980 to close Sydenham and Metropolitan Hospitals. Sydenham's location, west of St. Nicholas Avenue on 118th Street, made it in effect the emergency room for Central Harlem. Closing the hospitals didn't save that much money, and it added strain to Koch's already poor relations with the black community.

In 1980, Koch fired the HHC's president, and governance of HHC dissolved. The chairman could no longer control board meetings. Koch and Bobby Wagner, citing my work at Mt. Sinai and my experience running meetings, implored me to step into the chairman's spot until they could recruit a new president. There was nothing in it for me, and I thought they were setting me up for a possible death by stoning, but I had no choice but to accept until Koch could find a permanent chairman.

The board meetings were public, held in HHC's office on Worth Street. The directors sat on a platform, making them ideal targets for insults or hand grenades. The audience was usually in a high whine, screaming—justifiably—about Koch deserting Harlem. Two members of the local community boards served on the board of directors, mounting their attacks from both ends of the table at once. The meetings were so raucous that Ellen Weissman, my primary staff on HHC, advised me to have protection. I never did, but police were always in the audience.

At one meeting, one of the community representatives sitting across the table from me called Health Commissioner Ferrer an "Uncle Tacos," and a black board member who voted with me and the mayor an Uncle Tom.

Although I thought he was probably correct, I slammed my hand on the table on front of him and blasted him for his rudeness. Alarmed at my ire, Ellen leaned forward to grab my arm and told me to calm down. "Don't worry," I whispered to her. "Sometimes you've got to show righteous indignation."

The chaos and turmoil following the Sydenham decision tested my mettle at each meeting and affected the mayor forever. He confessed it was his worst decision.

Ed Koch was sometimes a lot more popular out of town than in New York City. His first two trips abroad were considerable successes. They took the Yenta out of City Hall and exposed him in all his zaniness to the world's media. I think he found them educational.

The genesis of Ed's first trip was my promise to my wife that in exchange for serving two years in his majesty's service, I'd take her to China. In 1978, the United States and China had not yet formalized relations. One of Ed's assistants had a Chinese friend who suggested a visit from the mayor to the proper authorities in Beijing. At first, Koch didn't have much interest, but he loved Chinese food. As he thought about it, visions of Peking duck must have danced in his head, because he finally consented to go as long as it wouldn't be too expensive. I asked for a firm commitment that he would set aside two weeks for China. He agreed.

There was another reason for Ed's trip: New York was fast becoming the world's leading international city, but it had not developed relationships with foreign governments. We wanted foreign investments, but Chicago, San Francisco, and Dallas were all ahead of us in forging relationships overseas. China was a new game. We could lead there.

During the fall of 1978, we worked on the trip. Wary of the assistance we were receiving, particularly from the sponsor—a Hong Kong Chinese businessman—I asked the US State Department to check out his credentials. The report that came back caused sufficient concern for us to cut ties with our Hong Kong connection. Since you couldn't travel to China in those days without a sponsor, we were nowhere.

A few months later, in January 1979, President Carter established diplomatic relations with the People's Republic of China. We could now make a formal approach to the Chinese embassy in Washington. I did this, and a few months later, we were informed that the mayor would be welcomed but that the Chinese could accommodate only a limited party.

Ed Koch was a media dream, and the chance to photograph and televise him live and in color from atop the Great Wall, along the Avenue of the Emperors, and in the Great Hall of the People, had both the American and Chinese press salivating. It had Chinese government officials apprehensive. We were given a quota of twenty. The mayor invited his close associates as well as Ed Sadowsky, finance committee chairman of the City Council, and Jay Goldin, the comptroller.

The original date was just after Labor Day 1979. In July, the Chinese, whose level of anxiety about Koch grew daily, wrote to postpone the visit to February 1980. The mayor, also nervous about any break in his routine, seemed relieved. We agreed on a February date. In the meantime, I told the Chinese embassy that, if it was possible, Mrs.

Solomon and I would use the original September date to "advance" the mayor's trip. I did not receive a reply from the embassy. I told Linda we were going to the People's Republic but there was a good chance they would not be expecting us, in which case I had no idea what we would do.

We landed in Beijing just as a lunar eclipse passed an airport so tiny that it resembled the one at Martha's Vineyard. No one was there to greet us as I waited for our luggage. Just as I was beginning to despair, I saw a man running toward us. "Mayor Solomon!" he called. I couldn't have been more relieved.

I delivered a letter from Mayor Koch of New York City to Mayor Lin Hujia of Beijing suggesting "exchanges in the economic, cultural and educational area" and the establishment of a Friendship City relationship. A month before the start of Koch's 1980 trip, Beijing agreed to be our sister city.

Linda and I spent a week touring the People's Republic. Small gray clouds of pollution covered the city of Beijing. I delivered several letters to appropriate ministries on behalf of New York companies, one of which was from Hank Greenberg, chairman of AIG, to the ministry handling insurance. AIG had begun as an Asian company, had had no contact with the PRC since Mao's victory, and, of course, wanted to return. My delivery of this letter, the fact that it resulted in Hank Greenberg's first reconnection with the historic base of AIG, and the fact that he never said thank you to me or the mayor became the stuff of legend. Many years later, I overheard Ralph Buultjens, the NYU foreign policy expert, regale a group with the anecdote. I was shocked, because I had not told many people about Greenberg's ingratitude.

Beyond Beijing, we toured Xian—where the terra-cotta warriors had recently been discovered—Shanghai, Nanking, Suchow, and Hangchow. We visited the Great Wall and other famous sites. At the Ming tombs, a coincidence of Thomas Hardy proportions occurred. As I looked over thousands of Chinese tourists, I casually remarked that I couldn't believe I didn't know anyone. Out of the blue, John McCarter, my Harvard Business School roommate, appeared. He was on a tour with White House fellows. We later saw John again in Kweilin.

China was a mass of blue Mao jackets and bicycles. No cars, no advertising. In Beijing, we toured the now familiar Forbidden City, Summer Palace, and Temple of Heaven. We stayed in the hotel overlooking the Forbidden City and Tiananmen Square. It was an exciting time; the West seemed to know so little about China. I asked to see the Underground City consisting of tunnels and subterranean living quarters built in the late 1940s, at what must have been huge expense, to shelter the population from a nuclear attack from Russia. We entered a haberdashery store, and one wall swung open, revealing a large stairway. In the cavernous rooms and extensive tunnels of the Underground City, there were still provisions to feed millions of Chinese.

The West was just beginning to learn about the Cultural Revolution. In Kweilin, we were told bodies floated down the Li River nightly. We met Chinese intellectuals just returning to the cities. Our trip was extraordinary, and the Chinese accommodated our every request. We also sketched out the trip the mayor would take and scheduled it for February 1980 with appropriate media.

Koch's trip to China was well documented. WOR-AM and WCBS-AM/FM toured with us, as did reporters from the *Daily News*, *Newsday*, and the *New York Times*. The AP had correspondents residing in the PRC who accompanied the party as well as a photographer.

The mayor's entourage arrived at Narita Airport in Tokyo, coinciding with the US Olympic Team's victory over Russia in the "Miracle on Ice," which we watched on television. The flight to Beijing had its own drama, as the plane's fuselage seemed to have a tiny hole, and the engine was emitting a shrill sound. Using advanced technology, the Chinese crew tried to stuff a towel around the hole, with the expected results.

The passengers loved the mayor. Americans constantly appeared to tell him, "My aunt Sadie once met you in Queens." Beijing had a spanking new and deserted airport replacing the Martha's Vineyard–type terminal that had greeted Linda and me just a few months earlier. The Foreign Affairs Institute was our host. The press had come to meet us, and I spied Fox Butterfield, the *Times* reporter, nearby. Fox had been a year behind me at Lawrenceville and Harvard.

The mayor had no plan. Although we had discussed our goals to promote business, neither he nor anyone else accompanying us had spent a moment studying China. At some point, Koch spontaneously decided to promote free trade zones, a phrase that he had picked up somewhere and that was irrelevant. It took two to three press conferences to convince him to abandon the concept.

The Chinese had changed our agreed-upon itinerary, and I didn't like it. Diane Coffey, the mayor's chief of staff, and I met with our hosts for hours to rearrange the trip, knowing that every aspect could be organized in seconds since the government controlled every hotel and mode of transportation.

Air pollution was worse than the previous fall. I was barely able to breathe. Our first meeting was with Beijing's deputy mayor. We reviewed the Sister City documents in detail.

The Chinese were dealing with Koch and New York as if he was the president and we were from Washington. They were taking the discussions seriously, which was more than Koch, Jay Goldin, and Ed Sadowsky were doing. They all acted like they were on an exotic junket. Beijing wanted to promote trade, finance, cultural exchanges through our museums, and tourism with Pan Am Airlines and hotel chains such as the Sheraton, China Air at JFK Airport, and finance. The Chinese had a real agenda. We didn't. The Chinese knew what industries and technology they wanted, and they were able to articulate them. As we went through our trip, it was obvious there would be competition between the capital and Shanghai over which would be important from a business standpoint. In 1980, Beijing was dominant commercially, but that would change as Shanghai pursued its agenda.

Koch, meanwhile, was a hot dog. Outside the Wall in his "I Love New York" muffler! Astride a stone elephant at the Ming Tombs! Greeting constituents in Tiananmen Square! But it was in the Great Hall of the People that he reached his zenith.

We met Mayor Lin Hujia there for the signing of documents pertaining to our Sister City relationship. It was pretty hard not to be impressed by our surroundings. We entered through gigantic doors opening onto Tiananmen Square and were greeted by Lin in front of a large mural depicting the red sun rising. We Americans were all feeling like Nixon or Kissinger on an important state mission.

Mayor Lin led us into the Beijing Room, an enormous rectangular hall with a large red enamel dish on one wall and a large carved ivory tusk in another corner. In the center was a green baize table with chairs for Mayor Lin, several deputy mayors, and other officials. On our side were chairs for Koch, Goldin, Sadowsky, Consul Bill McCahill of the American embassy, and me. Behind Mayor Lin was a table with other Chinese officials. Lin made a speech about Beijing's power to establish its own trade relations and conclude agreements. He said after the Cultural Revolution and after "smashing the Gang of Four," the country shifted to rebuilding the economy. Beijing was the political and economic center of the country, and it needed to develop trade.

He pursued specific ideas, and Koch actually followed the agenda, even suggesting a Chinese trade office in New York City. Goldin and Sadowsky kept chiming in, finally saying that they would do anything in their power to remove roadblocks to trade. Call me cynical, but to me this all sounded like a variation on, "We're from the government. We are here to help!"

Lin offered a toast in which he praised my contributions to the events. It was a lot nicer than anything Koch had said to me about the trip. Koch and Lin agreed to establish a two-person committee to push efforts ahead. Koch instantly announced that I would be one of them.

In the corner of the hall, sitting in an overstuffed chair, Ron Simoncini, the mayor's bodyguard, tried to stay alert and figure out why he was there. The police commissioner had ordered him to protect the mayor; the State Department had ordered him to leave his gun at home.

As the mayor was signing the documents, he turned to me and, on the only occasion I ever heard him awed, said, "Boy, I feel like a chief of state." The picture of Ed embracing Mayor Lin after the signing made papers throughout the world, including the front page of the *London*

Times. For a former congressman who used to scheme to get his name in the local paper, it wasn't bad.

That afternoon, we visited the offices of China Air to offer our encouragement for direct flights from the People's Republic to JFK. We reminded the China Air officials that JFK was not only the primary tourist entry port to America but also a significant freight center, receiving 40 percent of the freight entering the US. Goldin, as an aside, joked that I didn't tell the minister that, once it gets there, 50 percent of the freight is stolen.

We had arranged for Li Xiannian, vice premier, to meet with the mayor in the Greeting Hall. It, too, was an immense structure, with an entrance three times the height of a City Hall door. On one wall was a large scenic mural. The twenty-five-foot ceiling had twenty-five panels, and each of the panels had aquamarine designs. Five chandeliers hung from the ceiling.

But the meeting was depressing. The mayor, who could be so good in informal settings, acted insecure and pompous with the vice premier. He insisted on talking about Stalin and asking why the People's Republic venerated a butcher of millions. He mentioned Finland and Estonia. He asked what the premier expected from the Chinese plenum session. The mayor's Stalin ploy was not meant for the Chinese audience. Fox Butterfield, *Times* Peking correspondent, was impressed by Koch's feisty quality and his knowledge of history, and Koch started to come off better in his dispatches. The vice premier, meanwhile, treated the mayor like a fresh child: firmly and condescendingly. At one point, the vice premier said to his interpreter, "How should I answer this silly question?"

"Ignore it," Mr. Hao, our host from the Foreign Affairs Institute, replied, and he did.

As I walked alone back to our hotel, I felt a sense of what China could be. The air was chilly with traces of snow remaining in the great square. Children were flying kites, one with a long tail attracting a crowd. Two girls passed me, and for the first time I noticed suggestions of Western dress breaking the monotony of Mao uniforms. Change was coming to China.

After sightseeing and shopping, we flew to Xian. Ed had begun to relax and enjoyed the crowds. Sadowsky, on the bus to the plane, asked me how my office was organized and how long I was going to stick around. He said he didn't appreciate why a deputy mayor was necessary for economic development until he watched me operate. He realized it required authority to get projects done. I realized on this trip that everyone, except Koch, recognized that I was different from other people in the municipal government. I complimented Wagner and Leventhal, but Sadowsky dismissed them as "boys," saying they could never stand up to Koch.

Shanghai was not the city it is today. There were neither first-class hotels nor skyscrapers. There was one top antiques store. There was a prison, and it was filled with a number of wives who had killed their husbands.

The vice mayor of Shanghai hosted an event for us. Once again, Koch brought up Stalin, but by this time, word about the mayor's foibles seemed to have circulated, because the Chinese did not seem surprised or offended. Almost every official at the banquet had been exiled to fields or factories during the Cultural Revolution, and now most of them had learned English and spent time in the United States.

I met with representatives of the Shanghai International Trust Corporation (SITCO), which had not yet been announced officially, and the China Venture Investment Corporation (CVIC). They laid out specific needs and priorities in terms of products and technology. It became clear that Shanghai would not take a back seat to Beijing in terms of economic growth and was planning to become a principal investment center for China.

After Shanghai, we traveled to the lovely resort city of Hangchow. Bob Tierney, the mayor's counsel, and I took a walk around the perimeter of the city. We saw what we thought was a group of workers on a tea break. We talked to them, and they walked us through their embroidery factory. In fact, they had been gathering for a meeting to improve worker productivity. We asked if we could join the meeting. We were enthusiastically welcomed and offered sweets, sunflower seeds, and small local walnuts. A fortyish female worker rose and talked about improving output. The youngest worker then read a two-minute speech on training to be a good worker and noted how she was getting help from older workers. Another worker, the only male who wasn't at the head table, talked about how he was the oldest worker but he was doing the best he could. Then a professionally trained opera singer and factory worker sang a song. They then asked me to sing. Apparently, they had heard me singing to myself as we toured the factory on our way to the meeting. I sang the theme song of the ILGWU, "Look for the Union Label," and while I couldn't remember all the words, it was a great hit. Tierney told the newspapers about the incident, and the *Daily News* reported it.

Our last day was a return to Shanghai. After almost two weeks in China, I was worn down. The distance between Koch and me was considerable. We had little in common, but, I hoped, we did have mutual respect. He had made at least one aside thanking me for arranging the trip, and at one point, he mentioned to the mayor of Beijing that I might be mayor after he left office. Goldin had also approached me on this subject, but I told him that if I ran for office, I would never run in New York City because it was too rough. Almost everyone on the trip knew I had made a decision and that this was my swan song. I had done in city government what I was asked to do. I had learned much. It was time to move on.

Koch wanted to go home directly, but we had scheduled a three-day stopover in Tokyo to celebrate the twentieth anniversary of the New York City sister relationship with Tokyo. No one had paid much attention to this relationship, which had been started in 1959 under Mayor Robert Wagner. I had discovered it by chance as we planned the China trip. No one knew the Tokyo municipal government had been sending an intern each year to the city's Office of Economic Development for the past twenty years.

The Japanese press covered Koch with the same zealousness as their American colleagues. From the moment of our landing at Narita, he was on camera. The emotional highlight was our arrival at City Hall in Tokyo. We left the hotel in a motorcade precisely at the scheduled moment. As we drew near City Hall, we caught a glimpse of heavy traffic. Being New Yorkers, we assumed an accident had occurred. Then we realized the crowd was for us. Ever the politician, the mayor leaped from his car to be greeted by a band, a cheering crowd of several thousand, Governor Suzuki of Tokyo, and Miss Tokyo. It was a grand moment.

As always, the yenta in Koch had to be suppressed. He had pestered me to stay at a Japanese Ryokan instead of the Imperial Hotel. He had even asked Diane Coffey to call the American embassy to arrange it. I had vetoed the idea. As we went up the packed elevator in the Imperial, he announced from the back, "Thank goodness you kept me from myself." It was a sentiment the mayor's staff heard often.

Addressing the Municipal Assembly at the Okura Hotel, the mayor delivered a speech I wrote, and, for the first time in two years, said what I had written.

In the end, those two weeks in Asia helped the mayor's image and gave him stature beyond New York. We did manage to put the city squarely on the road to internationalization. We arranged follow-up visits from Governor Suzuki and other Japanese leaders to New York City. As a result, Japanese business felt even more at home in New York, and, in fact, a minor New York City boom began in Japan. The Chinese did expand their facilities in the city, and visiting officials from Beijing and Shanghai always called on the mayor. All this was good because it made Koch a hot topic, and in politics, the sizzle is the steak.

CHAPTER 18

To Washington

or

Always Leave Them Laughing

(1949 Musical Comedy)

Like almost every other story about city government, the story of my departure from City Hall is not straightforward. One of the bigger surprises occurred one morning in August 1979. As I was exiting the FDR on my way to City Hall, I heard on WINS News Radio that I was "returning to the private sector." In other words, I was fired. I was stunned. I hadn't announced any such plans, and I had taken steps, as any appointed official must, to ensure that no one would get the impression that I wasn't in my boss's good graces. As soon as I got to City Hall, I raced to the mayor's office. "What is going on?" I shouted at Ed Koch.

Before I go too far, let me say that I understood the political compact where the appointed official serves at the whim of the elected official. Underlings have to manage elected officials gingerly. Vernon Jordan, the well-known confidant of US presidents, once told me that in all his years of friendship with President Clinton, he never offered him any advice; he just listened. Elected officials don't often seem to like advice, even from those they have appointed. You are 100 percent dependent on your elected boss as you attempt to carry out your duties and appear competent to the press. It's not like the business world, where there is a two-way social contract between boss and underling, and often a severance bonus if the relationship doesn't work out. You can disagree with your elected superior, but you do so at your peril; disagreement, if it occurs too often, risks a cold shoulder. And cold shoulders in government are fatal to an appointee who is vulnerable to the quirky realities of political expedience or a more powerful person's mood.

I knew by mid-1979 that the mayor had an appointee problem. Early in his tenure, when he had an imprecise understanding of job titles and management, he had appointed a number of political pals, personal friends, and people he barely knew—but who were friends or relatives of people whose support he needed—as deputy mayors. Their presence had no great effect on me, other than that I sometimes felt I didn't have enough to do because we had so many of them. In several conversations earlier that summer, I told Koch that he might want to weed out some deputy mayors. I also mentioned that after another year or two, I wanted to leave city government to do something else. Exactly what, I didn't know yet. Koch's plan for getting rid of deputy mayors was as unfocused as my plan, and he made it clear that whatever he did, it wouldn't involve me. I didn't think much about it, until he suddenly started swinging his ax.

The idea of firing deputy mayors had occurred to Koch several months earlier, when Jimmy Carter fired part of his cabinet. Carter had the same issues of dissatisfaction, but he fired cabinet officers with whom he had no prior relationship: namely, secretaries Michael Blumenthal, Joseph Califano, and James Schlesinger. Koch, on the other hand, fired some of his longtime intimates. He also timed his housecleaning for August, when he thought fewer people would be paying attention. But news from City Hall is never ignored, and the media jumped on the announcement. The changes, in fact, were dramatic. Koch fired Deputy Mayor Phil Trimble, a close friend who had run legislative matters and who would never talk to him again. He fired Phil Toia of finance, whom I never heard talking to anyone about anything. He let go his rival in the primary and the leader of the Puerto Rican community, Herman Badillo. He shifted Herb Sturz from deputy mayor for criminal justice to chairman of city planning, promoted Bobby Wagner from city planning to deputy mayor, and elevated Nat Leventhal to deputy mayor of operations. Finally, he eliminated Ronay Menschel's deputy mayor for intergovernmental relations title. In essence, Haskell Ward and I were left. The way the press reported the changes, Haskell and I were being given the boot, albeit in slow motion. The early edition of the *New York Times* included me in its editorial; WINS and other stations broadcast it on the radio.

When I burst into Koch's office, his body language and tone of voice were unusually defensive. He explained that Ronay was in tears about her demotion. She insisted that all deputy mayors be included in the press release; Koch was trying to mollify one of his closest and longest-serving aides. Ronay had been on Koch's staff for ten years. Along with Diane Coffey, Ronay was and would remain one of Koch's closest associates. "Well, you told me you didn't have enough to do," he said. "I am firing five deputy mayors, and Ronay Menschel asked me to include all deputy mayors in the press release."

I was flabbergasted. "You're right," I said. "I didn't have enough to do, but that was because there were too many deputy mayors! I am not leaving now."

I confronted Ronay. I told her in life sometimes unfair things happen; when they do, nothing is more pathetic than trying to hurt innocent people to save yourself.

The press release and resulting publicity catalyzed members of the business community to chastise the mayor for letting me go. Their strong reaction impressed Koch and increased his respect for me. I didn't wait for the reaction and launched into damage control mode, calling various media outlets and mounting a counteroffensive. I stopped the story from spreading further. Koch was forced to say, over and over, that I could stay on the job as long as I wanted. But a negative story never goes away completely, and the rumor of my leaving haunted me until the day I actually left city government.

For Koch, the firings were politically positive. His elevation of Bobby Wagner was acclaimed. Bobby, a graduate of Exeter and Harvard College, was an intelligent man with a vast knowledge of New York political history, which you would expect from the grandson of Senator Robert Wagner and the son of three-term Mayor Robert Wagner. He had also been my constructive partner as chairman of city planning and became even better as deputy mayor. When the mayor needed to know the historical context of an issue or historic political relationships, Bobby always knew the difference between the truth and the perceived.

The press and public interpreted Koch's moves as a sign that his knowledge of the job was increasing along with his confidence level. In one swoop, he had streamlined the mayor's office, indicating that he was more comfortable running the city. When he walked the streets famously asking people, "How am I doing?" the most frequent response was "Great!"

Meanwhile, I soldiered on. City Hall duty is 24/7 and has been since 1965, when Mayor John Lindsay introduced the "night mayor," a concept assigning a deputy mayor or commissioner to duty throughout the night. By 1978, the duty officer sat at the City Hall police desk, but a deputy mayor was still designated each night.

In this smaller cadre of deputy mayors, I was the only married deputy mayor; in the era before cell phones, I was the most reachable at night. I never asked Nat and Bobby where they were. But the police and other emergency services personnel knew where to find me during nocturnal emergencies, and so it was me alone they called at two, three, or four in the morning.

I got accustomed to the wee-hour conversations with a police officer. They all had the same pattern.

"Deputy Mayor?"

(Groggily) "Yes."

"There has been a shooting, explosion, gas leak, Con Ed blackout."

"Have you called the police commissioner, fire commissioner, head of EPA?"

"Yes, sir."

"Good. Don't call the mayor, but call me again if you need me."

Back to sleep.

I had to laugh at myself. When I accepted Koch's offer of a job as deputy mayor, I had told him that I was the father of three young children, and I expected to spend weekends with my family and go to their after-school events. "I don't do weekends, and I don't do windows!" I had said, thinking I was being funny. But here I was now doing nights.

As I noted earlier, my departure story had several subplots. A couple of months before all the firings happened, I'd gotten an unexpected phone call from Lehman Brothers partner Steven R. Fenster. Steve, an ally of Pete Peterson and Lew Glucksman, was a former Department of Defense "whiz kid" with whom I had a cordial relationship. He asked to see me in my City Hall office. Without comment but with curiosity, I said fine. I had hardly thought about Lehman—or Wall Street in general—in the year I'd been away from the firm, working in my $57,500-a-year city job. With the exception of Harvey Krueger, who lived in my building, I didn't socialize with Lehman partners, so I wasn't current on the firm's politics. My job as deputy mayor was all-consuming, and I pretty much shut off that other part of my brain.

My meeting with Fenster was strange, for two reasons. One was that all of my meetings in that basement office in City Hall were strange, if only because the space was cramped and my desk had a weight-bearing pole in front of it, running from the floor to the ceiling. The other reason for the strangeness was that Fenster was so socially awkward. As smart as he was, he wasn't comfortable in his own skin.

After some cringe-inducing small talk about the weather, he finally got to the point. He represented Pete Petersen, Glucksman, and Bob Rubin. The corporate finance operation needed a leader. Harvey Krueger had decided he didn't want to run corporate finance, and the senior partners didn't think that the next partner in line, Bill Morris, was up to the task; would I, Fenster asked, consider returning to run the division?

Fenster's argument was that since Jim Glanville and his energy associates Ward Woods and Ian MacGregor had left Lehman to go to Lazard, there was finally the opportunity to run a rational business. There was truth in this argument; I might not have left the firm if these toxic partners had already departed. The fact that my absence had apparently made some hearts at Lehman grow fonder amused me. But at that point, I wasn't tempted to return. First, I had promised Ed Koch that I would serve for at least two years. The mayor would, of course, soon challenge the ground rules of our relationship with a press release. But even if I left City Hall, I was not eager to dive back into life at Lehman. I still had bad memories. Some people there had been glad to get rid of me. Not Pete Petersen but Glucksman, Glanville, Morris, and maybe even Fenster, who was now clumsily soliciting my return. I had many clients, but they didn't care. Lehman Brothers was an arrogant place. And as happy as they probably were to get rid of me, I was just as pleased to be free of them. When I left for City Hall, I didn't take a leave of absence like some financial people do when they join government. Taking a leave could have guaranteed my ownership position if I returned, but I didn't want to do that. I wanted to make a full commitment to city government—and a clean break with Lehman.

Other options were becoming available. I continued to meet with Stuart Eizenstat and Jack Watson on the second floor of the West Wing to explore joining the Carter administration. This option was appealing, although even the discussions made me uncomfortable. Carter was floundering, and the relationship between him and Koch was testy. Koch felt Carter was a weak leader, especially when it came to his commitment to Israel. During one of Carter's visits to New York in 1978, Koch dramatically handed the president a letter objecting to his actions toward Israel in full view of the press. On the other hand, the city remained dependent on the Carter administration to supplement its credit and operating budget.

By the beginning of 1980, I had decided that I would leave Koch after the budget was passed in June. I discussed with my friend Dan Lufkin, one of the founders of DLJ and a fellow director of General Cigar, creating a leveraged buyout fund and thought about reviving Lehman's approach. I felt I'd done my duty to the mayor. Washington, despite my misgivings about Carter, was an intriguing possibility.

The position of undersecretary of the Treasury had become vacant with the resignation of Anthony Solomon (no relation). The secretary of the Treasury was G. William Miller who had been trained as a

Cravath, Swaine & Moore lawyer, then became the general counsel for Textron, the Rhode Island conglomerate. With the deaths of several possible successors, he had risen to CEO. As happens too frequently, Bill Miller, with few credentials but with circumstances breaking in his favor, became a leader of the US business community. President Carter had appointed him to be chairman of the Federal Reserve Board, although he had no training in either central bank administration or monetary policy. After months of failure in that post, Miller became secretary of the Treasury.

Bill Miller was the shining example of the Peter principle, rising to one's highest level of incompetence. With his leadership at Treasury, interest rates had risen to 14 percent, markets were crashing, and unemployment grew. Miller clearly needed help.

No lesser figures than David Rockefeller and Senator Daniel Patrick Moynihan called the president to urge that I be appointed as undersecretary of the Treasury. Eizenstat and I also had a number of conversations about this appointment, but it became increasingly clear that either the White House didn't want to appoint me to that particular job or the Republicans, seeing a weakened president, had stopped confirming his proposed appointees. In any case, nothing happened. The Lehman option was now looking more attractive.

As I began to withdraw psychologically from City Hall, I turned over more of my duties to my staff and prepared them for an afterlife. I appointed the able Ken Schuman commissioner of the office of economic development and Phil Aarons as chairman of PDC. Fritz Favorule was working full-time on the Democratic Convention. Steve Spinola, later head of the Real Estate Board of New York, had assumed a leadership role at OED. I had negotiated a position for Paul Watterson at Steve Schulte's law firm. Judith Friedlander and Robert Herzog were in firm positions. In issues where my office and, say, city planning were involved, I let city planning take more of a lead.

The mayor and I discussed the timing of my departure and my successor. Ironically, while in China in February, I became convinced I should leave sooner rather than later, even as my relationship with the mayor became closer. With Koch's knowledge, I approached Robert

E. Rubin, then a partner of Goldman Sachs and a Harvard classmate. Rubin was active in Democratic politics. I met with Bob in his Park Avenue apartment as he lay on his floor to ease the chronic pain in his back. He told me that he couldn't make the move to deputy mayor and "You're interested in policy," he said. "I'm not. I'm interested in politics!" As the years unfolded and Bob became the author of "Rubinomics," otherwise known as Bill Clinton's economic policies, I have often thought of Bob's comment in 1980.

I next approached Lew Lehrman, the scion of a retail drug dynasty and a well-known political conservative. I arranged an interview with the mayor. The conversation got off to a pleasant start, until Lew couldn't resist lecturing the mayor on the evils of the city's personal income tax. I couldn't get him out of Koch's presence fast enough.

Apparently, my downshift in intensity became increasingly obvious. Within the government, my colleagues noticed that my office wasn't pushing as hard. Soon the press noticed as well, and stories appeared, wondering whether I was on the outs with the mayor. If getting into government at the right level is difficult, getting out with your reputation intact is equally daunting. The trick is to leave office at the height of your powers. I planted a story that countered negativity and demonstrated my authority. The next day, I announced my resignation. The *New York Times* printed a picture of me in my office with a big smile. "Always leave them laughing" was exactly my message.

In May 1980, I decided to return to Lehman. I called Pete Peterson, who was enthusiastic. It seemed right, even though a position in the Treasury Department had finally been offered. It was below the undersecretary level, and confirmation was not assured; Carter would probably lose his reelection bid in November. I would be in Washington for fewer than six months. Being deputy mayor was sufficiently disruptive to my family without now going to Washington, where I would live alone and commute to New York City on weekends and Martha's Vineyard for the summer. That seemed silly.

Stuart Eizenstat was disappointed in my decision. He wanted me to join the Treasury in any position because the White House felt it didn't have much control over the department. I told him that an interim position was not attractive even if we created a new title for the Treasury, "counselor to the secretary."

Senator Pat Moynihan did more than express disappointment. The senator and I had met each other when we were professor and student, respectively, at Harvard. We had spent time working on federal funding for economic development projects for New York City in the previous two years. Our few UDAG funds, such as for building the Portman Hotel (now the Marriott) in Times Square, were the result of Pat's influence. He had been my most active supporter in terms of a Carter appointment. In 1976, for example, he had written the president urging my appointment as chairman of the SEC.

"You idiot!" he shouted into the phone when I told him that I was going to turn down the Treasury offer and return to Lehman. "Don't you know there will never be another Democratic president? Look at the demographics of the country. With your careers in finance and government, you have to learn how the Treasury, the White House, and Washington work! This is your opportunity! It is precisely *because* Carter will lose that you should take the job!" I hung up feeling like I'd had the wind knocked out of me.

Rarely do you hear good advice at precisely the moment you're ready to hear it. *He's right*, I thought. *I am looking at this backward. I can always go back to Lehman. This is a new vista.* I had already taken a big chance leaving Lehman and joining a new and erratic mayor at a bleak moment in the city's history. That had worked out. Why shouldn't Washington work out just as well?

I called Linda; just the day before, I had assured her that I would resume my former life. I broke the news that I was reversing course. She was understanding. Pete Peterson, though, said he couldn't understand why I would turn down Lehman to take a lesser position in Washington, one with little apparent prestige. I told him it was a legitimate question, and if Carter lost, as I suspected he would, we would talk in the fall. Although skeptical, he graciously wished me luck.

The mayor was incredulous. He understood me leaving, but he

couldn't believe that I was quitting Ed Koch to go with "a loser." He thanked me for giving the city my help and also wished me well.

I had pondered my next move for about a year, come to a decision, then reversed it a few hours later. As I reflect on my life, there are themes or patterns that I recognize. I am drawn to risks. I will take a chance on my ability to work through a situation, whether taking a job in government, managing a theatre company, starting a business, or even getting divorced. I have confidence that it will somehow work out.

I think that confidence comes from optimism. I've always believed that if I apply myself, treat colleagues well, have a plan, and pay attention to detail, I will catch a rising tide.

I left city government on a beautiful June morning. My last official act was to formalize an agreement for developers to operate a recreational site on a pier at Twenty-Fourth Street and the Hudson River. Not surprisingly, and appropriately—since my first-day challenge involved a shady situation—the developers turned out to have unsavory ties. The piers weren't developed until years later when Tom Bernstein and his partner Roland Betts created the renowned Chelsea Piers.

In the subsequent thirty-five years, city government and the city are much improved. I was part of a team that changed the trajectory of the city. What could be more rewarding?

CHAPTER 19

US Treasury—1980

My arrival in Washington coincided with an invitation to attend a state dinner for King Hussein of Jordan. In a gesture unrelated to my appointment to the Treasury, Jack Watson, assistant to President Carter, had put me on the invitation list. When I later thanked him, Jack confided that he had proposed my name a number of times over the previous four years, but I had never been invited. The remark made me feel like Washington was greeting me with a grudging acceptance.

Bill Miller, the secretary of the Treasury, was as enthusiastic as he could be about my arrival. I was imposed on him by his boss, the president, and he didn't know me. Neither was it clear what my duties would be or how I would interact with the secretary. Having been thrust into a similar situation in City Hall, I knew that I had to stay calm, act confident, and simply start showing up at Miller's office daily at eight o'clock, and the relationship and my role would eventually work themselves out. I also commandeered a room across the hall from his and was fortunate to retain Nancy Feister as one of my assistants. Nancy was an old Treasury hand and later became the assistant to the next secretary, Don Regan. She was invaluable.

I had another strong ally in my close friend Bob Glauber, a renowned Harvard Business School professor of finance, who joined me as a consultant. Under President George H. W. Bush and Treasury Secretary Nick Brady, he would become undersecretary of the Treasury.

Senator Pat Moynihan had predicted that my stint in Washington would be a way for me to learn how things worked there, and that's the way things turned out. The last months of the Carter administration were a hard time to get things done. The president and the White House were captives of the Iranian hostage crisis. Inflation was raging. I did what I could, but my tenure in Washington did not affect the destiny of the nation.

The best aspect of the Treasury is that it is centrally located. The White House is across the street. Its thick walls keep it cool in the swelter of the Washington summer. I concentrated on a few areas where I thought progress might be possible. The first area was industrial policy. Manufacturing was ebbing, and jobs were being exported overseas. The domestic automobile industry was in crisis. Steel production was crumbling. Unemployment in Michigan and Ohio was nearly 20 percent, with cities such as Flint, Pontiac, Akron, and Toledo in dire straits. The Treasury under Miller had given the domestic defense contractor Lockheed a lifeline and was in the process of doing the same for Chrysler. But Felix Rohatyn and the unions wanted a number of specific programs tied up in the ribbon of an articulated industrial policy to revitalize domestic manufacturing. He advocated a new Reconstruction Finance Corporation, mirroring what President Hoover had established and had continued until 1945.

Curious about Felix's idea, I commissioned a thorough review of all aspects of Carter's efforts to help industry, including an analysis of the bureaus and programs established originally in the early 1930s under RFC. Brian Freeman, one of the most able people I have known, presented an analysis that showed that while the RFC itself had been disbanded, most of its programs still functioned within the federal government. These agencies included the Small Business Administration, Commodity Credit Corporation, and Economic Development Administration. Indeed, few of the programs had disappeared. There was no need to reinvent the RFC or create a new industrial policy; a policy and the programs, for all practical purposes, existed.

The analysis also concluded that while the RFC had invested the entire $3 billion from 1932 through 1945 in the equities of railroads, manufacturing, and related companies, under the able leadership of Jesse Jones, it had gotten back the entire $3 billion. It had been an unqualified success.

Freeman's report was instructive to me then, and again twenty-seven years later as the country approached the financial crisis of 2008. With it in mind, in 2006, I advocated a new RFC to support banks and financial companies in anticipation of an impending downturn. No one, not even Paul Volcker, seemed to support the idea. Eventually, the George W. Bush administration, in response to the collapse of Lehman Brothers, proposed the TARP program and used it to invest in warrants and equities of numbers of distressed banks, insurance companies, and financial institutions. It, too, got repaid and made a profit.

In 1980, the United States car industry was losing market share to Japan's newer manufacturers such as Honda and Toyota. There wasn't much Carter could do about this because quality was a management and labor issue. As part of the automobile task force, I met with Japanese diplomats and leaders of the Japanese Keidanren, the powerful business group. Japan Inc. didn't want to antagonize the United States but did want to sell more cars. The trips I'd made to Japan as deputy mayor and the resultant relationship I had with Governor Suzuki of the Tokyo metropolitan government underscored my credibility as someone with an understanding of Japanese/USA issues.

The use of government's procurement of goods and services can be a source of small business job creation. Bob Glauber and I analyzed the purchasing patterns of the Department of Defense to see whether the size and location of businesses were the criteria. We knew, of course, political influence mattered. We didn't do enough research to reach definitive conclusions, but it was clear that New York City wasn't getting its share of procurement dollars.

Most of my summer was spent on tax policy. The president was proposing a tax bill, although it was clear that in an election year, few would take it seriously. I was asked to help draft the substance of the bill.

Congress was more congenial and respectful in 1980. Seniority counted, and Senate committees were dominated by such formidable figures as William Fulbright of Arkansas on foreign relations. None was more informed and respected in the area of tax policy than Senator Russell Long from Louisiana, chairman of the Senate Finance Committee. Senator Long was *the* authority on taxation. Heeding Pat Moynihan, I called the legislative aide of Senator Long and introduced myself. Senator Long was gracious enough to spend two long sessions with me, reviewing the tax code in detail and explaining the reason for almost every single tax. I felt as if I had seen the movie. We met in an office under a flight of stairs in the Capitol Building. The office was unmarked and windowless. As we talked, the senator imbibed frequently; I also drank a bit but was not expected to keep pace.

Secretary Bill Miller was a formal and lonely man. He and his Russian-born wife had no children. He smiled easily and carried himself with a certain pomposity like a bantam rooster. When he walked, he pranced. His words and manner were crisp and precise, befitting a former Cravath, Swaine & Moore lawyer. And he was strong on details. While he had little sense of policy, the Treasury secretary, for all his failings, was the driving force behind the government guarantees that saved Chrysler and Lockheed. In both cases, Bill Miller crafted the deals, convinced Congress, and the government made a profit.

He knew how to stand his ground. In the middle of the Chrysler negotiations, Lee Iacocca, the company's flamboyant CEO, came to a meeting in the secretary's conference room. Miller hated smoke in an era where many still smoked, both cigarettes and cigars. Iacocca probably knew that. With an obnoxious bravado, he told Miller that he objected to the secretary's suggestion that he divest Chrysler of many of its private airplanes, all the while blowing smoke in the secretary's face. Miller calmly told Iacocca that, if he wanted Chrysler to receive congressional approval, there would be no planes.

But Miller's relationship with the president was unclear. Carter had appointed him chairman of the Federal Reserve, and then, after he couldn't convince David Rockefeller to become Treasury secretary, he moved him to Treasury. Miller, perhaps out of insecurity, seemed to put all of his energy into managing upward. He was distant to me and his staff. Glauber and I were with Miller in his office one day when the president called, not an unusual occurrence. Miller took the call, hurried into his bathroom, and closed the door as he continued talking.

My new colleagues in the Treasury were also off-putting. Roger Altman barely paid attention to me. Since I had been instrumental in his brief career at Lehman, I found this upsetting. It confirmed my suspicions about why I hadn't been approached for a position in the Treasury early in the administration. My only peers who went out of their way to welcome me were Betty Anderson, the undersecretary of the Treasury for administration, and General Counsel Bob Mundheim.

Stu Eizenstat made sure I was involved in proposals involving the Treasury. I spent time in Stu's office on the second floor of the West Wing. He took extensive notes on yellow pads, underscoring that he was listening to every word. Stu would continue on in Washington and have a distinguished career in the State Department and as deputy secretary in the Treasury under Larry Summers. I would kid Stu about a big spender ending up in the Treasury.

One of my contributions was to the SynFuel Program. In response to the energy crisis, the president had proposed the establishment of a corporation to invest in alternative energy. But the president now couldn't find a chief executive. My Washington role seemed to be evolving into a "free safety." When there was a problem relating to business that no one else could solve, I got called into action. In this case, I suggested Don Smiley, the retired chairman of R. H. Macy, whom the president appointed.

Washington seemed much too formal and status-conscious for my taste. I also realized how little time and accurate information federal policy makers had. I was the recorder of the Economic Policy Committee, chaired by Miller and including senior officials and Vice President Walter Mondale. At one meeting, the discussion centered on retail sales and consumer demand, but the data was out of date. I asked the secretary to be excused and, in the course of several calls, was able to talk by phone to a sufficient number of retail CEOs to provide more accurate and current data. It is amazing how quickly CEOs take calls from the Treasury or White House. Still, with few exceptions, I didn't get much respect in Washington, and I knew why: I had a title that no one understood, and it was late in the term of an unpopular president.

Occasionally, I would be invited to an important dinner or event because of my New York City connections with the Chinese or Japanese. At a formal dinner at the State Department for a Chinese leader, I was seated far below the salt. Chairman of the Federal Reserve Volcker was one of the prominent guests. After the main course was cleared, the chairman, to the apparent astonishment of the table, gestured for me to join him. Paul led me to the window. As he towered over me, he put his arm around my shoulder to draw me close to him in a most confidential manner. I was anxious about what he might tell me.

"Peter," he said, "the final episode of *Shogun* is on tonight. I don't want to miss it." *Shogun* was a miniseries about seventeenth-century Japan; in 1980, you couldn't record television shows. "So you and I are going to leave right now and together. They will all think there is a matter between the Fed and the Treasury which needs immediate attention."

With a sense of relief, I hurriedly said my goodbyes and followed Paul out the door. The next morning, my secretary, Nancy, rushed to my office saying that everyone wanted to know what the chairman wanted and why it had seemed so urgent. I said I couldn't tell them. It was a highlight of my Washington stay.

As campaign season heated up, the White House asked me to help. Because of my work with the automobile task force and my background in economic development, I was asked to make a swing through Ohio and Michigan, meeting with mayors and giving out economic development funds. (I had already determined that the prospects for near-term improvement in the employment levels of those states were nil.) Meanwhile, other parts of the country, such as Houston, were booming because of energy prices. People in the Midwest could not sell their homes and, therefore, could not move to where there were jobs. I proposed that the federal government buy homes in those economically depressed states, but the idea was viewed as too radical.

Ohio and Michigan had high levels of unemployment. Stu's young deputy Ralph Schlosstein joined me representing the White House. His friend Steve Rattner, a reporter for the *New York Times*, accompanied us. The trip took us to the heart of the tire, car, and manufacturing center of the United States. The low level of economic activity and the dreary prospects didn't augur well for Carter's reelection prospects. The most telling aspect of the trip was Rattner's front-page story, in which he quoted his friend Schlosstein instead of me. It reaffirmed my lack of importance in the Washington status rankings. The only positive result of the trip was my getting to know Ralph and Steve. I was instrumental in both of them joining me at Lehman Brothers after Carter lost.

The Monday after the election, I called Stu and, after commiserating with him, asked if he would mind if I left that week. He wished me well and thanked me profusely for coming to Washington for six months to help. I thanked Nancy and Secretary Miller, who surprised me by his compliments. He told me that he had hoped I would be in the cabinet if Carter had been reelected.

Before I left Washington, one more interesting event happened. I was packing my Treasury papers when Nancy handed me a blue envelope with the name Onassis printed on the reverse. I opened it to find a simple one-page note: "Dear Peter. You won. Jackie." In the middle was a Kennedy dollar, Scotch-taped to the letter.

I knew what this was about, but I could hardly believe it. Several months before, I had been in New York to attend a ribbon-cutting ceremony for Theatre Row, several stages of which were part of a theatre complex originated by Fred Papert and the Ford Foundation under Roger Kennedy as part of the revitalization of Forty-Second Street. As I entered the theatre that day, I saw three seats on the stage. Fred welcomed me and waved me toward an empty seat. I looked up and unexpectedly saw Jackie Kennedy Onassis. I greeted her by introducing myself. "I know who you are," she said. "Since you left Lehman Brothers, your career has been supersonic!"

I was dumbfounded. She asked me what I was doing now. I said I was working in the Treasury for President Carter but would be back in New York City when Carter lost in November. She said, "He isn't going to lose!"

"No," I said, "he is going to get killed by Reagan." I immediately regretted the word "killed," but Jackie didn't seem to notice.

Then she stuck out her hand. "I bet you a dollar Carter wins." I shook with her and agreed to the wager. The ceremony was short, and I went on my way. I'd almost forgotten about our encounter, but apparently she hadn't; here she was, just a few days after the election, making good on her bet.

I didn't have any more contact with Jackie until the following January. One day in January, I was in my office at Lehman on the fifth floor of One William Street, when my assistant Helen Burlew said Mrs. Onassis was on the phone. I had told the story about meeting her to a few friends and assumed one was putting me on.

The voice was distinctive, soft and breathless. "Peter," she asked, "could you come for dinner next week at my apartment?"

I was taken aback. Losing my cool for a moment, I committed a faux pas. "Jackie, thank you," I said. "I will check with my wife."

Instantly, I wondered how I could be so dumb. Why did I say this, when it was clear from her tone that the invitation was for me alone? Did she know I was married? Was she asking me alone in any case? Jackie was cool when I said I had to check with my wife. I knew I would have to say no. The next day, I called and declined to a butler.

Jackie and I never spoke again. We lived close to each other in Martha's Vineyard. I would see her at the Chilmark Store or in Menemsha. On Monday mornings, she would wait with the diamond merchant Maurice Tempelsman at the small Vineyard airport. Sometimes we stood next to each other as we waited for the plane to load. I always greeted her. She never acknowledged me.

But, Jackie aside, had the foray to Washington been worth it? It had certainly broadened my understanding of the federal government, and the knowledge I acquired and the connections I made would prove valuable. Years later, Tommy Tisch remarked that I must have had a mother who loved me a lot, because I was so secure that I never wanted to return to Washington. I laughed, but the fact is that I never did return to Washington. I haven't even visited the city much in the interim. It didn't suit my personality; it was too superficial, too transient. I didn't love it then, and, thanks to the rancor that infected the government beginning in the 1990s, today I love it even less.

Fashionable Mother, natty Dad—Boca Raton Hotel, 1930s

Richard and I dressed for Collegiate School—1944

JR—Mother's father—cofounder of Stop&Shop

Grandma Rose

My bar mitzvah with David Livingston and Marty Gross

Prof. Harry Austryn Wolfson of Harvard—my freshman roommate
(Harvard University Archives)

Nixon and Khrushchev at the site of the Kitchen Debate,
Moscow, 1959, photograph taken by me

With Dad on a fishing trip in Canada

Mother and five grandchildren at 1780 house in Stamford—1975

On the outskirts of Quneitra, Syria—Yom Kippur War, 1973

Elevation at Lehman—September 30, 1976

Dan Carpenter, the Hudson Guild Neighborhood House
(Photograph from *The Villager* for a brief obituary,
volume 73, number 47, March 24–30, 2004)

Burt and Chuck August—founders of Monro
Muffler Brake and wonderful partners

As usual, listening to the mayor—City Hall Blue Room, 1979
(Photograph by Holland Wemple)

DAVID W. BROWN
DEPUTY MAYOR

May 1, 1978

Mr. Peter Solomon
Lehman Brothers Kuhn Loeb Inc.
1 William Street
New York, New York

Dear Peter:

You asked me to sketch the range of
responsibilities if you were to be Deputy Mayor.
At the time of your designation, Ed would assign
you the leading role in his administration with
respect to the following matters related to
economic development:

1. formulation of tax policy (in
conjunction with Deputy Mayor Toia)
2. formulation of energy policy
3. review of government regulatory policy
4. application of UDAG and CETA funds
5. oversight* of

*"in charge of."
per discussion with
mayor + DWB on
5/2/78.

a.	OED	d.	PDC
b.	MOD	e.	ICIB
c.	IDA	f.	BMC

6. liaison with

a. UDC
b. Port Authority
c. State and Federal Commerce Depts.
d. Mayor's Representatives.

I will be glad to discuss these matters in
detail with you.

Sincerely,

*x Plus Ports + Terminals
on Econ. Policy matters.*

David W. Brown

"Get it in writing." —Peter G. Peterson

THE CITY OF NEW YORK
OFFICE OF THE MAYOR
NEW YORK, N.Y. 10007

M E M O R A N D U M

TO: Peter Solomon

FROM: Edward I. Koch

DATE: April 4, 1979

A carless Solomon would be a Samson
without locks and unacceptable. By
the way, sleeping in the car between
stops is definitely to be commended.
I do it myself. Indeed, I can sleep
on a subway between stations and wake
up automatically. How about that!

mg

Who says City Hall isn't fun!

On the Long Island Expressway during the independent truckers'
strike, 1979 (Photograph property of Peter J. Solomon Company)

Forbidden City, Beijing—1980
(Photograph by photographer using Peter Solomon's camera)

"Always leave them laughing." Last day in City Hall.
(Photograph by Neal Boenzi)

January 19, 1981

To Peter Solomon

Thank you for your warm note. I deeply appreciate your friendship and support over the past five years. I also want to thank you for your outstanding work at the Treasury Department, particularly your development of our Industrial Revitalization Program and your Chairmanship of the Automobile Industry Task Force.

You have served our Nation well. I know that in the years ahead you will look back with pride on your accomplishments.

As you return to private life, you may be sure that you take with you my very best wishes for every future success and happiness.

Sincerely,

Jimmy Carter

The Honorable Peter J. Solomon
Counselor
Department of the Treasury
Washington, D.C. 20220

President Carter was always gracious.

PART III

CHAPTER 20

Democrats Regroup

"... I'd still be governor."
(William Jefferson Clinton, 1981)

It's unusual to hear from wives and mistresses of powerful men, so when Pamela Harriman called me in 1980, not long after I'd left the Treasury Department, I was perplexed. Pamela, then wife of former New York governor Averill Harriman, told me she was organizing a group she was calling "Democrats for the '80s," and she wanted me to work with her. Reagan and the Republicans had swept the White House and Congress. Pamela's mission was to rebuild the Democratic Party.

It would have been impossible not to know of Pamela, but I had never met her. I still don't know how she found me, but after just a few minutes on the phone with her, I knew the score: I was going to work for her and not with her. Still, I was game, and she assigned her long-term aide, Janet Howard, to work with me.

Over the next three years, we held a number of events in New York and Washington, raising money and rallying Democrats to embrace new ideas. We had mixed short-term success—witness Fritz Mondale's run for the presidency against President Reagan in 1984.

Pamela was accustomed to having her way. Once she called me in the middle of the workday and ordered me to come to Washington that next evening for a soiree. I told her that it was my wife's birthday and I had planned a dinner in New York. "Nonsense," she said. "Be at Marine Terminal at LaGuardia Airport at 5:00 p.m. Averill and I will fly you both to Washington, and we will celebrate there." I did as instructed.

On this occasion at her luxurious Georgetown home, dinner was served first for about fifty congressmen, senators, and former appointed officials. Among the participants was Richard Holbrooke. He had lived with the Harrimans for a while. My former boss at the Treasury, Bill Miller, sat with us. At one point, motivated by I don't know what, he blurted out to the assembled group that I was one of the most capable people he had ever met in government, "the very model of a public servant." I was shocked. Not only did I think that was improbable, but he had ignored me for the six months I had worked for him.

At dessert, Pamela produced a cake with the correct number of candles. Sixty Democrats sang "Happy Birthday" to Linda.

After dinner, Pamela organized a discussion on the failures of the Democratic Party. At one point, a youngish-looking guy whom I had not noticed piped up. "The problem with the Democratic Party," he said, "is that there are too many old people in it!" He was sitting directly behind Averill Harriman, who was then eighty-nine and who was slouched down in an easy chair, hopefully asleep. No such luck.

As the group collectively gasped, the governor began to turn slowly in his chair. He resembled a crocodile coming out of the river mud. He turned around toward the speaker and growled, "What did you say?"

Without missing a beat, the speaker said, "Governor, if I didn't say things as stupid as that, I would still be governor of Arkansas."

Eleven years later, when Bill Clinton became president, his wise-ass remarks and his self-deprecating humor struck me as keys to his winning personality.

Random comments can reveal much more about someone's prejudices and personality than set speeches. Reporters understand that, and that's why an important lesson for both public and private life is that one's comments are rarely off the record. The most dangerous moment in an interview is when it is over. At that time, the subject relaxes, thinking more about how they performed than what they are saying. Remember that Jimmy Carter was walking his *Playboy* interviewer to the door when he made a remark about sometimes having "looked at a lot of women with lust." When you're in the presence of the media, you shouldn't say anything that you don't want to appear in the *New York Times*.

Nineteen eighty-one was an important year in my nonbusiness life. It began by Koch asking me to become finance chairman of his reelection campaign. He was a popular mayor, and I did not anticipate difficulty in raising money. Koch and I disagreed about one matter, though. I didn't want to solicit any real estate interests since I had been head of the real estate incentive boards as deputy mayor. I also didn't think we needed the extra campaign funds. Koch had no such qualms, which surprised me—given his aversion to "richies"—but he was taking no chances.

I made a stupid decision. To save money, and for my convenience, early in the campaign, I ran the fundraising from my office at Lehman Brothers. Seeing me spend time on a political project confused my partners and, I think, made them doubt my commitment to the firm.

Koch was reelected with 75 percent of the vote. I had no interest in rejoining him in City Hall.

In March 1981, I was notified by Harvard that I would be nominated to the Board of Overseers, once known as the most exclusive men's club in the United States. All Harvard alumni vote for six of twelve nominees; thirty-six overseers serve for one term of six years. John F. Kennedy was an overseer when he was elected president. I felt I had a reasonable chance of joining the board because of my government service and because I was the only male Jewish candidate. I was a director of the Lucius N. Littauer Foundation as a result of my previously described relationship with Professor Wolfson, and had been on the Visiting Committee of the Overseers to the departments of Near Eastern Language and Literature, also because of Wolfson. Of all the committees I have served, before and since, the Visiting Committee was the one for which I was least qualified. The discussions centered around the teaching of languages such as Hittite and Assyrian. Every other member was a professor of a major university and probably spoke a minimum of four current languages and three ancient tongues. Meanwhile, I'm pretty good at French.

The electorate for overseers was traditionally liberal and seemed to vote by block. Candidates were asked to write a short personal essay. Most of their submissions seemed pompous, so I decided to highlight my experience as a beekeeper. I pointed out that nothing concentrates the mind as quickly as forty thousand angry bees.

Somewhat to my surprise, I was notified in June that I had been elected and had, in fact, finished second in the voting behind Sam Butler, a former Harvard football captain and senior partner of Cravath Swaine & Moore. Sam, at that time, succeeded John McCloy as the unofficial head of the American establishment.

For someone who had been the last person admitted to the class of 1960, being elected overseer was an astonishing turn of events. I served until 1988. Sam Butler, who was elected president of the board in 1987, became a close friend. Our backgrounds and the way we look at issues have always been different, but we have usually reached the same conclusions.

Our time as overseers, regrettably, was dominated by the issue of divestment by Harvard's endowment fund of stocks of American companies doing business in South Africa while the apartheid regime remained in power. Ridding the world of apartheid was a noble goal, but the issue was absurd. To his credit, Harvard's president Derek Bok held the line arguing that Harvard's investment strategy had to be free from such political issues. If it wasn't, he argued, next year the university would be forced to divest chemical or other stocks.

President Bok's decisiveness, however, did not put an end to the crises that rattled the campus. One incident occurred during the celebration of the University's 350th anniversary. An elaborate dinner had been arranged in Memorial Hall with some three hundred attendees. As the overseers walked together toward the building, our path was blocked by a demonstration chanting prodivestment slogans. Harvard and Bok chose not to interfere with the demonstrators, who carried on to the point that the dinner had to be cancelled. We dispersed in our formal wear, and John Loeb Jr. and I ended up eating in a seedy Thai restaurant on Mt. Auburn Street. The next day, I was sitting on the steps of Fogg Museum reading about the incident. Fox Butterfield, my old friend from Lawrenceville and Harvard—whom I had last seen with Koch in China, where he was a *New York Times* correspondent—sat down next to me. He asked about the night.

I assumed we were chatting as friends. "Fox," I said, "if Ed Koch had been in charge, he would have had them arrested."

The next morning, the *Times* printed my quote.

There is an unwritten rule that no overseer criticizes or even comments publicly on the actions of the university, no less the president. I was mortified, and when I saw Derek the next day, I apologized. As always, he was unperturbed.

About six months later, the overseers had a dinner meeting at the Kennedy School. Sure enough, another group of demonstrators tried to stop traffic and disrupt the dinner, but the Boston and Harvard police intercepted them and made some arrests. As I sat at dinner, I felt a presence behind me. "I got them this time," President Bok whispered in my ear.

At the end of my term, the time had finally come for a vote of overseers on divestment. Bishop Tutu of South Africa had been elected an overseer by write-in ballot but didn't appear. A young woman who had been elected on a write-in three years before, and whose husband was harassed in South Africa, chose to present her case. Before the meeting, she approached me and asked me to sit next to her. "Why?" I asked. "You know I think this issue is ridiculous and a total waste of time." She said she knew that but she was so nervous she thought she might choke up and become inarticulate. She said she knew I'd be making disparaging but funny remarks under my breath during her presentation and thought that might actually be helpful!

I did as she asked. She did fine. I accommodated her by making sotto voce comments, and several times she giggled. I and others admired her devotion to her cause, but the overseers overwhelmingly voted to continue the university's endowment policy.

During the course of my years on the board, the overseers and the elite Harvard Corporation seemed to move closer together. I concluded that Harvard, like the Vatican, was structured so that it was impossible to change it too rapidly, and thus was inured from the influence of a single issue or group. If I wanted to make a contribution, I should focus laser-like on one or, at most, two issues. My own specialty became the Financial Affairs Committee, which I chaired for several years. Harvard did not use replacement accounting for its buildings and its other capital stock. Depreciation is a tax concept, and, of course, for a university and a nonprofit, depreciation was irrelevant.

Based on my recommendation, Harvard instituted replacement accounting that would allow it to estimate more accurately the useful life of its buildings and plan for replacements. It would avoid the fate of Yale, which had fallen behind in modernization. I would also continue to be chairman of the Friends of the Center for Jewish Studies to help assure the success of what we had begun.

Harvard had a governing shibboleth, "every tub on its own bottom." Basically, the different graduate schools and the undergraduate Arts and Sciences operated independently under their deans. The governance probably contributed to the strength of its graduate schools, but, perhaps equally, it created a weak president. It also seemed to inhibit the coordination of schools in solving complex problems that require several disciplines.

The Harvard Corporation, composed of eight people, including the university's president, acted as a collective chief executive group. It was self-perpetuating, having been established by the Massachusetts legislature in 1626. The overseers were merely advisory. Traditionally, the Corporation met frequently and in person. Thus, it was composed principally of Yankee men who lived in New England and were intimately familiar with the daily workings of the sprawling university. By the 1980s, though, the university was becoming more diverse in terms of gender and geography, and the Corporation was less representative, less relevant, and therefore less helpful to the president. It was clear that Harvard needed to change its governing structure and attitude toward the "tubs."

An event occurred that may have been irrelevant to the need for change but that nevertheless intensified the discussions. In October

1987, the stock market plunged. The decline did not seem to be related solely to economic conditions. It looked like the market had been manipulated.

At the time, the Harvard Management Company supervised the university's endowment of $5 billion. The university's sophistication had made it one of the early forerunners of hedge funds, and, as an alternative investor, it had increased its use of derivatives. A number of business writers, such as Harvard graduate Bob Lenzner, had begun to publicly question the endowment's risk profile.

At a cocktail party attended by the overseers at Harvard Medical School in 1985, I asked Derek Bok how he would feel if the endowment fell 20 percent. I didn't mean in a day but in a year. Linda, observing us from across the room, asked me later what I had said to Derek, because he had suddenly turned ashen.

Almost immediately after the October crash, rumors spread that Harvard's endowment, along with a few institutional investors, had caused the plunge by use of derivatives to "insure" their profits. The Bush administration commissioned a report under the aegis of former secretary of the Treasury Nick Brady. The report, written by Harvard Business School Professor Bob Glauber, confirmed that Harvard's actions had contributed to the crash.

For years, the Harvard authorities resisted change. Whenever the issue of broadening the corporation or giving the overseers more authority was raised, they said it would be impossible without action by the commonwealth's legislature, which Harvard prudently did not want to approach. Those same authorities noted that a vote of the Massachusetts electorate might also be required before the Harvard Corporation could be revamped.

Then one day in 2010, Harvard wrote to the alumni that it planned to expand the membership of the corporation from eight to thirteen. A new, more representative university government was at hand, and with no action by the commonwealth's legislature. My guess is Harvard had finally found a better lawyer.

Ed Koch never wanted to run for governor of New York State, but in 1982, he did anyway. He had been coaxed into the race by Rupert

Murdoch, with whom he had become close. Koch's relationship with the publisher of the *New York Post* was based on policy and commerce. Rupert appreciated the mayor's tough stand on crime and the death penalty, the issue that had allowed this unknown liberal congressman to become mayor. But commerce was equally important to him. The *Post* was having trouble attracting advertising from department stores. Rupert would invite the mayor to lunch with retail executives such as Marvin Traub, CEO of Bloomingdale's. I don't think it helped the *Post* much, but it did bolster Rupert's support of the mayor. We had similar lunches with Malcolm Forbes at his townhouse. Koch always performed to the host's delight.

Koch asked me if I would be finance chair of his campaign along with John Zuccotti. I knew John and respected him; he had been Abe Beame's first deputy mayor. He was, at the time, the chair of the real estate firm Olympia & York, owned by the Canadian Reichman brothers. John's history was a classic New York story. His father had been the maître d' at El Morocco, the famous nightclub.

I wasn't interested in being the mayor's finance chair. I had just finished the 1981 mayoral election, and, while raising money had been easy, I'd had enough. I had no intention of being viewed as a professional bag man. My interest was in policy, not politics, and any further involvement would be used against me by my enemies at Lehman.

It can be hard to say no to Ed Koch, though. He was insistent that Zuccotti—who felt the same way as I did but for his own reasons—and I remain as his chief fundraisers. Then we got lucky. At our first meeting at City Hall in the mayor's office, Koch told us that David Garth, his political guru, wanted a protégé of his, Ken Lipper, to be a co-chair. Before we could respond, the door flew open, and in bounced Lipper. With the chutzpah that had characterized his career as an investment banker, Lipper plopped himself on the couch between John and me.

We might have been put off, but, in fact, we were much relieved. From that moment on, Lipper attached himself to the mayor's side as they toured the state.

The primary was a disaster for Koch. Although the experts considered him an overwhelming favorite against Lt. Governor Mario Cuomo, Koch lost by about 3 percent or fewer than sixty thousand votes. A *Playboy* interview, in which Koch demeaned upstate residents and talked idiotically about calico dresses, showed his real feelings about the world beyond the New York City limits. But Koch was a superb politician and communicator; he didn't make those statements accidentally. He was, either consciously or not, challenging the citizens to elect him. He didn't want to leave the mayoralty. After a tumultuous term, and having righted the finances of the city, *his* city, and now in the midst of a renaissance, Koch, in his heart, wanted to stay where he was.

While Koch may have been throwing the election, his campaign staff was not. When Donald Trump upset Hillary in 2016, I could empathize with Hillary's staffers, who had virtually measured the offices in the West Wing of the White House.

What a shock loss is for those who bind themselves to a candidate—no less a presidential campaign—for a lifetime, then find themselves topsy-turvy. Instead of moving to Washington or Albany, they are forced to reassess their lives and find new work. At least, at the end of the primary, most of Koch's campaign staff returned to their consulting businesses or City Hall or, in my case, Lehman Brothers.

CHAPTER 21

Choices: Lehman Redux—1981

At a "Democrats for the '80s" reception hosted by Pamela Harriman at the Four Seasons restaurant in New York City in 1982, I happened to notice a sign of apprehension in the eyes of some guests I was greeting. Before I could turn around, I was in the grasp of a strong man hugging me roughly. He whispered in my ear, "Aren't you embarrassed being back in the private sector earning money instead of in the public sector helping us?"

Still in his grasp but no longer struggling, I said, "Could this be the governor of the Empire State?"

It was, but Mario Cuomo was probably not kidding. He had an aversion to rich people. He was a class warrior who, it is said, never got over not being offered a prestigious Wall Street job when he graduated from St. John's Law School. We had a cordial relationship. I was a member of his economic advisory committee, even though I was the co-chair of Ed Koch's failed primary campaign for governor against him. The governor's admonishment was not so off base.

When I returned to New York after the Treasury Department, I was at a crossroads, uncertain about career choices. And why not? The world was shaky at that time. In December 1980, the stock market was still in a seven-year drift, inflation was 12.5 percent, interest rates were soaring to 21.5 percent, the Iran hostage crisis was unresolved, and, as if to underscore bathos, John Lennon was assassinated in front of the Dakota.

I was not a wealthy man; my biggest bonus ever at Lehman had been $225,000. For the previous two years, I had been paid $57,500 as a government employee. A bellwether of values, my apartment, for which I'd paid $157,500 in 1970, was in 1980 probably worth about $125,000. And my Lehman partnership value when I left was six figures. I had a wife and three children in private schools. I wasn't complaining, but the 1970s had been a shock, and I wasn't secure.

At age forty-three, I pondered my options. I liked public service and could find an opportunity. But one lesson I had learned well was only elected officials matter and only they create policy. Otherwise, you operate in the shadow of the elected official and at his or her sole discretion. I could run for elected office, eventually even mayor of New York City. I had a good reputation, and I thought Koch would support me as long as I didn't run against him.

Of course, the opposite direction, the private sector, beckoned. The leveraged buyout business showed promise in 1980. I'd discussed the opportunities extensively with Dan Lufkin. Or I could return to investment banking, either at Lehman or a different firm. Salomon Brothers had once again approached me. I thought of leaving Wall Street and going into the media business. My banking experience could be transferred to building a media company.

There was a middle path. David Rockefeller had asked me to become CEO of the then new Partnership for New York City, a group of leading CEOs who worked for the economic benefit of the five boroughs.

Or I could do nothing at all for a while. In retrospect, it might have been the best choice, to take a deep breath and then explore the landscape more broadly. It is one of the few decisions I regret: namely, not taking three to six months off to consider options. In the last thirty-five years, it is advice I have given many times. When at a crossroads, take your time, look around, meet with people of different backgrounds, and, most of all, have confidence in yourself. Taking time allows you to think carefully about your values and your priorities.

Instead, I wound up back at Lehman Brothers. How did that happen?

First, I was worried about my future. For today's readers, it may be difficult to envision what the end of the 1970s felt like. I have tried to give a sense of all the trauma of the decade. Ronald Reagan spoke of the light at the end of the tunnel. To many, the light seemed to come from a locomotive heading toward us.

Second, I knew I could succeed at Lehman. I had clients and was confident in getting more. I discussed with Pete my desire to spend more time buying companies and even proposed a joint venture in which I would justify my partnership by advisory fees but primarily invest. Pete said he wanted the firm to do more investing, and I could do investing within Lehman. He had even appointed former Abraham & Co. senior partner George Heyman to direct investing.

Third, while I was in government, Pete had been diagnosed with a brain tumor, which, fortunately, turned out to be benign. He told me it had made him realize more about human relations, and it would affect his behavior favorably. I also convinced myself that the departures of Glanville, Woods, and McGregor would make the firm more secure.

Fourth, I chose to minimize the off-putting way Lehman asked me to return, which began with a call from Bob Rubin around Christmas 1980. Rubin was someone I thought I understood. In the three years I was working in government, however, I didn't realize Rubin had undergone a metamorphosis, transforming himself from an honest broker—a guy whom everyone respected—to Lew Glucksman's consigliere. As we discussed my return, he changed the terms that Pete Peterson and I had discussed before I went to the Treasury, offering me 10 percent fewer shares in the firm. "Wait a minute, Bob," I immediately said. "What's with this?"

"What can I tell you?" he said. "I guess that's what we think you're worth." As soon as I hung up, I called Peterson.

"What's going on, Pete?" I asked. "This is not the arrangement we discussed earlier this year."

"Well, Peter, you took a job in Washington that was less than we would've expected you to take."

He didn't explain further. What he meant was that if I had been named undersecretary of the Treasury instead of a mere counselor to the secretary, Lehman would have held to the original deal. Pete, even after seven years, retained his Washington status fixation.

I lunched at the India House in Hanover Square with Bill Morris, my contemporary at Lehman. Toward the end of our curry meal, for which the India House was famous, Morris said matter-of-factly, "Well, I really don't want you to come back to the firm, but I guess you'll do a lot of business, so it's better having you there than at Salomon Brothers."

Whatever my rationale, I ignored the warning signs. I made a major miscalculation in returning to Lehman Brothers.

I resumed my career at Number One William Street in January 1981. Helen Burlew once again became my faithful secretary.

With one exception, clients gave me a warm welcome back. I returned to the boards of Miller Wohl Company and Associated Dry Goods. Associated had acquired Caldor's, a competitor of Bradlees, owned by Stop&Shop, so I could not join both boards. Sidney Rabb told me to rejoin Associated. He assured me that I would always have Stop&Shop's business.

Within months, I realized that Pete's relationship with his partners had improved but marginally. They respected him more. He had brought in business and was widely respected by business leaders. There was little warmth, however, even without Glanville. Glucksman had neither mellowed nor lost his insatiable need for recognition and power. Despite my efforts to develop a cordial relationship—in an ultimate gesture, I gave him smoked salmon I had caught on the Restigouche River—he remained an adversary. By my return, he was using Rubin to build a corporate finance group more loyal to him than to Pete.

Meanwhile, my personal banking business flourished. My media efforts were rewarding. We represented the Outlet Company in its expansion into additional television markets, and Stanley Hubbard retained us to finance his satellite television initiative, later Direct TV. Oddly, my sole setback was at LIN Broadcasting. Donald Pels, chairman of LIN, did not ask me to return to its board. I had recruited Pels as LIN's CEO in 1969, and we socialized in Martha's Vineyard and New York City. But Pels harbored resentment and disrespect for me and my LIN partner Tom Unterberg. Pels reinforced these feelings with his actions. He chose Wasserstein Perella to sell LIN in 1986 and included neither Lehman nor Tom. Pels' actions remain a notable unpleasant chapter.

In the early 1980s, retail was undergoing seismic changes. The major chains, such as Federated, Macy's, Allied Stores, and Associated Dry Goods, and the former mail order retailers, such as Sears and Montgomery Ward, had been losing market share for thirty years. One cause was the widespread availability of credit to consumers because of the increasing use of credit cards. My father remarked as early as the late 1950s that one of department stores' most important competitive weapons was the extension of credit. Credit cards issued by independent finance companies gave shoppers the ability to consume in any store.

Credit cards and the expansion of regional shopping centers spawned specialty chains, such as The Limited and Petrie Stores, and tens of shoe chains, such as Bakers and Melville. As the decades went by, specialty chains got more hubris. Nine West, a popular shoe brand, opened its first store next to the entrance of Macy's, its largest customer, in the Stamford Town Mall.

Discount stores became serious competitors. Korvette's, run by Eugene Ferkauf, whom my father had admired, opened across the street from A&S on Fulton Street in Brooklyn in 1947. Korvette's challenged the "fair trade" practice, where manufacturers set retail prices. My father immediately understood the implications and challenged Korvette's on toys at Christmas in 1950. A price war was so unusual that *Life* magazine featured it.

Korvette's advanced beyond New York City and survived for a few decades. Other chains, such as White Front Stores on the West Coast, grew. In the Midwest, the Dayton Company founded Target. Caldor's and Bradlees were building in the mid-Atlantic, and Sam Walton opened his first Walmart in Arkansas in 1973.

By the late 1970s, off-price retailers, such as Marshalls, T.J.Maxx, Dress Barn, and Burlington Coat Factory, were absorbing excess inventories and offering consumers cheaper prices than department stores'. Lehman had an opportunity to underwrite Burlington Coat, but I was worried about its accounting. I thought the fact that it never took markdowns could result in an accounting disaster due to overvalued inventory. In theory, I was right about the potential for an accounting crisis but wrong about the timing. Thirty-five years later, the company has gone public, been bought in an LBO, and gone public again.

I was more accurate about Dress Barn, a Stamford, Connecticut–based retailer started by Elliot Jaffe. Bill Arnold, CEO of Associated Dry Goods, was interested in acquiring the company but didn't pursue it to conclusion. He introduced me to Elliot. In 1983, we underwrote the initial public offering of Dress Barn, which continues under his son David's leadership.

David Farrell, CEO of the May Company, felt the pressure on his department stores. The May Company was a distant third to Federated as a national chain. Although it had strong stores in Los Angeles, Denver, and Cleveland, it had no presence in New York. Like other department store chains, it had attempted to diversify. Farrell bought Volume Shoe, a discount chain, and started Venture Stores, a general merchandise discount chain.

Farrell knew he had to get bigger. His first objective was to acquire Allied Stores, the owner of seven department store chains with 190 stores. Two of the better-known Allied chains were the Boston-based Jordan Marsh Company, which was also the leading chain in southern Florida, and Stern's in New York. Allied was run by a tough-talking former Columbia University basketball star, Tom Macioce. Macioce also understood the need to get bigger. He had acquired three chains— Garfinckel's, Brooks Brothers, and Miller & Roades—in 1981, after buying the women's specialty chain Ann Taylor. Macioce had a lot of bluster and not much knowledge of merchandising. Like a number of his contemporary CEOs in the department store business, he was a finance person.

Stern's had a long lease on a store in one of New York City's worst crime areas: Jamaica, Queens. As deputy mayor, I had committed the city to revitalizing what had once been one of the borough's principal shopping areas. Now, as a Lehman banker, I arranged a meeting at Macioce's request with Queens borough president Donald Manes in Macioce's office. Manes outlined for Macioce the steps that he and the city were willing to take to keep Stern's open in Jamaica. Before Manes could catch his breath, Macioce launched into a diatribe against the city and Queens in particular. It was the type of performance—embarrassing and self-destructive—that occurs all too frequently when business leaders meet politicians. Manes left the office vowing never to help Stern's or any other entity affiliated with Macioce.

A second mistake led to the demise of Allied, which I will discuss in more detail later. An analysis of Allied's bylaws clearly indicated that the company had few defenses against a greenmailing shareholder or a hostile takeover. By the mid-1980s, the hostile takeover, a technique of acquiring a target company, was still frowned upon by polite society but was not uncommon.

At Lehman, we had the usual merger-defense practice where we analyzed a company's bylaws and other charter provisions and advised management on how to protect itself. A key defense tactic was to erect hurdles against aggressive tactics. The law, as it evolved, forbade such barriers, but law firms, such as Skadden Arps under Joe Flom's astute leadership, and Wachtell Lipton, driven by Marty Lipton's fertile mind, were developing intricate legal defenses.

Our firm had extensive conversations with Macioce about Allied's vulnerability. Despite our urgings, he refused to adopt the simplest defensive tactics. His refusal did not appear to be rooted in an ethical standard. He just thought of himself as a tough guy who would defeat any adversary. The position was consistent with his personality, but it was not good judgment. His intransigence eventually cost him Allied Stores.

David Farrell pursued Tom Macioce to the point where he would attend charitable events in New York where Macioce was being honored. Nothing came of that romance. Macioce would not sell to anyone, but particularly not to David Farrell, whom he did not like.

About the same time in 1983, Ed Finkelstein, the CEO of Macy's, approached me about merging with Associated Dry Goods. Finkelstein realized that Macy's strength resided in managing large department stores, something Federated had also concluded about itself after a number of missteps in discounting and smaller stores. ADG was a high-end chain including Lord & Taylor in New York City, L. S. Ayres in Indiana, Six Baer and Fuller in St. Louis, and Robinson's in Los Angeles. It was a quality business, much more upscale than Macy's but not particularly well run. Lew Seiler had been the CEO when I had replaced Joe Thomas on the board. The board was old-shoe Princeton; few directors had ever been in a department store of any sort, no less one owned by ADG.

Dick Pivirotto had become chairman, and Bill Arnold, president. Arnold had become frustrated by Pivirotto and organized a coup to replace Dick as CEO, but Dick stayed on the board. Bill Arnold and I became close, which negatively affected my relationship with Dick.

Both Finkelstein and Arnold trusted me. I was on ADG's board but had represented Macy's for years. As a result, I conducted both sides of the negotiations. Over the next few months, we worked out the financial terms. The difficult issue was the prospective roles of ADG principals—particularly Red Largay, whom Arnold had installed as president but whom Bill knew would never succeed him as CEO.

During this period, Arnold's health began to deteriorate. He had been diagnosed with stomach cancer, but it seemed to have stabilized, and the merger discussions were not motivated by his illness. Nevertheless, the illness made it more difficult for Arnold to concentrate and do his job. Eventually, however, we did solve all the issues, with Largay getting a senior management position running the combined Midwestern division.

Finkelstein and Arnold arranged a final meeting on a Sunday in Greenwich, Connecticut, at Arnold's home. I did not insist on attending, which turned out to be a fatal mistake for the merger. I waited for word from Arnold. No call came on Sunday. I went to bed concerned.

Early Monday morning, I called Arnold. In a plaintive voice, he told me he just couldn't do it; he had neither the physical energy nor the emotional commitment to have the discussions with his management and to undertake all the tasks necessary for a CEO to complete a merger successfully. I was deflated but understood what he was saying. My friend Bill Arnold was dying. Any deal would have to come later.

Bill Arnold died less than a year later, in September 1984, at age fifty-nine.

In 1983, three of the major department store retailers—May, Macy's, and Associated Dry Goods—had all known they had to do something strategic, but none had succeeded. The problem, hopefully, was not that they had an incompetent investment banker. Rather, it was that the companies had been independent and competitive for so many years that they couldn't make the necessary break. This lack of success was to have dramatic effect on the retail industry.

One of the lessons I learned from the experience with Bill Arnold is that health affects the ability to make important decisions. Bad health saps concentration as well as energy. That critical moment when one must make and execute a decision becomes more momentous and intimidating when coping with the debilitating effects of disease and the loss of confidence in having the will to execute.

CHAPTER 22

"Greed and Glory"

The political infighting at Lehman was more vicious and irrational than I anticipated. And it's not as if that was the price the firm had to pay for being blessed with a world-class brain trust.

Ken Auletta, in his excellent book on Lehman, *Greed and Glory: The Fall of the House of Lehman*, details most of the internal strife from 1982 to 1984, when, because of the failure of the principals to get along, the firm had to be sold at a bargain price to Shearson. There is no need for me to reiterate all the details of Auletta's narrative here, but my perspective as a primary participant in this epic battle might add to his account and to the history of the Street. I should say up front that I didn't cooperate with Ken until the end of his research. After he had his initial coffee at the Candy Kitchen with Pete Peterson in Bridgehampton, he called me, related in outline form what Pete had told him, and asked if I would help. I immediately said no. When I was at City Hall, Ken had never bothered to cultivate me or treat what I did seriously. But the other reason I withheld my full cooperation was that I knew the real story of what happened was so irrational, and our partners had acted so badly, that Ken's book was bound to hurt the firm's reputation.

September 30, 1982, Lehman's fiscal year-end, marked the beginning of the fall. The most intense time in an investment bank is the period up to and just after the end of its fiscal year. Since partners are paid a nominal draw during the year, bonus payments are the largest part of compensation. Generally, bonuses are tied to production of revenues, management responsibilities, partnership ownership, and seniority. In practice, despite such guidelines, there is also the part that is discretionary because the managing group likes or dislikes a partner. In well-managed firms such as Goldman Sachs, the discretionary portion of the bonus is minimized. Lehman was not a well-managed firm.

Traditionally, the division head decides how the profits will be distributed in terms of bonuses and the reallocation of stock. In September, Glucksman, who had become president of the firm just a few months earlier, approached Peterson with a radical plan so politically motivated and reflective of his self-destructive personality that it would trigger an avalanche of distrust.

Rather than consolidating power and acting as if he cared about the opinions of the four members of the executive committee, Glucksman attacked them. He proposed that the stock ownership as well as bonuses for Morris, Krueger, Istel, and me be reduced materially. This was surprising for any number of reasons. Krueger had been president and CEO of Kuhn, Loeb and had merged his firm only five years before. Neither he nor Morris favored Pete, and they were nominally Glucksman's allies. Yves Istel was a nonpolitical respected banker with an international reputation. I, of course, had rejoined the firm just two years earlier and had a smaller number of shares than the firm offered me before I went to the Treasury.

In *Greed and Glory*, Auletta reports a conversation that neither Pete nor I remember. He writes that Pete told me not to fight with Glucksman over a reduced bonus of $250,000. "I'll make it up to you," Pete supposedly said. To appease Glucksman, Pete cut his own bonus so that it was below Glucksman's and said he would arrange for my bonus and the others' to be restored to more reasonable levels. To satisfy Glucksman, however, he eviscerated the executive committee by combining it with the larger board of directors on which younger and financially less secure partners sat.

During the course of bonus discussions, Glucksman and Pete decided to pay Steve Schwarzman $25,000 more than Eric Gleacher, the more senior merger banker. Schwarzman, one of the most ambitious bankers I had ever met, was nipping at Gleacher's heels. I said that if Gleacher found out, he would be so insulted he would leave the firm. Glucksman and the others scoffed at me. Glucksman said, "No one quits over $25,000." I bet Pete a dinner at Lutece, New York City's best and most expensive restaurant, that Eric would, in fact, quit if he found out about this slight. (Pete bought dinner in 1984.)

As Thomas Hardy noted, coincidence often plays a decisive role in one's life choices. By chance, a day or two after this meeting, I was in my office on the fifth floor. I just happened to have the bonus sheet on my desk. Not expecting anyone in my office, I was on the phone with my back turned to the door. As I got off the phone, Eric Gleacher had entered my office and, like a good Lehman banker, was reading everything on my desk. Including the bonus schedule. He asked me point-blank what had happened and whether he was reading the documents correctly. Was Schwarzman really getting $25,000 more than he was? I replied simply in the affirmative. He asked me about my own bonus, and I told him the saga about me, Morris, and Krueger. As he left the office, I could sense he had just made the same decision I had made about leaving the firm. But Eric was going to do it immediately. Within a month, he became a partner at Morgan Stanley.

If only we applied the lessons we learned in school to our lives. The futility of appeasement was an enduring lesson for those of us who grew up in the 1940s and were schooled in the 1950s. The pathetic image of Neville Chamberlain returning from Munich, and the horrors of celebrities and diplomats browbeaten by a crazed Joe McCarthy in the first television spectacular were drilled into our psyches. Apparently, though, those examples were lost on Pete. He could have stopped Glucksman in September 1982. At the moment that he demanded higher comp than Pete and attacked Pete's executive committee, why did Pete appease him?

After years of discussions with Pete, I now understand why the mad president of Lehman was allowed to bully the distinguished chairman and CEO. It had to do with Pete's frame of mind. By 1982, Pete had had enough. He was thinking about retiring from Lehman. While he and his wife, Joan Ganz Cooney, hadn't set a date for his departure, he was tired of running an investment bank, fed up with the bickering, and not comfortable as CEO of a firm increasingly dependent on trading, which he didn't really understand, and Glucksman, whom he did not trust. In reality, of course, Pete didn't retire after he was forced out. He cofounded one of the twenty-first century's major financial institutions, the Blackstone Group. But these factors made him flee rather than fight.

Why couldn't Glucksman stop? Glucksman was a person whose own inferiority complex created a fever within him that could not be contained. He seethed—his shirt drenched in sweat, his clothes in disarray. He didn't as much talk as spew words. He was a bully who would not be stopped in any situation without a direct confrontation.

Within days of proposing to Pete that he take shares from me and others for himself and his acolytes, Glucksman called me. "Come see me," he said, without any preface. "You know what it is about." In fact, I didn't know because I was as yet unaware of his plans. I entered his small study with pictures of his fishing boat and saltwater fish with a fisherman's gaff on the walls. I sat across from him. There was no attempt at small talk, "Peter," he said, "we are going to take some of your shares from you."

I moved to the edge of my chair, leaned over the small table, and shoved my finger into his chest. "Fat man," I said, "if you take one share from me, you better be prepared to take them all!" With that, I left the office. He never raised the subject again, nor took the shares.

Meanwhile, Pete continued to cater to Glucksman. In the spring of 1983, Pete proposed that Glucksman become co–chief executive officer. Trading was becoming more important. More Lehman employees were now under Glucksman's aegis than Pete's. Lehman had enjoyed a profitable year.

Pete came to my office on the fifth floor, something he had never done before. He told me all the reasons Glucksman deserved to be co-CEO. I told him I understood but reminded him that Glucksman had almost bankrupted the firm in 1973 and had lied to the partnership at that time. I also reminded him that Glucksman was trying to demean and disenfranchise many bankers, including me. Nevertheless, I told Pete that I would not oppose his elevation. Even I, who knew what a rat Glucksman was and had criticized Pete for his policy of appeasement, misguidedly hoped that maybe the recognition would alleviate his anger and anxiety. Once again, I made a mistake.

Beyond his unquenchable need to attack anyone who could be a threat, Glucksman may have been driven by the reality that the structure of the Lehman partnership was certain to change and his ascent might be stopped by events beyond his control. It was clear as early as 1982 that the growth of trading could not be supported by the narrow capital base of Lehman Brothers. The capital problem was exacerbated by the death of Bobbie, the retirement of many senior partners, and the vicissitudes of trading and banking revenues. After Salomon had become a public company, I strenuously advocated for Lehman to consider going public.

Pete seemed to have some difficulties with the advantages of public ownership, but Glucksman grasped it immediately. He knew that his divisions needed capital to compete, that the only way to get sufficient capital was to go public, and that under public ownership, Pete was the ideal chairman. Glucksman knew he would never be the public face of Lehman. In my view, his recognition of this fact propelled his audacious final confrontation with Pete three months after Pete had elevated him. He demanded that Pete appoint him sole CEO, then leave Lehman.

It was a scant three months later, in July 1983, when Glucksman pushed Pete out of the firm. Peterson mishandled his response. Instead of going to the partnership with his case and telling Glucksman to fuck himself, Pete tried to deal rationally with the situation. This couldn't be done. Glucksman wasn't a rational person.

I have already noted Pete's appeasement, but when Pete resigned abruptly and without consultation with his partners, he was like Lord Jim, from Joseph Conrad's novel of the same name. He abandoned his partners and left them afloat but unprotected. As I am quoted as saying in Ken's book, "Attila the Hun had arrived."

Why did the partners of Lehman allow this takeover? For several reasons. They feared Glucksman's eagerness to avenge slights. He had, after all, humiliated Pete, his patron. If these younger partners stood up to him, and he forced them out of Lehman, what would they do? The partners were not confident of their own abilities. One of the curious facts about the "'masters of the universe" is that many of them are not sure they can do as well beyond the settings in which they found their initial success.

The partners also had scant loyalty to Peterson. He had cultivated younger associates such as Steve Schwarzman, but he rarely developed personal relationships with the forty-five- to fifty-five-year-old partners who were the heart of the firm. Harvey Krueger, for example, who should have been an ally of Pete's and could have stopped Glucksman dead in his tracks, was instead at the time a supporter of Glucksman's.

The board meeting on July 26, 1983, was a fateful occasion and probably the worst three hours of my career. I was not aware of the behind-the-scenes confrontation, nor that Peterson had already agreed to depart in exchange for a payment. He would not be defending his position or the partnership. He was, in effect, selling our firm to Glucksman, a man he knew was mentally unsound.

I have always faulted myself for not being more alert, more sensitive to the impending crisis. If I had been, I would have lobbied the partners, made things public, and rallied an opposition.

At the board meeting, Glucksman acted as if his ascension and Pete's departure were faits accomplis. All fourteen of the other board members went along. It was a coup—a takeover of our firm without our consent, a deal done between two people, neither of whom were the legitimate heirs to Robert Lehman. I had to try to stop it in any way I could.

My plan was to keep Peterson in place until I could work on other partners such as Krueger and Gordon. Those two were the keys to my strategy. While Harvey supported Glucksman, he was an institutional person. He was a lawyer and rose to be the head and unifying force at Kuhn, Loeb. Seven years earlier, he and I had started the process that resulted in the merger of KL and Lehman. With time, I believed I could persuade Harvey to stand up to Glucksman. Shel Gordon, meanwhile, was less known to me at the time and was viewed as Glucksman's man, but he and I shared a Boston and Harvard connection. I felt that I could reason with Shel. Gordon and Krueger were weak links in the chain of Lehman partners, but I had no other choices.

My other tactic was to use my government experience and acknowledged press relations savvy to warn the partners of the damage to our firm that would result from the sudden and not easily explained removal of Peterson. After all, we had been through the bad publicity that followed the firing of Ehrman ten years earlier, as well as other negative articles on the firm during the past decade; would we want to be back in the news with another story about turmoil and backstabbing?

I made progress on this aspect during the board meeting. I said that Glucksman replacing Peterson was so inexplicable that the press would keep coming back at the story like a wave crashing upon the beach until they learned the truth and it destroyed the reputation of our firm. While my language was dramatic in the extreme, it seemed to intimidate the partners. Although I'd been caught off guard by the developments, I was on the verge of stopping the Glucksman express. Then the partners asked George Ball to come into the meeting and opine on my charge about the press.

George, who, unbeknownst to me, had been negotiating for Pete, apparently wanted to throw in the towel. Pompous and white-haired, with a perfect State Department demeanor, he assured the group that the firm had nothing to worry about from a public relations perspective. This would be a one-day story, he said.

Did George believe this or was he just trying to get Pete as good a deal as he could and not prolong the agony? I never found out. George ended my case. When he finished speaking, I was defeated.

I have mentioned the importance of Bob Rubin. Without Rubin's support, Glucksman could not have gone as far as he did within the firm. Bob Rubin was a middle-class kid from Boston who went to Yale and then HBS. After a tour in the army in Oklahoma, he came to Lehman and distinguished himself by his excellent analytical abilities. He was the youngest of a group of senior associates I described earlier, who functioned as noncommissioned officers and who never attained partnership in the Bobbie Lehman era. In fact, only Rubin ever did, and only in the late 1960s.

When I came to Lehman, we became close, largely through his previously mentioned cousin Bunny Solomon, the government relations person at Stop&Shop, who was close to my uncle Sydney, the CEO of SHP. Auletta repeats statements from partners that Rubin grew to hate me because of comments about Bunny and his work for my family, but these aren't credible. Bunny remained close to me until his death, and Bob and I would talk about him fondly. In fact, it was the one area of civility between us.

His problems with me arose from something else. To this day, I do not know what. There was irony in Bob becoming such an ally and advocate of Glucksman. The partners had put him beside Glucksman after the 1973 debacle to watch over him and keep him honest. It was the same role that Arthur Schulte had been given but was found unable to execute. Bob became Glucksman's face to the firm. He may have gone over to Glucksman's side because he sensed that Peterson did not value him. Pete was, after all, a salesman, and Bob was not. Pete was not a financier, and Bob was a skilled analyst. They were different types of men, with different priorities. I could understand Bob's antipathy toward Pete, but I've never understood his antipathy toward me. I would occasionally ask Warren Hellman why he thought Bob turned on me, and he had no answer either.[3]

The year 1983, despite the internal turmoil, was a profitable period; my own business continued to be good, and the firm earned $27 million, up $7 million from the previous year. But bonus discussions promised to be contentious. My expectation was a bonus of $500,000. Glucksman proposed a bonus of $375,000. He dropped Morris's and Krueger's

---

[3] By a bizarre coincidence, Bob Rubin and Pete Peterson died with two days of each other in March 2018. Both men made major contributions to society after Lehman Brothers. While Pete's accomplishments were known internationally, Rubin became one of Brooklyn's most important civic leaders as a founder of St. Ann's School and chairman of the Brooklyn Museum. It was a pity that they never reconciled.

bonuses below mine and reduced their shares by five hundred each, leaving my shares as they were.

For the first time, Krueger and Morris, in separate meetings, joined me in telling Glucksman our bonuses were unsatisfactory. They stood on their hind legs, and Glucksman finally folded. He withdrew the stock reduction proposal and raised their proposed bonuses from $300,000 to $400,000. He also raised my bonus to $400,000. I characterized the extra $25,000 as a pourboire, or a tip. Meanwhile, Glucksman raised his protégé Dick Fuld's stock and Shel Gordon's ownership above mine. At that moment, I knew the end was near for me at the firm.

In the fall of 1983, two revelations augmented the worries about Glucksman's judgment. We learned in the bonus discussions that Glucksman and Rubin had signed a deal between themselves that set a formula for their relative compensation. Although Rubin was already known to have abandoned his original mission and gone over to Glucksman's side, this Lehman version of World War II's Molotov-Ribbentrop Pact stunned even Rubin's supporters.

The second incident happened when Glucksman asked Fuld to make a presentation to the board of directors on the equity and fixed income divisions' strategies. In doing so, however, Dick revealed that he had no idea how these divisions, which were just then beginning to lose money, would ever be profitable in the future. Fuld's floundering and clear inadequacy shook the partners.

Meanwhile, Glucksman once again showed an awkward sense of timing. Faced with losing money, with Gleacher and other partners leaving and taking their capital with them, and questions about his principal lieutenant, Fuld, Glucksman proposed lengthening the payout period of partners. A myth of a partnership is that one can withdraw his or her capital at any time. Obviously, if all partners withdrew capital at the same time, an investment bank would go out of business; it could not meet the capital requirements stipulated by the government's regulatory bodies. Lehman had faced this issue in the early 1970s after Bobbie's death and Glucksman's losses. It had raised preferred capital from two European banks, but the firm's trading had grown, and its capital base was barely adequate. It was for this reason that I had proposed that the firm consider public ownership.

Glucksman was not wrong about extending the partners' capital, but he proposed it at the worst moment, when suspicions about his motives were greatest and when his support was again in decline. Clearly, he was a self-destructive human being who had no strategy other than to keep hurling himself at issues until someone stopped him cold.

By December 1983, Lehman Brothers' equity capital had declined to $150 million, a reduction of $26 million in two months. The board, which Glucksman had worked so hard to pack with his loyalists, turned against him. As much as they had feared his vengefulness, they now were more afraid of losing all their capital through defections and bad investments. They decided to sell the firm.

The period from Christmas 1983 to the eventual sale in May 1984 was dreadful. Ironically, the board insisted that I be on the sale committee because after several years of ignoring and deriding me, they concluded that I was independent of Rubin and Glucksman. During this interval, Glucksman actually handled himself well. He apologized to me a number of times, not only for his behavior toward me but especially for Rubin's, which had become increasingly harsh. Glucksman couldn't understand how Krueger, Gordon, and I had formed an alliance. As Auletta notes, Glucksman said, "The only thing Krueger and Solomon had in common is that they were both members of Our Crowd." It was a perfect Glucksman statement: so ignorant, so paranoid. Krueger and I had a lot of things in common, and one of them was that neither of us was part of Our Crowd. I was a Russian Jew who, as a kid, was never invited to the Our Crowd German Jewish parties, and Harvey was a New Jersey boy who came from modest means.

In 1984, Lehman Brothers began to lose money rapidly. Owing to the inability of Glucksman and Fuld to outsmart falling markets, our attempts to sell the business were not going well. Political instability and modest profits scared off the firms and investors who would later wish they had bought Lehman. Remarkably, Glucksman and I worked well together. I didn't insist at being at any meetings I wasn't initially invited to. When we were together, I was respectful.

In the early spring, there was a mention in *Fortune* magazine that the firm was for sale due in part to internal strife. As always, my detractors blamed me for the leak, but I was skiing in Aspen and was as surprised by the item as anyone else. In any case, for me to leak this news would have been exceedingly dumb. Why would I want to hurt my chances of getting someone to buy me out of a firm I was going to leave if all else failed?

The outcome is well known and well documented. Steve Schwarzman provoked Peter Cohen of Shearson, then a subsidiary of American Express, into buying Lehman Brothers for about $300 million. It was one of the great purchases in history, and Peter, for all his later gaffes, should be congratulated on a brilliant and perceptive move. Shearson, though not one of the exalted names, acquired one of the great brands in the history of the securities industry.

My emotions about the sale were decidedly mixed. I had returned to Lehman because, for all its faults, it felt comfortable. Because of my experience, because I was one of the few people with ties to the era of Bobbie Lehman, and because I was a good business generator, I felt that one day I would run the firm. I felt let down: with the sale, Lehman became something fundamentally different. It felt like four years shot to hell.

On the other hand, I had $8 million of cash and AMEX stock, which was the first capital beyond the relatively modest money I had made through LIN Broadcasting, SHP, and Lehman's compensation. It seems odd to say now, but $8 million was a lot of money. A great New York apartment still cost less than $1 million in those days.

As part of the sale, Shearson required the partners to sign three-year noncompetition agreements. Because they were division heads, Shel and Fuld were required to sign five-year ones but took larger shares of the bonus pool. Shel refused. I suspected he wasn't going to be with the firm for much longer.

I decided that I would be as cooperative as possible with the new owners. The Lehman partners had an obligation to make the acquisition look good. Cohen had taken a big gamble, and if it weren't for him, I would have left Lehman with no capital. To their credit, many of our partners felt the same way.

I had no illusions about my position in the new firm, called Shearson Lehman. I knew Sherman Lewis, who ran Shearson's banking division. I liked him and had met him two years earlier when Gleacher and I had dined with Shearson people to see if we could interest them in buying Lehman. Jim Robinson, the chief executive of American Express, which owned Shearson, was a long-term acquaintance. But he always treated me as a "younger" person, though he was only three years my senior.

Shortly after the acquisition, Peter Cohen, chairman, called me. He asked me to meet him and Shel Gordon for breakfast in Peacock Alley at the Waldorf Hotel. This was another one of those cases where I had no idea what might happen. Was I going to be fired? At breakfast, Shel told me that he and Peter had decided that, with Gleacher gone, there was no one to take over the mergers and acquisition department of the firm. They asked me to take the job. I had no ambitions to run a mergers department. Indeed, I had always distrusted the gunslinging M&A guys who had no loyalty to a single client and few long-term relationships. Their ambitions were to complete the most deals, not the best ones. Tender offerings, both hostile and friendly, had also begun to replace negotiated transactions. M&A guys did little more than parrot the legal tactics and strategies of the increasingly important lawyers, such as Joe Flom of Skadden Arps and Marty Lipton of Wachtell Lipton. In short, the idea wasn't terribly appealing.

But Cohen and Gordon kept talking. By the time breakfast was finished, they offered me an increase in compensation, a chauffeured car, and use of the company plane. Having forgone a car since I left city government six years before, I found this to be a great inducement. Besides, I had already decided to honor the three-year noncompete agreement. So, I figured, why not? Despite misgivings, I accepted.

CHAPTER 23

Guide to Surviving Betrayal

One of the more potentially valuable bankers in our new merger and acquisition department was Steve Schwarzman. I had recommended hiring Steve when I ran associate recruiting at business schools for Lehman in the early 1970s. A graduate of Yale and HBS, he had talent and, in the course of a decade, had built a close relationship with Pete Peterson. I was happy to have him on our team. But then I learned that shortly after Shearson's acquisition of Lehman, Steve had gone to Jim Robinson, the CEO of American Express, and Peter Cohen, the CEO of Shearson, and gotten them to let him out of his noncompetition agreement for having instigated the Shearson purchase. He would join Pete at his new private equity and advisory business.

What Jim and Peter did outraged me. We had thirty-five bankers with noncompetes, and all of them were senior to Steve. I told Jim and Peter that if they let Steve out of his noncompete, I would tell all the people who worked with me that I didn't believe their agreements were binding. Shel Gordon agreed with me.

Confronted by me, Jim and Peter backtracked on their consent. Steve's reaction was to quit working and to sit, day in and day out, in his office doing nothing. He had made an unreasonable request, and he had almost succeeded. It was hard enough to motivate bankers in a firm after it had been sold without having one of them acting like a jerk.

I didn't know what to do about Steve until one day Bruce Wasserstein, then still at First Boston, called me. Although I didn't know him well, he was aware of Steve's performance, and he offered advice. "It's a hard enough job to recreate Lehman's M&A business," Bruce said. "You can't have Schwarzman acting like Hamlet. Get rid of him—and soon."

I decided to talk to Shel and Peter Cohen about moving Steve. Peter agreed that this was probably the best alternative. Peter talked to Steve and Pete Peterson; I was told they entered into an agreement whereby Steve would join Pete, but Steve and Pete would share profits with Shearson for the three years remaining on Steve's noncompete. It was a satisfactory resolution. I don't know, however, if Shearson ever received a cent pursuant to this agreement.

Steve's departure was a setback but was not fatal. We had talented people such as Tom Hill and Steve Waters, and I brought in Bill Shutzer from corporate finance to be my deputy. Gradually, through 1985 and into 1986, our business grew.

In the middle of 1986, Wall Street and beyond was shocked by the arrest of the famed arbitrager Ivan Boesky for violating SEC rules about insider trading. Implicated with Boesky was well-known merger professional Marty Siegel, then head of Kidder Peabody's M&A department. Siegel was apprehended on a New York street with a valise filled with about $450,000 in cash.

Boesky's illegal trades resulted from use of information on unannounced deals. The fear of anyone running a merger department is that bankers at their firms are involved in the spreading scandal. Soon Dennis Levine surfaced as a key participant. Levine had been a middle-level banker in our department. He was liked by his clients but evinced little interest in the details of deals. He had been recruited away from Lehman by Michael Milken, the Drexel junk bond king. I had mixed emotions about his departure. Suddenly, his inability to remember details of our transactions took on a different meaning. Clearly, his accounts in the Bahamas and the running of his conspiracy had consumed all his attention.

The SEC published a list of deals in which Boesky had traded on inside information. One deal in particular was troubling. It was the proposed acquisition of Standard Brands by Nabisco; only Steve Waters, one of my top lieutenants, Ira Sokolow, a merger associate, and I knew about it. Waters was beyond reproach. But what about Sokolow?

I discussed my worries with David Hershberg, Shearson's general counsel. I didn't want to accuse anyone without evidence. Hershberg sent an advisory memo to bankers in the merger and acquisition department, in essence saying that if by chance they had done something stupid, it would be wise to tell him. We had no responses, and I then met with each banker.

In an active firm, bankers frequently travel. Ira Sokolow wasn't in the office, but I expected him on the following Monday. He did not appear. I called his home but got no answer.

Ira was friendly with Ken Tuchman, another promising associate. I asked Ken to do an important service for the firm: to go to Great Neck, where Ira lived, and find Ira. He drove out and didn't find Ira but remembered that his in-laws lived close by. Ira was there.

Ken told me that Ira was clearly worried about something, though Ira wouldn't say more. Based on this information, early the following morning, I went to Hershberg's office. David called the US attorney. We told him that we thought we had a problem but didn't know the extent of it. Minutes after we hung up, a lawyer called to say that he represented Ira and he was going to turn himself in to the US attorney. Ira was eventually convicted of violation of the securities laws and spent eight months in prison.

A lot of lessons could be taken from the scandal. Most of them are obvious. One can't be too careful; even then, bad guys will figure out how to beat the system, at least temporarily. But what the experience taught me more than anything else was the value of moving swiftly, getting ahead of the issue, and taking action. Throughout the investigation of insider trading, every time the US attorney or SEC interviewed me and would begin to get aggressive, I reminded them that I had called them regarding Ira. They hadn't called me.

We at Shearson Lehman suffered no adverse consequences because of the speed of our actions. Contrast our reaction to that of Salomon Brothers and John Gutfreund during the 1991 Treasury government bond scandal. For three months, John knew that the traders had hidden their purchases of treasuries. John took no action. The delay in reporting the violation, among other actions, caused John to lose his job, and Salomon suffered damage to its reputation.

In October 1987, I was in Tokyo with Peter Cohen when I opened the *Wall Street Journal* and stared in shock. The opening sentence of the lead article, by James Stewart, described Dennis Levine as a protégé of mine. The piece stated that Leon Black of Drexel Burnham Lambert had hired Dennis on my recommendation. I had never spoken to Black about Levine, and I was surprised when he was hired. I inherited Levine when I became head of the M&A department. I would never have endorsed him, even before I knew he was unethical. His disregard for details ensured that he would never become a partner at Lehman.

It didn't take long to learn the truth. Fred Joseph, a Harvard Business School classmate of mine, was at the time still CEO of Drexel and Black's boss. After a TV interview that we did together with Adam Smith, he told me that Leon had, in fact, told Stewart that I had recommended Dennis. "He shouldn't have done that," Fred added.

When I complained to Stewart about six months later, he sent me a one-line note from the SEC files maintaining that someone had said Black hired Levine after speaking to Peter Solomon. I was disappointed that Stewart, a Pulitzer Prize–winning journalist, had not called me for comment or confirmation.

This incident, however, reaffirmed a suspicion. A group of merger bankers and reporters—including Stewart, Bryan Burrough, Bruce Wasserstein, and others—routinely used the pages of the *Wall Street Journal* to leak information and otherwise promote their agendas. I wasn't shocked because there was hardly a profession that didn't use newspapers. In City Hall, the mayor routinely used the press to disseminate information and persuade. The difference was, in cases where press manipulation could affect the price of a stock, it was against the law.

The scandal of the late 1980s, which eventually ensnared Mike Milken and led to the bankruptcy of Drexel, destroyed a generation of bankers. Talented young people like Sokolow never worked in finance again. Marty Siegel served no time but only because he fled to Florida. Bob Freeman, a Goldman Sachs star, went to prison.

We ran an honest business, but that doesn't always protect you. I never felt threatened until years later, when my friend Federal Judge Milton Pollack said something startling to me over lunch. Judge Pollack was a formidable jurist and lawyer. I first met him in 1957 as the father of my Harvard College classmate Daniel Pollack. Before going on the bench, Judge Pollack had been a renowned lawyer who represented Bobbie Lehman. Over the years, I lunched with the judge many times, and we had a close relationship.

On this particular occasion in 1995, Judge Pollack told me that during the scandals of the late eighties, Rudy Giuliani—who had made a big show as US attorney in taking alleged felons in handcuffs from Kidder Peabody's office and prosecuting the insider trading cases— had tried to tip him about me. "I keep running into the name Peter Solomon," Giuliani said, "and I hear you are a friend of his. I want to warn you that I think he is involved in these crimes."

The judge told me that he calmly said to Giuliani, "You are entitled to go after Peter Solomon. But I will tell you one thing. If you do, it will end your career."

I reacted with horror, relief, and gratitude. The story underscored how closely run events are in life. If Giuliani, while trying to make a name for himself, had launched an investigation against me, he would have found nothing, but the mere fact of his looking might have tainted me. How fortunate I had been to take anticipatory action. How good it is to have solid friends who will push back against ambitious politicians.

There were other challenges during that period, from within the firm.

One day, Sherman Lewis—the cohead of the investment banking division—and I both got a call from Bob Barbanel, a senior executive in the lending area of Bankers Trust. Bob asked whether Shearson was working on the leveraged buyout of Save Mart Supermarkets, a Northern California chain run by Bob Piccinini. We said the deal wasn't familiar. "It's odd," he said. "Bankers Trust is looking at a proposal from Dick Bingham to acquire Save Mart. The selling memorandum is written on blank paper, but on the back of one page is the letterhead of the Shearson San Francisco office." Barbanel had smelled a rat and, as a friend, called us about his suspicions.

Dick Bingham, who sent out the letterhead-less memo, was a skilled banker about my age. He was a senior partner who had been at Kuhn, Loeb and later managed the Lehman, Kuhn, Loeb M&A department. I had known his father, Wheelock Bingham, who was a senior executive at R. H. Macy. Dick was from San Francisco and had wanted to return to the Bay Area. He developed a sizable office there. We sent a number of promising younger bankers, one of whom was Sterling Brinkley, to work with him.

Sherman and I called Brinkley and asked him if anyone in the San Francisco office called on Save Mart. He said he didn't know of any calls. We now knew we were onto a bigger lie.

Two days later, Brinkley called us and confessed to the scheme. Bingham, he said, was leading a private buyout in which he'd been involved. We summoned Bingham to New York. Sherman and I, with the approval of the executive committee, fired him and Brinkley. We called Piccinini and said we would be prepared to go forward with the buyout, not telling him that they had been doing this without authorization. The deal never happened.

Our authority was tested again a few months later. One of the younger managing directors who had benefitted from the sale to Shearson informed us that he was going to Morgan Stanley, a direct challenge to the noncompete agreement that had been signed by thirty-five of our bankers. We had dealt with the Schwarzman challenge and the Bingham deceit, and we were not going to be beaten in this case. We warned the managing director that he was about to violate his agreement; he told us to shove it. We sued him. My partner Alan Finkelstein, before and later a successful lawyer at Cravath, told me we would never win the suit. I said we didn't have to win the damages part. We simply had to win the initial ruling that the MD could neither work for Morgan Stanley nor be in New York City. We did prevail in the early decisions, and he was unable to join Morgan Stanley. Eventually, Morgan prevailed but not before the MD had to move to Los Angeles.

In 1986, Shel Gordon, my boss, decided to retire. Shel's training had been in investment management, and he had never been a banker. Glucksman had made him head of investment banking after Peterson was forced out. It wasn't a good fit, but Shel stayed in the position because Lew was never going to make me the banking head, and Bill Morris, my rival, had a following but not enough personality or interest in new business to run the division.

Now with Shel leaving, a new banking head would have to be appointed. Once again, Peter Cohen and Shel approached me about taking on additional responsibility. I didn't ask for any increase in compensation or additional perks. I was to become one of a dozen vice chairmen of Shearson, and while the move was an honor of sorts within the firm, because Shearson had never been considered a premier firm, it was not a distinguished position. I had only one request. I wanted Sherman Lewis as my co-chairman.

Sherman was a Shearson banker I had first met as Eric Gleacher's brother-in-law. Eric and I, on our own initiative, had approached Shearson to acquire Lehman in 1982. We did this before the blowup between Glucksman and Peterson but because we could both already sense that internal political struggles were making the firm unsustainable. We met with Sherman and another Shearson executive in an Italian restaurant in Queens so we wouldn't be recognized.

The discussions did not advance at that time, but I was impressed by Sherman as a person. Solid, Midwestern, he had been schooled at Northwestern and lived in New Jersey. His wife, Dorothy, by coincidence, had worked with my brother, Richard, at Clairol. He loved football and ran a fantasy league. He was trusted by the Shearson guys and, while not a natural leader, seemed to have qualities I lacked, such as patience. Most important, I enjoyed his company and could laugh with him.

James D. Robinson III was not convinced that Sherman and I were important enough to be heads of the investment bank. Jim, a former White Weld banker not much older than Sherman, had become head of American Express in 1977 after my friend Howard Clark retired. Jim was the progeny of a distinguished Atlanta family. His father, Big Jim Robinson, had been chairman of the first Bank of Atlanta. Robinson was on the Business Council and the Roundtable, the leading business groups representing the American business establishment. He had an annoying habit of referring to me as "young man." Jim was capable and smooth as silk but not a good combination with Peter Cohen, the rough-and-tumble CEO of Shearson, a major subsidiary. Basically, Jim didn't seem to trust Cohen's judgment but was too cautious to confront him.

When Cohen told Robinson that he was appointing Sherman and me to run his investment bank, Robinson, given his establishment background, insisted that Cohen recruit a Fortune 100 business establishment CEO as chairman. Robinson didn't think we could do the job on our own. Cohen settled on Phil Caldwell, a former naval officer who had been the first non-Ford CEO of the Ford Motor Company. In his quiet, professional manner, he had turned Ford around. He was the perfect choice, except for a few key things: he knew nothing about investment banking, he wasn't at all a finance guy, and he wasn't from the East.

Cohen—along with Jeff Lane, his closest associate at Shearson—and I flew to Detroit to recruit Caldwell. The plane trip produced one of the oddest conversations of my career. While Cohen was in the bathroom, Lane turned to me across the aisle and said, apropos of nothing, "I have told Peter that making you head of the banking division is one of the worst moves he has ever made—and it might cost him his career."

I was too flabbergasted to say anything in reply, nor did I mention it to Cohen until a year later, when he came to my office to ask if I thought making Jeff Lane president of Shearson was a good idea. I told him the story and added that, in 1983, Pete Peterson had come to my office for the first time ever to ask whether I thought making

Lew Glucksman president of Lehman was a good idea. At that time, I hadn't thought so but agreed anyway because I saw no harm in it; Glucksman ran a division that was important to the firm's success, and I figured the title might alleviate his inferiority complex. But I had been wrong. Not wanting to make the same mistake, I told Cohen what I honestly thought: that making Jeff president was absurd. He had bad judgment and produced nothing at the firm. It was simply a payoff for loyalty. I appreciate loyalty as much as anyone, but rewarding it by this promotion was a bad idea. Cohen proceeded against my advice but fired Jeff two years later.

As for Caldwell, his office was in a modest commercial suburban office building outside Detroit. It seemed to be empty except for his suite. There was little on his desk besides framed photographs. Our conversation was stilted, and it became clear to me that Ford exiled its former CEOs to remote locations somewhat like a benevolent dictator might imprison his predecessor.

Nevertheless, Robinson hired Caldwell, ensconced him in a house in New Canaan at great expense, and gave him an office on the nineteenth floor near Cohen and all the senior management of Shearson except Sherman and me. (We insisted on remaining on the banking floor in the midst of our banking colleagues.) Caldwell never produced a piece of business and, as far as I could tell, never even generated a lead. He was a nice man but a great expense.

The Shearson Board of Directors I joined when I became co-chair of the Investment Banking Division in 1986 was an odd collection that included the inside vice chairman, executives from our parent company, American Express, and so-called independent directors, most of whom had been appointed by Sandy Weil. These included Dina Merrill, the movie star heiress of the Merriweather Post family; Malcolm Wilson, the former governor of New York State; and Gerald Ford, the thirty-eighth president of the United States. None of them had the foggiest idea of Shearson's business.

The regularly scheduled Shearson board meeting took place the day after the 1987 stock market crash. At a break, President Ford gestured to me to follow him. He headed directly to the men's room. As we stood side by side at the urinals, the president said, "Peter, Howard Baker just called me." (Baker was President George Bush's chief of staff in the White House.) "He wants to know what the president should say about the crash."

I told President Ford the same thing I had told President Carter through Stu Eizenstat in November 1976: "Say nothing."

That moment demonstrates how your imagination is, at best, a rough draft of how life actually works out. When I was twenty-four or so, I had envisioned myself someday sitting in the White House advising an incumbent president on affairs of state. Instead, I wound up in a men's room telling an ex-president what to say about a blip in the stock market.

Gerald Ford loved golf but wasn't good. One day in 1986, while I was playing with him at the Shearson Invitational at Torrey Pines, his drive off the first tee hit a spectator standing almost directly behind his back.

At dinner the same night, Edgar Cullman and I were seated at the president's table. He and Edgar began to discuss Tryall, Edgar's home in Jamaica. President Ford, when discussing the golf course there, turned to Edgar and, pointing to me, said, "The eleventh hole is so tough, even Peter can't par it!"

At that time, I had not visited Edgar in Jamaica, so I didn't know the golf course. But, with my contrary nature, I replied, "Of course I can!"

The president said, "I'll bet you a buck you don't." Edgar and I took the bet.

That winter, I visited Edgar. We played golf in a drizzle. By the eleventh tee, I was wet and playing badly. As we reached the eleventh tee, it began to rain harder. Eleven is a par five. The drive goes over vegetation and a drainage ditch, and the fairway curves uphill to the left and climbs to an elevated green.

My drive went through the fairway into tropical vegetation, stopping by a small palm tree. The rain only increased as I chopped a seven iron into the fairway. A three wood careened up the hill, up the green, and, with luck, rested on the back edge of the green. I needed to get down in two putts for a par, but I had sixty feet downhill on a slick green with a line curving sharply left for a par. With trepidation, I stroked the putt and watched it snake its course toward the cup, hoping it would stay on the green. As it neared the hole, it slid, turned left, disappearing into the cup for a birdie four!

No one was more surprised. President Ford sent a dollar each to Edgar and me, claiming we had cheated "an old man."

Sherman and I built a respectable investment banking business for Shearson. But the low morale of our former Lehman bankers continued. Gershon Kekst, at lunch, suggested taking advantage of the American Express ownership by getting our bankers invited to its sponsored events. Cohen agreed, suggesting we hire Fran Kittredge who became invaluable.

I was also discouraged by the challenge of creating a Shearson identity. A chance encounter one night on my way home with Gene Mercy, a Goldman Sachs partner, lifted my spirits. He assured me there was no reason to feel defeated. "Peter, it is all marketing," he said. "And you are one of the great marketers."

For days afterward, I thought about this remark and the strengths of Lehman and Shearson. Lehman was known for its imagination and intellect; Shearson for its access to public capital and distribution. At some point, it struck me that we should reinvigorate the old English banking phrase "merchant bank" and promote the ability of Shearson to combine these capabilities on behalf of clients.

To augment our ability to compete with Drexel with its junk bonds, as well as Goldman Sachs and Morgan Stanley, Sherman had recruited Dan Good, an experienced banker. Not long afterward, Dan told us that Ted Turner asked if Shearson would finance a hostile takeover of CBS, then controlled by its founder William S. Paley. We met with Ted, one of the world's most charismatic and visionary people—almost everything he foresaw eventually happened, including CNN—and he laid out ways he felt he could improve CBS.

Cohen then spoke to Robinson, who understandably saw a challenge to CBS, the essence of the business establishment, as a bold move for the firm. Jim proposed that Cohen, Good, and I bring Ted to an Amex senior management meeting that weekend at the Boca Raton Hotel.

We arrived as instructed. Ted flew down with Justus Moore, the head of Robinson Humphrey, an Atlanta brokerage firm owned by Shearson. Jim and Lou Gerstner, Amex president, were joined by a number of senior management people.

Ted began by giving a detailed analysis of CBS and the changes he would make. The Amex executives were impressed; Cohen and I, standing against the wall, were much relieved that the discussion was going well. After a few perfunctory questions, Jim paused. Then he said, "Ted, I want to ask you the vice presidential question. Is there anything we should know that might embarrass us if we back you?"

This is a standard question that hopefully elicits a speedy no. Ted, however, didn't answer. My sense of foreboding increased. I didn't know my new bosses that well. What was Turner thinking? "Yes," he finally said. "There is one thing." He paused again. "I love to fuck. I know I shouldn't fuck so much, but I can't resist. I fuck everything I can!" He went on for a while describing this robust enthusiasm for fucking.

Robinson, recently separated from his wife, was like every straight single guy with any money in his pocket in New York City. But he tried to keep a serious demeanor.

The meeting ended politely, and I wasn't sure how Robinson would react to Ted's philippic. Robinson, however, was impressed enough by Ted to approve our representation. As the news of a possible takeover spread throughout the business community, CBS began to fight back.

Sam Butler, my pal from the Harvard Board of Overseers and the senior partner of Cravath, which represented CBS, called Robinson. Sam told Jim that he would be thrown off the Business Council if Shearson supported Turner. Unable to stand the heat, Robinson reversed his decision. This was a blow to our program to position Shearson as the alternative to Milken and Drexel. Ironically, Paley eventually sold control to Larry Tisch, who carried out many of the ideas Turner proposed.

Running the banking division had its lighter moments. Fred Frank was one of the stars of our profession. I had first heard of Fred in the late 1960s, when he was the hottest equity analyst at Smith Barney. In those days, the "in" places to have lunch were Delmonico's and the Coachman across William Street from Lehman. Fred was a regular at both places and was so influential that if he touted a stock at lunch, it rose that afternoon. His specialty was pharmaceuticals; he was the institutional investor research all-star.

In 1968, Lehman poached him. Soon, he moved from research to investment banking. Few have made the transition as smoothly as Fred. Soon, he was the outstanding new business banker, using his research knowledge and reputation to garner initial public offerings and advising emerging pharmaceutical and biotech companies such as Roche and AstraZeneca.

Fred became a partner before I did. We worked well together. We could always count on him for business. Fred developed a good group of subordinates, including Larry Leeds' daughter Tracy and Mary Tanner.

By the time I became cohead of investment banking, Fred was still going strong. The sale to Shearson was good for his business, because having the larger, more productive equity sales force facilitated his advocacy of Lehman as a lead underwriter.

By the early 2000s, it had become a cliché on Wall Street that many bankers married their colleagues. But in the 1980s, it was still unusual for professionals within the same firm to date.

Steve Waters one day told me that he had seen Mary and Fred in what appeared to be a romantic tête-à-tête at a restaurant. It was no business of mine, so I didn't think anything more about it.

Then, one Sunday in 1986, Fred called me at home. My first reaction was that he was going to quit. My fear was not far-fetched. We were vulnerable. Instead, Fred greeted me warmly and asked nervously if there was a rule at the firm prohibiting partners from marrying associates.

"Fred," I answered, "you are one of our thirty-game winners. You can marry the elevator boy as far as I am concerned."

He replied that he was marrying Mary, and I congratulated him.

Mary and Fred have been married for decades. Eventually, Mary left Lehman to go to Bear Stearns. After the Lehman collapse, and after I had pursued Fred for more than twenty years, he joined PJSC.

In the late 1980s, I also made a decision that I came to regret. Dan Good brought into the firm two young brothers, Mitch and Stephen Rales. They seemed to have scant experience, yet they wanted to do a hostile tender for an industrial company, Danaher, located in Washington, DC. At the time, many speculators with little background and no experience were being financed by Milken to do hostile takeovers. Some of these "investors," such as Ron Perelman and the Rales brothers, subsequently built important businesses. Others—such as Herbert Haft and his son, owners of Dart Drugs in Washington, the Canadian Belzbergs, and the investor Paul Bilzerian—turned out to be irresponsible. It was difficult to get a sense of who was worth trusting and who wasn't. Jules Kroll, who had reinvented the investigatory business, was having a banner time helping firms investigate the rash of new clients.

In this context, Shearson had an opportunity to finance the Rales. We did not, and it was because of me. I was opposed to financing clients who had no plan other than to control a public company and who proffered no strategic vision. While I wanted to build up Shearson's banking business to compete with Drexel, I couldn't bring myself to suspend my basic suspicions and to support hostile takeovers. Sherman agreed with this view, and Peter Cohen, though he was inclined to be more aggressive, deferred to me. The Rales built Danaher into a major industrial company that, in 2018, had market equity of over $71 billion. They also became major art collectors. I take responsibility for the misjudgment.

In the business of investment banking, you must acknowledge your errors in judgment even as you remember your brilliance. You should also learn from your mistakes, though in this case, I didn't learn anything. If I were meeting the Rales for the first time today, I still would not see them as the sort to stick with the company they acquired and achieve great success. But they did, and I congratulate them!

CHAPTER 24

Setbacks and Successes

During the early 1980s, I began to work with companies that I had gotten to know in City Hall. The most interesting of these was Pan American Airways, then run by Bill Sewall. Although I hadn't worked with them, Pan Am was hardly a new account at Lehman. Juan Trippe, who founded the company in 1927, was close to Bobbie, and the firm had represented it throughout its history. Lehman had, in fact, been instrumental in the founding of the airline industry in the United States. It had participated in the formation of the Aviation Corporation of America, which at one time owned a number of carriers. Led by partner Johnny Hertz, it had acquired Trans World Airlines in 1934 and sold it to General Motors and then Howard Hughes. Hertz later started the rental car company bearing his name. He was also known for owning the champion thoroughbreds Reigh Count and Count Fleet. The horses' trophies for winning the Kentucky Derby and the Belmont Stakes were displayed prominently in Lehman's eighth-floor dining room.

By the 1970s, Pan Am had serious problems. It was overleveraged and only an international carrier. It was competing against foreign national airlines, each of which was subsidized on its routes. It had bought the Inter-Continental Hotel chain and owned the mammoth Pam Am Building above Grand Central Station. An equity infusion was necessary, but there were no domestic sources. Peterson and George Ball had traveled to Iran in 1975 to entice the Shah of Iran to invest in Pan Am. They had to cool their heels by the hotel pool for days, waiting in vain for the Shah to meet with them. In 1978, Pan Am got into a bidding contest against my HBS classmate Frank Lorenzo to buy National Airlines. They finally got a badly needed domestic feeder, but the fleets weren't compatible, and the integration went badly.

To address the problems, Lehman in 1982 sold Pan Am's Pacific routes to United Airlines and paid off some debt. But then the company made a fatal mistake. It continued to sell assets and routes to reduce its debt. It sold its Atlantic division to Delta. It sold the hotels and the Pan Am Building to Metropolitan Life. It even tried to sell its flagship terminal at JFK, but there were no buyers.

Pan Am's debt, while reduced, was still much greater than what its unprofitable route structure could sustain. With prospects for profit seemingly nonexistent, the banks foreclosed on Pam Am. It filed for bankruptcy in 1991 and was eventually dissolved.

America had lost its flagship overseas carrier as well as an iconic brand. New York City had lost a major contributor to the economy and the business establishment. Lehman lost a core client.

From Pan Am's decline, though, we can at least take some lessons. First, it is surprising how long an unsustainable business can survive. By the early seventies, it was clear Pan Am could not compete without domestic routes, and yet it lasted another eighteen years or so.

Second, desperate companies take desperate actions. The bidding contest for National caused it to leverage itself to a point that exacerbated the strategic dilemma. Acquisitions of public companies are, by their nature, expensive; the buyer must always assume it is paying a premium—that is, an amount over the daily price in a rational trading market—to gain control. I once noted this obvious point to Larry Tisch, himself a skillful acquirer. He asked me why no one ever says this in a deal. The calculation every acquirer should make is how quickly it can create savings or synergies to recapture the premium. Sometimes the stock market accommodates the merged companies by valuing the equity at a higher multiple. Pan Am got neither savings nor synergies; it ended up only with more leverage.

A third lesson is the need to merge cultures. Because of the company's proudly glamorous heritage and the marketing campaign that reinforced its image, Pan Am employees viewed themselves as superior to National's. Pan Am found it almost impossible to integrate the resultant workforces.

Finally, if you are overleveraged, make a deal with your lenders before you start paying off debt. When you owe lenders disproportionate amounts of money, the lenders have a problem. When you pay down the majority of your debt without making an overall settlement, you, the borrower, have a problem.

$$\approx$$

Ed Finkelstein, the CEO of R. H. Macy, may have been the first retail executive to realize that the department store sector needed consolidation. Or maybe he was simply the greediest.

As I related in chapter 21, Finkelstein in 1983 attempted to acquire Associated Dry Goods and would have succeeded except for the illness of Bill Arnold. In 1984, he took matters into his own hands.

Not only was Finkelstein frustrated by his inability to conclude the ADG acquisition, he was also jealous of his colleague Phil Schlein, CEO of Macy's San Francisco, who had made a fortune as a director of the emerging technology company Apple. Finkelstein had headed Macy's California before moving to New York City to become the senior executive. He thought the Apple seat, and the money that went with it, should have been his.

In October 1984, Finkelstein announced that he and Mark Handler, his president, would lead a management buyout at the premium price of seventy dollars per share. Macy's earnings had declined from the previous year. The offer was three times book value and fifteen times earnings per share, both premiums to the market.

Finkelstein also announced that Goldman Sachs would be the company's adviser. For Shearson Lehman Brothers, and for me in particular, that was a serious blow. Lehman and Goldman had been joint managers of Macy's financings since the 1930s, when Lehman partner John Hancock (yes, that was his real name) and Goldman senior partner Sidney Weinberg signed an agreement to share clients. Loss of a major client to another investment bank is always traumatic; investment bankers often fear client loss more than they take joy in a new deal. But in 1984, so soon after Lehman's sale to Shearson, our firm was sufficiently fragile that a loss, particularly to our archrival Goldman Sachs, was devastating.

From my perspective, Finkelstein's decision could not have been worse. I was the primary contact with Macy's, having worked on the account for two decades. Don Smiley, the former CEO, and I were close; I had arranged his appointment to the Carter administration. In 1970, it was my pleas and my argument that the Thirty-Fourth Street location was a valuable asset—not a liability—that kept Moody's credit rating agency from downgrading the bonds of Macy's. A decade later, as I've already described, I risked my reputation protecting Macy's during the Legionnaires' disease scare. The shock of our exclusion was a low point in my business career.

I immediately called Finkelstein and set up a meeting in his office. He was in his mid-fifties, not more than five nine in height, and overweight. I pleaded my case. "Your firm is finished," he responded angrily. "And everyone knows it." It had been a long time since I'd been so dismissed.

My reaction at such times is not to show the anger I feel but to be calm and firm. "In that case, I wish you well," I said.

Finkelstein, amazed, said, "You're wishing me well after what I just said to you?"

"Yes," I replied. "You are going to need it."

The saga of the Macy's management buyout lasted eight years. It began badly for Macy's. It was not until 2015 that Rob Kaplan, an associate at Goldman in 1984 and later vice chairman of Goldman, told me that in doing the feasibility analysis to determine the buyout price of seventy dollars per share, Goldman made a mistake. They classified Macy's deferred taxes as a cash-generating item rather than as a use of funds in its cash flow projections.

Once they spotted their mistake, various bankers and accountants spent a weekend confirming it; on Monday morning, Goldman partner Fred Eckert informed Finkelstein of the error. In light of the information, Eckert pleaded Macy's should reduce its seventy-dollar offer to sixty dollars per share. Finkelstein refused.

Without knowledge of these discussions, as I tried to maintain my position and that of the firm's, I unfortunately gained a modest position in the financing of the buyout on Lehman's behalf. The most perceptive person invited to invest in the equity was Walter Cabot, then head of the Harvard Management Company. When Finkelstein told him of all the savings and efficiencies that the Macy management could effect as a private company, Cabot asked him why he didn't institute them anyway. Finkelstein, apparently, had no answer. The Harvard endowment did not invest.

Macy's loaded their board with luminaries such as Henry Kissinger, none of whom knew anything about retailing.

By the late 1980s, Macy's would get caught up in the aftermath of the Campeau capers (described ahead) and the dislocations within the declining department store business. It would go bankrupt in 1992. Ed Finkelstein would disappear in disgrace. I lost $1 million, but Lehman was still standing.

❧

Michael Eisner, CEO of Disney, was much more successful than Finkelstein. I had known Michael since he was a child. His family lived in an apartment overlooking Park Avenue on Eighty-Ninth Street, and we lived in the back of the building facing Lexington Avenue. I was friendlier with his older sister Margo, but I was aware of his successful career at ABC and at Paramount Pictures.

One day, John Angelo, a friend since our twenties and then head of arbitrage at L. F. Rothschild, asked to bring Michael to see me. At the time, Rothschild's office was several floors above my Lehman office at 55 Water Street. John explained that Disney was looking for a new CEO, and Michael wanted to be considered for the job. There was a catch: Michael couldn't get an interview.

John knew that Phil Hawley—CEO of the Los Angeles–based

department store chain Carter Hawley Hale, a director of Disney and, most critically, the chairman of the Disney Search Committee—was my friend and client. He asked me to call Hawley on Michael's behalf.

Phil and I were close enough that a call was not an imposition. He could always say no.

With John and Michael in my office, I got Phil on the phone. "Phil, are you head of the Disney Search Committee?" Of course he answered that he was. "Could you do me a favor?" I asked. "I want you to interview Michael Eisner. Before you reply, I know you think he is from Hollywood, but he is really from Park Avenue. We grew up in the same building. He is a preppie. He went to Lawrenceville, where I went, and he is married to his first wife." Disney stood itself apart from the movie industry and the Beverly Hills crowd. Phil was a prominent member of the California Club, the bastion of the Los Angeles gentile establishment. Phil was married to Mary and had seven children.

I kept talking so he couldn't say no. "Phil, I know you are talking to Dennis Stanfill," I said. "He isn't your man. We were together at Lehman. He is the guy Darryl Zanuck had in mind when he said don't say yes until I finish talking."

Phil finally got a word in, asking, "Peter, what do you want me to do?"

"I want you to see Eisner," I said. "He will be in your office tomorrow!"

Michael got the job, of course, and had a successful twenty-year run at Disney. Many self-absorbed people create history to conform to their self-image. In Michael's autobiography, he tells a different version of how he became head of Disney, with no mention of me. Nor did he ever say thank you or return the favor. And he had his chances.

When I started the Peter J. Solomon Company in 1989, Michael, as CEO of Disney, promised to retain the firm but didn't. Michael asked me to meet his CFO, Gary Wilson. Accordingly, I made an appointment with Wilson in his office in Burbank. After my plane from JFK landed, I learned that Wilson had cancelled the meeting and flown east to Washington, DC. Dismayed, I reached him in DC, and we made a date for breakfast for the following day at a hotel adjacent to then National Airport. The overnight red-eye got me to breakfast. After the briefest of welcomes and only the offer of coffee, Wilson said Eisner and Disney didn't need more financial advice than he, Wilson, could give. When I related our conversation to Michael, he did nothing.

Over the next five years, PJSC represented Reed Elsevier in buying business magazines from Disney and Children's Place in buying the Disney Stores. But Michael never hired us.

My lack of success extended to philanthropy. I was on the board of the American Museum of Natural History on Central Park West. The museum has one of the most extensive dinosaur collections, and its provost, Michael Novacek, continues the tradition of dinosaur exploration on the Flaming Cliffs of Outer Mongolia every summer. In 1995, the museum decided to build a new dinosaur gallery on the fourth floor.

The museum needed $4 million to finance the project. It decided to ask Disney to name the halls even though there was worry that the Disney Hall would be viewed as a little promotional and commercial. The museum, after all, was a scientific institution, not an exhibition park like Disneyland. But it needed the money.

Joseph F. Cullman III—a museum trustee, CEO of Philip Morris, a friend of Eisner's deceased father, a mentor to Michael, and a director of Disney—suggested I go see Michael. Joe seemed to have surrounded the "ask." As the museum's emissary, I flew to Burbank. Major solicitations must be made in person. But they are not always successful, even when you are prepared.

Michael's desk was, as always, paperless and pristine. He was on the phone with famed director Barry Levinson. Katzenberg, the studio head, was away, and Michael sounded like a caricature of a Hollywood producer.

When he hung up, I made my pitch. "Michael," I began. "The museum would like Disney to consider naming these new halls. It is right up your alley, a mixture of science and entertainment."

He listened for about three minutes, then cut me off. I had noticed something on his lap, and it turned out to be a copy of *Newsweek*.

He whipped it out and opened it to a spread depicting a variety of dinosaurs. He had circled one. "I don't want your dinosaurs," he said, pointing to his favorite. "I want my own!"

I flew home defeated. Joe was upset with Michael for turning the museum down and for wasting my time and money, but, as in the Wilson case, Michael remained unresponsive.

Ultimately, the museum did get the money from the Dewitt Wallace Foundation. And Michael demonstrated the perseverance that contributed to his success. He did get his own dinosaur, or at least part of one. By coincidence, in 1997, the Field Museum, under John McCarter's direction, bought at auction a dinosaur skeleton named Sue. Mac got Disney and McDonald's to put up the $8.36 million for the winning bid. Sue is in the center court of the Field Museum today.

&

My friend Tom Unterberg says deals are like subway trains: a new one appears every twenty minutes. That's probably true, but you have to be lucky to find the right combination of timing, a good management, and an affordable price. You don't want to get on the wrong train.

In 1984, Murray Foreman walked into my office at Lehman Brothers, saying he'd come to see me on behalf of some friends. I'd known Murray for a long time. My father worked with him in the late 1920s at his family retail department store business, B. Foreman Company, in Rochester, New York. The friends in question were Chuck and Burt August of Rochester, who owned a small under-car service company called Monro Muffler/Brake. They wanted to find capital to buy out their third partner.

Monro had sales of $30 million done through fifty-two shops. Forty-five percent of its sales were mufflers, with the remaining sales aligning wheels and fixing brakes. The Augusts valued 100 percent of Monro at $8 million and would reinvest alongside the buyer.

I asked George Heyman, the partner in charge of the leveraged buyout business at Lehman, if the firm had interest in this $8 million investment. He replied that it was too small. When I asked him if I might invest myself, he said it was fine.

Over the years, my close family friend Don Glickman and I had made a number of investments in private companies. We had owned a peach-pitting company and several window companies. Don was interested in investing with me.

The under-car business had a number of positive characteristics. Cars on the road were aging, averaging over ten years. Dealers kept shorter hours than Monro and were closed on Sundays. Labor sales were also higher at dealers. More affluent American car owners were turning to the do-it-for-me repair business at the expense of the DIY business.

It has been proven time and again that two of the most important contributors to a successful company are favorable macro trends and excellent management. The former is probably the more important, but the latter cannot be overestimated. Management is essential to maximizing opportunities. Monro had the trends, and it also had the astute August brothers. Liking what we saw, Donald and I bought control of Monro at an $8 million value.

After a honeymoon period, in the late 1980s, Monro, at my urging, expanded rapidly from its base of one hundred stores, opening forty more annually for three years. Les Wexner, the genius behind the success of The Limited and Victoria's Secret, has spoken about the difficulty of increasing store count more than 100 percent in any one year. But in our case, even 20 percent was excessive. The company's management was incapable of opening numbers of stores profitably. Management also expanded into unfavorable geography. Monro opened a number of stores in and around Pittsburgh, a market fragmented into diverse micromarkets. As famed realtor Bill Zeckendorf stated, real estate is about location, location, and location.

Even the best analysis of quantitative data will not guarantee a productive retail location. Monro has a number of stores in Youngstown, Ohio. It's the headquarters of the DeBartolo Corporation, a major real estate developer and one of our first PJSC clients. On one trip, after a meeting with Mr. DeBartolo, I was complaining to his two senior executives, Rick Sokolov and Tony Liberatti, about the losses at Monro's two Youngstown shops. Tony Liberatti, out of the blue, commented—"No Jews." I was immediately offended and asked him what that meant. Liberatti said, "There are no Jews in Youngstown; there are Italians, and they do their own car repair work." This was a good explanation of why some locations don't perform well. It illustrates why local knowledge is so important and why local retailers often perform better than chains.

Retailers generally rely too heavily on their real estate departments, and the real estate vice presidents rely too heavily on real estate developers. A typical lease has a term of ten to fifteen years with fixed minimum payments. Boards rarely focus on individual leases because leases are a routine matter. Yet the boards of directors will scrutinize the details of a placement of debt, which may be a far lesser commitment. Additionally, because of the reliance on developers, the analysis of prospective store locations is frequently faulty. The developers feed information to the future tenants. I know ours did. Given my background, Monro should not have made these mistakes.

There are certain truths about store expansion. One lesson is that while a retailer can predict the aggregate sales volume of all stores opened during a year within 5 to 10 percent, management is incapable of predicting accurately plus or minus 10 percent the opening volume of any one store.

It is also true that in the past twenty years in the United States, virtually every store opened by a chain after its first one hundred stores has opened with a lower sales volume and ramped up more slowly. This is true because of the growth of available selling space footage throughout the USA compared to the growth in disposable income. By the twenty-first century, there was twenty-five feet of selling space for every person in the US, compared, for example, to five feet per person in Europe. These facts explain the decline in retail profitability without e-commerce and Amazon.

It's also more expensive to open a store due to environmental regulations, zoning laws, and construction costs. The return on equity, therefore, has declined. Retailers frequently have compensated for the decline in equity by employing more debt. Many have gone bankrupt due to the lethal effects of more debt and lower returns.

How did Monro grow despite the pitfalls of expansion? It changed its strategy. Instead of opening new stores, it bought existing ones operated by competing chains. Because volume purchases of oil, tires, and parts entitled Monro to lower prices, the company was able to reduce its cost of goods and increase gross margin. Monro thus became a "margin" strategy, coupled with the use of its balance sheet to enter new markets.

The company had also changed its service strategy. A successful retailer leads consumer trends. Some retailers are able to innovate through new merchandising techniques or offerings. Some—such as Walmart, TJX, or, of course, Amazon—create or capitalize on new concepts.

In 1984, cars had mufflers that deteriorated after five to seven years. By 1990, manufacturers began to supply vehicles with stainless steel mufflers whose life expectancy was nine years. A one-time change was unfortunate but not catastrophic.

Stainless steel muffler installation caused a steady decline that lasted not an additional four or five years, as one might expect, but twenty years! Reacting to the challenge, Monro initially added chemicals like brake fluid and looked into rebuilding transmissions. Management soon realized that it needed to build an additional product line.

Monro had always sold tires but decided to expand more rapidly into that business through acquisitions. Using its positive cash flow from the muffler shops, management financed acquisitions of independent tire and service operators.

Today, Monro opens about five stores annually and closes an equal number. It uses debt to buy stores when its debt is between 25 and 40 percent of total capital. Tires represent almost 50 percent of total sales, and mufflers, which have finally stopped declining, now represent about 7 percent.

Monro's ability to adapt its model required changes in top management. We have had seven CEOs since 1984. The latest, Brett Ponton, joined in 2017 and is doing an excellent job bringing Monro into the digital and mobile age. As the business evolved, we needed leaders with different strengths.

Orchestrating change positively in a public company is hard because of disclosure and scrutiny. Employees and shareholders are apprehensive. It requires meticulous planning regarding reaffirmation of culture and timing the rationale for change. No detail is too small.

Monro has given me considerable satisfaction. Our investment has paid off. Today, Monro has 1,200 stores. Sales exceed $1.1 billion, and its enterprise value is $3 billion. It has 6,500 employees and is still headquartered in Rochester.

I have been fortunate to have had many excellent partners over my life, personally and in business. But no partnership has surpassed the friendship that Don and I have had with the August family. Chuck died in 2005, and Burt died in 2017 at 101.

CHAPTER 25

Beginning of the End

(Department Store Mergers—1980s)

Department stores entered the 1980s as the dominant channel of retail distribution. Although their aggregate share had declined from 60 percent in the 1960s, even with the emergence of discounters, the 150 different department store nameplates held a 30 percent share. But the senior executives could see the growth of competing outlets.

Segments of industries and companies have life cycles. The department store industry was ripe for consolidation. By 1984, most of the larger companies—such as Associated Dry Goods, Allied Stores, Federated Department Stores, Broadway Hale Stores and Dillard's, May Company, and R. H. Macy—were all in motion.

ADG was the fourth-largest department store chain in the country, but it had the most specialty and high-end units: Lord & Taylor was run by Joe Brooks, a flashy merchant; Robinsons was the quality store in Southern California; L. S. Ayres of Indianapolis and Hornes of Pittsburgh were established leaders in their cities. Knowing the need to diversify, in 1981, ADG bought Caldor, the profitable regional hard goods discounter and, in 1983, Loehmann's, the famous soft goods discounter with origins on Fordham Road in the Bronx.

I had joined ADG's board of directors in 1977 and rejoined in 1981. By 1985, Bill Arnold had been dead for a year. Joe Johnson, the former chief financial officer and a genial southerner, was CEO, but he was not a strong leader for a fashion retailer.

There were problems of leadership at ADG. Few members of the Associated board had ever been inside one of the company's stores. Indeed, the board resembled a 1940s Princeton College eating club with NY Life head Manning Brown, industrialist Rodney Gott, Goldman Sachs partner Arthur Altschul, Chemical Bank CEO, Donald Platten, and previous ADG CEOs Lew Seiler and Dick Pivorotto. As a group, they were too old and not invested enough in ADG. Bill Arnold had never been comfortable with his own board.

When Carl Bennett, who had built Caldor, and George Greenberg, of Loehmann's, joined the board, they were placed on either side of me so I could assure them about Associated. More than once, the thought that we were sitting in the Jewish section crossed my mind.

Compounding ADG's problem was the departure of Mike Gould, who had been CEO of Robinsons. Mike quit when he was not made president, a position Arnold had promised him. Bill Fine, the former head of Bonwit Teller's and a close friend of Arnold's, pleaded with Mike to stay. In doing so, he used a phrase that has stuck with me. "In life, sometimes you get a check cancelled, and you just have to deal with it." I, too, had a heart-to-heart with Mike, flying to have breakfast with him at the Beverly Hills Hotel. He wouldn't listen, though, and maybe that was just as well. Life worked out for Mike. He succeeded Marvin Traub as CEO of Bloomingdale's and flourished there for twenty-two years.

Frustrated by his failure to seduce Tom Macioce and Allied Stores, David Farrell, CEO of the May Company, wasted little time once he decided to acquire Associated. Since Goldman Sachs and Lehman were both May Company and Associated bankers, he could not retain us. Instead, he chose Morgan Stanley. His legal representation was the already famous Joe Flom, the dean of hostile offers.

In the spring of 1986, Farrell wrote a letter to the Associated board proposing a stock merger. The terms depended on the accounting treatment of "pooling of interests," thereby avoiding the item of "goodwill." Pooling required a melding of assets and a continuity of management. Because it involved the exchange of common stock, the Associated shareholders would not pay a tax on the shares they received in the May Company. May offered a generous premium.

Farrell was perceptive. Associated's retail properties faced fewer challenges than many department stores. Unlike the May Company or Allied's stores, which were oriented more to the middle class, Associated's stores were better positioned, appealing to more affluent customers. The problem with Associated was that with Arnold and Gould gone, it didn't have enough executive talent.

The ADG board rejected the sixty-six dollars per share May offered, even though ADG's shares had been selling at forty-six dollars. Farrell then made a cash offer for 51 percent of the stock. We knew this was a feint because the May Company couldn't afford to buy the whole company for cash. We also knew that for the deal to increase May's earnings per share, it needed "pooling of interests" treatment.

As negotiations proceeded, it was clear to me that we could torture Farrell indefinitely, but our client didn't care about getting every last dollar or winning every last point. For example, May offered to put only three Associated board members on the May Company board and then for only three years. Given the fact that Associated was the fourth-largest department store chain and May the third, Associated could have insisted on several more directors serving for unlimited terms; they could have also insisted on chairing of some board committees. But they were fine with May's initial offer and seemed more interested in retaining the 40 percent discount at Lord & Taylor and the charitable matching gifts program.

Even with a wavering board, we got Farrell to raise his price to seventy-one dollars per share, or almost $3 billion. It was then the largest retailer merger in history.

The postscript played out as we expected. Farrell fired the three distinguished former Associated directors immediately after the three-year commitment expired. He also canceled the discounts and stopped the charitable match. For the next eighteen years, the May Company continued to buy, sell, and trade department names in Houston, Boston, Philadelphia, Kansas City, Salt Lake City, and Chicago, until it finally merged into Federated Department Stores in 2004.

While the CEOs of department store chains were trying to rationalize their businesses, their commercial partners, the major regional mall developers, began to worry. The growth of the suburban store and the spread of regional malls went hand in glove. There is no stronger demonstration of countervailing power than the relationship between the developers who created the environment for expansion and the stores that anchored the centers and held high credit ratings that permitted the developers to obtain financing. It was a symbiotic relationship but also a competitive relationship. The stores and developers were constantly negotiating.

The three largest developers were Alfred Taubman in Detroit, Mel Simon from Indianapolis, and Edward J. DeBartolo from Youngstown, Ohio. Added to this mix, in 1985, a Canadian real estate developer, Robert Campeau, came to New York. Campeau was not the first Canadian developer to try to break into the American market. In 1977, the Reichmann brothers appeared at the bottom of the New York real estate market to acquire the former office buildings of Percy and Harold Uris. With the recovery of the city, they had made several billion dollars.

Bob Campeau was brash and confrontational even by standards of Canadian real estate people. He had developed residential and office buildings originally in Ottawa and had begun to operate throughout Canada. He had even attempted a takeover of the Royal Trust, a part of the Canadian financial establishment. Now Campeau came to Shearson Lehman Brothers to meet with Tom Hill, then co-chair of the merger department under Sherman and me. Campeau told Tom that he wanted to buy a major department store chain in the US. He approached us because we represented many of the major companies. Tom, immediately sensing the potential for conflicts and having a good nose for serious people, listened politely and then recommended he talk to Bruce Wasserstein at First Boston. Tom knew Bruce well, having worked for him; he understood Bruce's ambition and his apparent lower standards.

☙

Thus began a series of events that, depending on your point of view, either destroyed the department store business in the United States or accelerated its rationalization. In either case, companies were taken over, rivals merged, some went bankrupt, nameplates were traded, managements fired, a great deal of money lost and some gained, employment declined. Over the succeeding thirty years, the total market share of department stores fell from 35 percent to less than 10 percent. Where there were once 150 name plates, by 2015, there were thirteen.

E. J. DeBartolo began his career paving asphalt driveways in Youngstown, Ohio. His stepfather was in the construction business. His first projects were in the Ohio area, but he was one of the first developers to recognize the potential of Florida. DeBartolo centers spread across Florida and, by the 1980s, owned about 10 percent of all US shopping center square footage. He viewed his tenants as partners and was close to the CEOs. He also owned the San Francisco 49ers.

By the time I met E. J., his wife had died, and he seemed lonely. He continued to live in Youngstown, had a secretary named Edie, who always asked me for my phone number, and for the ten years of our relationship, almost always called me at four o'clock on Friday afternoon.

He had a son, Eddie, who ran the football team, and a daughter, Denise, who was married to Richard York, a doctor who thought he was an investor.

DeBartolo came to see me at Shearson when he had heard rumblings from Macioce that Campeau might try a takeover. I felt I got his trust because, as our conversation wound down, I walked him not only to the elevator but down the Amex building escalator to his waiting limo. To this day, I insist that the employees of Peter J. Solomon Company walk the client to the elevator. I myself often take the client to the front door of the building on the pretense that I need the air.

Within two months of the Associated sale, the rumors about Campeau became true. In September 1986, Campeau, financed by First Boston, launched a hostile takeover of Allied Stores. It was somewhat ironic. Of all the major national department store chains, Allied had the weakest roster of stores, servicing, in the aggregate, the lowest economic bracket of customers. Yet its anchor locations in major shopping centers were enviable. An attack by an outsider such as Campeau, an unknown Canadian real estate developer, was a challenge to which the American retail and real estate establishment had to respond.

Everything about the hostile tender was unusual, including how I was informed. Harvard was celebrating its 350th Commencement. September 4, 1986, was a moment of extraordinary pomp and tradition held in the Tercentenary Theatre, an open space within Harvard Yard flanked on one side by the imposing Widener Library and by Memorial Church on the other. The sea of alumni, faculties, and distinguished guests powerfully underscored the continuity of Harvard.

That year, the nation's oldest university had invited Prince Charles to be the featured honoree. We overseers, the members of the corporation, senior faculty members, the administration, and honorees were seated on the expansive platform facing the audience. The sheriff of Middlesex County, in full regalia, stamped his staff thrice, calling the meeting to order.

While listening to the welcome of the master of ceremonies, I became aware of a rustling on the stage. From the whispering, it sounded as if someone in the crowd of perhaps twenty-five thousand was being sought. I thought I heard my name, but why would that be? Then I noticed a gown-clad faculty member pointing me out. Someone I didn't know gestured to me and beckoned. What could be going on?

Finally, a security guard reached me in the front row—where, as a more senior overseer, I was sitting—and told me to call my office immediately. It's hard to imagine an era before cell phones, but I asked for the location of the nearest public phone. It was in Sever Hall, a hundred yards away. As I ran to the door of Sever, my brother, Richard, approached. He, and apparently the entire audience, had seen me leave the stage.

"What's wrong?" he asked.

"No idea!"

When I reached my office, my assistant, Bruce Diker, said, "Campeau has just tendered for Allied Stores!"

"You called me off the stage of a Harvard graduation to tell me *that?*"

"Yes," Bruce said. "You told me to be sure always to inform you about important developments!"

I returned to the stage, but throughout the day, people asked me what had happened. I just shook my head.

E. J. DeBartolo reacted quickly to the Campeau tender. He had a material interest in Allied Stores, as well as a personal connection. He had developed many of Allied's retail mall stores, and he and Allied's CEO, Tom Macioce, were both Catholic and Italian. E. J. was willing to help Tom in any way he could; one way would be to make a competing offer for Allied at a price higher than the fifty-eight dollars per share Campeau was offering. Working with Shearson Lehman as part of our merchant banking strategy, we arranged to finance $1.6 billion of debt for DeBartolo, allowing him to offer sixty dollars per share.

E. J. and I arranged a meeting with Tom and his legal adviser, George C. Kern Jr., a well-known merger lawyer at the distinguished firm of Sullivan & Cromwell. There, E. J., in Kern's presence, made the firm, fully financed offer.

As E. J. outlined the proposal that we had worked on together, Kern interrupted him. "Ed, we appreciate the offer, but we think we can defeat the Campeau offer."

Surprised by his smugness, I said, "George, this is a firm offer, and you have to take it seriously." George turned to Tom and basically said they were going to put this offer in their pocket—in other words, not disclose it. E. J. didn't object, and the meeting ended.

After E. J. and I left the meeting, I told him that what Kern had proposed violated the disclosure rules. We had made a real offer, fully financed by Shearson, and it had to be disclosed to the Allied shareholders.

After Kern and Macioce rejected E. J.'s private offer, Campeau continued his assault. Without knowing that E. J. had offered sixty dollars per share, he raised his offer modestly to sixty-two dollars.

Macioce finally realized he was in a war that he would most likely lose. He turned to E. J. and Shearson Lehman. E. J. had a relationship with investor Paul Bilzerian, who offered to provide equity for a higher offer. He also turned to Les Wexner, one of the most successful specialty store operators and a lessor of considerable space in DeBartolo centers. As a result, on E. J.'s behalf, we offered sixty-seven dollars per share in cash.

As of the end of October, it looked as if the DeBartolo group had prevailed. The securities rules governing tender offers are laid out in the Williams Act, named for the chairman of the Senate Banking Committee. The rules prohibited, among actions, the purchase of stock during the tender period. During the tender period, Jeffries, then a marginal brokerage firm, had accumulated more than 48 percent of Allied's shares in anticipation of selling them to the eventual winner of the fight, presumably the DeBartolo group with the higher cash offer.

But no one counted on the hubris and ingenuity of Bruce Wasserstein. With Wasserstein's guidance, Campeau terminated his tender offer. Twenty-seven minutes later, on October 26, Campeau purchased the entire Jeffries block of Allied shares to gain ownership of more than 50 percent of Allied shares and, thus, control. The tactic was the first of what became known as "drop and sweep." First Boston provided a bridge loan of $1.8 billion to a man they hadn't known twelve months earlier.

Of course, we went to court with DeBartolo to protest an obvious breach of the rules dictated by the Williams Act. Ironically, the case was heard by one of my oldest friends, Judge Pierre Leval, in the Federal Southern District Court. Our parents had been close friends at the North Shore Country Club. Pierre and I had competed against each other annually in the club's tennis and golf tournaments.

Our goal was for the judge to issue a temporary restraining order (TRO) against the voting of these shares. In a ruling that may not have achieved the result Pierre wanted, he decided against the TRO and scheduled a hearing on the merits of the case for the following Tuesday. Sensing, perhaps incorrectly, what he would rule at the later hearing, the markets and DeBartolo swung toward Campeau, who won the day with a sixty-nine-dollar-per-share offer in cash and other securities. He also paid the DeBartolo group $116 million, made a deal with E. J. on future real estate development, and promised to retain Macioce for three years. The press reported that all parties looked like winners.

Conversations with Pierre Leval over the past years, the most recent in May 2015, revealed that the judge was surprised by the reaction to his ruling on the TRO. He had been leaning toward the opinion that the drop and sweep was a violation of the Williams Act. He hadn't issued a TRO against the purchase of the shares because he thought the issue could be heard in a timely manner. Regrettably, like war, success and failure are near run things.

Shortly after Campeau won, when it didn't affect the outcome, an administrative law judge ruled that Kern violated federal disclosure laws for not disclosing the offer. I was always surprised that no one asked me what happened at a meeting where I was one of four participants.

With success under his belt, the ambitious Campeau would become a major force in US retailing. He had been a breath away from failure.

In 1988, Campeau went after the largest and most prestigious department store chain, Federated Department Stores. My father had worked for Federated at Abraham & Straus for most of his business career. I had worked on the Federated team at Lehman since 1963. Ralph Lazarus, the son of the founder Fred Lazarus, had wooed me to become the chief financial officer in the mid-1970s. I knew all the executives and stores. While Shearson Lehman no longer had a director, we remained its banker. The CEO was Howard Goldfeder, a burly man with little charm. Federated's results were undistinguished, and there was no concentration of ownership.

Campeau had sold fifteen of Allied's twenty-two units, including Joskes, its Texas chain. He had created some open-to-borrow, but he had also demonstrated erratic behavior with the banks and analysts.

He launched an unsolicited tender for Federated in the Allied manner. Unlike Allied, Federated had at least the standard defenses to slow down an acquirer. Goldfeder's initial response was similar to Macioce's—the tough guy approach—but we convinced him that he could not survive. We began discussions with the May Company and with Macy's, both of which were run by ambitious executives who had demonstrated their understanding that the department store sector would benefit from consolidation. In fact, we negotiated a deal with the May Company, which *Fortune* magazine later described in detail. At the last moment, at May's board meeting, David Farrell decided that his management was not capable of taking on the enormous management challenge of Federated. This happened only one other time in my career – 1993 when the management of Office Depot decided that it was not capable of managing Staples, with which we had negotiated a merger, two years before the public merger agreement.

The bidding process followed the Allied pattern, but, in this case, both May and Macy decided the price for Federated was more than they could afford. Macy's eventually bowed out of the bidding but not before managing to acquire Bullocks and I. Magnin, two of Federated's better divisions, and giving a strong entry into Southern California and a specialty chain in San Francisco.

Because I was managing the division, I didn't run the defense of Federated. Jim Stern and Tom Hill dealt with Goldfeder; as Campeau raised his offer from forty-eight dollars to sixty to sixty-nine, it was clear that Federated was lost. The fight has been documented, and there isn't much to add to the takeover of the classiest of all department store chains. For me, of course, it was the final break with a company for which my father had worked and helped create.

During the Federated conversations, I suspected E. J. was talking to Campeau. Finally, toward the end of the two-month fight, E. J. came to me to tell me that he had invested $350 million into the Federated-Allied combination. I told him that it was dangerous to be a minority investor with a man who looked like he might end badly. Campeau was paying too much and leveraging the business excessively. E. J., in his modest manner, told me that he wanted an option to develop the future Federated-Allied store in malls and that he was protected by an option. I pointed out to him that he had little protection. The option would be without value if Campeau defaulted.

E. J.'s business rationale for investing with Campeau seemed secondary to personal reasons. His business relationships were disappearing. Tom Macioce had left Allied within three months of the takeover. The top management of Federated was about to be ousted. Socially, he was alone in his office. He was a widower, and Eddie Jr. was away from Youngstown running the San Francisco 49ers. Loneliness made him desperate to be part of the action. At sixty-five, he didn't want to be left out.

❧

My grandfather Joseph Rabinovitz ("JR") joined his brothers Jacob and Julius, who founded the Economy Grocery Stores in Boston in 1915. JR was joined in 1918 by his oldest son, Sidney, who purchased Jacob's shares, and later by his two other sons, Harvard graduates Norman and Irving. My mother was the only sibling not directly involved, but Dad was on the board of directors.

Despite a near-bankruptcy experience, by the 1960s, its successor, the Stop&Shop Companies, had attained a leading market share in much of New England. The supermarket landscape, however, was intensely competitive with pretax profit margins an unsatisfactory 1 to 2 percent.

To increase supermarket profitability, Sidney had taken the bold step of abandoning the Top Value stamp program that, for decades, had been the promotional vehicle of Stop&Shop and other major grocery chains. Additionally, the company diversified into the emerging discount business by acquiring Bradlees, a soft goods discounter; Perkins, a tobacconist; and later, Off the Rack, a nascent off-price retailer. It also started Medi-Mart, a drug retailer.

My brother, Richard, as JR's oldest grandson, had always been expected to join the family business; in 1958, immediately upon graduation from HBS, he became an apprentice butcher at the Stop&Shop on Memorial Drive in Cambridge. Over the next decade, he worked his way into higher management positions. He managed a traditional SHP in Quincy, then a discount supermarket in a GEM Club store, and eventually opened and managed a number of Bradlees discount supermarkets. These stores became successful, and Richard was appointed sales manager for the company. His accomplishments were clear.

Sidney Rabb was the CEO and dominated the business and his brothers. His power was not derived solely from his aggressive personality and his early ownership; when his mother had a nervous breakdown in the 1920s and Norman, Irving, and Mother were dispersed to live with relatives, Sidney had assumed some of his parents' responsibilities.

Regrettably for my brother, Sidney's daughter Carol Goldberg joined SHP in the early 1960s. Carol had no business experience and was Richard's contemporary. Her husband, Avram, became a lawyer at the company just before Richard arrived.

Sidney grew increasingly critical of Richard. It was clear that he aimed at harassing Richard to the benefit of promoting Carol. Given my father's business reputation, his status as a board member, and the fact that he was Richard's father, he would have the right and opportunity to challenge Sidney Rabb on his treatment of Richard. While SHP was a public company, Mother was a large shareholder and had legitimate interests.

Richard left the company in 1969, moved to NYC, and eventually founded a successful fine arts business. He never forgave Dad for his lack of support.

Avram became chief operating officer in the mid-1970s. Over the next decade, Bradlees finally improved despite competition from Caldor. After years of frustration, management enlarged the footprint of the supermarkets to create Super Stop&Shops with, among other amenities, more prepared food. Pretax profit margins doubled.

Sidney Rabb died from cancer in 1985. He was mourned but not missed. He had built a major company and transformed an industry. The top award of the Food Market Industry bears his name. He was a force, sharing Massachusetts political and cultural power with the Kennedys, Boston Brahmin leader Ralph Lowell, and Cardinal Richard James Cushing. He was admired and feared, but few, including my mother, felt affection for him.

In 1985, Avram became chairman and CEO, and Carol became president. I had rejoined the board upon the sale of Associated Dry Goods and its subsidiary Caldor. Perkins and Medi-Mart were sold in order to concentrate on Bradlees and the supermarkets, which, by 1987, had total sales of $4.2 billion.

In 1961, the New York Stock Exchange forced the dissolution of the Rabb family trust agreement. By the 1980s, the family owned about 25 percent of the stock.

Enter the Hafts, a Washington, DC, father and son who controlled Dart Drug, a local retail drug chain. Encouraged and financed by Mike Milken, they became the prototypical corporate raiders and greenmailers of the 1980s. By the time they focused on Stop&Shop in 1988, they had already made hostile offers for Safeway stores and Dayton Hudson Company.

In 1984, Avram, advised by me and Dick Beattie of Simpson Thacher, began to discuss a defensive leveraged management buyout. It was clear that with only 25 percent ownership and a clean balance sheet, the company was vulnerable to raiders. Over half a dozen dinners in Boston, we prepared a plan.

Avram was tentative about initiating a management proposal. The reason for his hesitancy has never been clear. My suspicion is that he was unsure of his ability to run a leveraged company and felt that, as the son-in-law of Sidney, he would be perceived as stealing the company from the families of Norman, Irving, and Mother. The latter reason would be odd because Julian Edison and I were both directors and would have supported him.

On January 21, 1988, the Hafts launched a hostile tender for all the shares of the company at thirty dollars per share. Later, they raised the offer to thirty-seven dollars. Until the final acquisition of Stop&Shop by Kohlberg Kravis Roberts two months later—in March 1988—at forty-four dollars per share, as the investment banker for the company, I worked ceaselessly to find an alternative.

Our initial strategy was, of course, to fend off the Hafts. As greenmailers, their objective was to get bought out of their stock at a premium. They had been successful a number of times, and they would repeat the tactic many times in the future.

However, unless Avram was willing to lead a buyout, we would be acquired.

Because of the situation's importance to the family, I moved into the Four Seasons Hotel in Boston. I had my work cut out for me. It was unlikely that one strategic buyer would buy both Bradlees and the supermarkets, so I needed to find separate buyers. I knew that Bradlees, with its less dominant position, would be the more difficult to sell. One night, I had a long conversation with Sol Price, who had started Price Club, a membership club retailer based in San Diego. I begged Sol to buy Bradlees for its 169 East Coast retail locations. He said firmly that he had no interest in any part of the company. "Sol," I said, "you're missing my drift. I understand that in reality you don't have any interest, but that is beside the point. I need you to say you might have interest!" I had to get some competition going between strategic buyers. Despite Sol's eventual help, I could not induce any company to buy Bradlees.

I had more luck with financial buyers. Both Thomas H. Lee and KKR were interested. Tom Lee had the inside track. The family knew him. He was from Boston, and the first company his fund had acquired was a wholesale fish business owned by Esther Rabb's family.

On the final night when the bids were due, Tom had the highest offer. But I lost contact with Tom for almost twenty-four hours. As the deadline approached, KKR put in a final bid of forty-four dollars. In that era before cell phones, I could not find Tom. If I had, I would have gotten him to raise his bid.

We sold the business to KKR for a total value of just over $1 billion. In retrospect, it seems like a small amount for such a dominant company. The family and Tom felt that Dick Beattie's participation had given KKR the inside track because he had often represented KKR. I am sure Dick was pleased that KKR won, but he didn't influence the decision. I made the decision to accept KKR's final offer.

I negotiated with KKR on behalf of our family and Norman's and Irving's to "roll over" 7.5 percent of its stock into the leveraged equity of the new company. Sidney's family, Avram and Carol Goldberg, as part of management, were making their own deal with KKR.

At a meeting held at the Somerset Club on Commonwealth Avenue, we asked each family if they wanted to subscribe for their full amount. Richard and I acquired the stock Norman's and Irving's families did not want. In 1996, when KKR sold Stop&Shop to Koninklijke Ahold N.V. of Belgium, the three families made more money than on the initial sale.

Mother was remarkably unemotional about the sale. Richard had little regard for Avram and Carol, given their past, and welcomed the liquidity. I had mixed emotions. I would miss the cohesiveness of the family and the influence that comes from a successful business.

As a business decision, though, it was timely. The competitive supermarket industry was about to face a new entity: Walmart.

Over the ensuing years, through weddings, bar mitzvahs, and funerals, the Rabb first cousins—Hope, Jane, Betty, Jim, Richard, and I—have remained close. Norman died in 1997, Mother in 2006, and Irving in 2008. All in their nineties.

We have had less contact with Sidney's family. Avram and Carol were pushed out by KKR shortly after the sale. Helene, Sidney and Esther's oldest daughter, died in 2010. Her husband, Norman Cahners, a great business success whom I represented for years, died in 1995. Sidney's granddaughter Deb is treasurer of the Commonwealth of Massachusetts, the last glimmer of Sidney's political clout.

❧

The four years between the May 1984 sale of Lehman and May 1988 had been exciting and exhausting. Although Lehman had been sold, I had emerged as a vice chairman of the new firm, Shearson Lehman Brothers. Ken Auletta, in a TV interview, compared me to Churchill emerging from obscurity to lead Britain in WWII. (The comparison to Churchill seemed a little much.)

I had been involved in almost every merger in the US department store business. The Lehman retail legacy, built over the years by my predecessors, had been obliterated. Fortunately, the department store legends—such as Fred Lazarus, my father, Jack Straus at Macy's and Buster May of the May Company—were not alive to witness the destruction of their companies. Even the Stop&Shop I knew ceased to exist.

As if to add an exclamation point to the close of this chapter, the closing dinner for the SHP sale and my final dinner as overseer, in Boston and Cambridge, were on the same night, May 25, 1988.

My family was also moving on. Joshua was at Harvard College, Abigail was about to enter Williams, and Kate was having a good high school career at Taft. But I could sense the end of my marriage to Linda.

It was time to turn the page.

CHAPTER 26

Shearson Lehman Brothers

(Barbarians Within—1988)

As I approached my fiftieth birthday in the summer of 1988, I had been an investment banking adviser long enough. I wanted to return to my ambition from almost a decade before, of being an investor.

The investment banking division had climbed the rankings to the fourth position in the industry and didn't require both Sherman and me to chair it. It was satisfying to realize that we had merged dysfunctional Lehman bankers with Shearson to create a smooth-running operation.

We had accomplished this feat by a number of steps worth noting.

First, we had told all our bankers that we would have one culture. We would neither brook cliques nor elegiac longings. We were now a combined firm.

In my experience, most mergers fail because top management fails to impose a single culture. A better culture is preferable, but the key issue is one culture, tolerating no variations. What culture did we impose? The principal components were integrity, accountability, teamwork, responsibility, honesty, and optimism. Investment banking isn't that hard. If a banker calls on a potential client consistently, using the resources available at a firm the size of Shearson, they will eventually be successful. We harped on these characteristics. Political speech writers tell you that themes need to be repeated seven times in a single speech. We kept repeating that if the bankers worked to incorporate these values, we would be successful.

After I had delivered one of my exhortations, when we were alone, sometimes Sherman would shake his head in wonder. I had learned something from Pete Dawkins and von Clausewitz; namely, a leader must always be optimistic. The troops look at the leader and gauge their sentiment. I could cry in my office when the door was shut, Dawkins cautioned me, but on the way into the office, I must always smile.

We didn't tolerate bankers who didn't cooperate with their partners or do what we asked them. This, of course, was evident in the way we handled the issues such as the Bingham subterfuge. The relationship Sherman and I forged demonstrated the culture and values we sought. I should emphasize that few—except to his credit, Peter Cohen— thought the combination would be successful, because Sherman and I seemed to have different personalities, interests, and strengths. *Investors Daily Digest*, an industry magazine, pictured us on its cover, labeling us the odd couple and describing how our leadership had restored Lehman to a leading position. Of course, it was our complementing strengths and our genuine liking of each other that made us successful.

Peter Cohen had great strengths but also critical weaknesses. He had emerged from the shadow of Sandy Weil when Sandy became president of the parent, American Express. People are often what they look like. Cohen was small and muscular with a crew cut and the noxious habit of chewing on an unlit cigar. He looked like he was always ready for action. He wasn't Ivy League, and he didn't fit the mold of a major firm CEO. He was bold enough to acquire Lehman, but he always wanted more. In December 1987, ambition led him to the unfortunate acquisition of E. F. Hutton, run by the eccentric Robert Fomon, for $1 billion. Sherman and I warned him that Hutton had no value to the banking business, but his objective was to acquire a retail equity sales force of sufficient size to propel Shearson Lehman beyond Merrill Lynch. Merrill Lynch poached most of Hutton's salesmen, and Fomon left Shearson with a number of undisclosed contracts—including, ironically, one to Sidney Kahn, who had long since been pushed out of Lehman.

Cohen had risen to power surrounded by cronies who were not sufficiently competent to run a firm as diverse as Shearson Lehman. His protection of them reminded me of Koch's relationships with some of his crew in City Hall. Cohen had made his pals vice chairman. Their frat-like behavior affected Sherman and me in a number of ways, including Cohen's policy of compensating all the vice chairmen equally. Nice in theory but bad in practice, particularly when we were running the most profitable division and handling revenue-producing clients as well.

Cohen refused my requests for higher compensation but gave me permission to talk to Jim Robinson. Accessibility was one of Robinson's strongest characteristics. I lunched with Jim in the executive dining room on the top floor of our office tower. He listened to my case sympathetically but said he couldn't go over Cohen's head. Then he asked a curious question. What else might he do for me?

My response was spontaneous. "Jim, I would like you to give a million dollars to Harvard." Without batting an eyelash, he remarked that it was an interesting idea. I mentioned that Harvard was establishing an ethics program under Professor Dennis Thompson. Within six months, Amex president Lou Gerstner and Harvard University president Derek Bok announced the American Express Fund for Curricular Development in Ethics.

The way was open to change the direction of my career. Cohen had been murmuring about competing with some of the securities firms, as well as the emerging leverage buyout firms, in buying companies. Certainly Shearson's access to capital as a subsidiary of American Express would facilitate such a move. I approached Cohen with a suggestion that I head a new division, the Merchant Banking Division, and raise a $1 billion fund. We would approach endowments, public pension funds, and banks. With Robinson's approval, Shearson would seed the fund with $200 million.

Don Glickman, my partner from Monro Muffler, joined our team, as did Alan Washkowitz. We spent a year traveling the globe in search of capital.

In 1988, the leveraged buyout business was in its infancy. Raising money wasn't easy. We were a first-time fund. I was embarrassed at a meeting of the common fund, the investing entity of a number of college endowments, when a principal of Clayton Dubilier scoffed at our inexperience. Success was partially a matter of the number of meetings before you collapsed. On one foray, Alan and I flew to Paris, changing clothes on the plane to be on time for a meeting with Société General. When we arrived, we were not even offered a cup of coffee. After the meeting, Alan and I lunched quickly on the Left Bank and flew home. Surprisingly, Société General invested $25 million.

A broker in Shearson's San Francisco office indicated that the Colorado State Pension Fund had heard about leverage buyout funds and might be interested. On this cold call, we raised $50 million.

For the most part, financial institutions hoped for reciprocal business from Shearson Lehman Brothers. That is certainly why Nippon Life Insurance Company, then the largest company in the world, invested $250 million.

There was an interesting sidebar to Nippon Life's investment. At dinner at the Waldorf Hotel with Nippon's chief executive, I asked about Japan's financial dominance. Nippon was the world's largest company, and five of the top commercial banks were Japanese. Japanese industries, particularly autos, were outperforming their American counterparts. He assured me that this domination would not continue. "How can you be so sure?" I asked.

"After the war," he said, "my generation worked all the time to lift Japan from the ashes. But the new generation doesn't have the same will and drive to succeed. They will not work weekends!" Over time, he said, Japan's prominence would fade.

With an investment by Shearson itself and commitments from commercial banks Bankers Trust and Manufacturers Hanover, and insurance companies such as Connecticut General and Mass Mutual, we had raised $1.25 billion, making the Shearson Lehman Merchant Banking Fund the largest fund among investment banks at that time. The closing was scheduled for December 1988.

F. Ross Johnson had been a Lehman client at Standard Brands

since Lehman represented him in the 1981 merger with Nabisco. Subsequently, Nabisco had been acquired by the large tobacco company RJR. In 1986, Johnson became CEO of RJR Nabisco. He was not only a client but also a friend of Jim Robinson.

In the spring of 1988, I heard some discussion of a possible RJR Nabisco "going private" transaction. As a roughly $20 billion deal, it would be the largest management buyout. I assumed that if it happened, we would act in our traditional role as adviser.

At a social board dinner, Johnson apparently mentioned that he was thinking about a management buyout. At that time, there was definitely no plan, no financing, and, in fact, no price. Regrettably, Peter Atkins, a protégé of Joe Flom at Skadden Arps, insisted that since Johnson told the board, he was obligated to announce it publicly.

I think that Akins' advice was too conservative. The idea had not yet crossed the threshold of a plan. No steps had been taken; neither Shearson nor legal advisers had been retained by Johnson.

Johnson unfortunately also had as an informal adviser Andy Sage, then no longer a full-time employee of Shearson Lehman. He had left Lehman before the Shearson merger to invest his own money.

When I first joined Lehman Brothers in September 1960, Andy was the operating head of the small syndicate department. Syndicate departments, in those days, were clubs staffed by personalities who socialized with one another. Fred Whittemore, head of Morgan Stanley's syndicate department, was the de facto leader of this exclusive group.

A scion of famous banking families and a member of Piping Rock, the tony gentile country club near Oyster Bay, Andy commuted to Wall Street by seaplane daily. Andy had many admirable qualities, but he wasn't a top intellect, lacked sufficient discipline to graduate college, and didn't want to lead anything. He had given up the post of president of Lehman when Fred Ehrman was fired in 1973.

The story of the RJR Nabisco fiasco, chronicled by Bryan Burrough in *Barbarians at the Gate*, doesn't bear repeating. Burrough detailed the fight for ownership and the principal characters. Yet, as in the case of

Ken Auletta's account of Lehman Brothers' demise, the book does need some clarification.

Because the process began before there was a plan, Johnson, advised by Shearson, was scrambling from the first tee. They had not even decided on a price to offer shareholders. RJR stock was trading around fifty-seven dollars. Johnson decided on a bid of seventy-five dollars, thinking, I suppose, that it gave him more room to increase later. But KKR immediately countered with a bid of ninety dollars.

Cohen needed a win. RJR and merchant banking offered an opportunity. Combined with Robinson's friendship with Johnson, the mixture created a combustible environment. Shearson's business judgment went up in flames. Fortunately, I was no longer the merger maven, nor even involved in investment banking decisions. Cohen and Tom Hill ran the RJR-Nabisco deal.

One of Cohen's motivations was to rival Henry Kravis as one of Wall Street's power hitters. Kravis had approached Cohen to join in the bid. I believed then, and still do, that Kravis was playing Cohen and never wanted to give Shearson the status of a joint bidder. It was a moot point, though, because the deal quickly became a battle.

My involvement was solely through the $1.25 billion merchant banking fund. As the deal was shaping up, with a topping bid by KKR of ninety dollars per share over Johnson's and Shearson's seventy-five dollars, it was going to need a lot of equity. The logical place for Cohen to get it was from our fund.

The fund had not yet closed, and the limited partners' commitments had not been funded. The prospective limited partners had cautioned against using the fund to benefit Shearson as opposed to benefitting them. Repeatedly, I assured them that I would protect their interests. That is, I wouldn't allow the fund to invest in a deal that wasn't advantageous to the limited partners. My word was already being challenged.

In *Barbarians*, Burrough wrote that "Cohen froze Solomon" out of the deal. The facts are contrary. Cohen wanted to involve me, but I narrowly defined my role. I was no longer part of the banking division. I wanted to distance the fund from Shearson, the adviser to the management group.

Because of my relationships, however, I approached Mark Solow, chief of leveraged financing at Manufacturers Hanover, and Bob O'Brien at Bankers Trust to provide the senior debt to finance the offer. Burrough must have known this, since he reported a call Solow made to Dick Beattie of Simpson Thacher, trying to locate me to discuss the bank's position. I have no idea why he missed this inconsistency.

To advise me—and thus, the fund—I picked Jim Stern, a protégé of mine and manager of Shearson's financing desk. Jim had been a summer associate during college, then joined the firm after graduation from Harvard Business School in 1974. He had distinguished himself working on many of our retail accounts. I trusted his judgment. My instructions were to analyze the bids and to tell me when one exceeded a reasonable price for the deal. While I would not have chosen the RJR buyout as our initial investment, I might be willing to support an investment under the right circumstances.

The importance of making the correct judgment can't be overstated, for both my own reputation and the firm's. As part of the fund's partnership agreement, the limited partners had put their faith in my independence by insisting that I personally approve each investment.

Even with equity from the fund and other sources and senior debt, Cohen would need additional long-term subordinated debt financing. Drexel Burnham was financing KKR. Salomon Brothers was an alternative source. Its CEO John Gutfreund was in his prime, its President Tom Strauss was Cohen's close friend, and, with its balance sheet and expertise, Salomon was a powerhouse.

When Cohen and Johnson raised their bid to ninety-two dollars per share, Stern flashed the warning signal. At that price, with the normal debt leverage of four to five times EBITDA, the deal barely met the fund's targeted return of 25 percent. I told Cohen that I was not sure we would approve an investment above ninety-two dollars. He was shocked. Shearson was committed to the purchase, and he needed equity from the fund. How, he demanded, could I deny him this capital since he was CEO of the firm? We had dinner at a Chinese restaurant on the Upper East Side. He praised me as the firm's star and hoped I would reconsider my position on the investment. Of course, I was torn.

My decision was as difficult as any I would have to make in business. Peter, unlike Glucksman, was a supporter and friend. He had promoted me twice on his initiative, clearly without the support of senior management and some of his closest advisers. I had finally achieved what I wanted, namely, to run a major leveraged buyout fund at what I perceived was the beginning of a positive cycle. I had also recreated a major investment banking business and was loyal to my colleagues in my small merchant banking group and the larger banking division.

On the other hand, I had given my word to our limited partners that Shearson Lehman would not use the fund to advance its own business, and that was exactly what we were doing. I also recognized immediately that even if Shearson didn't acquire RJR, another Shearson deal would appear and create the same pressure. Independence was not going to happen. Finally, Peter still hadn't agreed to a compensation structure for our group. This underscored the lack of independence. If I was not independent, then I would be trapped inside a global bank.

After weighing the issues, I concluded that I did not want to compromise my independence and integrity. Despite my loyalties, I could not simply roll over. I told Peter that if our group decided RJR was not a good investment for the fund, we would not support him. The only way he could get to the money for this investment was to replace me.

The timing of the bidding war coincided with my birthday. We had a Sunday-night party in the newly renovated Rainbow Room in Rockefeller Center. And Linda surprised me with the gift of a week at the New York Yankees' fantasy camp, playing baseball with former and current Yankee greats. It was the only camp not run by the Major League team itself; rather, it was run by Mickey Mantle and Whitey Ford. Few baseball experiences could beat being with these two Hall of Famers daily. My friends Fred Roberts and Mike Danziger joined me. Whitey, in 1988, had an enormous pot belly and could barely walk, but his curve still broke hard and away. And Mickey looked like the longtime drinker he, in truth, was. Still, the ball coming off his bat sounded like thunder and lightning combined.

Other Yankees—Moose Skowron, Mickey Rivers, Johnny Blanchard, Dick Howser, Hank Bauer—all veteran World Series players, joined them. Gene Monahan, the Yankees and Jets trainer, ministered to the camp. The only active player was Ron Guidry, known as Gator or Louisiana Lightning. They all seemed to simultaneously respect and fear Mickey.

We played games daily in Kissimmee, Florida, with Whitey pitching for both teams. His first pitch was over the middle, and you were expected to swing. If you didn't, the next pitch was faster. By the third pitch, he threw a curve at your head. After one time at bat, you swung on the first pitch.

One day, Guidry decided he would pitch. By that time, we had played on the same team and become chummy. Guidry was, in 1988, the active pitcher in the American League with the most wins. His first pitch to me was around eighty-five miles per hour. I couldn't lift the bat off my shoulders in time to swing. A batter has four-tenths of a second to swing at an 85 mph fastball. I decided to swing on his windup. I don't think I ever saw the pitch, but I lined it off the right center field wall. The catcher was so shocked he leaped up and yelled, "Holy shit!" Mantle, umpiring at second, was laughing as I slid safely into second base.

After the game, Guidry was on the trainer's table getting a rubdown from Monahan. He was complaining to Fred Roberts and me that George Steinbrenner, the Yankees owner, was offering him just $400,000 for the 1989 season. He wanted $800,000. I had just hit a double off the wall off his fastball. "Gator," Fred said. "Do you know how long it takes a taxi meter in Lafayette to reach $400,000?"

Guidry ultimately got his $800,000.

Mickey's former teammates knew how volatile he could be. After one game, we were sitting around drinking, as usual. During the game that day, when Guidry was pitching for our team, I had dropped an easy pop fly behind second base. Two runs had scored. I asked Guidry and Whitey, who was sitting next to me, if they ever got mad when a fielder dropped a fly ball or made an error. Guidry said he never got mad unless the fielder came into the dugout complaining about a lousy pitch that made him look bad.

From across the table, Mickey attacked Whitey verbally. "I got mad sometimes," he fumed. "I'm still mad about that shitty curveball Whitey threw Robinson in Baltimore." Even Whitey, who knew Mickey better than anyone, was taken aback. The story, apparently, was that in 1953—then a scant thirty-five years earlier—Brooks Robinson, later a Hall of Fame third baseman, had hit a ball to right center field in Baltimore. Mickey had leaped against the wall and caught his spikes in the chicken wire at the base of the wall. Mickey had badly hurt his knee, in the first of many injuries. Fred and I thought Mickey was kidding. His former teammates knew he wasn't and dispersed.

The fantasy camp was memorable. Fred kept up with Mickey and his wife, Marlene, until Mickey's death in 2003. Whitey was so shaken by Mickey's death that he stopped drinking and lost a lot of weight. The last time we saw him was at Joe Garagiola's annual BAT dinner for the old timers' pension fund. Blanchard kept up with me whenever he saw my name in the press.

The longer-run benefit to me was I realized what bad physical shape I was in. While I hadn't gotten fat, at fifty, I had slowed a great deal. During the week, I pulled a hamstring. Recognizing that I couldn't run the bases with abandon or swing a bat without creaking was a wake-up call. After the camp, I began to work with a trainer, a practice I have continued ever since.

Meanwhile, as Cohen and Johnson schemed, a new group led by First Boston entered the bidding. The deal had become a donnybrook. No firm wanted to be left out. First Boston proposed a plan stitched together by my close friend Dan Lufkin. The viability of the deal depended on a favorable tax ruling that seemed unlikely. The price might be between $105 and $118.

The new offer, as far-fetched as it was, allowed the RJR Special Committee to delay making a decision. It was clear later that the board had no intention of letting Johnson and thus Shearson buy the company. First Boston's scheme was just a lucky diversion that gave KKR another opportunity to bid.

At that time, much was made in the press of the shrewdness of Henry Kravis, who gave all the appearances of leaving town and abandoning the contest. In fact, this was irrelevant to the outcome.

In late fall 1988, the bidding resumed, escalating from $94 to $100, and then to $106, $108 and $112. KKR and Shearson each proposed combinations of cash, payment-in-kind ("PIK"), preferred stocks, and debentures.

When the bidding reached one hundred dollars, our group decided we would not support our own company's bid. It is difficult to describe the tension between Peter and me. I told him the only way he could use the fund's capital was, in fact, to fire me. I had tried to avoid such a train wreck outcome but now saw no alternative.

On a Sunday at the end of a frantic week, the RJR Nabisco board met to decide the winner. It decided to sell to KKR but not because its bid was higher; it had the same value as Shearson Lehman's. Nor did it pick KKR because KKR offered to "reset" the value of the securities if the market proved them less valuable, as was reported. It chose KKR because it didn't want to sell to Ross Johnson. KKR became the owner but not the winner. There were no unequivocal winners in the RJR deal.

The KKR fund, with the RJR investment, did poorly, although Kravis did retain his title as king of the buyout guys—until Pete Peterson and Steve Schwarzman at Blackstone grew bigger—if anyone cares about that status.

Johnson got fired but left with a lot of money. He emerged with a reputation as one of the greediest men on the planet. The first paragraph of his obituary was assured.

Ironically, Lou Gerstner, who was president of Amex at the time, became CEO of RJR Nabisco.

Peter Cohen looked like a kid playing a grown-up's game. He had gambled once again, hoping to match his Lehman coup, but he ended up looking more like a Hutton replay. Shearson's reputation, both because it didn't win and it had backed Johnson, suffered a major setback.

Once again, my life would have to change.

Sherman Lewis, a great partner—Shearson Lehman, 1987

Edgar, John Angelo, and daughter Kate

Under Edgar's watchful eye

With Edgar at Saratoga

A happy Susan with a Missouri River rainbow

Capt. Tom Langman on our whaler

Dan Lufkin

John Eastman

Rock Ringling and Dick Beattie in Yellowstone

The Yankee on the left hit 536 home runs

The king and I at Bay Hill, Florida

Playing golf, talking fishing with Jack Nicklaus and Scott Hedrick

Sixtieth birthday party at the National Golf Club

Judy Vance and John McCarter at PJSC

Pete Peterson on a CFR trip to Libya, April 2005
(Photograph taken by Peter J. Solomon)

Sacred Valley, Peru—2017

Joshua, Abigail, Josh, Kate, and Laura

Justin Schiller guided my children's literature and illustration collecting

Celebrating MTC's Tony Award for *Doubt*—2005
(Photograph by Anita and Steve Shevett)

Ann, Abby, and John

Everyone should have a great brother.

Sara's Dalton graduation with the family

The first dozen

The second dozen

PART IV

CHAPTER 27

New Challenges: 1989–1990

In the decade of the 1990s, my life broke sharply with the pattern of my first fifty years. Until then, I had lived a conventional life for a middle-class Jewish kid from New York City. Except for my years in government, I had followed the career path and personal life expected by my parents and anticipated by my friends.

We often tritely remark that we are lucky to be alive, but one incident proved how true that comment is.

In April 1988, on the afternoon of Passover and the first night's Seder, Abigail and I drove from North Stamford to Watertown to pick Kate up. Abigail was learning to drive, and I thought this would be a good time for her to get some road experience. We were nearing the exit to Watertown, driving within the speed limit on Highway 84. Abigail must have passed another car, and she was near the center barrier.

I made an almost fatal error. "Abigail," I said, "you are too close to the metal divider. Move back to the right lane."

In response to this comment, Abigail must have pressed the accelerator, not the brake. The station wagon shot forth. Startled by the surging vehicle, she turned the wheel sharply right and flew across the highway. As she neared the barrier on the right, she turned left; the vehicle's right wheels went up the sloped end of the steel barrier and were propelled into the air. As the car rose from the ground, I said to myself, "Oh my God, we are going to die." Oddly, I felt no fear, only sadness that my life was ending unfulfilled. The wagon then did a somersault, flipping over to the left before coming to rest facing back down the highway.

The last moments I can only deduce because at some point I lost consciousness. I woke up upside down in the passenger's seat with the car's roof below me. Disoriented, it took me a minute to realize I was looking at the shoes of people coming to help us. As I moved my hand, there seemed to be blood everywhere, but I couldn't find a cut on me. Later, I realized I had a cut on my finger and where I put it was blood.

My head was wrenched to the outside, but with effort, I turned toward Abigail. I consciously said to myself that this might be the worst moment of my life. My darling daughter could be dead or maimed. Hesitantly, I called "Abigail, are you okay?"

Amazingly, she replied, "Yes."

The front window had fragmented, but the window on Abigail's driver's side had disappeared. With effort, we both slid upside down through that window. I had to navigate over the steering wheel. The car was flattened. We sat on the side of the highway as people surrounded us. After a few moments, Abigail got up and returned to the smashed wreck. She was removing her music cassette from the car.

Emergency crews arrived and insisted that they examine us, although we told them we were fine. We had an exam in an ambulance but refused to go to the hospital. A flatbed truck arrived to haul the wreck away. We asked him to take us to a car rental place, which, not surprisingly, was a sideline of the wrecker.

We were forty-five minutes late to pick up Kate at Taft. We didn't have a cell phone, and we didn't want to alarm her. Kate was waiting patiently in her room.

"I worried you had an accident," she said.

There were minor cuts on our faces, and fragments of glass embedded in our faces and bodies.

"We did," we said, "but when we get back to Stamford, don't tell your mother. We'll tell her later."

It took me about a year to recover from anxieties, even when I was driving. When the kids drove, I was fearful.

That day impacted my life. The terror of near death and, worse, the death of my child had a lasting influence on my later life. It stimulated me to make my subsequent series of decisions and lessened my anxiety about any less consequential events. It led me to change the pattern of my life. I wonder whether I was dying and something pulled me back.

While change coincidently occurred around my fiftieth birthday, it was not related to age. Then and now, my decisions were the culminations of thoughts and plans I had contemplated for a decade and my renewed confidence.

In December 1988, I told Peter Cohen I was leaving Shearson Lehman. My reason was simple and obvious: he had violated our agreement on the independence of the merchant banking fund. I didn't believe he had any interest in having an independent fund, and I didn't want to manage a fund where investments were made for any reason other than a good return to the limited partners. I could also see where Shearson and similar diversified securities firms were headed.

I had predicted that, with beefed-up balance sheets and global ambitions, the securities firms and commercial banks would commit their capital to private investments and engage increasingly in proprietary trading. Advisory work is harder than investing. With access to public capital and increased borrowing, the temptation to invest would be irresistible; Mike Milken, as well as Salomon Brothers, had shown the potential for enormous profits.

In a financial institution, if you emphasize proprietary trading and investing, you will increase the temptation to compete with your clients. Securities firms and commercial banks denied their conflicts with their clients for decades, but in 1989, the increasing conflicts were evident.

It was also clear that the profits from proprietary investing would make these activities more important within firms. And with firms going public and partners having limited liability for losses, their bets would become less prudent. Credit default swaps, which Lehman had first used in a bond offering for Freddie Mac in the early eighties, became prevalent toward the end of the decade. Since each swap required a counterparty, the firms were sometimes taking on risk from counterparties they had not vetted. Derivatives, generally, were becoming commonplace. These financial instruments added complexity and required capital. Seeking fertile markets, firms spread their trading around the world. At the beginning of the 1980s, most firms' foreign operations centered on London. By 1989, the firms had increased their overheads by expanding to the major financial centers of Hong Kong, Singapore, and Tokyo. They were trading 24/7.

There are at least two ramifications from an overreliance on priority trading. First, when there is a conflict, a firm will probably choose its interests over those of its clients. And second, over a period of time, the smarter professionals within the firms would migrate to proprietary activities. That point was particularly important in my thinking. As a collateral result of public ownership and lessening influence within firms of bankers, there were fewer senior bankers.

To avoid a harsh breakup, I suggested to Peter that I simply say what I believed: I didn't want my money or reputation dependent on trading securities I barely understood, with people I hardly knew, in times zones I rarely visited. He was disappointed and repeated his plea about my importance to Shearson. But in negotiating my termination, George Sheinberg, chairman of the firm's Commitment Committee, was particularly antagonistic toward me and my college classmate Daniel Pollack, the noted litigator who negotiated my separation agreement.

❧

I founded Peter J. Solomon Company, LP in February 1989. I hoped that clients would share my vision of an investment bank. Its ethos was an advisory business that offered experienced, independent, objective, and unbiased advice to senior executives and owners. It would not tolerate conflicts among its clients. Its culture would be steeped in the values of a partnership, both with its clients and within the firm. I told prospective clients that we were running against Goldman Sachs and the culture of conflicts.

One of my premises for PJSC was that CEOs needed a trusted

adviser who had been around the block. When I began at Lehman, the Street was populated by seemingly old men. While younger bankers, like myself, scorned these older pre-WWII bankers, clients favored their insights and were loyal. Over the decades of the 1970s and 1980s, investment banking, like most industries, became a game for young, smart business school graduates. The average age dropped and, with it, a lot of judgment. Law firms continued to have senior partners with broad experience, like Dick Beattie at Simpson Thacher and Sam Butler at Cravath, but even that breed was diminishing. More ambitious lawyers, such as Bruce Wasserstein, were leaving law firms for careers in finance.

Now, new CEOs had few contemporaries and fewer advisers more experienced than they. I meant to address this experience gap.

PJSC would also have a leveraged buyout fund. As part of my termination, Shearson Lehman paid me a fair sum. I should have asked Cohen to invest in my new fund. I was too tired to spend much time raising limited partner capital; besides, I would not have had much credibility since I had just assured institutional investors that I was in control of the Shearson fund, only to immediately lose control and leave. I didn't have the bandwidth to raise money and attract and service advisory clients simultaneously.

I decided on a pledge fund, where investors make a loose commitment and provide capital on a deal-by-deal basis. Connecticut General, through David Marks, and Manufacturers Hanover Bank, through Mark Solow, became my two pledged partner institutions.

To my sorrow, Helen Burlew, my long-serving assistant at Lehman and City Hall, was ill with cancer, retired to Florida, and died shortly thereafter. Kathryn Besarany, my second assistant, and Steve Signeavsky, my driver, became my first colleagues. I wasn't sufficiently confident to ask others to leave secure positions, and it seemed not quite right to approach people from an organization I had held together for five years. Donald Glickman remained at Shearson for several months, until I had enough revenue to pay him. He then joined as a founding partner.

The principles behind PJSC made sense to me but not to everyone.

When clients and friends heard I was leaving to start an "independent" investment bank to compete against Goldman Sachs and its peers, they were supportive but skeptical. Larry Phillips, chairman of Phillips-Van Heusen, one of my initial clients, pleaded with me not to do something so foolish as to start my own company, especially at the beginning of the George H. W. Bush recession. He told me to stay at Shearson and become head of the firm. Later, I would say that the only person who thought that my new firm was a good idea was my mother, and I didn't trust her judgment.

It was terrifying to be faced with a new venture and no assured income. My initial goal was to advise on one $500 million merger and to generate $5 million in fees. I made a deal with Cohen for a small amount of space at the former E. F. Hutton. He charged me ninety dollars per square foot, which was usurious, but it didn't matter. I didn't plan to be there for long.

As eager as I was for clients, I had been careful not to approach Shearson clients before I announced my departure. This approach cost me at least one valuable account. Kmart Corporation was facing exactly the strategic decisions my new firm was trying to address. CEO Joe Antonini had diversified into home improvement and other specialty fields and needed to determine how to create value. He came to my office and listened as I described what I was doing but with sincere regret said he couldn't hire me. He needed just the kind of independent perspective I could provide, he said; the problem was that he had just hired Jim Wolfensohn's firm. Despite this disappointment, I kept moving. As always, Edgar Cullman told me he would do anything to support me, a statement consistent with the way he treated me and my family throughout our forty-year relationship.

In April 1989, I flew to London. The English banking landscape was in transition, with major UK firms such as S. G. Warburg and N. M. Rothschild in decline. American firms like Lehman and Goldman were a presence there but were not yet a force in mergers and acquisitions. The only firm that resembled what I wanted to create was Hambro Megan.

Sir Peter Davis was the CEO of Reed, a major London-based

international publisher. Reed owned Cahners Publishing, which had been founded by Norman Cahners. As an associate at Lehman in the 1960s, I had worked on Reed's initial investment Cahners. I had represented Cahners and Reed in a number of acquisitions. Ron Segal, Cahners' CEO, was a proponent of mine. Davis wanted to acquire McGraw Hill; through my relationship with Harold McGraw Sr., I had initiated merger discussions. Davis became my third $250,000 annual retainer.

For years, I had made periodic visits to English retailers. One of the most flamboyant but forward-thinking was Sir Ralph Halpern, CEO of the Burton Group. (A year later, Sir Ralph was joined at Burton's annual meeting by his young model paramour. In an interview, she gave Sir Ralph the nickname "five times a night!")

Burton owned Debenhams, the major department store retailer, with which I had become associated through Sir Anthony Burney. Burton also owned a series of specialty chains, including Next, a junior soft goods company, and Topshop, a teen fashion retailer. The sales of the various divisions were mingled. A number of the chains operated as licensees in the stores of other Burton divisions. Almost every division had a shop in Debenhams. Ralph hired us on our $250,000 retainer to help him determine the sales, earnings, and value of each division.

I left London with my overhead covered. I had five paying clients, DeBartolo, General Cigar, the Burton Group, Reed, and Van Heusen. I then flew to Los Angeles to see Phil Hawley, CEO of the Los Angeles–based department store chain Carter Hawley Hale. Phil, as I have written, had been through a number of challenges. While he had never hired Lehman or me, we had become close friends. Phil had encouraged me to leave Shearson in 1985 and had even called other retailers to retain me. Phil immediately agreed to a $250,000 retainer.

Don Glickman, then, joined me. Apart from two competent commercial lenders—Jeff Kuhr and Lisa Toomy—whom Donald had brought with him, I had no support. I hired the headhunter Barry Nathanson. He found Henry Jackson, then an analyst at First Boston. Henry was a perfect choice. Wharton trained, he had worked in First Boston's corporate finance department. At twenty-three years old,

Henry was ambitious, personable, smart, and a self-starter. When I interviewed him, he asked what I was going to do in five years. It is a question that I have heard frequently in the last twenty-five years. Because I had spent time in government, people assumed that I would eventually run for office or accept an appointment. I told Henry that I doubted I would return to government at any level. I told him the story of how Tommy Tisch assumed my mother showered me with love, which is why I never felt compelled to return to Washington.

I also told Henry he had less risk in joining our firm. All he had to worry about was me and whether we would be profitable. And it was clear we would be. In a large firm, he would always have political risk. His boss may quit or be fired. The firm might deemphasize retailing. It might be sold. Twenty-five years later, it is clear that well-constructed "boutiques" have, in fact, been more stable than the large securities firms and commercial banks.

In 1989, my longtime friend Francis T. "Fay" Vincent became commissioner of baseball. A year later, he asked us to do a study of baseball finances. Oddly, baseball owners don't share financial information with one another, and, unlike in football, there is not much revenue sharing among them. It has frequently been said that while most baseball owners are successful businessmen, when they buy a team, they forget everything that made them successful.

Fay arranged for all the owners to send us their historical financial data. PJSC formulated the data to make it consistent with GAAP accounting, the standard business accounting system.

The results were clear. Teams in major markets—the Yankees and Mets and Dodgers and Angels and Chicago White Sox and Cubs—made money. Three other teams were in the black: Atlanta, because Ted Turner also owned national television distribution; the Toronto Blue Jays, the first franchise to recognize the talents of Dominicans and the profits that could be reaped by scouting, developing, and selling them to other teams; and finally, the Red Sox because of the strong New England television market.

Some of the conclusions were obvious. First, while a fat payroll did not assure a winner, a low payroll almost always assured a loser. Small markets like Kansas City and Cincinnati didn't seem to have a chance. Second, unlike football, baseball's sharing of broadcasting revenues did little to alleviate the disparity. The formula didn't yield enough to make a difference to the poorer teams.

Third, a new ballpark really helped profitability, not only because it was an attraction in itself but because of the phenomena of skyboxes, better concessions, and parking.

Fourth, as the book *Moneyball* would later confirm, large contracts with high school or college undergraduate pitchers rarely work out.

We offered to share this information with the two leagues and their teams, but the owners did not want it. Nothing more came of the study. Several years later, to considerable fanfare, Paul Volcker did his own baseball study and showed the same results.

As part of our work with MLB, I served as adviser to a committee comprised of Bud Selig, owner of the Milwaukee Brewers and later commissioner, Fred Wilpon, owner of the Mets, and Fay. One of the key systems MLB was trying to introduce was "pay for performance," in which a player would receive a base salary plus additional cash for achievements such as a batting title or, if he was a pitcher, twenty wins.

A perfect test arose. Fred was negotiating with Dwight Gooden, a great young pitcher for the Mets. Fred said he would test out a series of "bonus for milestone" arrangements with Gooden. The committee was encouraged.

At a subsequent meeting, Fred reported that he had indeed reached an agreement with Gooden based on the type of contingent payment we wanted. With great satisfaction, Fred said Gooden had agreed to a base salary of $2 million with $100k bonuses for twenty wins, the Cy Young Award, and maybe the World Series. We waited for the punch line. There was none. Gooden was getting what he would have gotten anyway, plus bonuses. Fred's contingent package wasn't one at all.

Baseball hasn't met the challenge of reigning in compensation to reasonable levels. It continues to pay tens of millions to players who haven't proven themselves or have already peaked, and it has few outs in the case of underperformance. It is one of the few industries whose comp programs are worse than investment banking's.

Fay's tenure as commissioner was marked by a series of disputes in which, for the most part, he took the right side. Maintaining the ban on Pete Rose because he bet on his own team and was still refusing to acknowledge it provoked a lot of heat. (We had a similar case in the securities industry with Mike Milken. To this day, Milken, who served two years in prison for racketeering and fraud, insists he did nothing wrong.) Fay's ultimate undoing, though, was the issue of realignment, or moving some teams to the Western Division. I never understood why Fay regarded league alignment as a moral issue, but he regarded everything about baseball with the same seriousness, and the owners pressured him relentlessly. I flew from Martha's Vineyard to the Cape on September 2, 1992, to persuade him to hang in, and John McMullen, owner of the Houston Astros, flew from Texas and arrived minutes after me. With a grin, Fay met us at the Hyannis Airport, telling us we were too late. He had already resigned. It was a loss for baseball.

Soon after, Fay joined PJSC. I decided to hold a dinner celebrating the event at the Lotus Club in New York City. Among Fay's friends in attendance were Yogi Berra and Ralph Branca.

After dinner, Berra rose to tell a story about Branca. Every year, the night before opening day, the Dodgers held a dinner at the St. George Hotel in Brooklyn Heights. At the 1952 dinner, as the Dodger players took questions from their fans, a nine-year-old boy rose and asked Branca about the pitch he had thrown to Bobby Thompson, when Thompson hit his famous "shot heard 'round the world" into the left field stands, which beat the Dodgers in the one-game playoff the previous October. Politely, Branca answered that he had two strikes on Thompson, and he knew he could strike him out with another fastball, but because he was ahead in the count, he threw him a curveball to waste a pitch. Unfortunately, Thompson homered. Berra continued with the story; he said, as the Dodgers left the dais, Sal Maglie, the gruff-looking right-hand pitcher for the Dodgers, known as the Barber because he threw so close to batters' heads, said to Branca,

"You dumb guinea bastard, if you can get 'em out with a fastball, throw the fastball!"

That is a real-life lesson!

☙

Strawbridge & Clothier, founded in 1868, had been part of the evolution of department store retailing. In 1930, the company began to expand into the suburbs, a revolutionary move at the time. In 1971, it created the Clover discount chain in anticipation of the growth of more value retailing, locating Clover stores in strip malls.

As part of my new business efforts at Lehman in the 1960s, I began calling on G. Stockton "Stock" Strawbridge. Stock viewed Dad as a mentor from the Associated Merchandising Corporation board meetings. I also knew some of his sons and nephews, who were my contemporaries. Stockton's nephew Frank Strawbridge, who was co-CEO of the company with his cousin Peter, was a friend. When I founded PJSC, Stockton encouraged me, although he had no business to give our firm. Later, when I sent out a mailing describing our early deals, he wrote back on the flyer, saying he was insulted that we did not describe Strawbridge as our first client.

Stockton, who turned the family dry goods store into a retail giant, was a visionary who wanted to make Philadelphia as important as New York. His idea of an upscale shopping mall in downtown Philadelphia continues to be a dream of that city. Strawbridge & Clothier also experienced the effects of retail consolidation in the 1980s. A raider named Ron Baron launched a hostile takeover in 1986. Under Stockton, the company fended off Baron.

While publicly owned, Strawbridge & Clothier continued to be controlled by the family. Stockton remained chairman. The board had no outside directors. It was composed of nine members of the Strawbridge family: two from the Clothier family and five former company executives. If judged by the terms of the later Sarbanes-Oxley legislation, which radically altered the composition of boards and their functioning, Strawbridge's board would have failed every test. Yet in terms of fiduciary responsibilities and making important decisions in a deliberative manner, it was one of the most conscientious boards I have known.

Despite the patriarch's wisdom and intentions, by the early 1990s, the days of the independent department store were numbered. Geographic concentration was too risky; finding sufficient talent was increasingly difficult. The department store share of the overall retail market was continuing to decline. Most upscale independent stores, such as L. S. Ayres in Indianapolis or Sibley's in Rochester, had sold to Associated Dry Goods or other chains or had liquidated.

Despite Stockton's exhortations to do better and simply run the business more profitably, Frank and Peter Strawbridge were sure they could not return to earlier profitability. The competitive pressures were too intense.

With Stockton's blessing, they hired PJSC to find acquisitions as the preferred alternative. We looked at the other similarly positioned companies, such as Bon Ton Stores, but they had identical problems and were less well situated.

From 1993, we worked with Frank and Peter to convince Stockton of the inevitability of a sale. We met frequently with the full board to review progress and alternatives. At each meeting, Stockton voiced his vociferous objections to a sale. The tensions were high, and the board understood that it was moving in a direction the patriarch opposed. I don't know what occurred beyond the confines of the store, but within it, the conversations lay just within the boundaries of civility. Frank was respectful to his uncle but persistent. He demonstrated extraordinary leadership in moving a family and a company to a difficult decision. Unlike many other situations involving family businesses, the strife did not become public. With the valuable assistance of Henry Jackson, I would meet with Frank, Peter, and their cousin Steven; I would also meet alone with Stockton. After months of these meetings, the board voted to seek a sale. As if in a Shakespearean tragedy, Stockton almost immediately suffered a stroke from which he never recovered. He died soon afterward.

The sale itself was triggered by the bankruptcy of Woodward & Lothrop, a Washington, DC–based chain that had acquired

Wanamaker's in 1986. Woodies had previously been acquired by regional mall developer Alfred Taubman, who, like E. J. DeBartolo, aimed to control anchor tenants and their real estate development. Taubman overleveraged Woodies, which had to file for bankruptcy in January 1994.

The bankruptcy of one's competitor might be a positive development, but it was not so for Strawbridge. In the consolidating department store world of the 1990s, the bankruptcy gave Federated the opportunity to buy a major position in the DC/Baltimore market. Federated offered to include Strawbridge in the acquisition group so Strawbridge could acquire Wanamaker's and dominate its home market. It was a more perfect solution to our dilemma than a sale because, with a larger share, it might survive. We negotiated an arrangement with Federated, Boscov's—a local chain that could buy some of Wanamaker's suburban locations—and a real estate developer. The tie to Federated was comfortable. The two companies knew each other well through a joint buying office, Associated Merchandizing Corporation.

In June, we completed the deal, but it had to go before the bankruptcy court. The deal we'd negotiated was for $350 million. We knew the May Company was interested in the assets, as was JC Penney. The May Company needed to bolster its Baltimore store, Hecht's, and moving Hecht's to Philadelphia made sense.

After our group negotiated a price, the May group offered $410.9 million. Our group raised a package that Woodies' creditors valued at $439.1, more than $80 million above our initial offer. We were able to entice Sears into our group by selling it a Tyson's Corner store and promising to retain 1,200 more employees.

On August 9, in a sweltering courtroom in downtown New York City, the bankruptcy judge presented our offer to the creditors' committee. The newspapers reported that more than two hundred lawyers, executives, merchants, other agents, and principals crowded into a courtroom that would normally accommodate seventy-five.

I had never been to an actual auction of bankruptcy assets. Once our bid was presented, May Company conferred and returned with a bid of $480 million. After that aggressive move, our team left to caucus.

Despite our urging, Federated declined to raise its bid, and the May Company bought the assets of both Woodies and Wanamaker's.

It was immediately clear to Frank and Peter and to the board that with May Company in the Philadelphia market, we could not compete. Strawbridge's independence would end.

We began the sale process immediately thereafter. Federated was not interested in Philadelphia. There were no other buyers for the whole company, so we decided to divide the business, seeking a buyer for Clover and another for the Strawbridge department stores.

We thought Kohl's was the most logical buyer for Clover, but it was reluctant to acquire. After an exhaustive search, we sold the Clover stores to a public real estate company that eventually redeveloped them into various other stores.

Finally, we negotiated the sale of the Strawbridge stores to the May Company. The financial result was pleasing to the board; at the shareholders' meeting in the store, attended by hundreds of shareholders and analysts, Frank explained why the sale was necessary and described the steps management had taken to find other alternatives. While Henry wanted to sit in front, I advised him that we would be better off sitting to the side or in the middle of the shareholders so we were less open to attack if shareholders decided to vent on an agent.

The meeting was not angry but civil and sad. The shareholders accepted the inevitable and the goodwill of Frank and the board.

That was one of our most important assignments. We were dealing with a family, its generational relationships, and an important tradition. I was proud of how we handled ourselves and of our ability to handle delicate, less quantifiable issues. Henry, once again, showed himself to be extremely able and thoughtful.

Of course, I regretted having to represent positions that Stockton himself opposed, and I regretted his death. He was a great friend and supporter. Frank and I continue to be good friends, and he served as a director of Monro Muffler for many years. Every Christmas, I ask him if he has second thoughts about the sale or not being in the department store business, and he affirms his decision. Then and now, I view this relationship and our work as one of the high points in PJSC's history.

CHAPTER 28

Lost Opportunities

> The perfect is the enemy of the good.
> (Voltaire)

Starting a new business isn't easy, but sometimes even the setbacks reinforce the premise. In our case, the premise was the need by senior executives for investment banking advice from a trusted and unconflicted source. Such was the case of Dunkin' Donuts, Inc.

Bob Rosenberg and I sat in alphabetical order next to each other in Section B the first year of HBS. A graduate of the Cornell University School of Hotel Administration, Bob grew up under his father, Bill, who had started Dunkin' Donuts after World War II. "Rose" and I were friends, but Goldman Sachs was Dunkin's banker.

In early 1989, a Canadian raider announced a hostile tender for Dunkin' Donuts. I called Rose and suggested he could use our help. He needed someone he could trust, someone who would supply strategic thinking, not simply defense tactics. I knew our value would be a hard sell. We were in start-up mode, and in those days, Goldman was lionized by managements and directors. But I had an advantage. Rose trusted me. I would call him at night to discuss changes in conditions and ideas about strategic options and tactics.

One night I suggested that Rose didn't simply have to defend. He could take positive action in a sophisticated variant of Pac-Man defense. "What acquisition would make sense for you right now?"

331

I asked. Answering my own question, I suggested Mister Donut, the second-largest doughnut chain, by chance headquartered near Dunkin' in Boston. I had solicited business from Mister Donut as part of our new business and sensed management might be making its own strategic decisions.

Rose liked the idea and called Goldman. What a coincidence: Goldman had been retained by Mister Donut to find an acquirer. Here was Goldman representing direct competitors, both making strategic decisions. Was there a conflict? Certainly there was ample cause for suspicion. Clearly, PJSC's own strategy was on the right track.

Of course, life isn't always fair. The hostile attack was rebuffed. Goldman got a larger fee. Rose didn't tell his directors that he was getting advice from us, and he didn't have the nerve to ask them to authorize a larger fee for us.

Afterward, however, he did ask us to raise private equity for Dunkin', and we placed a convertible preferred stock with the General Electric Pension Fund, for which he paid us well.

The large firms generally, but particularly Goldman, intimidated clients. In the 1980s and '90s, directors would not defy them. Until research was separated from investment banking by SEC mandate in the year 2000, the implicit threats by the firms to use leverage against clients would represent a hurdle for independent firms. In time, however, Goldman, due mostly to its own actions and regulations, would suffer in terms of power and reputation.

It was only logical that PJSCs first clients were people with whom I was already familiar.

Sumner Feldberg, whose family had founded Zayre Corp., a lower-end discount chain based in Framingham, Massachusetts, had been a client of Lehman Brothers for thirty years. The Feldbergs were, along with my family, the Rabbs, and the Smiths of General Cinema, one of the leading Jewish families in Boston.

Zayre had created an off-price apparel and home goods division called T.J. Maxx in 1976. In 1988, the Zayre name and discount stores were acquired by Ames, a competitive discount chain, for $431.4 million in cash, a note, and a convertible preferred stock. Unfortunately, Ames couldn't compete and filed for bankruptcy in 1990.

The newly named TJX Companies initially had set aside a $185 million reserve against future losses. When Ames went bankrupt, TJX still was liable for leases and, compounding the financial effect, lost the anticipated value of the note receivable and preferred. In the midst of this financial chaos, Sumner stepped back from management and appointed Ben Cammarata as chief executive officer.

Sumner asked me to come to Framingham. He immediately grasped the value of an experienced adviser, particularly to a new CEO, and introduced me to Ben, who was equally welcoming.

Ben's first request was for help in shoring up TJX's balance sheet by raising equity. We agreed that it might be possible to sell a preferred stock convertible into TJX stock. While we had raised a similar security for Dunkin' Donuts, I told Ben that I wasn't sure we were sufficiently experienced to place this security. We were, after all, essentially a merger advisory firm. But Ben said he had confidence in us, and his faith paid off for both TJX and PJSC. We placed the security; it provided the needed leeway for TJX, and, nicely, General Electric, the buyer, did well.

TJX is still a client of our firm. In the ensuing thirty years, its market equity has grown from less than $300 million to $60 billion, its sales have grown from $513 million to $40 billion, and its earnings from $14 million to $3 billion.

Soon after Donald Glickman joined me in 1990, we had our first opportunity to invest in a management buyout. Linda Wachner, as tough as they come in the apparel business, called with an opportunity right up my alley. Regrettably, I botched it. The lesson here is that sometimes too much analysis can paralyze.

Linda Wachner and a partner had acquired Speedo International Ltd., the predominant swimwear manufacturer. It was an iconic brand. Every Olympics champion swims in a Speedo. She wanted to buy out her partner.

Headquartered on Santa Monica Boulevard in Los Angeles, Speedo had EBITDA of about $15 million. She could recapitalize the business for about $100 million. Speedo also owned White Stag, a ski brand that had been prominent in the 1960s but had since lost its cache.

There were half a dozen facts that made me wary, but there always are. The key is to know which are manageable and which you cannot control. First, of course, the country was in the midst of the George Bush recession. Not clear how long that would last.

Second, the management was unimpressive. I had no idea whom we could recruit to strengthen the leadership. I asked Bruce Klatsky, then COO of Phillips-Van Heusen, to become a director as a backup.

Third, I was afraid of Linda Wachner. She was extremely knowledgeable but was a lot tougher than I. We got on well when we traveled to England to meet with Stephen Rubin, the owner of the Speedo license outside the US, but I wasn't sure I could work with her.

Fourth, since Speedo already had such a large swimwear market share, the growth business plan was to open Speedo retail stores. I doubted whether a retail store devoted solely to swimsuits and accessories was viable, particularly since this was one of the few categories that department stores still dominated.

Fifth, White Stag was supplying about 20 percent of EBITDA. It sounds strange given today's multiples, but paying a six multiple for these earnings seemed excessive for a brand with no growth.

Finally, Mark Solow of Manufacturers Hanover did not like the deal. He thought the price was excessive. Our other pledge fund institutional partner, David Marks of Connecticut General Insurance Company, said he would finance the whole purchase.

Uneasy with this division, we passed.

Ultimately, Wachner bought it herself with financing from GE Credit. The deal was a home run for more than five years until the stores ceased to grow and the company faded. Speedo went public in 1994 and, at one time, reached a value of $800 million. But the stores did not perform. The management had to be replaced, and Wachner was as difficult as possible, eventually buying Speedo for Warnaco in 1999.

I was right on many counts but wrong by $80 million, the amount our partnership would have realized.

Our experience with Speedo caused us to look seriously at two other deals. The first was Hibbett Sports, a small-store sporting goods company owned by the Anderson family of Birmingham, Alabama. Smith Barney was auctioning it for $55 million. I liked the business, but it had begun to open superstores that competed against Sports Authority, Oshmans, and other large-box sporting goods companies. I didn't want to back this plan, and we passed.

Hibbett was bought by Saunders Karp & Megrue, a private equity fund specializing in retail deals. Its market equity at one point rose to $2 billion, and it operates only the original smaller stores that I liked. Some years ago, I asked Tom Saunders how he got the company to abandon the large store concept. He said he let them open several that failed, and the management figured it out for itself. He was smarter than I.

The second of these two deals involved lumber. We were convinced in early 1990 that the economic climate in the southern states was about to accelerate and that the lumberyard business combined the attributes of home building with a real estate play. Donald Glickman and I were approached through an intermediary by Ken Miron, whose family was in the business around New York. We had the opportunity to buy a number of yards in North and South Carolina, Georgia, and Florida from Arthur Goldberg, a shrewd investor. The fact that he was selling to us made me cautious. Donald was responsible for our financing, and I told him that we had to be sure that we could survive a recession or any abnormal period. This was a long-term play.

Then, shortly after the investment, on August 2, 1990, the Gulf War broke out. How could this affect our lumberyard business? The South, thanks to some formidable politicians representing it in the US Senate and Congress, has a disproportionate number of military bases. When the war began, thousands of service people were shipped to the Middle East, and their spouses and children returned home to their parents. Economic activity in the area all but ceased, but our interest payments did not.

As devastating as this was to Donald and me, we felt the yards were viable if the business could be restructured. We were naive. Today, we would have hired a restructuring firm to approach the creditors. Instead, we did it ourselves. We walked into CIT's office and met with the chief lending officer. We explained the situation and asked for some forbearance while we ran the business, basically on its behalf. By the time we returned to our office, though, CIT had essentially pulled its financing and put the company into bankruptcy.

The history of the Peter J. Solomon Company is intertwined with the growth and decline of Office Depot, Inc. The relationship provided constant work and welcome fees. Through it, we experienced innovation in retail, wholesale, and, eventually, e-commerce distribution. We learned how to negotiate better between competitors, a skill that became a competitive distinction of our firm. We learned more than we ever wanted to learn about the vagaries of antitrust law and how to advise our clients to anticipate and minimize antitrust objections. We experienced the value of good management and the costs of not adapting quickly enough in a vortex of changing consumer habits.

Can one generalize about an industry from the saga of one company in a single segment? Clearly, not every detail is relevant, but the macro trends in the competitive environment, the need to innovate constantly, and the aging of a once-novel approach are all illustrated by Office Depot and the office products superstore segment.

Prior to the founding of Staples, Inc. in 1986, office products were sold to businesses through wholesale distributors. Every city of a certain size had its own, catering to local businesses much the same way local supermarkets and department stores dominated their markets before consolidation.

Tom Stemberg, whose career had begun with Star Markets, the major competitor to Stop&Shop, had an idea to replicate the supermarket concept in stand-alone office supplies stores that he called Staples. Segmenting a market wasn't an original idea, but selling in a retail format to small businesses at wholesale prices was novel. With retail locations and enough volume, Stemberg reasoned, he could "disintermediate" the office supplies distribution system, shorten the supply chain, and outcompete local purveyors.

As with every successful innovator in retailing, Stemberg had a number of copycat regional competitors within a short time. In this case, though, they weren't just doing something similar; they were so alike that customers could barely tell them apart. Location was the main—and sometimes only—distinguishing factor. OfficeMax was in the Midwest, Office Club, Inc. in the western states, Businessland was based in Texas, and Office Depot in the Southeast. Clearly, not all could survive. Eventually the industry consolidated around three companies: Staples, OfficeMax, and Office Depot.

Through a recommendation of a friend, I met David Fuente, Office Depot's CEO, in 1989. Little did I know that it would be the beginning of a twenty-five-plus-year relationship.

Dave had not been the founder of Office Depot. He became CEO after the 1987 death of the founder, Pat Sher. Quickly, he saw that there would be a race to create a national chain, and that size would matter in terms of purchasing and marketing. His first strategic move was the acquisition of Office Club, a chain of fifty-one stores with sales of $285 million in 1990. Given its location in the West, Office Depot now had a national reach.

The super store was an efficient way to reach small businesses, but the majority of office supplies are bought through the wholesale channel by large companies and governments. To enter this arena, Office Depot acquired Eastman Office Products, a contract stationery company headquartered in Long Beach, California, in 1991 and, in 1992, the Great Canadian Office Supplies Warehouse Chain.

Both Staples and Office Depot were expanding in stores and in the contract business. By 1991, Staples' volume was $763 million in 133 stores, but Office Depot's was bigger, with sales of $1.3 billion in 228 stores. In every consumer sector, there is a race to consolidate. I've often wondered whether it is better to be the consolidator or to be acquired. Whatever the answer, in the office supply business, Staples and Office Depot were going to be the consolidators, with OfficeMax a distant third.

By 1993, Staples and Office Depot were on a collision course. Tom Stemberg approached David Fuente to discuss a merger. Tom, a visionary, saw the eventual commoditization of the industry—the lack of any perceived distinction between brands—and was bored. He wanted to get out of the business and go to Europe.

We negotiated a merger. Jack Levy of Goldman and Ken Moelis of DLJ represented Staples. I made the presentation to the Office Depot board in Boca Raton, and it approved the acquisition. Dave called Tom and congratulated him on the merger. But that wasn't the end of the story.

Inexplicably, after the board had agreed to the deal, Alan Wurtzel, a director whose father had founded Circuit City, asked Dave whether Office Depot had the management depth to consolidate Staples. It was a legitimate question posed at an inappropriate time. Oddly, Dave, instead of brushing aside the question, turned to his management team and said, "Go to lunch and discuss Alan's question and let us know after lunch." I assumed this was a pro forma response to a question with a foregone yes as the response. After all, it was Office Depot's management that had recommended the merger.

But an hour later, they stunned me by saying they weren't certain that they were capable of successfully managing the combined companies. More amazingly, Dave decided to listen to them! Not that I needed it, but here was further proof of the adage, "Don't ask questions you don't want the answers to."

Dave then called Tom, who had already informed his board, and explained that the merger was not to be. It was one of the most awkward moments in my career, as Office Depot's reversal was inexplicable. The problem with the inexplicable is that it is difficult to explain.

Over the next two years, Office Depot and Staples continued to expand rapidly and were increasingly competitive, especially in the area of distributing to large companies directly from warehouses. While fulfillment of orders was critical, price was the primary selling point. State and municipal governments were important customers.

By 1996, it became clear that the proposed merger of 1993 had, in fact, been a good idea. Once again, the two companies entered into merger discussions. Initially, the merger was conceived as a merger of equals. Dave Fuente would become CEO, and Staples' Martin Hanaka president of the merged entity. The economics of the deal were clear: elimination of enormous amounts of duplication and the lessening of competition in markets that now had Staples, OfficeMax, and Office Depot. Staples was represented by Steven Heller, "Mac," the able co-chair of Goldman's merger department. For hours, he and I debated issues such as location of headquarters, the structure of the board of the combined companies, the committee composition, and even the name of the company. This was in the era of Ira Millstein's corporate board reform adopted by General Motors with the new concept of a lead director.

As the negotiations continued, Office Depot's business worsened, and its earnings declined relative to Staples. As a result, conversations intensified. Dave was concerned about the trend in Office Depot's sales. He was worried about the risks of not reaching an agreement with Staples and, of course, apprehensive about the FTC blocking the merger. Concomitantly, Staples' board of directors was beginning to lose confidence in Dave. The tenor of the negotiations changed, from a merger of equals and an exchange of stock leading to proportionate ownership, to less for Office Deport shareholders and an acquisition by Staples.

In every merger, there is a moment where the deal comes together or talks end. The last week of August, the moment arrived. Dave and his wife, Sheila, were spending Labor Day with Susan and me at our 2,100-square-foot rented house on Georgica Pond in East Hampton. I invited Tom, Marty, and Mac for an informal visit on the Friday before Labor Day. Mac arrived at seven thirty in the morning; Tom and Marty arrived thirty minutes later at eight o'clock at the tiny East Hampton airport. A hurricane was racing toward us. Dave was clearly nervous as I arrived with the Staples team. Sheila and Susan had laid out bagels and salmon for our guests and left. I suggested to Mac that we, too, leave.

I reflected on the time in 1984 when I left Ed Finkelstein of Macy's and Bill Arnold of Associated Dry Goods alone and the merger had collapsed. But Dave needed a deal. Reenergizing Office Depot would be an effort. He had fired his last president, Mark Begelman, and restocking the company with talent would require time. We knew that there were periods where even growth companies don't grow and that Office Depot was in one of those periods. Dave was initially asked to be CEO of the new entity and was disappointed that he now would not be, but he put the company's need before his ambition. He would be a hot commodity for another CEO job.

Ninety minutes later, Mac and I returned briefly, then left again for another hour. Upon our return, the principals had reached an agreement. At noon, I drove Mac, Tom, and Marty back to the airport.

We knew the FTC would question the reduced competition and what it meant for the consumer. In office products, superstores competed with every discount chain, drugstore, and specialty stationery store and, in the sale of computers and printers, with companies such as Circuit City and Best Buy. I believed the realities of the marketplace were on our side; the total share of all office supply superstores was miniscule in every category. We were confident that we could satisfy the government.

The deal was announced on Wednesday, September 4, 1996. Both stocks soared. Six months later, in March 1997, after intense negotiations, the Federal Trade Commission staff recommended to the Commission that it approve the merger subject to the sale of sixty-three stores to OfficeMax. But on April 4, the Commission, by a vote of 3:2, rejected the staff's recommendation, then sued to get a temporary restraining order (TRO) and preliminary injunction to prevent the merger. After a trial in federal district court, Judge Thomas F. Hogan granted the preliminary injunction on June 30, 1997. Several days later, the two companies terminated the merger agreement.

The month of June was a nightmare for our firm. Ken Berliner attended every session in Washington, DC. The decision was, of course, a setback for our firm. We lost an $11 million fee and a boost in the ranking of merger firms. As a director of Office Depot, I now had to deal with a less competitive company in a more intensely competitive world.

This case offers a number of important lessons, applicable to all mergers between competitors.

The companies lost the case because of their own internal data. They were hoist by their own petard. The FTC proved its case using marketing and pricing data from the companies' own files. Understand that the FTC had a tough case. It sued based on consumable office supplies such as pens, pencils, Post-it Notes, computer discs, and toners. These products represented 5.5 percent of the sales of both companies. It ignored products such as computers, telephones, and furniture, which represented most of Staples' and Office Depot's sales.

Both Staples and Office Depot made the fatal mistake of comparing themselves principally to each other and the other major superstore, OfficeMax. With all their marketing material referring to the other office products superstores, the FTC could define a submarket of office products superstores, ignoring every other seller of these disposable supplies. For example, the judge wrote in his opinion, "Office Depot notes all competitor store closings and openings, but the only competitors referred to for its United States stores are Staples and OfficeMax."

The two companies also priced their consumable office supplies differently depending on the presence of one of the two other superstores, even though they proved that they competed generally against a broad array of other sellers. Quoting Hogan's opinion, "This evidence all suggests that office superstore prices are affected primarily by other office superstores and not by non-superstore competitors such as merchandisers like Walmart, Kmart, or Target."

The court agreed that there was competition from a number of sellers but not that that competition affected pricing. What determined pricing was the prices at the superstore competitors.

The court granted the FTC the preliminary injunction after expressing "sympathy for the plight of the defendants." All its reasoning toward reaching its conclusion flowed from data from the companies' own files.

The moral is clear. Any company considering a strategic consolidation is well advised to create a documented history of a broad competitive landscape. Concomitantly, its pricing analyses should cast a wide net. Strangely, while I have had this conversation with a number of clients, I have found them unusually obtuse on this particular subject. Anticipation is so cheap, and the adverse consequences are so expensive.

Second, during the interregnum, while the FTC pondered and the companies negotiated with it, Office Depot's management deferred excessively to Staples, providing more information than necessary. By the time the deal collapsed, Staples had learned much from Office Depot—especially about sports marketing and information systems—and Office Depot had lost its competitive edge. It was not a coincidence that subsequently the downtown Los Angeles sports arena was christened the Staples Center.

Management supervision must intensify, not lessen, during interregnum. While the merger was pending, the companies continued their pricing policies, apparently unaware that the FTC would obviously check prices. In fact, at a critical point, a Tampa housewife sent the Commission two ads demonstrating the differential pricing. Someone hadn't gotten the word.

Finally, we know our enemies, but sometimes our friends can kill us. Both companies let their antitrust counsels manage the negotiations with the FTC within sufficient oversight. Donald G. Kempf of Kirkland & Ellis antagonized the staff and was uncompromising in his approach. While the court commended both counsels for their excellent performance, from our firm's perspective, Kempf's approach prior to the trial reduced the chances of settlement.

After the termination, Office Depot and Dave Fuente had to regroup. Over the next year, we tried to acquire Corporate Express NV, a public company and one of the largest contract stationers. We made a "bear hug" offer in April 1998; and similar to the 1986 Allied Stores situation, Wachtel Lipton, Corporate Express's lawyers, opined that the bear hug was not sufficient to warrant disclosure. Regrettably, we got a similar result when David did not pursue a public approach. He has said he regretted not being more aggressive.

In 2000, to keep up with the changing distribution patterns of the business, Office Depot acquired Viking Office Products of Long Beach. Bruce Nelson, who replaced David, was Viking's president.

Staples kept pace with Office Depot, acquiring competitive distributors, but in the ensuing sixteen years and after David's departure, Staples had more consistent management and achieved better results.

It would not be until 2013 that the industry finally consolidated, first with a desperation merger between Office Depot and OfficeMax, and then in another attempt to merge with Staples in 2015. By that time, the two firms were barely profitable. Staples, while doing better for a number of years, also faded in terms of growth and profitability.

But once again, the FTC intervened and sued to halt the Depot/ Staples merger. Having been clearly wrong about the 1997 decision, it now sued on behalf of America's one hundred largest companies, arguing that the combination of the two largest so-called contract wholesale businesses would disadvantage these major corporate customers. The court granted a preliminary injunction, against the expectations of the Street who had concluded that, between Amazon and other wholesalers, the likes of Goldman Sachs could bargain successfully for vital paper products such as notepads.

In 2016, Staples and Office Depot/OfficeMax were still adrift in a hostile world. Staples was sold to the private equity fund Sycamore Partners for $6.9 billion in June 2017.

CHAPTER 29

Coping with Tragedy

Few days in one's life are so joyous or horrible that they remain frozen in memory. Joy is the birth of your children or your wedding day. The horrible days include 9/11, JFK's assassination, and the out-of-sequence death of a relative. These moments are indelible.

August 15, 16, and 17, 1991, were three days that changed my life and the lives of others close to me. Linda and I had separated several weeks before, in early August. One minute we were in Stamford having lunch, and minutes later, I had left. Tension had been building for months, caused primarily by me. But walking out of our home reminded me that long journeys begin with a single step.

I had not taken this step lightly. I had thought about the implications for our family, particularly Joshua, Abigail, Kate, and my brother's family. No one except my cousin Jane had been divorced in our family. Given the connections between our families, my divorce was not an isolated act.

A week after I left Cascade Road, Linda and I agreed to meet at our home on Quitsa Lane in Martha's Vineyard. The weekend was a cacophony of emotions. By Sunday, however, I was certain that we would separate permanently.

On Sunday night, Bob Millard flew me and Donald Glickman to New York in his plane. We dined at the Post House on Sixty-Third Street. Hurricane Bob was projected to strike the Vineyard on Tuesday. Our plan was for Linda, Abigail, and Kate to evacuate the Quitsa

Lane house due to its exposed location on the cliffs by Squibnocket Beach. They would stay on North Main Street in Edgartown with Gretchen Glickman and her kids, Victoria, Priscilla, and Douglas. The Glickmans and our kids were the same ages and our closest family friends, with whom we spent vacations.

Donald and I had met on our first days at Lehman in September 1960. We had become friends and partners and had invested together in a pickle company, an apple corer company, and a window manufacturer. And, of course, we had bought Monro Muffler in 1984. He was my fellow founding partner at PJSC.

Hurricane Bob hit Tuesday with force, but the Vineyard escaped extensive damage. The Glickmans' house had lost power but was otherwise not damaged.

On Wednesday, relieved, I flew to St. Louis to attend an Edison Brothers Stores, Inc. board meeting. Linda's brother was CEO, and her father, cousins, and uncles were directors. I was apprehensive about my reception, but the clan treated me politely. Meanwhile, Donald was working in our Park Avenue office.

On Wednesday morning after breakfast, Linda, Abigail, and Kate returned to Chilmark. They drove the ten miles cautiously, watching out for downed electrical lines. Our house was hardly damaged, with the most harm to the flora from salt spray.

The day after a hurricane is generally clear and bright, as the storm system clears out the atmosphere. In sunshine, Gretchen and her family biked toward the beach at Katama on the outskirts of Edgartown to see the turbulent ocean and storm damage. As Gretchen rounded a corner, she saw her daughter's bike on the road. Priscilla had been hit by a truck and lay immobile.

Orange-haired, vivacious Priscilla was dead on the ground. Inconceivably, at twenty-one, this star child was gone. She had been an outstanding student at Spence and later at Andover, with perfect grades her junior year. She had matriculated at Princeton and was the first woman admitted to the prestigious Ivy Club.

Abigail and Priscilla were the same age and were closest friends. In June, they had traveled to Eastern Europe together.

What a horrendous turn of events. A divorce is acknowledgment of a failed union, but life goes on. Priscilla's death was a lethal blow to our families. Abigail had, in the course of weeks, dealt with the breakup of her family and the death of her closest friend. The effect on the rest of our family was less but only by degrees.

Within months, Donald withdrew from our business. Our business plan to create a firm that would be both a principal and an adviser was dashed. Without a trusted partner, I could not be successful in both businesses. I relied on Donald's judgment and financing skills, and I knew I needed to share the burdens and successes of our enterprise.

Thirty months after stepping out on my own and weeks after becoming separated, I was alone and coping with the aftereffects of these terrible days.

❧

Set back emotionally, I had to adjust to new realities. Nineteen ninety-two was a critical year to prove PJSC was a sustainable business. It was one thing to have an idea and another to validate it through the retention of clients and the acquisition of new assignments. We had to survive the departure of our partner Don Glickman and the realization that private investing was not an immediate strategy. We had to build a firm.

Henry and I realized that we might not be tough enough to prosper independently. We also understood that we needed to create a "factory" capable of handling a number of simultaneous transactions. Our first hire, Ken Berliner, brought to the firm a more systematic method of analysis and presentation.

We were then fortunate to find Jeff Hornstein, a graduate of Yale and HBS. He came from Kidder Peabody & Co., one of the best smaller investment banks when I entered the securities business, run by Wall Street icon Albert H. Gordon. Mr. Gordon died in 2009 at 107 and was known to work well into his nineties. When I stressed control of expenses, I would relate how I met Mr. Gordon on a plane from Los Angeles to JFK in the 1970s. Squeezed into my coach seat on the 4:00 p.m. flight, I was bemoaning my fate when I noticed Mr. Gordon squeezed even more tightly next to me into the center seat. More pointedly, he was returning from a Carnation Company board meeting, and his travel would have been reimbursed.

Because of Kidder's acquisition by General Electric, we found a number of colleagues, including our receptionist, Jean, there. I would tell Jean that her position was critical, as she had the first interaction with our guests, reminding myself of Sonia Meiller, Lehman's gracious third-floor receptionist.

At last, Diane Coffey, whom I had tried to lure to Lehman from City Hall, joined as our administrative partner in 1996. When Marc Cooper, Ken Baronoff, Anders Maxwell, and three additional associates joined us, we really began to expand. (Marc, Ken, Anders, Jeff, and Diane are still with the firm. Marc is chief executive officer, and Ken is chief operating officer. Jeff and Anders are senior bankers.) By the later 1990s, we had evolved from a boutique—which, to this day, the press continues to call smaller firms—to the firm I had envisioned.

The investment banking advisory business is relatively easy if you work hard and make new business calls. In some ways, it epitomizes Woody Allen's comment that "80% of life is showing up." The other 20% is timing and luck. While we had a number of successes, we also suffered setbacks and disappointments.

When I founded PJSC, I visited a number of long-term corporate clients. Some had no immediate banking business, but I had worked with them for many years. I told each that I had limited resources. If they would commit to using our firm, I would spend my time working on their financial issues.

I had been close to Albertsons Companies LLC, the supermarket chain, since the mid-1960s. I had developed a close relationship with the founder, Joe Albertson; even after he retired, he would come to his office when I visited just to say hello. In the 1970s, I had represented Albertsons in a series of conversations with Staggs Companies, a supermarket competitor located in Salt Lake. Albertsons headquarters was in Boise, Idaho, so it wasn't easy to get there, but I visited with regularity. Henry Jackson covered the account, and he and Gary

Michael, the CEO of Albertsons, had developed a nice relationship. I had known Gary for decades, since he had been the CFO when Bob Bolinder was CEO.

In 1998, we knew American Stores, which had merged with Skaggs, was interested in talking again. I asked Michael what our role would be, naturally assuming we would represent Albertsons. He was elusive. When I pressed him, he admitted to me that he had hired Merrill Lynch to represent the company.

He said Sam Skaggs had hired Blackstone to represent American Stores, and he didn't think it would be appropriate for boutiques to be on both sides. What bad luck. Tom Hill, my former Lehman colleague and then at Blackstone, represented Skaggs. Michael confessed that he realized that he had betrayed me. He had told his CFO that I would never speak to him again, and I didn't for twenty years.

The $11.7 billion deal would have been important to our firm's prestige, as well as its income.

Henry was appropriately discouraged. He wondered whether he could do as well as an adviser as he could as an investor. That is a common longing of investment bankers. He decided to look for another opportunity. I introduced him to Donaldson, Lufkin & Jenrette, which he eventually joined, moving to London. The American firm's benefits to expats, including housing and school tuition, permitted an enhanced standard of living. During an interview, Tony James, president of DLJ, said DLJ would pay Henry a bonus for PJSC clients he brought to his new firm. Henry told me he didn't think he could join a firm that acted in that manner. I told him not to worry about it. It didn't surprise me, given Wall Street's ethics.

I regretted losing Henry. He contributed enormously to our firm. He has realized his dream by founding a successful investment firm in London and building a robust family. We see each other frequently.

CHAPTER 30

Love and Other Emotions: 1993–2001

By 1993, we had established Peter J. Solomon Company, but virtually all of our clients were old friends or people who had come to us through personal connections. I had thought the business community would respond quickly and decisively to the promise of experience and integrity. I was wrong. A few years after our founding, it still wasn't clear that anyone, even the clients we had, truly appreciated the threat to their business interests from the inherent conflicts in the larger securities firms.

In the years since I'd started our firm, conflicts had become an even larger problem. Proprietary trading and investing had mushroomed. Most firms now had private equity funds, which allowed them to invest and potentially compete with their clients. And then there was a new kind of transaction called "stapled financing." An investment bank such as Goldman, after it had been hired to sell a company, would approach buyers, many of which would be private equity firms. As part of its sales process, Goldman would offer to finance the buyer's acquisition of its client at a multiple of earnings before interest, taxes, depreciation, and amortization (EBITDA). To the casual observer or the less sophisticated client, the fact that an agent was offering to finance a buyer seemed advantageous. But, in fact and in practice, the seller's agent was acting on behalf of a buyer as well. Representing a buyer and seller in the same transaction, even with the best intentions, is, of course, a clear-cut conflict of interest.

In the 1990s, the practice of stapled financing became a competitive tool for large banks and, increasingly, a hurdle for firms like ours without a balance sheet. It remains so to this day.

The other flagrant conflict was the use of stock research to promote investment banking business, particularly initial public offerings. Supposedly, firms maintained a Chinese wall that prevented research from being tainted by business considerations, but in practice, as everyone on the Street knew, the wall was as porous as cheesecloth. "Buy" ratings had become a tool for keeping clients happy. I had been the beneficiary of this practice at Lehman, so I knew it well. When pitching a prospective client, one offered to provide equity research with the tacit understanding that the research would be favorable. Of course, within the firms themselves, there were sometimes conflicts on this point. The research department might be proud of its record and might not want to be ordered by another part of the firm to recommend stocks it did not actually favor. To get around this problem, many firms created a new department; at Lehman, we called it Corporate Client Services. CCS turned out glowing reports on clients that the real securities research department would never have endorsed.

In one case that became infamous, Sandy Weil, then chairman of Citibank, directed Jack Grubman, a top telecom research analyst at Smith Barney, a leading securities firmed owned by Citibank, to do favorable research on AT&T. Sandy was trying to woo Michael Armstrong, the CEO of AT&T, who was contemplating a stock offering, and he knew that there is nothing that warms the heart of a CEO more than an endorsement from someone like Grubman. Besides, Sandy wanted Armstrong's vote—they were on each other's boards—to depose John Reed as CEO of Citibank.

The curious part of the story—and, no doubt, why it gained notoriety—is that Grubman, in an email sent to a friend, boasted that Sandy had "bribed" him into raising his rating on AT&T's stock with the promise of getting his child into the nursery school at the Ninety-Second Street Y. As Grubman noted, it was harder to get in there than Harvard.

Grubman at that time was already under scrutiny from regulators for his advice on the telecom company WorldCom. In his self-aggrandizing manner, he had flaunted his disdain for the Chinese wall, saying publicly that it kept investors from being fully informed. Despite Grubman's endorsement, WorldCom-MCI went bankrupt in 2002. That same year, Grubman was fined by the SEC and barred from the securities industry for issuing fraudulent, misleading, and otherwise flawed research reports under Salomon Smith Barney's name. In 2004, after Sandy had also left Citibank, Citibank settled with retail customers who had bought stock based on Grubman's inaccurate research reports.

A couple of years before that, I was playing golf with Deryck Maughan, the former CEO of Salomon Brothers. Deryck had replaced John Gutfreund after the Treasury scandal of 1991, when a Salomon trader had submitted false bids in an attempt to circumvent the rules regarding the purchase of Treasury bonds. Maughan was then the chair of Citibank International. As we reached the sixteenth hole, I raised the issue of conflicts such as fake research and stapled financing.

Deryck was polite. He said simply that Citibank could afford to lose the research argument. It was helpful to its business but not essential. Under no circumstances, however, could it afford to be restricted from providing stapled financing. Lending to both its clients and those who might acquire its clients had become the sine qua non of its business model.

❧

Meanwhile and more importantly, during the 1990s, I rebuilt a family. On January 17, 1993, I was finishing work on a grim day when I received a call from Ken Brody. I didn't know much about Ken except that he had an unusually varied career as a partner at Goldman Sachs, being successful in several areas, including real estate and banking.

"Peter," he said with no introduction. "I don't know you well, but I have always heard good things about you! I have a friend, Susan Rebell. She is going out with someone inappropriate. I want you to call her and take her out!"

I replied that my Harvard classmate Harry Wise had mentioned her name and that I would call her. Ken obviously didn't hear the necessary urgency in my voice.

"No," he said, "not sometime. Now." He went on, "I won't hang up until you tell me you are going to call her right now."

I told him I would call her as I scribbled her number. And Ken finally hung up.

I dialed Susan's number, and she answered. "Where do you work?" I asked.

"The Seagram Building," she said.

"Oh, I work directly across Park Avenue at 350. What floor are you on?"

"Tenth."

"Come to the southwest corner of the floor, and we should be able to wave to each other."

I could see her wander around the floor trying to figure out where the southwest corner was located. Finally, she was across from me, and I waved.

We arranged to have a drink at the Drake that evening. While we missed each other because I arrived a few minutes late, we got together almost immediately thereafter.

Sometimes you get really lucky, and this was one of those times. Susan had two children, Laura and Josh, who were about the same ages as Kate and Abigail and had similar interests, such as fun and theatre. The families melded beautifully. Kate and Laura even traveled together through South America when Kate was in the Peace Corps in Paraguay.

In 1995, the American Museum of Natural History decided to celebrate its 125th anniversary with a trip by private plane around the world, visiting a number of its far-flung sites. By then I had enough confidence in the stability of our business and my colleagues to sign up for the thirty-five-day sojourn, out of sight and out of contact.

Even if we had had cell phones or the internet, we couldn't have used them. The only means of instant communication were satellite phones.

Susan and I had been dating for two years at that point. She had a senior executive position at Mercer Consulting, where she was also a director. I asked her if she wanted to go. Her colleagues were not sympathetic, and she knew a prolonged absence could hurt her career. But Laura, with unusual prescience for a twenty-three-year-old, told her she wouldn't remember what she did at work that month, but she certainly wouldn't forget this trip. So Susan decided to come.

The trip was to begin in Tikal, Guatemala, but the plane couldn't land, so we spent the first night in a hotel in Belize City. The organizers had failed to limit luggage. Clay Frick and his wife, Pemmy, had ten pieces of matching Louis Vuitton luggage delivered to their tiny room.

At Tikal, as Susan and I gazed at the moss-covered pyramid trying to decide whether to climb it, Pemmy scampered up its narrow steps in high heels, carrying a Hermes bag. It was an unplanned, memorable sight.

The next stop, Manaus, was uneventful, except our chartered airplane was temporarily confiscated by the Brazilian government. Apparently, Madonna had skipped out of Rio on this plane without paying some taxes, and now the government wouldn't release it without payment in full of $150,000.

Somehow the bill was paid, and the plane's tail number was repainted to avoid a recurrence. From Brazil, we began a crossing of the Pacific Ocean, stopping first on Easter Island, the remote eastern end of Polynesia and the site of the large stone statues known as moai.

We stopped briefly in the Cook Islands, coming to rest in Papua, New Guinea.

One of my principal reasons for joining the trip was exploring New Guinea's famed Sepik River. The villages along the river haven't changed much for centuries. In one stop, Bill Beinecke, then seventy, mentioned to a tribal elder that he had been in the US Navy along the New Guinea coast during WWII. The elder had also fought against the Japanese. Beinecke happened to mention it was his birthday. That night, the entire village appeared at the Sepik River Lodge to celebrate Bill's birthday, at one point carrying him on their shoulders.

Outer Mongolia is the land of dinosaurs. Each season, the American

Museum of Natural History sends an expedition to the famed Flaming Cliffs to dig. With the fall of the Berlin Wall, Russian democracy, and the melting of the Cold War, Outer Mongolia was no longer strategic, and aid to it had stopped. The president of the new Outer Mongolian Republic asked our delegation for financial assistance. Accustomed to asking for money, we demurred on the foreign aid.

Walking with Lewis M. Cullman, Edgar's brother, we passed the Ulan Bator stock exchange, which was set to open the following month. As we entered the small building, a guard barred our entrance to the trading floor, God knows why. Today, the Ulan Bator stock exchange trades thousands of stocks.

We then left a freezing Mongolia and flew south to Peking and then to Yangon (formerly Rangoon). Myanmar (formerly Burma) was trying to reenter civilized society. We flew to Pagan, one of Buddhism's principal cities and an area with thousands of pagodas, many in crumbling condition. On a day that remains a highlight, museum provost Mike Novacek, Susan, and I biked through this mystical landscape. Susan considered starting an import business centering on Burmese lacquer ware, but problems with the US embargo of Burmese goods ended that vision.

Borneo, our next stop, was the site of an orangutan breeding program. After that, we flew west to the island of Madagascar. Antananarivo, its capital, ranks with Papua's Jayapura as one of the world's most poverty-stricken capitals. The French were terrible colonialists, leaving behind weak economies and incompetent civil servants. The US ambassador called it a "pit." Like Outer Mongolia, it had lost its Cold War value as a strategic spot.

Separated from mainland Africa, Madagascar has developed unique animals and flora. The museum supports Berenty, a breeding site for lemurs, those remarkable mammals that walk on their hind legs.

Two days later, we flew to Arusha, Tanzania, to observe the antipoachers program before our final stop in the Dordogne, France, where we saw the famed Caves of Lascaux with their prehistoric paintings. Entering the caves, which had been closed since 1961, brought me full circle: in 1962, Bob Glauber and I had taken the train to see the paintings, only to learn that the caves had just been closed to prevent deterioration.

A month had passed. Meanwhile, back home my business continued peacefully. The only negative effect of the trip was that Susan's bosses, put off by her monthlong absence, removed her from the firm's board of advisers. Times have changed. She was the only woman. I doubt they would be so intolerant today.

Susan and I were married in my mother's apartment in April 1996. It was a great day. I figured if she survived New Guinea, we could survive anything. In a throwback to the 1950s, our reception was a tea dance with, among other delicacies, cucumber tea sandwiches, while my childhood friend Peter Duchin and his band entertained.

❧

The work that Henry Jackson and I had done for the Macy's creditors and the Strawbridge experience convinced us that the restructuring business was consistent with our merger advisory business. To put it in psychological terms, it is the dark side of the confident, upbeat merger world. While I'm not a dark person by nature, the need to restructure balance sheets in the always-evolving consumer business is permanent. We had also seen that the fees paid in bankruptcy, though subject to court approval and credit objections, could be equal to fees from merger advice. Another attractive aspect, monthly retainers, could help cover overhead. By cultivating a restructuring business, we might also lessen our dependence on merger advisory retainers, which are always hard to get.

The marketing pitch technique used by Arthur Newman of Blackstone and the other bankruptcy specialists seemed to offer an opportunity. Their argument centered on their intimate knowledge of the bankruptcy process, not on the ability to value the eventual postbankruptcy worth of the assets in a sale or merger.

After mulling the idea for a year, we decided to hire a restructuring banker and also to base our appeal on our capacity to value beyond bankruptcy. At the time, it was a novel approach. Through Jeff Kuhr, we met David Resnick, a vice president at Lazard. Resnick joined the firm in 1996, and we gave him the latitude to recruit additional bankers, one of whom was Todd Snyder. Snyder was an associate at Weil Gotshal, then and now the leading bankruptcy firm.

For the next four years, PJSC built a solid bankruptcy practice, not only in retailing but also representing debtors and creditors as diverse as Schlumberger, Zenith, and Home Place. The diversity of income, as well as of clients, broadened the base and reach of our firm.

Resnick was an excellent processor, and Snyder had the potential to be a good new business getter, but he did not learn enough about the details of the value proposition until shortly before he left the firm. In Resnick's case, he rarely cultivated business. Ken Berliner and I sourced most of our business. Our biggest breakthrough came when we represented LG, the Korean-based owner of Zenith, which filed for bankruptcy in 1999. The consulting firm McKinsey was already working with the company. The week of Thanksgiving, McKinsey, with the LG executives in tow, called Blackstone to meet. Arthur Newman was not available, and, for some reason, neither was Steve Schwarzman nor Peter Peterson of Blackstone. Because of Ken's relationship with McKinsey, they called him and asked if we could meet with them and the LG executives the day after Thanksgiving. We did. I am certain that McKinsey/LG hired us because of my name on the door and the fact that they met the principal. This pattern continued on almost all our restructuring business. PJSC supported Resnick fully and successfully.

Resnick was initially paid $400,000; by 1999, we were paying him $4.4 million. Our business has excellent economics, which is one reason the number of independent boutique firms has grown over the last twenty years. But every year, David, like most investment bankers, wanted more money and a higher payout on restructuring fees. Our conversations became increasingly unpleasant.

In 1999, Tom Unterberg and John Gutfreund, who were by this time working together at Unterberg Towbin, asked if I would be interested in talking to Gerry Rosenfeld, a former partner of Gutfreund's at

Salomon Brothers. Gerry had become CEO of Rothschild & Co. in the United States. He was interested in building the firm that, while strong in Europe and England, had never reached its US potential.

I had a brief history with Rothschild. In 1990, John Angelo had asked me to meet with Baron David de Rothschild and his cousin Evelyn, about merging our new firm and serving as CEO of Rothschild America. I knew the firm was struggling in New York, and, at the time, I had no desire to go to work for anyone, particularly without an equity interest.

I agreed to meet with Gerry, but I was aware that he knew Resnick and Berliner. I told John it had to be clear that if I met with Gerry, Gerry was prohibited from recruiting Resnick and Berliner. John told me he conveyed that message explicitly to Gerry.

Why would I meet with Gerry under any circumstances? In 1989, I had determined to build PJSC for ten years and then go find another activity. A decade had passed, and our firm was doing nicely. I thought Rothschild also had unlimited potential and my partners would profit.

Tom, John, and I talked with Gerry for about two hours, but the meeting was inconclusive. Before we parted, I repeated my comment about approaching Ken and Resnick, but something in Gerry's response made me apprehensive. After the meeting, I told Gutfreund my concern and asked him to call Gerry and remind him again of the basis on which the meeting was held. John did that.

Several months later, in March 2000, Resnick and Snyder walked into my office and resigned. They were leaving to go to Rothschild to work for Rosenfeld. At the same time, they had recruited the other key professionals in the PJSC restructuring group to leave with them. Six of them disappeared the same day.

Snyder professed to have some conscience. He told me his father was concerned about his actions. He agreed to meet with me at EAT on upper Madison Avenue for lunch. He said he would abandon Resnick if I guaranteed him the same $4 million Rothschild had guaranteed him for the following two or three years. That seemed to be the cost of his conscience. I told him I couldn't do that.

The mass exodus was an extraordinary blow to me and the firm.

John called Rosenfeld, who blew him off. John and Tommy were embarrassed and also felt deceived, but their sense of betrayal paled compared to mine. Resnick had gone beyond recruiting our whole team. He had called our clients, trying to shift fees to Rothschild. I called every client and, in the case of Schlumberger, threatened legal action if it didn't send our $6 million fee to us. All paid what they owed our firm.

I sued Resnick and got a small settlement. At times such as these, you learn who your true friends are. Willkie Farr, who had been one of our principal law firms, chose Rothschild over us, and I tried never to use them again. Dick Beattie arranged for Simpson Thacher to represent PJSC, which I appreciated.

We rebuilt our restructuring business but missed the boom of the 2000s.

Baron David de Rothschild, meanwhile, had become a friend. He continued to try to lure me to run US Rothschild. On the day his father, the famous Guy de Rothschild, died, David insisted that I keep a luncheon appointment with him at the firm's Paris office and walked me to the door, always a gracious gesture. Six months later, over a drink at the Waldorf in New York City, he repeated his offer.

"David," I said, "you know my first act as CEO will be to fire David Resnick and Todd Snyder."

"Oh, Peter," he replied, "that was a long time ago."

"David," I said, "it was a long time ago for the Rothschilds but very recent for the Solomons!"

I turned down David's offer, again.

ಶ

In late 2000, I received a letter from a French banking executive whom I didn't know, Jean Peyrelevade, the CEO of Credit Lyonnais S.A. Credit Lyonnais had an investment banking group, Clinvest, and Peyrelevade wanted to know whether I had any interest in doing a transaction. It seemed to be a form letter fishing for a connection. It made me think of the story Mort Sahl would tell about the note a man received saying, "Darling, I will kill myself if we don't see each other." The recipient couldn't figure out who sent it. Then he looked at the envelope and saw it was addressed to "Occupant." That's how I viewed Jean's letter.

Some weeks later, I received a call from an executive from Clinvest, Jean Laurent-Bellue, who asked to visit me in New York. Jean turned out to be an erudite banker with a wonderful sense of humor. I liked him immediately. As a result of our meeting in August 2001, Clinvest bought a $10 million convertible preferred security in PJSC.

For the next eight years, we developed a cordial and profitable relationship with Jean and his colleagues, and with Peyrelevade and his close associate Alain Papiasse. I attended board meetings of Clinvest four times annually in Paris and saw Jean and his colleagues socially. Together, we helped Office Depot buy Guilbert SA in Europe. It was the association with Clinvest that allowed us to develop a relationship with PPR (now Kering).

On every deal, I learn something new. One day in 2003, I awakened to read that the French government, which had assumed control of Credit Lyonnais when it was in financial trouble, and had installed Peyrelevade as CEO, had sold its ownership in Credit Lyonnais to Credit Agricole Group. My agreement with Credit Lyonnais had no outs for me. I was now partially owned by a rural French Bank that had no interest in developing a US merger business.

Guy de Panafieu, one of two brothers in a distinguished French family, was one of the remaining senior bankers still at Credit Agricole. Through his good services, in December 2009, I repurchased our preferred shares at a discount from Credit Agricole. Not surprisingly, in the financial crisis, Credit Agricole suffered substantial losses. It seemed to be an incompetent group.

❦

The millennium was traumatic for the stock market and then for the world. The internet bubble burst in 2000; while I didn't take it personally, the crash showed the idiocy of some of my investments.

My friend Dan Lufkin, normally one of the best investors I know, induced me to invest with three friends who had little knowledge and less judgment. The professional venture capitalists mostly on the West Coast seemed to be the only investors who timed this cycle. Ten years later, Kleiner Perkins and its pals got it right again, but with Facebook, Google, et al. And they got it right in billions.

With the defection of the restructuring team, we needed to regroup. For the first time, our revenues declined, but we remained profitable. Our contained overhead enabled the firm to survive, and I knew we had a stable business. I just had to keep making the new business calls.

On September 11, 2001, I flew from Teterboro to Cleveland to call on the conglomerates Parker Hannifin and the Eaton Corporation and have lunch with Jim McMonagle, a director of Owens Corning. It was a crisp, beautiful late-summer day when we took off at 7:30 a.m. As we approached the Cleveland airport, our pilots said something odd was occurring. They were told to land immediately. Apparently, a plane was over the airport. I assumed it was Air Force One.

We landed just before nine o'clock. Judy Vance, my able executive assistant, emailed me that a plane had hit the World Trade Center Towers. I, of course, thought it was an accident, remembering the B-25 that crashed into the Empire State Building in 1945. Alan Wilkinson and I traveled in our Hertz car to Parker Hannifin. As we waited for our ten o'clock appointment, we watched the destruction of the Towers.

The meeting was perfunctory. I don't remember much about it. And we never followed up. We drove downtown for a quick lunch with McMonagle, found a Hertz—since all flights were banned—and began to drive back to New York.

By that time, we knew the third plane had crashed in Pennsylvania. The reports made it sound as if it crashed along the route of the Pennsylvania Turnpike, so we set out to New York City by way of Buffalo. Soon it became clear that we could take the more direct turnpike, so I turned south. Six hours later, we arrived in New Jersey. I drove to Teterboro to pick up the car we had left that morning. It was dark, and the smell from across the Hudson was acidic. The parking lot was guarded now. My associate Michael Parham lived in New Jersey, and we spent the night in his basement.

The next morning, we took a ferry to the West Side and a bus to Fifty-Eighth Street and Fifth Avenue.

We all know the stories of the destruction and the near-death experiences. My former Lehman colleague Alan Washkowitz went to the bathroom in the Lehman building I used to occupy across the street from the World Trade Center. He emerged in darkness to find the southeast corner of the building sliced away.

For days, the acid smell of destruction wafted up the East Side. On September 14, using my deputy mayor's badge, Susan, Bethany and Bob Millard, and I visited the site. Ruins were smoldering. Cranes were lifting large strands of steel. The area was organized for emergency relief.

Meanwhile, Governor George Pataki had moved quickly. He had designated Safe Horizon, the organization of which Susan was chairman, to handle the emergency response for the victims of 9/11.

Safe Horizon had been created by Herb Sturz during the Koch administration as Victim Services. It dealt with a variety of ills but had distinguished itself in the area of domestic violence. Susan had joined the board in 1989 and by 1998 had become chairman. She hired a talented executive, Gordon Campbell, and together they reshaped the agency and expanded its scope.

Pataki was a lazy governor who accomplished little. In fact, shortly after he left the governor's office, I walked down Fifth Avenue with him, and no one seemed to recognize him even though his height—about six feet, five inches—should have distinguished him even if nothing else did. My view of government is that its main function is to act in crises and take control. To Pataki's credit, without hesitation, he appointed Safe Horizon as the lead agency to deal with the victims of the attack. This was a brilliant move because it was not a government agency and, therefore, could cut through a lot of red tape. In a crisis, you need direct action, not bureaucracy.

United Way collected $180 million to help the victims. Ten thousand dollars was given to anyone who lost a relative, a job, or housing. Operating out of Pier 95 on Fifty-Fourth Street and the Hudson River, Safe Horizon had representatives from relevant government agencies and volunteers who could speak twenty-four languages. Each morning, hundreds of victims lined up to be helped quickly, fielding few questions other than rudimentary documentation.

After a week, it occurred to me that the staff was distributing money so efficiently that Susan would be well advised to hire an auditor to be sure there was no major scam. Amazingly, after giving out the $180 million there, the auditor found less than $15,000 in fraud.

Several weeks after the attack, our firm organized a visit to the city for twenty-three friends and clients from the US and abroad. I billed it as "New York Is Still Open." We visited the site, met with security officials in charge of the recovery and the head of the New York Stock Exchange, saw a Broadway show, and Mayor Giuliani spoke at one of our breakfasts. It was attended by German industrialists, the Le Figero publisher Yves de Chaisemartin, American CEOs such as Ed Ludwig of Becton Dickinson, Ronald DeFeo from Terex, Terry Lundgren of Macy's, and Sam Butler, among others. When Yves de Chaisemartin saw the Safe Horizon center on Pier 95, he remarked that only Americans could mobilize so completely to deal with such a challenge.

As a postscript, in January 2002, Giuliani ordered the center to be closed and told Safe Horizon to vacate the pier. Susan told him that many victims were still lining up each day to get assistance. "They are alive, aren't they?" he replied. So much for empathy. Fortunately, Bear Sterns had built a new headquarters, and its former space was available on Lexington Avenue. Safe Horizon moved there.

New York mayors have one big legacy (if any) and several small ones. For Koch, it was saving the city from bankruptcy, restoring a jaunty optimism, implementing a $5 billion housing program, and, lest we forget, an edict ordering dog owners to acquire "pooper scoopers." Bloomberg brought a businessman's professionalism to City Hall, accelerated the real estate rebuilding of the city, and focused on health.

If not one of my favorite political leaders, Giuliani did reduce crime and corruption in New York. As a former prosecutor, he went after the mob. He was so successful that some years later, when I asked Deputy Mayor Dan Doctoroff how much time he spent on corruption, he replied, "None!" This was an amazing statement. When I was in City Hall, corruption on the piers and in government had consumed a considerable amount of my energies.

Dan Doctoroff, by the way, is one of the most able people I know. Dan had been a star analyst at Lehman Brothers. As a result, I assigned him to work with Pete Dawkins, who was responsible for our new business program. Dan was so frustrated with Pete's bureaucratic style that he asked to be reassigned. I had sent him to work temporarily for Bob Bass, who was creating a leveraged buyout fund. Dan made a nice success there and never returned to Lehman.

Shortly after Bloomberg was elected, I got a call from Dan. He said he had been asked by Nat Leventhal, my former deputy mayor colleague and the head of Bloomberg's transition team, to become the deputy mayor for economic development, my old job. He said he was turning it down and wanted me to know.

I immediately told him he was making a mistake. Rather than giving all the reasons on the phone, I told him I would write him to explain why. The next day, I sent him an eight-page handwritten memorandum with—as he well remembers—only one word crossed out. I essentially gave Dan the same advice Pete Petersen had given me in 1977. He had accomplished a great deal in the private sector, and this was an opportunity to take his training and his interest in the world and put it to use for the general good. He would be successful, I was sure, and it would elevate him in people's minds and create opportunities for him afterward.

In recent years, Dan has credited this memo with changing his mind and remarks that he is amazed I handwrote an eight-page memo with only one word crossed out.

Dan did a superb job leading the rebuilding of New York, and it did open opportunities. He became CEO of Bloomberg and later entered into a joint venture with Google to invent a new model for "smart" cities.

҈

Wall Street was changing as the century rolled over but not necessarily evolving. Let me tell you a story that illustrates what I mean.

John Levin had merged his asset management business into a public company, BKF. John A. Levin Company was BKF's only asset. Levin managed over $13 billion, a considerable amount of which was related to the Loeb family. He was a favorite of John L. Loeb, the family's patriarch.

BKF would have been better off as a private company, but unfortunately, that was not the case in 2004. In that year, Warren Lichtenstein, the forty-one-year-old partner of Steel Partners, a hedge fund, began buying stock in BKF, running the price up from the low twenties to forty-three dollars. In what would appear to be a violation of the Williams Act, which required "groups" bound together by a common purpose be identified, another hedge fund, an obscure San Francisco–based fund named Cannell Capital, also bought BKF stock. Well-known fund managers Mike Price and Mario Gabelli next bought positions in BKF.

The new investors challenged three directors of BKF then up for reelection—including Burt Malkiel, author of *A Random Walk Down Wall Street*, and, most important, John Levin himself. BKF had a distinguished board of directors, including Anson Beard, formerly the head of retail for Morgan Stanley; Barton Biggs, a renowned strategist also lately of Morgan; Jim Tisch, CEO of Loews; Malkiel, a tenured professor at Princeton University; and Dean Takahashi of the Yale endowment. BKF's issues weren't governance.

I assumed that the outside hedge funds had a plan to merge their funds into the public company, thereby achieving liquidity. I could not see what else they thought they could achieve in this public investment management company with a market value of about $250 million.

364

In the 1990s and early 2000s, proxy advisory companies, the most recognized of which was Institutional Investor Services (ISS), were gaining prominence as arbiters of good governance and public policy. The hedge funds attacking Levin put up a slate of three directors and appealed to ISS for support. Now, just imagine the situation. The hedge funds are running against the CEO of the company, a person who controlled about 60 percent of the assets—assets, I should add, represented by investment management accounts that could be transferred on a moment's notice.

Levin asked me to talk to ISS. I found myself dealing with an analyst who was no more than twenty-five years old. He had little experience in any business and, as far as I could tell, less knowledge of investment management. He told me that ISS's position was that John Levin was not doing a good job as a manger, and it was likely these hedge funds would do better, though he admitted that none had ever managed a public company. I reminded him that Mr. Levin personally controlled about 60 percent of the assets. I warned that if Mr. Levin were defeated, he would probably leave the company and take the assets with him. He assured me that this would not be the case. "Look at Blockbuster," he said. "Carl Icahn ousted the CEO, and he stayed at the company."

I asked whether, in that case, the ousted CEO controlled the store locations and could take them with him. He dismissed my question as irrelevant. "Oh," he said defiantly, "Mr. Levin will stay!"

Levin, thanks in part to ISS, was defeated. He left the company and took his assets with him. When the company collapsed, someone from ISS criticized him publicly for leaving the company that had rejected him and where he had been chastised unmercifully by the activist funds.

After Levin's departure, I begged Anson Beard to become chairman. He, Jim Tisch, and I felt an obligation to try to salvage the company. Lichtenstein, however, went to Europe for the summer. He never attended a single board meeting in person. One other director, Ronald LaBow, attended only a few meetings. The third director, Kurt Schacht, supposedly a governance expert, soon realized that governance wasn't the issue. The other investors never contributed a thought or effort but left us to deal with their elected directors.

After a year of struggling and with the decline of assets to about $3 billion and the stock below five dollars, Tisch, Beard and I left the board. I was assured by our counsel that we had done all we could do and would incur no liability in resigning. Months later, the company filed for bankruptcy.

A handful of awful lessons came from this debacle. First, don't assume smart people know what they are doing or have a plan. The activists had no plan and never did. They simply thought they were buying assets cheaply.

Second, don't assume right will prevail in the financial markets, which are often subject to irrational behavior. Even the brightest investors make decisions that defy careful analysis.

Third, advisory groups such as ISS—and, as we found out in the 2008 financial crisis, rating agencies such as Moody's—make bad decisions. We must remember that they are for-profit organizations, their staffs are often inexperienced, and their procedures are not geared solely to the public interest. ISS morphed into a profit-making business owned by private equity. It began to charge companies for advice on how to win ISS support on matters ranging from compensation practices to board independence. ISS became structured to make money and create equity value. The people who work for them have no special insight.

As times changed on Wall Street, the tension between profits and objectivity became apparent. In 1960, Moody's and Standard and Poor's were part of publishing businesses. Those rated did not pay for the rating. Al Esokait at Moody's and Russ Fraser at S&P were the arbiters of ratings. They were formidable and incorruptible. Presentations to them were, in practice, interrogations of CEOs.

Around 1968, I accompanied Dick Dempster, the CEO of then fast-growing Black & Decker, to a ratings presentation in front of Esokait. I warned Dick to tone down the growth prospects of the company and focus on the stability, but like all good salesmen, Dick couldn't contain his enthusiasm. By the end of the meeting, Esokait was clearly disturbed. I later had to assure him that the growth plan would not entail undue risk.

Over time, the ratings agencies converted to a pay-for-ratings plan. By 2006, they were rating every issue sold by banks but demonstrating little knowledge. Rather than being arbiters of security, the rating agencies, as in the case of ISS, became coconspirators.

The final lesson here is that many companies shouldn't be public. In the case of Peter J. Solomon Company, there have been times when I thought we would be better off going public because it would allow my colleagues to build net worth at a capital gains rate, give us a currency to acquire other talent and other companies, and provide liquidity for me and my family. I decided to remain a private investment banking partnership until I could find a better alternative.

CHAPTER 31

Family Businesses Are Unique

Although Tim Zagat and I were undergraduates at Harvard at the time, I was not an original contributor in 1979 when he and his wife, Nina, founded the Zagat Survey, the famous rating system for restaurants. Over the years, I frequently provided ratings in New York and Paris and helped Tim and Nina with financial decisions. When they sold a minority interest to the venture firms Kleimer Perkins and General Atlantic, they asked me to become a director.

Tim is a wonderful marketer. Nina is the perfect partner, keeping an eye on the business.

By the mid-1990s, Zagat surveys covered Los Angeles, Chicago, and other US cities and morphed into rating golf courses, hotels, and even movies. The red pocket restaurant guide, however, continued to butter its bread.

Being associated with the Zagats was fun. Annually, Susan, Nina and Tim, and I would tour New York restaurants confirming their location and their menus. As the Survey became more renowned, we couldn't just drop in. Every chef greeted Nina and Tim, offering food and a hug. We reached the point where, after a number of stops, we were too sated to keep going. And Susan and I attained one of the most valuable perks for a New Yorker: we were always assured of a reservation at even the hottest spots.

Zagat's revenues grew nicely, but as Tim and Nina passed sixty-five years of age, we discussed selling the business. I assumed that when they were ready to make a deal, I would represent them.

Regrettably, I assumed incorrectly. At a board meeting, to my shock, I learned that the venture investors had prompted the company to hire Goldman Sachs to sell the business.

In a word, Goldman failed. It ran the typical sell-side auction, but Zagat did not lend itself to an auction. Unusual businesses, ones not appropriate for leveraged financial buyers but appealing to corporate strategic buyers, need to be marketed with the sales pitch tailored to each prospective buyer.

While I had a sense of satisfaction from Goldman's failure, my friends the Zagats had been ill advised. At a subsequent lunch with Tim and Nina at Nougatine, Jean Georges' café on Central Park West, I explained why selling still made sense but how we would be successful. We resolved to go forward but in a process more likely to succeed.

Mother was fond of saying, "A prophet is without honor in his own country." I had seen this truth when Bill Miller tried to convince E. J. DeBartolo to use another banker to sell Ralphs. Big banking brands have enduring strengths, even after years of client abuse. But when smaller clients deal with big banks, they don't get the tailored attention they need. A Zagat survey of investment banking services would have alerted them to a low rating for Goldman in this category.

We agreed that two companies, American Express and Google, had strategic reasons to acquire Zagat Survey. We knew we might have a problem since Goldman had canvassed the globe. But we had a precedent. In the case of Lands' End, there was a similar fact pattern. Goldman ran a failed auction, but within two years, we had found a buyer at a good price.

Conceptually, I estimated that the Zagat brand was worth a multiple of the value based solely on its capitalized cash flow. We needed to tailor a sales process emphasizing global value of the brand.

Luck and timing are often critical in deals. Tim and Nina happened to be at a conference with Google management. This chance encounter led to a series of meetings after which Marissa Mayer, who then headed the Google team, indicated that Google was interested in an acquisition.

This time, Tim and Nina asked me to represent them.

Our strategy was not to justify an asking price using an index or multiple. We focused on the opportunity for Google. Google, of course, wanted both Zagats to remain. We reinforced the Zagats' confidence in the future by accepting that condition. It is always reassuring to the buyer when the seller is eager to remain.

Despite such insistence, I gave Tim and Nina my customary form of "Miranda warning," advising them that the buyer will likely find their presence unnecessary and annoying, and will want to fire them within six months.

Nina skillfully concluded the negotiations, and the deal was made and signed on September 8, 2011. At the closing dinner, Susan sat next to Marissa Mayer's assistant. The twenty-something woman kept talking to her about business matters and throwing in all sorts of acronyms, none of which Susan recognized. The assistant also continually referred to the acquisition of ZAG-at, not knowing that Tim and Nina pronounced their name za-GAT. Finally Susan had had enough. A name-dropper is bad enough, but a letter-dropper is worse. "If you tell me what all those acronyms mean," Susan said, "I will tell you how to pronounce the name of the company you just bought."

Google sold Zagat Survey in March 2018. At that time, Tim and Nina were still at Google.

As the Zagats' episode demonstrates, dealing with owners of private companies and founders and control shareholders of public companies requires specialized skills. PJSC was established targeting owners and (or) chief executives of public companies who owned— or thought they still owned—the businesses. Given my history at Lehman and my families' history at Stop&Shop and Edison Brothers Stores, our firm had accumulated experience in these situations. Public companies, such as Dunkin' Donuts, Burton Group, and Carter Hawley Hale, retained the governance of a family business. (Others, such as Culbro, were publicly owned but controlled by the founder's family.)

Many family businesses such as DeBartolo were private but with public investments. There were many variations on the theme.

I favor private ownership. My most quoted speech was one I made to a group of apparel and retail business owners at the Princeton Club, where I pointed out how much owned businesses define the social lives of the owners and how bereft many owners become after the sale. I said they become "just one more schmuck with $50 million and nothing to do walking around the streets of New York." An audience member jumped up and said he'd like to be such a "schmuck." The *Wall Street Journal* commented favorably on the speech while omitting the word "schmuck."

Private family businesses have decided advantages, including the ability to plan for the longer term and an option to be indifferent to short-term volatility in earnings or stock prices. They get little public scrutiny when making strategic decisions. And when those decisions turn out to be wrong, the adverse consequences are usually less noticeable, even when they have material impact on a family's fortunes.

There are times when it is smart for owners to sell their private company or control of a public company. The question is asked frequently: how does the banker convince an owner to sell a business and how do they reach agreement on price? Put another way: doesn't the owner always have an inflated view of the company's value? How does a banker move the owner to a realistic value?

The truth is that no one can convince an owner to sell at any price if the owner doesn't want to sell. Once again, process is important, and the first step in the process is getting the owner to trust you. Without a bond of trust, an investment banker will not be privy to the reasons behind the sale and the goals the owner wants to achieve through the sale.

As I have indicated, the sale of a business results from both quantitative and qualitative motivations. An outsider can understand the driver as age or succession and can perceive the need for capital and competitive positioning, but a banker must be helped to understand the other forces at play, such as the relations within the family. Thus, trust and the open dialogue between banker and owner are critical to a successful process. Easier said than established. I succeeded in cases such as Strawbridge and Clothier, Zagat Surveys, and Lands' End. But I failed with Claire's Stores, where the sisters who inherited control from their father distrusted all their advisers.

After establishing an open dialogue, the question arises always, "What is the value of my company?" In public companies, comparisons are easier, and stock market values set parameters. In private companies, there are fewer neat comparisons and principally general guidelines. With companies that appeal to private equity, approximate value is dependent on the tolerance for leverage. But many owners don't want to burden their businesses and aren't appealing to financial sponsors. I have given illustrations of how to think about value in these cases—namely, through a triangulation of factors. These help structure the conversation but are rarely decisive in agreeing with a private owner on the price he or she will sell.

The sale of control of PJSC is illustrative. I had established the amount of capital I needed to accomplish my dollar goals. I had also determined how I wanted to remain active in my business and to assure that my colleagues had an opportunity to accumulate capital while protecting them from too much interference from the acquirer. In my case, as in many of my clients', my nonfinancial goals were as important as my financial ones. Understanding this difference is critical to completing the sale for an owner. My career is littered with failures when owners could not differentiate between the two types of objectives and realized late in the process that the sale might immediately lessen their standing in the community or change the daily dynamic of their lives.

Trust, an open dialogue, and a clear disciplined process will usually convince the owner that the offers reflect the buyer's view of value. The banker's job is to help the owner understand that the market has spoken, and the owner must measure the market result against their objectives. Closing the circle and completing the transactions depends on an enlightened owner.

Most of the disadvantages of private ownership, such as more limited liquidity for family members, the concentration of assets, and the more limited capital available can be lessened by planning.

A lethal threat to the survival of a family business, public or private, is the expectation that family members will join the business and, in most cases, eventually manage it. Edison Brothers Stores is just one example that did not end well.

EBS was a high-fashion, value-oriented women's retail shoe company started by five brothers in Atlanta in 1922. In 1929, the brothers moved to St. Louis, the shoe center of America, and from 1948 to 1973 grew from two hundred stores to one thousand stores, principally under the show banners of Chandlers, Bakers, and Burt's Leeds. Mark Edison, the initial CEO, died in 1958, and his brother Harry, the financial genius of the family, became the chairman, with Irving as president. The two remaining brothers, Sam and Simon, were in top management, but they deferred to Harry.

EBS had come close to bankruptcy during the Depression, bailed out by a timely public offering. Scared by the near-death experience, Harry made sure the company had a solid balance sheet. I first met Harry at an engagement luncheon for Linda Newman (Mark Edison's granddaughter and Eric and Evelyn Newman's daughter), and Harry took the occasion to boast to me about his ability to lend money to banks.

Harry's children were not in the business, so when he died in 1966, he was succeeded by his brothers and two members of the next generation, Bernard (Bunny) and Julian Edison. The younger Edisons were graduates of Harvard College and HBS, and bright and capable executives. They had worked in the company since graduate school. But neither was a merchant in terms of instinct, and EBS' business, after all, was primarily women's shoes.

For years, the company continued to grow, but it missed the seminal shift in women's footwear to casual shoes and sneakers. It began to mimic the trend in specialty retailing, expanding into additional retail lines such as Jeanswest, a chain of pants stores; 5-7-9, a retailer of small sizes for women; Wild Pair, retailing unisex shoes; Handyman, a hardware chain; and United Sporting Goods.

In a negotiation on one of these acquisitions, Bunny admonished his lawyer to "protect him but not too much." A statement worth remembering.

Bunny and Julian left their management positions in 1985. During their tenure from 1972 to 1985, the company's sales had grown from $250 million to over $1 billion, and it operated over 2,400 stores. They were succeeded by Andy Newman, Linda's brother, and his HBS classmate Marty Sneider. Andy Newman is also a graduate of Harvard College. His first job was in the Pentagon with the whiz kids who staffed the secretary of defense. At EBS, Andy had been responsible for, among other tasks, building new businesses. His interest in gaming and electronics led him to acquire Dave & Buster's, a sports bar/restaurant concept, and to become the US distributor for "Virtuality."

The early 1990s was a tough period for Edison Brothers and for me. After Linda and I separated, I resigned from the board.

The company's business continued to be difficult. In 1995, the company was forced into bankruptcy. Sneider, in a memoir, blamed a number of policies and people for the demise. Unfortunately, despite Andy's efforts to diversify, the organization had been too successful for too long to adapt to changing conditions.

When the bankruptcy happened, those inside the management structure suffered in terms of cash and reputation, but the reverberations reached other members of the family with devastating results. Uninvolved cousins who were not allowed to sell their stock because it was needed to support the active insiders lost assets and income.

At Stop&Shop, our family faced an ownership situation similar to the Edisons', but we didn't require that each family member hold all their shares. Anyone could sell. One can argue that if we had retained all the shares, we would not have been attacked by greenmailers, or that when attacked, we could have defended ourselves without selling the business. But in my opinion, when noninvolved family shareholders own more shares than family members who are in the business, the noninvolved family members should be able to sell their shares. Dynasties are entities rooted in blood and heredity. If the business of a dynasty is business, hereditary criteria are a mistake.

Feuding among families because of real or imagined hurts are widespread. The Binghams of Kentucky, owners of a newspaper, Louisville's *Courier-Journal*, are an example of assured destruction. I mention the saga only because I watched the unfolding debacle through the moods of Barry Bingham Sr., the patriarch with whom I served on the Harvard Board of Overseers during the most heated period of family hostility. He and his wife, Mary, were the sort of elegant couple one envisioned as quintessential southern aristocracy. Barry Sr. had the carriage of a Kentucky colonel, a title his father actually had. The fight among his children over the destiny of the Bingham business no doubt shortened his life. He died in 1988.

Books have been written about the Bingham family debacle. The issue was simple, but the causes were sibling rivalry and jealousies. In 1984, Sally and Eleanor, the family's two daughters, both my contemporaries, attacked their brother Barry Jr., who was then titular head of the Bingham family. The daughters wanted to sell the *Courier-Journal*, the television and radio stations, and the other properties and distribute the assets to the family. When Barry Jr. forced Sally off the company's board of directors, she escalated the fight, publishing a book that belittled her brother and other members of the family.

The feud was ugly and expensive. In 1986, Barry Sr. gave up and sold the company, distributing the substantial proceeds to his children. Barry Jr. continued to manage the *Courier-Journal* after its sale to Gannett. His death in 2006 ended a great family dynasty.

Family businesses can survive and prosper despite the potential pitfalls. Medline, a multibillion dollar distributor of medical supplies, has prospered and sustained family control because they recognize the issues that may divide and the components of unity. For example, family management operates consensually, respecting opposing opinions and disavowing postdecision dissension. Compensation and perquisites are set lower than industry standards, minimizing envy.

Family businesses with public ownership under assault from the *outside*—from ISS and activists—don't have to capitulate or self-destruct. Certain defensive strategies can be considered. Having two classes of stock with voting favoring insiders, for example, is a structure that is scorned only by those who do not own the inside shares. When Dick's Sporting Goods was preparing for an initial public offering in 2002, Goldman Sachs and Merrill Lynch, its prospective underwriters, told Ed Stack, Dick's founder, that they had a policy of not underwriting companies with two classes. This view was based on the prohibition of the New York Stock Exchange and the belief that two classes inhibited shareholder democracy, a worthy position. I pointed out to Ed, however, that Monro Muffler Brake was a public company in which I personally held the golden share, controlling the critical decisions such as dividends, sale of assets, and election of directors, and its stock also traded at a comparatively high price/earnings ratio. I told Ed to tell these two firms that he would find an underwriter that didn't mind the two classes of stock. As expected, Goldman and Merrill withdrew their opposition.

Experts have published volumes on family-controlled businesses. Let me state a few points:

- Domestic tranquility is more assured when the business is expanding.
- Growing businesses obviously generate jobs for family and thus the promise of more income and net worth accretion. Once a business ceases to grow, family scrutiny and anxiety will intensify.
- Having smart, well-educated children is not a guarantee of sustainability. Heirs may not be interested in—or cut out for—a particular business.
- Parents preaching family unity can sustain family cohesiveness but only up to a point.
- Treat daughters and sons, sons-in-law and daughters-in-law equally.
- Jealousy and envy are natural conditions. Don't treat them as diseases to be cured. Rather, expect these emotions to occur

WASTING TIME CONSTRUCTIVELY

in a family business and factor them into your discussions and strategy.

- Business has to be viewed separate from family. It shouldn't come before family, but it is a precarious balance. Be sensitive to human concerns but make a commitment to run your company professionally.
- Promote people on their merits, whether they are family members or not.
- Encourage prospective family employees to train and gain a positive reputation elsewhere.
- Provide liquidity for family members if they need or want it. Don't begrudge the sale of stock for a relative not involved in the business. There are ways to provide liquidity without endangering the balance sheet of the company.
- Keep your pride in check. Recognize when evolving industry conditions require a change in ownership. Dynasties are subject to termination.
- Divorce can upset a family business, but divorce is a fact of contemporary life. It has to be anticipated and accommodated.
- Outside counseling and intervention may be helpful in anticipating and dealing with family issues.

$$\approx$$

The velocity of management transitions in the United States has accelerated. In the 1990s, the average chief executive's tenure was about ten years. Today it is about five and a half years. Increased board scrutiny, emergence of activist shareholders, and the complexity of business have kept the revolving door in motion. But whatever the cause, transitions pose challenges to any investment banker. To a smaller firm such as PJSC, with more personal and less institutional loyalty from its clients, the risks of losing a client in a transition outweigh the opportunities of forging a relationship with his or her successor.

In cases where the founder decides to sell the business in its entirety, we usually get the job of negotiating the sale. Even when the founder has relinquished the CEO job to a successor, he or she is often able to convince the board that their investment banker should handle the assignment. But boards are so jealous of their prerogatives these days that any variant of an outright sale can cause them to hire their own banker.

Consider the Cato Company, a retailer of women's ready-to-wear. In 1986 at Shearson, I had handled Cato's initial public offering. The company hadn't done well, but I had maintained a professional relationship with the founder, Wayland Cato, and his successor son, John. Wayland retired, remarried, and moved to Wyoming. John Cato called to tell me that his father was going to sell a large block of stock back to the company, and the board would need a fairness opinion. He asked us to provide it. When his board learned that he had requested our services, however, it decided we had to audition for the role, which we did in Charlotte. Over the objections of the CEO and the major shareholder, the board decided to hire the locally based Bank of America, arguing we were too close to Wayland Cato to be independent. Meanwhile, Bank of America was, at the time, the chief lender to the company, a situation with obvious conflicts. Our experience with Cato demonstrates the finicky nature of relationships with boards even in controlled companies.

Still, nowhere is there more danger to an investment banker's relationship than when a retiring founder or principal shareholder decides to retain a control stock position but anoints a successor CEO. Tension between the founder and successor will inevitably occur.

Jack Robinson of Perry Drug Stores; Gary Comer, founder of Lands' End; Larry Phillips of Phillips-Van Heusen; and Michael Bloomberg of the media giant Bloomberg L.P. are four examples of founders who appointed talented successors but were not able to let go emotionally. In Perry's case, changes in the competitive environment justified the conclusion to sell. In the case of Lands' End, the company needed to adjust both to e-commerce challenges and to the opening of more retail stores, but the sale was driven by Comer's personal estate considerations. Bloomberg, with no political outlet for his energies after being mayor of New York City, needed to return "home." Dan Doctoroff, who'd been running the company in his absence, immediately understood his dilemma. While Dan had done the job Mike needed during his years as mayor, Dan knew his authority would be undercut by the presence of the owner. There is no place for a creative and energetic CEO while the founder and majority owner is in the building.

Most companies understand the impossibility of a hovering former CEO, even if it is a case of one hired chief executive succeeding another. Few boards allow the departing CEO to remain a director for more than a year after the successor is chosen. Some companies exile the departing CEO immediately. When Jim Robinson sent Peter Cohen and me to speak to Phil Caldwell, the recently retired CEO of the Ford Motor Company, in 1985, we were driven to a remote suburban office building. Inside this three-story pristine building, we found Caldwell ensconced in a large suite of offices with several secretaries. But there was no one else in the building, and his desk was clean. He was in the corporate version of the gulag.

Equally, it is a bad idea for the former CEO to remain on the board and own a lot of stock. Larry Phillips of Philips-Van Heusen was a friend and client. His father had sold goods to my dad at A&S, and Larry and I had bonded on the trip to Israel during the 1973 Yom Kippur War. Larry had done a terrific job converting PVH from a prosaic manufacturer of shirts to an outlet retailer. PVH was a core account when I founded PJSC.

Bruce Klatsky, a career PVH employee, was Larry's designated successor. In 1992, Larry was still nominally CEO, but Bruce, who was doing the job, wanted the title. Crystal Brands was a company in distress that PVH had considered buying. I was playing golf with David Fuente on the Monterrey Peninsula in California. We were about to tee off on the third hole of Spyglass when my cell phone rang. Larry, in an obvious state of agitation, was calling to tell me that Bruce had confronted him with an ultimatum. Larry could retire immediately and appoint him CEO, or he was joining Crystal Brands as CEO. I put down the phone, hit an eight iron to the green, picked up the phone, and told Larry to tell Bruce to go to hell.

Larry, of course, didn't take my advice. Instead, he promoted Bruce. I could understand why. Larry, while CEO, wasn't actually running the business, and without Bruce, he would have to return to the grind of managing an apparel retailer. Being CEO of PVH meant flying around the country visiting department store chains, entertaining buyers, and servicing customers, difficult jobs that Larry no longer wanted.

Months later, Bruce was doing an excellent job as CEO. He would, in fact, build PVH into a powerhouse apparel company. But Larry was unhappy about losing his grip on the company and the concentration of his wealth in PVH stock. Once again, the issue came to a head on the golf course. We were playing in Boca Raton, and Larry, this time in person, was kvetching. Exasperated, I yelled at him to sell the stock and be done with PVH. He could reinvest it in equally good ways, and he would eliminate his anxiety. I also suggested he give a portion of the stock to Beth Israel Hospital with which he and his family had long been associated. This time he took my advice. Today, the Beth Israel Hospital Phillips Ambulatory Care Center for inpatient and outpatient service is at the corner of Union Square and Park Avenue South. PVH has thrived and has remained a core account of our firm. Bruce and I became close friends.

One more example of how succession can be so dicey. Helene and Marvin Gralnick founded the women's clothing chain Chico's FAS, Inc. in1983. They incorporated their hippie sensibilities into fashionable clothing that fit larger-sized women and jewelry that reflected Helene's interest in the Mexican aesthetic. After their business became successful, the Gralnicks would sometimes disappear into Mexico. Often they would leave their headquarters in Naples, Florida, to drive to the ocean, sip a beer, and watch the sunset. Why shouldn't they? By then, their successor, CEO Scott Edmonds, was running the business and doing a good job of it. And yet Gralnicks, who couldn't make a complete break, also frequently gave into the impulse to wander into his office and give him advice.

One day in 2002, Edmonds called me, describing his needs

for banking advice but, more tellingly, outlining his troubled relationship with the Gralnicks. He asked me to meet with them and help them come to terms with the fact that they had handed over the reins. I immediately recognized the behavior common to founders who hadn't sold stock. Over a short period, I developed a trusting relationship with the Gralnicks, and they came to New York to have dinner at our home.

At dinner, I asked them if they had heard of the provision in the securities laws that allowed controlling shareholders to sell stock periodically and told them that Bill Gates at Microsoft used this method to diversify his holdings. The marketplace adjusts to these expected sales, I said, and they wouldn't be giving the impression of a lack of confidence in the business.

The Gralnicks embraced the idea. It was as simple as uncorking a bottle. The tension between them and Edmonds dissipated. They were not abandoning their creation, after all; they were just becoming a little less connected.

Chico's continued to grow, although Edmonds was eventually replaced by David Dyer, formerly CEO of Lands' End, when we represented it in the sale to Sears.

The stories I've told about succession involve different circumstances and varying results. The common thread is an ability to be straightforward in situations, understand the personal dynamics in the interactions between founders, successors, and boards, and hope for the best. In almost every case, our firm eventually got rewarded for loyalty and honesty.

CHAPTER 32

Fees

Let me show you my art.
(Donald Fisher, CEO, Gap Inc.)

In 2002, the Gap was struggling. The ubiquitous and profitable men's and women's retailer had abruptly run out of fashion magic. In 2001, its earnings per share had dropped 26 percent. It was also consuming cash. Its debt had doubled, and it had a negative cash flow of over $700 million. Over the previous three years, shares in the Gap had fallen from the midfifties to the low teens.

Warren Hellman, founder of Hellman & Friedman and a leader of San Francisco's establishment, called to alert me to a call from the Gap's founder, Donald Fisher. Fisher had asked Warren for advice and capital, and Warren had told him to call me.

On the call, Fisher was anxious. He wanted help—and quickly. It was ironic. For years, I had tried to see Fisher but had never even been granted a moment. Goldman had underwritten the Gap's initial public offering and was still its adviser. But Fisher explained that Goldman and the Gap's commercial banks were worried about the deterioration of credit due to negative trends in cash flow and earnings. In fact, Fisher said Goldman had refused to use its own balance sheet to support the Gap. Goldman had clearly resolved which interest was paramount.

I reassured Fisher. There was no real danger of the Gap going bust. While Edison Brothers Shoes and other fashion retailers had gone bankrupt, it was vendors refusing to ship goods and the inability to extend short-term debt maturities that triggered failures. Fashion volatility is a given. Retailers endure when they take inventory markdowns quickly, free up cash, and use it to buy goods that will sell with a fuller mark-up. I was certain the Gap could survive its fashion blip and that financing was available. Working with Sabrina Simmons, Gap's treasurer, we approached Bank of America and JPMorgan, both eager to replace Goldman. Through them, the Gap sold privately $1.38 billion of senior convertible debentures. The financing gave the Gap enough time to turn around.

Since Warren had introduced me, I asked him what fee he thought I should charge the Gap. He suggested $750,000, but I told him I thought $500,000 was more appropriate. "Too low!" Warren bellowed, but I said it seemed like enough, and hopefully Fisher would use our firm subsequently. In the advice business, there are guidelines but not formulas for fees. You have to think of what's fair.

Fisher was flabbergasted by my fee. He said he couldn't believe we would charge so much. He acknowledged our role in warning him about Goldman, directing him to commercial banks, and imagining a senior convertible security. But as clients frequently do once you have served them, he stressed the time we worked on the project and not the value added.

When a client negotiates with me by focusing on the numbers of hours I spend on its project, I reflect on an incident when I was nine years old and had a terrible stomachache. My parents, on the advice of our family general practitioner, Dr. Sam Karelitz, diagnosed appendicitis and scheduled an appendectomy at Mt. Sinai Hospital. To confirm the diagnosis, however, my parents asked a specialist to give a second opinion, and he examined me at home. After several minutes of probing my stomach with his icy hands, he told my parents that I didn't have appendicitis, just severe gas and stomach cramps.

My parents and I were relieved—until the specialist gave a bill to my father for one hundred dollars. My father was stunned. The specialist had been at our house for less than ten minutes, and one hundred dollars was a lot of money in 1947. Over the years, I realized that there is no price too large for expert advice. To prove it, I have no surgical scar.

Advice from an expert is not a matter of time. It's a matter of value. Few clients remember this lesson when the crisis has passed and their financial well-being is no longer hanging in the balance.

About a week after our conversation, I received a letter from Fisher enclosing a check for $100,000. In it he acknowledged our role and hoped that we would accept his payment, which "we feel is fair." He also said he had spoken to John Lillie, his vice chairman, who agreed with the amount of the payment. He didn't mention then still president Mickey Drexler, whom he publicly fired a few months later. That was also interesting because Lillie was clueless about the financing. Finally, Fisher's letter included a postscript, inviting me to call on him the next time I was in San Francisco "as I'd like to show you our personal art collection." Translation: while I am chiseling you on the fee, I have art worth millions.

I have Fisher's letter framed and hanging in my office. Mickey Drexler relishes the letter for its bad judgment and utter lack of sensitivity.

Fees are the lifeblood of an investment bank. Since at PJSC we only do advisory work, fees from clients provide our only source of revenue. But fees are a fraught subject for both banker and client. When I started PJSC, it was immediately clear to me that clients couldn't differentiate between paying a fee directly to me and paying the company. They felt that every dollar was going directly into my pocket. I realized I should never ask for a fee myself but, rather, let my younger associates—and later my partners—negotiate our fees. That helps clients understand that my colleagues have to get compensated.

What are the industry's fee guidelines? Over the years, bankers and clients have relied on the "Lehman formula," a term that amuses me because we never had a formula at Lehman Brothers. In any case, this method charged 5 percent on the first million of proceeds, 4 percent on the next million, then 3, 2, and 1 percent thereafter.

Fees on larger deals are always negotiated. Usually the fees are calculated to be about 1 percent for $200 million mergers and scale down, so on billion-dollar mergers, the fees are a fraction of 1 percent.

Initially, clients resisted paying small firms like ours the larger fees associated with firms such as Morgan Stanley and Goldman. But, over time, as big hitters Bob Greenhill and Eric Gleacher set up boutiques, clients relented.

For an investment banker, it is fortunate that in the last fifty years the absolute dollar size of fees has mushroomed as the stock market and enterprise values of firms have grown. One would have expected the fees, as a percentage of deal size, to have declined ratably. But this decline has not happened. Since 1965, it is not unusual for the enterprise value of a NYSE-listed company to have increased twentyfold. The fee on a $1 billion deal in 1965 might have been in the range of .8 percent or $8 million. In 2015, on a $20 billion merger, not an unusual size merger, an investment bank received a fee of $82 million or .39 percent of the deal size. The merger fees in recent years exclude financing fees, which might dwarf the merger advisory fee.

How does one account for the power of investment banks to sustain such a fee structure? Probably it reflects the power of the financial community in American economic life.

Another reason that fees have grown is that in most cases of widely owned public companies, no one feels they are paying the fee. First, in a stock merger, there has never, to my knowledge, been a case where the per share amount received by the seller has been affected by the size of the fee. A corollary is that in a cash acquisition, no buyer has ever lowered the amount paid to the seller because of the size of the fee.

Of course, this seems counterintuitive. Why wouldn't they care and adjust the payment? It doesn't happen. Such indifference to fees by buyers would suggest that it would be easy for a banker to negotiate a larger fee with a client who is selling a business; oddly, this also may not happen. Sellers sometimes negotiate fiercely to reduce the percentage fee even as the banker explains that they are not, in fact, paying the fee. It makes no sense, but this is just one more idiosyncratic aspect of investment banking.

"Idiosyncratic" doesn't necessarily mean "fun" though; the

inherent irrationality can lead to bad feelings. In 2001, we were hired by the two Claire sisters. Their father had built the business, and with his death, they wanted to know their alternatives. The board of directors had been nominated by their father, and they were not active in management.

We determined that Claire's had saturated the world with jewelry stores and that there was literally only one other country for growth: Spain. The sisters and board authorized us to sell the business.

We estimated the value of Claire's at $3.0 to 3.5 billion and suggested a fee of $16 million, part of which we would owe to a Boston firm that recommended us. We explained the reasons for the fee, showed them comparable analyses, and explained that, in fact, they would not even be paying the fee. Likely the company would be bought by a financial buyer, and it would finance the fee and the purchase price.

Eleven years later, in March 2018, and after being structured once before, Claire's filed for bankruptcy and reduced its debt by $1.9 billion. It had shown no growth, as predicted.

Nothing was unusual except the sisters' reaction. They became enraged and accused us of gouging them. We and their lawyer, Adam Chinn of Wachtell Lipton, had clearly done an inadequate job of taking them through a discussion of our fees; as a result, both his firm and ours were fired by the client.

Claire's used Goldman Sachs, which charged a higher fee, and was sold to the Apollo Group, a private equity firm. We received a modest fee for our opinion on the fairness of the $3.1 billion price. Apollo retained control of Claire's even after its 2018 restructuring.

To a degree, it was our fault. We should have laid out the fees early in the discussions. The less sophisticated the client, the more important it is that they understand every aspect of the process.

Adrienne Vittadini, a beautiful Hungarian woman in her midfifties, was a designer of women's ready-to-wear. Her line was in the bridge category, spanning the price point between haute couture and better. Mother loved Adrienne's elegant and simple lines and the drape of her often white fabrics. So did a lot of other stylish women.

Dick Beattie was Adrienne's lawyer. He asked if we would represent

Adrienne in the sale of her company. While we frequently represented apparel companies, Adrienne's business seemed at first glance too small for us. Dick insisted, though, and because of our friendship, we agreed to be retained.

Gianluigi Vittadini is Adrienne's husband and business partner. Gigi, as he is known, is a true charmer with good fashion instincts. He was instrumental in Adrienne's success.

Negotiating with Gigi should have been simple. Our firm has a standard retention letter, and our fees conform closely to industry practice, usually a retainer credited against a commission based on the selling price. Our terms were neither unusual nor excessive, but Gigi applied his Seventh Avenue negotiating strategy. Every sentence was a battle. At long last, we concluded an agreement that we both signed.

Jeff Hornstein handled the sales process. None of the major apparel firms had any interest in buying the business, but we concluded a sale to Marisa Christina, a moderate-size dress manufacturer. Gigi and Adrienne were pleased with terms that included their continued employment.

Fees are due and payable at the closing. A few days after the agreement was signed, Gigi called. "I would like to discuss the terms of the fee," he cooed.

"What exactly do you want to discuss?" I asked. "It is time for you to pay what we agreed on."

Gigi came to our office and began a tedious explanation about how little they had received for their life's work. It was a lot of talk, concluding with the statement that he had no intention of paying the agreed-upon fee. Finally, he got around to asking for a 15 percent discount. He offered no reason for the amount, only giving the impression that Gigi Vittadini never paid retail.

There is no rational retort to a client who simply refuses to pay a fee. You either accede or you sue. I don't know why it has taken me so many years to understand certain life lessons, but after forty years, I finally figured out a response.

"Gigi," I said, "when we negotiated endlessly over the terms of the retention letter and you signed it, did you think that was the start of the negotiation on fees or the end?"

Without missing a beat, he replied, "The start!"

Knowing I was beaten, I told him to cut 10 percent off the fee and pay it that week. He did.

Marisa Christina eventually disappeared. As part of the process, the creditors were selling Vittadini. Naturally, Gigi called. "Would you represent me in reacquiring our business?" he asked.

"Gigi," I said. "You must be kidding."

My world has allowed me to span different characters, from Gigi Vittadini to Warren Buffett.

Over the years, I've found Warren Buffett surprisingly accessible. When I call, I am put through to him immediately. When I talk to him, he listens closely. He tells you if he is interested in your idea and, if so, at what price. But he doesn't readily pay fees.

I met Warren in the summer of 1988 flying from Martha's Vineyard to Chicago through Boston. On the small Vineyard shuttle, everyone looks vaguely familiar, but I didn't think much about it.

On the Boston-Chicago leg, I was in first class plowing through the memoranda daily thrust upon me as vice chairman of Shearson. I wasn't paying attention to my window seatmate, but I did notice that he seemed interested in my reading material. He ordered a Diet Coke; when I heard his voice, I realized it was Buffett, then a legendary investor but not yet the Sage of Omaha. We started chatting, and he invited me to visit him in Nebraska. In January 1990, soon after I left Shearson, I flew to Omaha.

I couldn't wait to ask him about some of his life lessons. For example, he was quoted as saying that he would never give money to his children. "Why not help them out financially if only for estate purposes?" I asked him.

"Oh," he said, "of course I give my children money. I don't know why I said that."

He also said he didn't have a private plane. But flying into and out of Omaha is difficult.

"Did I also say I have no plane?" He said, "Oh, yes, I have a plane."

Warren cultivates his folksy mystique.

Warren and I spent about six hours together. Late in the afternoon, he drove me to the airport and didn't use his seat belt although the roads were slick. "Warren," I said, "it is dangerous to drive without a seat belt, particularly in these conditions!" He buckled up and assured me he wears his seat belt.

Driving with a seat belt may have saved Warren's life, but other advice I gave him helped enhance his many Berkshire Hathaway shareholders' standard of living. In 1991, I called Warren about buying American Express. In truth, the proposal was self-serving. I had received Amex stock in the Shearson buyout of Lehman. The stock had not done so well, and I was nervous about the concentration of my net worth in Amex, a company that in the early 1990s looked like it was going nowhere. I thought Amex was an opportunity.

"Warren," I said, "Amex is an undervalued situation; it fits into your concept of a solid company growing with America. It would be an intelligent buy for you." He thought about it for a minute or two and demurred. At least he said he wasn't interested.

About six weeks later, an SEC filing revealed that Berkshire Hathaway had bought $300 million of a nontransferable issue of preferred stock convertible into 2.6 percent of Amex common stock. The Amex press release stated that Warren had called Jim Robinson offering to invest up to $500 million in American Express. I was perplexed. What a coincidence! Warren must have been buying stock at the time I was mentioning it, and he didn't want to tip his hand to me. Too bad I didn't call earlier, I thought. Maybe he would have paid our firm for the idea.

I brooded on this for some time and one day mentioned it to George Heyman, a former Lehman partner who was a friend and adviser to both me and Warren. "Can you believe the coincidence?" I said.

"Nonsense," George said. "That was no coincidence. You gave him the idea."

"I don't think so," I said. "I can't believe he would take that information from me and not acknowledge it."

"Of course he would," says Heyman, "and he did!"

I continued to call Warren with investment ideas. Each time, he would look at what I was suggesting, consult Value Line, and respond that the deal was too small, too expensive, or had something else wrong with it. I never got discouraged, though; turndowns are part of our business.

At no time did I have the nerve to raise the Amex issue.

Then, one day I called him about McKesson Corporation. McKesson is a major medical distributor and one of our clients. In 1998, it made an unfortunate acquisition of HBOC, a software company based in Atlanta. Fortunately for PJSC, McKesson used Bear Stearns as its adviser. We were disappointed at the time, but we were not implicated in the disaster that ensued.

HBOC turned out to be a fraud. McKesson's stock plummeted, and Mark Pulido, the CEO and our principal contact at the company, was fired. Fortunately, he was replaced by John Hammergren, with whom we had an excellent relationship and who has subsequently rebuilt McKesson into a major distributor.

With the stock at thirty dollars in 1999 after being as high as ninety-three dollars the prior year, I called Warren to suggest he might want to take an ownership position. I thought I'd also use the call to elicit some comment on his Amex purchase, if I could.

As always, Warren came on the line immediately. "Warren," I said, "I have an idea that is as good as the idea I gave you on American Express several years ago."

"Yes," he said without missing a beat, "that was a great idea."

There, I had my answer. I was wiser but no richer.

As of June 2017, Berkshire Hathaway owned 17.47 percent of Amex, worth $14.52 billion, its largest holding.

Warren turned down the McKesson idea, or at least he said he did.

A lot—probably too much—has been written analyzing the success and failure of mergers. Some pundits claim that most are unsuccessful. In my experience, that isn't true. In fact, the companies that make the most acquisitions within an industry tend to be the most successful, and their stocks sell at the highest price/earnings ratios. But what makes for an exemplary merger? There is no single answer, but there are some clues to increasing the probability of success.

Mergers and acquisitions are terms often used interchangeably. In practice—except in the case of private equity where a fund acquires a company—almost every combination of one company with another is a merger. Mergers don't depend on whether a large company acquires a smaller company or the two companies are of equal size, the so-called merger of equals. Mergers don't depend on the currency to effect the combination. While usually in larger mergers common stock is used to defer a taxable gain, the currency can either be cash or a security.

Private equity invests rather than acquires. Its objective is a return on equity that may be achieved without sales and earnings growth. On the other hand, no strategic acquirer can regard an acquisition as successful without achieving sales and earnings growth.

Most companies need to acquire as part of their growth strategy. The growth of the American economy is too slow to allow managements to achieve growth targets without accretive products or technology beyond their core competences. Technological innovation is too swift and growth in countries beyond the United States is too compelling to permit managements to rely solely on internal development.

Google, Facebook, and Oracle are serial acquirers, but it is not just technology companies that assure growth by acquisition. A number of years ago, A. G. Lafley, the CEO of Proctor & Gamble, noted that his stock price assumed a rate of growth that was not possible with P&G's portfolio of products. After all, 15 percent of the company's total volume was sold to Walmart, then growing at less than 10 percent. To align P&G's growth with the expectations of the stock market, P&G would be required to make $15 billion of acquisitions. Despite his plans, he couldn't find a more modest portfolio, so he ended up acquiring Gillette for $57 billion.

Every management at some point faces the issues of "strategic alternatives," the moment when it must decide between buying or selling itself. What considerations determine whether the decision taken will render the desired result?

First, a management needs to structure the analytic process

correctly. Investigating merger opportunities should be viewed as a "line of business," something no different from opening new stores, launching a new product, or introducing a technological innovation.

To establish the process, the merger department should report directly to the CEO or, in a conglomerate, to the head of the division. Filtering merger discussions through the CFO implies delegation of this important strategic function. It relegates the process to a lower priority, which can be a costly mistake. Former secretary of defense Bob Gates notes in his memoir, *Duty*, that if a cabinet officer wants to make changes in the bureaucracy, he himself must supervise the function, not delegate it. It is no different in the business world. Only the boss can convey the necessary sense of priority and provide the energy to succeed.

It is essential to have periodic meetings of top management reviewing merger options. Because of the longer-term time frame involved in the hunt for an acceptable acquisition, without established periodic meetings, the spotlight will dim as attention is focused on more immediate concerns.

As you might expect, I think an investment banker should work as an integral part of the acquisition team. Retaining outside advice and expertise broadens the talents, reach, and experience of the management team. It also keeps the pressure on. Sometimes managements think that retaining an investment banker will keep other bankers from showing them ideas. This is rarely, if ever, the case. Competing bankers are not that deferential. If they think they have a good idea, they will call you.

Looking for appropriate acquisitions is a grinding process. An investment bank serves as an outsourced development department containing the kind of talent that would otherwise be difficult or expensive to find. Only in companies that acquire serially is there talent comparable to experienced investment bankers. The hired development function is especially valuable when the objective is to diversify through an acquisition.

When Phillips-Van Heusen decided it needed to diversify, our firm looked at more than one hundred candidates over five years.

Eventually, management acquired the business of Calvin Klein. In the early 1990s, Cintas Corporation, the industrial laundry company located in Cincinnati, retained PJSC to call on dozens of local laundry entities throughout the United States. It didn't have the time to comb all these entrepreneurial operations that we could provide. In both cases, managements made accretive acquisitions.

A CEO's instinctive reaction to an acquisition idea tends to be decisive. Never pursue an idea that the CEO immediately rejects. The CEO's instincts deserve respect. The successful CEO knows what he or she needs in terms of an acquisition. The bankers' roles are to alert the CEO to opportunities and to advise on timing and techniques.

Due diligence is a critical part of any acquisition. In our business where we frequently negotiate between competitors, it is more complicated but not impossible. In some situations, we have used third-party consultants to analyze issues of synergies and cannibalization. An infamous case of bad due diligence was McKesson's acquisition of HBOC, which I mentioned earlier. Software companies like HBOC are notoriously difficult to analyze. McKesson thought HBOC was earning $1.4 billion annually. But HBOC earned nothing and was soon liquidated. The number of technology investments that are written off, in part or whole, by sophisticated acquirers testifies to the value of independent verification.

The acquisition of AOL by Time Warner in 2001 is an example of a deal in which due diligence seemed to have been purposely avoided. No one involved wanted to think too hard about what they were doing. By chance, I gave a speech at the Yale Club on the snowy morning that the deal was announced, labeling it a misalliance. Time Warner was leaping into a technology where it had no experience, at a price and size that would too radically change its business. The move seemed like a desperate attempt to appear current. Of course, it ended disastrously.

Purchasing power in the marketplaces can be key to a successful merger. Consider Monro Muffler. As the company acquired more units and expanded, its purchases of tires and oil could command price reductions from suppliers. The market price adjusts by supply and demand, and no place is this more evident than in the relationship between a purchaser or commodities and supplier. Monro's success is partially a result of successive reduction in its cost of goods.

Remember also that when two businesses merge, *someone* has to be in charge. Wall Street hates "heads-up mergers" in which two companies of roughly equal value exchange shares at little or no premium to the market. Stockholders don't see an immediate benefit from such an exchange, but a bigger problem may be that no single management is left in charge. When companies merge, one management must dominate. Every business or form of enterprise differs in culture. Some are tougher and emphasize hitting quantitative goals. Others include softer goals. There are organizations where the environment is subtly hostile to women; others are more enlightened. There are as many cultures as there are entities, but when companies merge, one culture must be imposed upon the other, and the employees must understand who is dominating whom. There can be no ambiguity.

When Lehman Brothers was acquired by Shearson in 1984, Lehman had a fractious culture. The firm had to be sold due to its unfixable, dysfunctional environment. Lehman's business would have to be righted under stable leadership. When Sherman Lewis and I took over the investment bank, there were thirty-five partners under a noncompetition agreement preventing them from going to other competitive firms but not from leaving. Sherman and I addressed them. I told them the fighting was over. They might not like the result, but Sherman and I were now the bosses. We were going to manage the banking division fairly and on the merits. We would not tolerate backbiting or malicious gossip. If the then managing directors could not function in that environment, they should leave. After my talk, Sherman told me he couldn't believe that I said that. But of the thirty-five MDs, only two left.

How does an investment banker figure into a merger? Our role involves process judgment and breadth of experience. Because I feel process influences the chances of success, a management must be assured of the integrity and experience of their investment banker. This seems such an obvious fact, yet many investment bankers haven't had sufficient training. I have written that one reason bankers were so successful after leaving Lehman was the discipline instilled by Ed Kapp in the industrial department in the 1960s.

At PJSC, we stress writing clearly, with presentations creating a storyline delineating assumptions, options, and the probable effect of strategic and financial choices.

The job of an investment banker is to get the merger completed once the client has decided to move ahead. The banker must push the deal through the inertia and fears that often freeze the acquiring managements. In every merger, there is a moment when both sides want to terminate the discussions. Personal slights, government objections, shareholder questions, unforeseen moves in financing cost, and premature leaks are some of the reasons. A seasoned banker has to be steady enough to condition the client to the possibility of these hurdles and knowledgeable enough to calculate the effect on the projected merger benefits.

I am often asked whether an investment banker always favors a transaction since most of our fees are based on the closing of a merger. Clearly, we prefer a closed acquisition. But a bad merger often results in your client ceasing to acquire for a period. Since it is so hard to get clients, and since clients that acquire tend to repeat, it is costly to the banker for the client to experience a setback. That's why my posture over the years has been to be cautious about acquisitions. But even caution must be exercised in moderation. It is important to move on a merger when the time is right.

Coach, Inc., the leather-goods retailer, was in its heyday when we suggested it might consider buying Kate Spade & Company, then a small handbag company that had been partially owned by Neiman Marcus Group Inc. during a period when Neiman's was trying to create unique offerings. The price was about $120 million. At meetings with Lew Frankfort, Coach's experienced CEO, we emphasized the hedging potential of Kate Spade. Coach passed. It didn't think it needed more handbags to grow. Liz Claiborne Inc. bought the brand. In the ensuing five years, Coach's growth slowed as a result of intense competition from Michael Kors and Tory Burch and the ubiquitous presence of its bags. Meanwhile, Kate's small handbag company has become a billion-dollar brand, and Liz Claiborne has changed its name to Kate Spade. And in 2017, Frankfort's successor, Victor Luis, acquired Kate Spade for $2.4 billion.

Mergers are like the forward pass in football. It's always exciting when you see the action unfolding and imagine the possibilities. But then as Woody Hayes, the famous Ohio State coach, said, "Three things can happen. Two of them are bad!" The bad options for a merger are happening and failing or not happening at all. It's one of my enduring frustrations that some of my best ideas never got beyond the drawing board. Here are four merger ideas that never happened.

Nike and The Limited

In the mid-1990s, two superlative consumer companies, Nike, Inc. and The Limited, were taking differing strategies to assure growth.

Nike, which was founded in 1964 as a shoe distributor called Blue Ribbon Sports, expanded from sneakers into exercise apparel. The strategy would extend its brand authority to buy shirts, shorts, and activewear bearing the famous "Swoosh" logo. Nike's reputation was based on performance running shoes. Apparel requires different sourcing and fit. The Nike soft goods of that day were shoddy.

The Limited, on the other hand, is a superb fashion apparel company. It had even branched into women's lingerie with its acquisition of Victoria's Secret. The CEO, Les Wexner, had adopted an aggressive real estate strategy. The Limited and its affiliated companies leased anchor-sized square footage in regional shopping malls. Given its diverse retail strategies, Limited could use the space, and on lease terms more comparable to the lower rates of the department store anchor tenants than to specialty stores.

In a meeting at Limited's Columbus, Ohio, headquarters, I proposed that the company join with Nike to form an activewear company. The combination of Limited's merchandising talents and, as of then, underproductive space, and Nike's prominence in sneakers would create a mall-based activewear company. (At the time, there was no Lululemon.)

For months, I tried to get the companies to meet. Finally, I gave up. Clearly, it wasn't a priority, and I wasn't even getting a fee.

Both companies have adjusted to changing markets in other ways, but they missed the opportunity to create a formidable active wear retailer years before the competition.

Au Bon Pain and Starbucks

Louis Kane bought control of Au Bon Pain, the urban coffee and croissant chain, in 1981. He and his partner, Ron Shaich, made fine coffee, but it was their ability to produce good croissants and sandwiches that distinguished their company from Dunkin' Donuts and Starbucks.

Starbucks had become a national chain serving expensive coffee. It had beaten Dunkin' Donuts and Au Bon Pain to the growing coffee market. However, its food, mostly rolls and sandwiches, were like Nike's apparel: not up to its own standards. I proposed to Lou and Ron of ABP that they consider merging with Starbucks. They weren't opposed to the idea. For months, I called Howard Shultz, CEO of Starbucks, to set up a meeting with Lou, but in vain. Meanwhile, life went on. In 1993, Au Bon Pain bought the St. Louis Bread Company for $24 million in cash with additional consideration in a payout. ABP was subsequently split into two companies, Au Bon Pain and Panera Bread (successor to St. Louis Bread). Panera was sold to JAB Holding Co. for $7.5 billion in April 2017. Closing the circle, in November 2017, JAB acquired Au Bon Pain.

Crate & Barrel and Neiman Marcus

Crate & Barrel, built by Gordon Segal, is one of the world's premier home businesses. I called on Gordon for decades at his office in suburban Chicago. In the mid-1990s, I convinced him that it was time to merge Crate & Barrel with a quality company that could provide the capital to expand, and that it was time for him to get some capital out of the business.

I suggested that he pursue a deal with Neiman Marcus, which was then controlled by Richard Smith through General Cinema. Gordon liked the idea but hired another firm to represent Crate. Nevertheless, I proposed the idea to Dick Smith, who also liked it. Usually, in a company controlled by a strong individual, this should have been decisive. In this case, though, it wasn't. Smith hired the consulting firm McKinsey & Company, which concluded that Crate was not the same quality as Neiman Marcus. Somewhat embarrassed but not enough to overcome the McKinsey conclusion, Smith turned down the opportunity. Gordon eventually sold control of Crate & Barrel to a German mail order company.

In retrospect, I shouldn't have been surprised by the way things turned out. Dick seemed to have a problem pulling the trigger. Several years earlier, we had an idea to sell General Nutrition Company to Neiman Marcus. GNC was just emerging in the supplement field at the time, and there was some controversy over its products. Although Dick liked the idea in principle, he came to the conclusion that GNC was a "round hole in a square peg," meaning he couldn't quite figure it out. So his reaction to the Crate & Barrel deal did indeed fit a pattern. At least he sent us a check for $250,000 for suggesting the merger, even though I had not billed him.

Gannett and MCA

In 1983, as cable grew and expanded the number of options for consumers, it was becoming clear that content in broadcasting and all forms of media was going to be king. There simply wasn't enough programming to go around.

Gannett Newspapers was one of Lehman's key accounts and part of my broadcasting responsibilities. We worked on a number of mergers, including annual discussions with the Knight and Ridder newspaper chains, at the annual Associated Press dinner. Eventually, Knight and Ridder merged without our help. Gannett was left to its own devices, and it would need to acquire content.

MCA, the major film studio and distributor, had access to content. I had gotten to know Lew Wasserman, the chairman of MCA, during my government service. He was a major Democratic contributor and a major force in Hollywood. Lew Wasserman and Dr. Jules Stein, the founders of MCA, didn't seem to be interested in a merger, but they were wise men, and they were not getting younger. I thought a merger would be a smart move for both sides.

Felix Rohatyn, a legendary partner at Lazard Freres, was an MCA board member. I called him and suggested a meeting. Felix was reluctant to call Mr. Wasserman but didn't object to me calling him. Without much resistance, I arranged a luncheon at Lehman Brothers with Mr. Wasserman and his president, Sidney Sheinberg, and Gannett's CEO, Jack Purcell, and Doug McCorkindale, Gannett's CFO. Felix and I joined them.

It was clear that the MCA team was intrigued by the idea. They were forthcoming about their new films and answered all questions politely. The body language was promising. Meanwhile, the Gannett executives were attentive and seemed interested. As the promoter of the merger idea, I was encouraged.

Several days later, I followed up with my Gannett clients. They told me that they weren't impressed by Sheinberg. They concluded that MCA's best days as a "content producer" were behind it. The deal was stillborn.

In the years after this luncheon, MCA released *ET, Raiders of the Lost Ark, Star Wars,* and *Jaws,* four of Hollywood's most successful films. So much for Gannett's judgment.

❧

Completing a merger takes a combination of perception, timing, chemistry, and stamina. Without all four and a dash of luck, even good ideas don't happen.

CHAPTER 33

Investment Banking Primer

When I was a sophomore at Harvard College, I took McGeorge Bundy's course on foreign policy. With one exception—me—the 150 undergraduates in the lecture hall were brilliant. But when it came time for the first exam, the highest grade in the class was thirty. I got an eleven. That's because Bundy chose to ask questions such as, "What day of the week did the Korean War begin?" It turned out that he saw the test itself as a teaching aid. Bundy's lesson was that every big picture is made up of a countless number of details—which should not be ignored.

This is the case in the profession in which I've spent the last half century. Investment banking is all about noticing little things—body language, tone of voice, firmness of handshake—so you can get insight into the human component of a business situation. Understanding the motivation and values of the participants is essential to good advice on mergers or acquisitions.

My world of investment banking is based on long-term relationships. Joe Stein, one of my partners at PJSC, once told me that he had realized that "your clients are your friends!" I told him it was the only way I knew how to operate.

I remain in touch with my bunkmates from camp, classmates, former colleagues, and people I have hired along the course of my career. At my surprise seventieth birthday party at Gramercy Tavern

Restaurant, Dick Beattie and Tom Brokaw created a T-shirt saying, "Oldest and Closest Friend" memorializing my large circle of friends.

For me, a transaction is the result of a relationship, not the reason for one. Most of my clients become friends before they become clients. Even if we had not done business together, I would still be seeing most of them in social and philanthropic settings. They know that, and it is one reason they became clients. I have few purely business relationships. In my experience, relationships require at least three years of cultivation to take hold. Because of my long involvement in their personal and professional lives, clients tend to view me as part of the family. Thus, as managements change and individuals come and go, I tend to stay with a company over the long haul. Some clients and I have been together for decades. While it is an accomplishment to get business, it is more telling to sustain it.

I am often asked what advice I can give to graduates hoping to enter my field. What makes a good investment banker? Obviously, brains and integrity are essential characteristics. Brilliance is helpful, as it is in most trades. If you scan the banking field, you'll find few summa cum laude graduates. Investment banking depends more on energy and focus and less on intellect. Seeking clients in a competitive world requires constant motion, concentration, and dedication, centered on superior organization of one's time.

The ability to write and present ideas clearly and concisely is a way to establish authority. School tests usually require a minimum number of words—"write five hundred words describing"—when the student would be much better served by being given credit for brevity. I urge my colleagues to avoid the type of adverbs I used in the first sentence of this paragraph. Adverbs slow the thought process, and words such as "significant" and "substantial" have no meaning in financial analysis.

When I mentioned to John L. Howard, general counsel of W. W. Grainger, Inc., that I was writing a memoir, he told me to include a discussion of networking. Networking with clients and prospects is essential to success. The word "networking" might have negative connotations associated with the deliberate cultivation of someone for a specific goal. I do frequently call or visit someone with an agenda.

Often, however, I call or visit to catch up on their lives or ask their opinions. My kind of networking involves finding a common bond around which we can form a relationship. I urge my colleagues to find personal connections with prospects before they begin a business discussion. This might involve charitable work, political causes, or hobbies. Successful networking involves connecting with people on their terms.

Wasting time constructively is an essential component of networking. An unexpected call often reinforces a relationship or leads to a conversation about a matter that later results in a fee. You can keep in touch via email, but there are moments when a banker must physically appear in a client's office or, hopefully, in front of their board. Timing sensitivity is a critical element to success.

Self-motivation is the sine qua non of success. Investment banking offers freedom to succeed. It is not hierarchical. There are layers of authority, but as one moves upward, the organization flattens. Anyone at any age can have and deliver new business. I tell our younger analysts that I had some of my best ideas immediately after entering the business, when I was twenty-five years old. Lehman invested in LIN Broadcasting in 1964. I made my first extensive new business trip along the West Coast to call on supermarkets in April 1964, less than a year after joining Lehman.

Only self-motivation can propel you out of bed and onto an airplane for a trip to see someone you have never met, to sell them a service or promote an idea they haven't yet conceived of themselves, knowing from the moment your alarm clock goes off that they will most likely say no.

To succeed in investment banking, it helps to like to visit new cities and meet new people. The TSA, planes without meals, and fewer flight options all can make the days long and difficult. There is no way around this; you must be on the road. In terms of getting business, a day in the office is a day wasted.

In the 1960s, it was a big deal for a New York banker to fly to Colorado or the West Coast. This was one reason regional firms thrived. California investment banking, for example, was dominated by brokerage firms Blythe and Dean Witter. Not even law firms were national. Today, bankers are expected to fly across the country and to foreign lands for lunch. My mentor, Paul Manheim, hated traveling, but when I went along with him, I realized he had found a way to ease the pain. In every city, we also went to at least one art museum or exhibition. I have kept up this tradition and extended it to presidential libraries or cultural sites.

When you are fortunate and get retained to negotiate a sale or acquisition, there are techniques to increase the probability of success. For example, process does affect the outcome in any negotiation, whether you are dealing with a multimillion-dollar acquisition or, by the way, dealing with your children. There was an ancient Roman saying that the winds and tides always favored the better navigator.

Here are some guidelines that seem to improve the odds of success:

First, be sure of the facts. A surprising number of times, even experienced business people begin a negotiation without digging hard enough to confirm the facts. They rely on secondhand sources or hearsay. Later, when facts emerge, they are surprised; their positions are undermined, and their credibility reduced.

Second, anticipation is essential. The best bankers develop a sense of the flow of a deal. They anticipate the twists and turns. Anticipation permits time to prepare your client and to develop alternative approaches. Anticipation also allows the banker to maintain the rhythm of the deal. Every negotiation develops a unique pace. Changing the timing may alter the outcome.

Third, the day of the week may become important. Don't take tough positions on Fridays and never give anyone bad news on Fridays. Your adversary will brood and conspire during the weekend. By Monday, their positions will have been hardened by the emotions of anger or pride.

On the other hand, don't call your adversary on Monday mornings. In fact, my advice is to delay until Tuesday. Calling on Monday indicates that you have been thinking and probably plotting what to say. This indicates too much pressure and the desire to resolve the issue. By waiting until Tuesday, you have socialized the issue, and the timing indicates a more measured response.

I've long thought that an investment banker and a golf instructor have a lot in common. What makes an ideal golf pro? It's someone who brings out the best in you but doesn't substitute their personality for yours. They make improving enjoyable and keep it front and center as the goal.

About fifteen years ago, Maury Povich introduced me to Peter Kostos, one of the world's best golf professionals. Peter is known widely for his commentary on PGA televised tournaments. I arranged to have a lesson with Peter at Boca West in Florida. Susan drove me to the lesson, and I told her to pick me up in an hour or so, when I assumed we would be finished.

Peter is a gentle soul who doesn't look much like an athlete. He asked me to hit a few balls. He told me to change my grip slightly and turn my body away from the ball a little more. I hit a few balls with these suggestions. After fifteen minutes, he said, "Great, that's all you need."

My friend Nelson Long, the golf professional at Century, has the same approach: a quiet, gentle manner without complicated strategies. He knows what my goals are. He adapted his instruction to my objectives and my potential.

Life's passage has made me better understand the importance of this approach. In investment banking, understanding the personality of a client and their goals is critical to a happy outcome of the relationship. Nelson's method is measured in yards and inches. Mine is in millions of dollars. Otherwise, we are the same.

Finally—and I list this last only for emphasis—the quality an investment banker should possess is integrity. Several years ago, our client Paul Finkelstein, former CEO of Regis Corporation, called to tell me he had recommended our firm. I later asked what he had said. "Did you tell them we were smart?" I asked.

"No," he replied. "Every investment banker is smart. I told them you were honest!"

My partners are frequently frustrated by the fact that the larger firms are able to serve competing clients. My daughter-in-law Geula Solomon runs Barclays' conflict resolution department. She works around the clock to resolve conflicts. Despite the exceptional job she does, Barclays paid plaintiffs $90 million stemming from its conflict in the Del Monte buyout in 2010. Who knows how many settlements it and other firms have made. For the big firms, paying fines and settlements is merely a cost of doing business.

PJSC has stood for the proposition that there is no case where representing conflicting or competing companies is beneficial to either company. Chinese walls, the theoretical edifice constructed by large banks to convince clients that different teams can represent competing and conflicting interests, are an illusion. A client who believes in this fairy tale deserves an unsatisfactory result.

❧

Halfway through the first decade of the twenty-first century, PJSC had established itself. We assumed that if we made the calls, were reasonably smart, avoided conflicts, and were honest, we would be successful. That's been our story for thirty years, and we are stuck with it. In the area of all forms of retailing and distribution and in terms of reputation, we had achieved our business goals. Our growing media banking business encompasses entertainment, theatres, and advertising. We have honest partners and associates who continue the culture of fairness and mutual respect and who value our clients.

We made a strategic decision to combine media and retailing in response to the challenge of the internet and e-commerce to our distribution clients. I had learned the hard way that without a unified approach, our clients might not think PJSC had the necessary exposure to new technologies and structures. You often learn more from failures than success. TJX was one of our earliest clients. But when its management began to explore e-commerce opportunities, it hired Merrill Lynch due to its technology expertise. Fortunately for us, TJX's relationship with Merrill didn't work out, but it made me realize that we needed to market better. Managements acknowledge our expertise in retailing but not technology. While we insist that the challenge to retailers is from e-commerce marketing and organization, clients were not convinced. Instead, we created a merged media-retail task force that proved successful. Over the next years, we represented Walmart, Home Depot, eBay, Christie's, and TJX among others in internet-related acquisitions. Thus we defended our turf and opened new channels for new business.

Through Dad, our family's retail businesses, and my investment banking work, I have been watching and engaging in retailing all my life. There have been selected moments when the relationship between stores and customers changed. Paul Mazur, in *The Standards We Raise*, pointed out the impact of the car and the six-day week in the second decade of the twentieth century in terms of the mobility of customers and the spread of retailing to the suburbs.

In 1949, Diner's Club International introduced a universal credit card. In 1958, American Express issued its first card to consumers. By the late 1950s, the credit monopoly of department stores was over.

The ability for consumers to have credit in any store facilitated the growth of specialty stores and shopping centers. New types of stores, however, were not seminal changes. They were natural evolutions.

The internet was a disruptive change that caused retailers to rethink their businesses in fundamental ways. Within a period of years, the explosion of information facilitated by mobile devices and new mobile payment systems affected every retailer. Even Monro Muffler, in an auto service and tire business, has to worry about the challenges from Tire Rack, an internet distributor of tires and, of course, Amazon.

At first, my colleagues at PJSC, so accustomed to the rapidly evolving world of computer technology, viewed the internet as just another improvement. Being less schooled in technology, I viewed it as a development as dramatic as the first television in our home on Park Avenue in the late 1940s, and maybe more revolutionary than cable television in the home. I persuaded my Harvard classmate Richard Marcus to help us transition into the new era.

Our education was timely. Retailers and real estate developers such as Steve Roth, the founder of Vornardo Realty Trust, asked about the impact e-commerce was likely to have on occupancy and traffic in his shopping centers. Seminal change forces every party to take a new look at how they operate.

The rapid sales growth of Amazon made clear that people would shop from their homes. What was initially less clear was how many consumers would buy clothing and other soft goods in addition to books and records. It turned out that a great many would.

Second, as we noted and Steve Roth worried, there is too much selling square footage in the US per consumer dollar. Such an overstored condition has existed for over two decades. E-commerce exacerbates this excess.

Third, shoppers don't immediately change their habits. The internet is not going to replace the traditional shopping experience of going to a store, but it would modify consumer buying habits. A successful retailer had to offer brick and mortar as well as internet options.

Fourth, we determined the immediate e-commerce challenge facing retailers was not technology. Rather, because of the complexity of the digital systems as well as the ages and the training of the people running the operations, the challenge would be the integration of their e-commerce operation with traditional management structures. At lunch one day, I asked Roger Farah, then CEO of Ralph Lauren, how he was structuring his e-commerce business. With confidence, he said he had appointed a veteran RL executive to oversee both operations. About six months later, I asked Roger how his new structure was working. He said he had abandoned his initial plan.

Indeed, catalog companies such as Williams Sonoma were the most immediately successful at integrating their offerings. They were experienced at dealing with parallel distribution channels, and they didn't have a traditional store management structure.

Walmart, on the other hand, demonstrated the problems of integrating e-commerce. Years after realizing that its primary competitor is Amazon, Walmart finally integrated its e-commerce operations with its store business by acquiring Jet.com and a number of specialized online businesses.

Finally, the proliferation of mobile devices has made the consumer, not the retailer, the master of pricing. The ability of consumers with mobile devices to compare price, value, or efficacy will increase the competition among retailers, lessen geographic dominance, and tend to lower prices and squeeze profit margins.

In terms of PJSC's business, the pressures on retailers and distributors of all business and consumer products have led to increasing numbers of strategic mergers. There is a natural process of geographic or horizontal consolidation as markets grow more slowly and synergies and savings are necessary to sustain profit margins. In retailing, for example, a 2–3 percent same store sales increase is needed to cover the administrative expense increases. When companies run out of room to add new stores, consolidation becomes attractive. Supermarket and drugstore companies have been active merger partners, partially because neither of these sectors sell goods that are exclusive to their operations.

The degree of change has also led to a number of specialty retailers selling to financial sponsors. Lack of expansion opportunities, aging principal shareholders, and the difficulty finding successors capable of managing in the more complex multichannel world have sparked sales. Confident in their ability to manage more successfully in the private world and awash with uninvested funds, private equity funds have pounced on retailers with as yet unseen investment returns.

CHAPTER 34

A Balanced Life

My goal was always to balance family responsibilities, career ambitions, and civic involvement.

One aspect of my public career was as a director of twenty-one boards of directors of public companies and not-for-profit entities. If Sidney Weinberg of Goldman Sachs was the king of boards, I was the jack. My first directorship was at LIN Broadcasting in 1964. The LIN tumult of 1968–69 sensitized me to the obligations and liabilities of board membership. It was the only time I was sued in a board capacity. With luck and prudence in the fifty years since, I have avoided most controversies and all liabilities.

Corporate directorships gave me an edge in getting banking business. Advisers are cautioned to be independent, and conflicts of interests are taboo. Congress enacted Sarbanes-Oxley to give more teeth to the obligations of board members and to add transparency to possible conflicts of interests. The law, however, deprives boards of much experience and knowledge.

I resigned from my last boards, Office Depot and PVH, because their counsels advised the CEOs that my directorship would prohibit PJSC from acting as their investment banker. Obviously, it is more lucrative to be the investment banker.

Public boards have morphed from being consultative and supportive of management to overseers and critics. One hears much about lead directors, independent audit, compensation, and special committees spotlighting corporate governance. It is hard to argue against these developments, particularly since PJSC is an independent investment bank, but we will see in a decade or two whether companies' governance and results have actually improved as a result of this more antagonistic approach.

My invitations to the boardroom resulted from my business, social, and charitable involvements. In Miller Wohl's case, I came onto the board because I did the banking at Lehman. At Edison Brothers Stores and Stop&Shop, I was a relative. Murray Foreman, a friend of Dad's, led me to Monro. At Office Depot, Dave Fuente decided paying me a director's fee was cheaper than paying me a retainer. Edgar Cullman chose me in a beauty contest. At Associated Dry Goods, I succeeded Lehman partner Joe Thomas. LIN Broadcasting was a Lehman investment. Larry Philips invited me on the PVH board because of a friendship born out of our trip to Israel during the Yom Kippur War. In almost every case, I became the lead director or an important director, and sat almost always on the compensation committee, a locus of board power.

The CEOs of the companies on whose boards I served—including Larry Philips, Bill Arnold, Heinz Eppler, and David Fuente, in addition to Edgar—became lifelong family friends and supporters.

Of course, not every one of my experiences with boards has been positive. Over the years, there have been times when the CEO and I clashed, or when he never came to rely on my judgment or turned to either Lehman or PJSC for banking advice. Earlier, I discussed my rupture with Don Pels, CEO of LIN Broadcasting.

My board experience with Century Communications under Len and Claire Tow was also disappointing. I knew Len and Claire socially. They rented our home in Martha's Vineyard and lived near us in Pound Ridge. Len was an entrepreneur who had been TelePrompTer's CFO before starting his own cable television company, Century Communications, backed by Sentry Insurance of Wisconsin. Because of our relationship, Lehman had underwritten Century's public offering in 1986.

Len and I had different views on corporate governance. For

example, Len and Claire collected director's fees, which is unusual in public companies. When the company bought cable systems in Kentucky, they personally bought an affiliated radio station. Two of their three children worked for Century. Finally, the chief operating officer of Century, who was also the chief executive officer of an affiliated cellular company, exhibited erratic behavior. Len recognized the situation but did not address it.

Over a period of several years (before Sarbanes-Oxley), I tried to convince board members to impose more prudent governance consistent with public company standards. Having no effect, I resigned. It was the only time I have taken this action. One can imagine how strongly I felt, since I knew Century would eventually be sold for over $1 billion; by resigning, I was eliminating any chance that Len would retain PJSC.

Century was indeed sold in 1999, retaining DLJ. It was sold for stock to crooks who controlled Adelphia Communications Corporation. In 2002, Adelphia filed for bankruptcy. Because I still held the merged company stock, our family lost money but, obviously, not as much as Len and Claire did. Fortunately, the Tow family sold stock held in its family foundation and are now generous philanthropists, with major contributions to Memorial Sloan-Kettering, New York Public Radio, Lincoln Center, and a broad range of charities. Len and I have renewed our friendship.

The dynamics of a board can affect the fortunes of a company. Being a CEO is a lonely job in the current investment milieu. Quarterly improvements are demanded, although no company grows smoothly. Accounting standards are demanding, giving CEOs and CFOs less flexibility. Audit committees preempt board time, and the Sarbanes-Oxley Act has heightened the liability of officers and directors.

Compensation committees had a cozy relationship with managements but are now required to be distant. This should not be surprising since comparative lists of compensation are published widely, with few observers claiming any CEO is fairly paid. As previously noted, proxy consultants like ISS and activist shareholders have gained influence and pressure boards. There is widespread need for better governance, and the markets have not been harmed by more transparency, fewer conflicts, and undisclosed relationships; the "old boy" network needed a shove into the modern age. But ISS as the arbiter of good governance and proper behavior is a sham. It is a for-profit company owned at one time by a private equity firm that charges clients for "advice." It often opines on the companies it is advising, and its analysts often don't have a clue. Ironically, it is a model for some of the worst behavior it purports to eliminate.

❧

I had been enthralled by the theatre since I saw *South Pacific* in 1949 but never considered a career. My voice is not musical comedy quality, and in the 1950s, Jewish kids from Park Avenue didn't go into the theatre unless they were academically challenged. At the Collegiate School, one student, Peter Bogdanovich—"Bugs," as he was known—ended up with a film career. But Bugs rarely went to class.

Abigail did perform in school and, later, college theatre. One of the things not taught at the HBS is that a parent should do almost anything to discourage a child from the theatre. It goes like this: "Dear, you are terrific, but you don't have enough talent for the stage." This admonition may bring hysterics for a short time as well as hours of psychological counseling, but it will save years of frustration and failure.

Despite my misgivings, Abigail is an actor and producer and can deal with constant auditions and frequent rejection more effectively than I cope with the same process pitching investment banking services.

One day, Rodger Hess, who had gone to Camp Kennebec with me, asked to have drinks with me and Barry Grove, the executive producer of a well-regarded Off-Broadway theatre company, the Manhattan Theatre Club.

The purpose was to ask me to join MTC's board. In the conversation at the Williams Club, Barry, several times, mentioned how helpful I had been to MTC. I had no idea to what he was referring and, in fact, became convinced that he thought I was my brother, who had been a subscriber to MTC since the earliest days in 1970s, when it was housed on Seventy-Third Street in the basement of a church.

At our second meeting, Barry said, "When we came to City Hall, you were so helpful." At first, I had no idea what he meant. He related to Rodger how he and Lynne Meadow had come to see me in 1979 in my basement office and had told me MTC's plight. Its lease in the church on Seventy-Third Street was terminated, and it had nowhere to go. Could I help them find space?

The movie and theatre office of the mayor was under my supervision, and our administration was committed to rebuilding Broadway and Forty-Second Street. We were ridding Times Square of its porn shops, putting more cops on the street, and were supporting Fred Papert's proposal for a new set of Off-Broadway theatres, "Theatre Row." City Center, a run-down municipal facility on Fifty-Fifth Street between Sixth and Seventh, was being renovated after a series of disastrous starts, and the city was going to put some of its limited capital budget in its renovation. My memory of Lynne and Barry's visit was hazy, but their recollection was clear; I called out to my assistant, Fritz Favourle, and told him that we should see if we could put a stage in the basement of City Center for MTC. As a result, MTC had moved to the refurbished City Center and now had two stages in the basement.

I went on the board of MTC in 1993. Lynne and Barry have a relationship guiding the theatre that has lasted more than thirty years. Their special position is nurturing new playwrights and actors. Terrance McNally, John Patrick Shanley, Charles Busch, Richard Greenberg, and Donald Margulies are some of its best known playwrights, while Nathan Lane, Cherry Jones, and Cynthia Nixon are some of the stars who have appeared frequently in MTC productions. I served as a director for five years until the capable chairman, Michael Coles, asked me to become president. His wife was ill, and MTC has numbers of events requiring a senior officer. I accepted with the proviso that I would not become chairman. I was too busy with my firm.

Terrance McNally, one of our most important playwrights, had written a play, *Corpus Christi*. Lynne did not feel it was worth producing and asked Terrance to rewrite it. The play would be controversial because it centered on a gay Jesus Christ. Lynne, Barry, and I discussed how to urge Terrance to postpone the play until next season, giving him the opportunity for rewrites. This is a common practice in the theatre, even when a play is in rehearsal; Terrance, in fact, often rewrote an entire play just before rehearsals. In this case, though, we were dealing with three issues. First, the play simply wasn't good, in Lynne's judgment—and MTC's reputation was based on Lynne's judgment. Second, Terrance McNally was not only a Pulitzer Prize–winning playwright but closely identified with MTC. Finally, that this play was about a gay Jesus would surely arouse the ire of a number of theatregoers and subscribers on whom MTC depends. The last point was less important but was a consideration. The fact that it had a gay theme was immaterial to MTC. We produced plays with gay themes; a number of our most prominent playwrights, board members, and actors are gay.

Lynne and Barry returned from a meeting with Terrance much relieved. He had agreed to postpone the play to the fall. All was fine, they explained.

Two days later, the world of MTC was threatened with collapse. Athol Fugard, the renowned South African playwright, told the *New York Times* that McNally had said MTC was "censoring" his play because of its gay Jesus theme.

All hell broke loose. The press led by noted *Times* arts correspondent Frank Rich attacked MTC. Playwrights threatened to boycott MTC. It looked like MTC's world was disintegrating.

Howard Rubenstein, the prominent head of the most politically sensitive PR firm, was an adviser to MTC. We briefed him and noted that since the announcement, MTC had received a number of threatening calls.

Howard proposed that Lynne call a press conference and tell them the whole story of what had happened. Lynne immediately called a press conference at MTC's larger stage at City Center.

Michael Coles, MTC's chairman, called me and said he had to resign. He said that the religious part of the play disturbed him, and he didn't feel right in continuing. Perhaps equally important, Coles said that he had no experience in managing such a crisis. He said with my background as deputy mayor, I knew how to cope. Obviously, his resignation and asking me to become chairman was contrary to our agreement. In September 1998, I accepted, seeing no alternative. And once again, the unexpected led to a significant experience in my life.

Lynne's press conference started badly. The theatre was filled with at least seventy-five reporters, and they were hostile. Lynne discussed the potential danger of putting on *Corpus Christi*. The press pooh-poohed the risk. Then, in a theatrical moment, the recorded menacing voice of a crazed caller blared from the sound system. The man was threatening to blow up City Center if *Corpus Christi* was produced. Instantly, the tone of the press changed. Even Frank Rich became sympathetic, understanding the dilemma of MTC.

We went forward with *Corpus Christi*. In the days before the opening, we received 350,000 letters stimulated by the Catholic League protesting the play. We needed to protect theatregoers. We put in standard metal detecting screening. But what would we do if a problem arose during a performance?

Standard procedure in the theatre would be for the stage manager to clear the stage of actors. He would then notify our house manager, who would notify our landlord at City Center, who would call the cops. Obviously, by that time, mayhem could have occurred.

Years ago at the Dana Farber Cancer Center, a pharmacist gave a patient named Lehman a lethal dose of a drug. In subsequent studies, it appeared that seven doctors and nurses had signed off on the drug and dose. Upon analysis, a consulting firm concluded that when more than three people are responsible for any decision, no one takes sufficient responsibility. Moral: shorten the chain of command.

I made a decision. If a disturbance happened during a performance, the stage manager would clear the stage, turn the hall's lights on, and call the cops. I spent the run of the performance of the play worrying that a nun would rise to go to the bathroom in the middle of this endless and boring play, and we would have her arrested. In reality, nothing happened.

Thus began my twelve-year run as chairman of MTC. It was one of my most rewarding experiences.

During that time, the MTC grew from two Off-Broadway houses to three, including a rebuilt Biltmore, the original home of *Hair* and *Butterflies Are Free*. We produced the Pulitzer Prize–winning *Proof,* written by David Auburn and starring Mary Louise Parker, in 2000. Five years later, we staged another Tony and Pulitzer Prize winner, *Doubt* by John Patrick Shanley, and, in 2007, produced *Rabbit Hole* by David Lindsay-Abaire.

In 2003, I had mentioned to Lynne that MTC's perfect play would have four characters (so we could afford it), one act of ninety minutes (to avoid the difficult second act and to end earlier so our patrons would be home by ten o'clock), and have a soupçon of homosexuality (our patrons had no phobia, but they didn't want to have sexuality of any kind be a dominant theme of an eight-play season).

During the summer of 2004, Lynne called. "We have a play by Shanley that fits exactly your criteria."

"That's a relief," I said. "But is it any good?"

"Yes!" she said. That play was *Doubt*.

Doubt became one of our most successful plays, winning awards for the playwright and for Cherry Jones as best actress. At the party following the premier, I saw Shanley and effusively said, "John, this play is fantastic. How did you do it?"

Without missing a beat, he said, "You know, Peter, sometimes it just all comes together." True, on the stage and life!

The relationship of Shanley and MTC exemplifies the collaboration that can be realized between a not-for-profit theatre company and a playwright. During the previous twenty years, MTC had produced six Shanley plays, some better than others, as he developed his craft.

Lynne and Barry were agitating to find a Broadway home. They wanted to be Tony-eligible, but the rules are odd. To qualify, a show has to appear on a Broadway stage, defined geographically. Some not-for-profits, such as Lincoln Center, have used clout to get on the official list of Broadway theaters. But MTC was not as powerful; City Center was beyond the Tony pale.

For five years, we looked at every theatre, turning down some on Forty-Second Street because of the size and others because they were too expensive. Finally, Lynne looked at the burned-out Biltmore on Forty-Seventh Street, derelict since 1987. We hired James Polshek, who had designed a number of public spaces. The estimated cost was $25 million, an enormous undertaking for a group that had never raised more than $3 million.

Most of my adult life, I have been engaged in fundraising. The challenge facing MTC was whether it could convince donors to build a landmark theatre for a group that catered primarily to a white, older, middle-class audience. A Broadway theatre, after all, was not a hospital, nor even a venue for experimental theatre.

Our first step was to convince the owner of the burned-out theatre that MTC had enough fundraising capacity to rehabilitate the Biltmore. Considering MTC's lack of financial resources, it was a legitimate concern.

With Barry Grove, I met with the Parker Organization's owner, a young Yale graduate who was Jack Parker's grandson. He questioned our financial capacity, at which point I removed from my coat pocket a sheet of paper with some names and numbers. Flashing the paper with probably the same tenacity of Senator Joe McCarthy's act in the Senate, I told him I had a list of commitments sufficient to fund the reconstruction. The Parker Organization agreed to let MTC acquire the theatre.

Getting support from the Giuliani administration was not easy. In the end, because of the support of City Council Speaker Christine Quinn and, later, Borough President Scott Stringer, we received $8 million in capital funds. The Bloomberg administration, through Commissioner Kate Levin, continued the support.

There are always disappointments in fundraising. The chairman of our Finance Committee and a member of a large family foundation could not deliver a promised $2 million. Worse, his foundation gave it to a competing theatre. The reason? His sisters felt neglected. (He later, in the next mini campaign, did deliver!) In another case, a close friend, enthusiastic supporter of MTC, and leading member of a foundation died before we could formally submit a proposal. He had urged me to go ahead despite my trepidations. After his death, when I applied for funds, the executive director of the foundation asked if he had formally committed to funding. Answering truthfully, I said not formally but he had encouraged me and said the funds would be there. The executive director turned MTC down.

We raised $36 million, but the renovation cost that much, leaving MTC with no endowment and a structural annual loss of $1 million. (We subsequently sold the naming rights to the theatre to the Friedman family for $12 million, thus creating an endowment.) The move to a Broadway theatre meant more single tickets to sell and more risk. Producing on Broadway is different from Off-Broadway. The audience expects more. The critics are tougher. Friends of ours, Barry and Fran Weissler, producers of *Chicago,* among other hits, changed the Broadway formula. Today, to attract an audience, the producers have to have a TV or Hollywood name on the marquee. MTC learned that we couldn't bring a play to Broadway without a tryout at a regional theatre, or we'd better stick to revivals, where at least the product is tested.

Lynne got her Broadway theatre. You have little choice other than backing talent when it wants to do something. It's the pact one makes with genius.

Susan and Lynne created a blowout final MTC act for me. We raised more than $2 million at a party at Cipriani. Bernadette Peters performed. I had to give money to her Broadway charity for wayward animals. Nothing is free. Everything is a deal.

CHAPTER 35

Train Wrecks—The Financial Crisis

There are always financial crises. They are a destructive by-product of the US financial system. By 2006, few people doubted that a crisis was imminent. The only questions were when and how severe. The larger investment banks and commercial banks were competing to lend to leveraged buyout groups at alarming multiples of cash flow, reaching an average of nine times. Competition among Lehman, Goldman, Citibank, and JPMorgan was fierce. Jimmy Lee, the chief lender of Morgan, boasted about the bank's capacity for lending; although once censured by the bank, he was later restored to a prominent position so the bank could lead the lending tables.

How did we get to that point? The inventor of the special investment vehicle (SIV) was Lew Ranieri, who in the 1980s was head of the mortgage operation at Salomon Brothers. With these instruments, banks bundled mortgages and sold the package to the public. SIVs quickly became the borrowing vehicle of choice, despite their opaqueness.

On a summer day in 2007, Bob Millard, the chief investor officer for Lehman Brothers, and later chairman of MIT, asked me to lunch at his Park Avenue office. As I ate a sandwich, he walked around the table reading me the indenture covering the sale of a recent SIV. He asked whether I knew who owned what and to what were the various lenders and investors entitled in the event of nonpayment. I hadn't a clue, I said. He admitted, neither did he.

What we could see plainly was that the risks were growing in the bond markets. Banks and securities firms were leveraging themselves on too little capital, then recommitting their capital themselves through the use of derivatives. In 2002 in Phoenix, I had given a speech to the Economic Club for my friend Jimmy Adler. In that talk, I noted that Alan Greenspan, the Federal Reserve chairman, had deemed derivatives important to the market because they provided additional liquidity. At the end of Greenspan's speech, however, he dropped a cautionary note: the derivative exposure of the top banks totaled 85 percent of their total capital.

Before the SEC banned fixed brokerage commissions in May 1975—at which point commissions on a share of stock dropped by 67 percent—the equity business dominated Wall Street. By the late 1970s, issuance of debt sold to the public emerged as the chief source of profitability. Salomon Brothers broke into the major underwriting syndicates through its power in the debt market. As the public debt market exploded, Wall Street invented an instrument called the interest rate swap, a method for issuers to hedge the cost of debt or speculate on the movements of interest rates.

In 1981, Lehman arranged an interest swap, the first of its kind, for the Federal Home Loan Bank. By the mid-1980s, interest rate swaps, credit default swaps (through which buyers or speculators could buy a form of insurance against failure to pay), and other forms of derivatives were being sold to chief financial officers throughout the world. Many clearly didn't understand the transactions. This fact became increasingly evident over the next thirty years.

At one point, after a meeting with the clueless CFO of a major New York utility, I thought our firm should create a business unit advising CFOs and boards on the potential benefits—and, more importantly, risks—of swaps proposed.

In any case, Wall Street took advantage of these ill-informed corporations and sovereigns. There is no clearer example of this than the suit in 2014 initiated by Libya against Goldman Sachs. Libya maintained that it lost its entire $1.5 billion investment through derivative transactions in which Goldman earned $350 million. When

I heard that, all I could think was that Goldman was lucky that Qaddafi was dead.

I first became aware of the accumulating liabilities in the system in the mid-1990s, through Peter Sacerdote, a senior partner of Goldman. Goldman was then still a partnership, meaning each partner had joint and several liabilities for any losses. Peter told me that while sitting in a meeting at Goldman, he had realized that the Goldman partnership didn't have a precise idea of its total liabilities for its swaps. Worse, most swaps were customized to fit the exact circumstances of the parties. There was no conformity and little accountability. Peter said he panicked, realizing that his personal net worth was liable. Soon thereafter, he appointed himself chair of the firm's commitment committee.

There were many and seismic changes in the structure of finance in the decades leading up to the Lehman collapse. The most notable was the repeal of Glass-Steagall and the enactment of Graham-Leach-Bliley in 1999. The legislation allowed the banks to expand into insurance and brokerage. Some argue that step was a decisive moment and Glass-Steagall should be reenacted. The world had moved beyond the barriers of brokerage and banking. GLB codified reality.

The growth of unregulated mortgages and of hedge funds changed the role of banks. Banks had become packagers of mortgages into SIVs, extending their balance sheets and leveraging their capital. Hedge funds, their partners in these endeavors, were unregulated.

The growth of private equity and the move of banks and brokerage firms into proprietary investing reduced liquidity and created more leverage but did not cause the Great Recession. When Obama embraced the Volcker Rule to limit proprietary trading and investing, I opposed this prohibition.

The regulatory system did not keep up with the changes in the financial institutions it was regulating. Since the New Deal, the financial regulatory system had changed little. Regulation reflected function. The SEC regulated the brokerage or securities industry. Firms such as Lehman and Goldman were under its supervision. While the securities industry harbored the myth that it was self-regulated, it reported to the SEC. The commercial banking industry was under the supervision of the Federal Reserve System and the Comptroller of the Currency. The insurance industry had no federal regulator but was supervised by state agencies. Investment advisers were registered with the SEC under the 1940 Securities Act. Commodities and commodity exchanges were regulated by Commodity Futures Trading Commission (CFTC). Derivatives, such as credit default swaps, were under the purview of the commodities regulator, as they were initially primarily a mechanism to hedge price volatility of commodities.

Congressional oversight reflected the functional system. The SEC and the bank regulators were overseen by the Senate banking committee. The CFTC was overseen by the agriculture committee.

The merging of activities in the financial markets led to overlapping regulators and agencies. Functional regulation gave way to activity regulation with some activities falling between regulators. The SEC, for example, had responsibility for JPMorgan's securities activities, but the comptroller and Federal Reserve for its lending functions. The Commodity Futures Trading Commission regulator should also have looked at its derivative positions. Given the complexity of the financial institutions and the overlapping of functions and personnel, good regulation never had a chance.

In March 2008, Bear Stearns collapsed. The Fed rushed in to rescue it, although Bear was a secondary player in every aspect of Wall Street. It had always been a firm that couldn't quite shoot straight. In the early days of our firm, I had testified in its defense in a case regarding the duties of an investment banker. But Bear's leadership in the age of Jimmy Cayne wasn't what it had been in the time of Alan Greenberg, "Ace," and John E. Rosenwald Jr.

Bear was forced into the arms of Jamie Dimon at a bargain price. Later, John Rosenwald told me that Jamie had wanted to buy Bear several years earlier at multiples above the price he paid, but Cayne had ignored the offer. John told me he had then sold his stock.

During the summer of 2008, I wrote an article arguing that the government should have let Bear Stearns be liquidated. Why should the shareholders receive anything? In another article, I called for credit default swaps to be conformed and traded through a clearing house. If the swaps were cleared on a regulated exchange, it would increase the transparency of the system. It would be possible for not only regulators but, more importantly, managements to monitor the leverage in the financial system and in each bank. Going back to Greenspan's observation in 2002, regulators and managements would know the relationship of equity to liabilities at any time.

I also wrote that it was now time to consider a new Reconstruction Finance Corporation as a vehicle prepared to bolster the financial system. I had worked on a history of the New Deal RFC during my time in the Treasury. The RFC had been remarkably successful, sustaining financial institutions, railroads, and even the defense industry from 1933 to 1945. Under Jesse Jones, it had lent $3 billion to the private sector, all of which it recovered. A number of former RFC agencies still existed, and there was no crisis.

The year 2008 was a different time. The US banking system was headed for disaster with overleveraged balance sheets, indeterminate and undisclosed liabilities through derivative contracts and excessive mortgage lending. When Lehman collapsed, it had leveraged its equity twenty-twofold. Its combination of excessive mortgage financing and illiquid real estate investments proved fatal. Yet, despite signs everywhere of impending doom, no one seemed interested.

Train wrecks have always fascinated me. We are taught in game theory the value of maximizing gains while minimizing losses. Business schools don't teach the loss to each party that occurs when negotiations fail. We see the results of failed negotiations every day. Amazon's abrupt withdrawal from Queens, bitter divorces, gridlock in Washington, and war are all examples of deadlocks that result in more damage to participants than a negotiated settlement with necessary compromises. Lehman Brothers' bankruptcy was a train wreck.

On the debacle of Lehman Brothers, much has been written. I have just three additional points.

First, I fault Treasury Secretary Hank Paulson for his lack of action leading up to the mess. We know the litany of excuses for inaction: the lame duck president; a divided Congress; the White House's desire not to get further involved in saving Wall Street firms; antipathy between the secretary, a former Goldman partner, and Lehman, a traditional rival; lack of legal authority; bad luck that the Bank of England stopped Barclays from rescuing Lehman; and maybe, finally, a judgment call that the collapse of the third-largest brokerage firm wasn't such a big deal.

The fact remains that the collapse was a big deal. One of the principal roles of government is to act in times of crisis. As I said earlier, the pertinent axiom is "Don't ask for permission. Ask for forgiveness!" History, which continues to reveal interesting facts through lawsuits and memoires, will record that Dick Fuld knew he needed capital for at least a year and that while he tried to raise capital from Koreans and others, he was not able to find a lifeboat. Paulson was clearly frustrated by Fuld.

Paulson had also used his powers to rescue Bear Stearns, which he need not have done. Tim Geithner at the Fed was not a strong partner. While people thought he came from Goldman Sachs, he had always been a civil servant, as he himself points out in his autobiography. He was not a deal guy.

In 2014, I had an opportunity to ask Geithner about his decisions in 2007–2008. While he graciously rejected my criticism of his inaction in 2007, he admitted that the Federal Reserve and administration could have been more proactive in 2008 as the crisis grew.

Paulson repeatedly claimed he did not have the legal authority to intervene. Even assuming he was not prepared to ask for forgiveness, by the summer of 2014, we learned that his underlings and those at the Fed had concluded the government did, in fact, have the legal authority to rescue Lehman. But it is unclear whether these subordinates informed their superiors of their findings.

Once Lehman cratered, the government acted promptly and well. It could not have been easy for Paulson and Geithner to make the decisions during the election campaigns. Witness the extraordinary meeting President Bush called at the White House with candidates Obama and McCain, where McCain had apparently nothing to say.

TARP, vilified by almost everyone because of the anger at the financial world, was the right program; if enacted in the summer of 2007, it might even have averted the crisis. Like the RFC, the government has received most of its money back and all from the largest companies. I, myself, would have been more dramatic and tended toward more material ownership and supervision of the banks.

In the first week of February 2009, I received an unexpected invitation to join a group meeting with Don Gips, head of the White House personnel office, to discuss staffing of the top jobs in the Obama Treasury. I was joined by Steve Koch, who had worked with me at Lehman and later became deputy mayor under Mayor Rahm Emanuel in Chicago, and Orin Kramer, whom I had first met in the Carter administration.

Gips showed us a management chart of the Obama Treasury. When he saw me smiling broadly, he asked why. "The chart shows only two people, the deputy and the counselor, reporting to the secretary," I said. "When I joined Secretary Miller, I created the title of counselor, borrowing it from the Department of State. No one knew what to make of it. Now you have institutionalized it, and at a high level. You have assured me of a more prominent obituary!"

Gips asked us if any of us would like to join Secretary Geithner. We all demurred. He then said that the Obama administration believed that the Treasury might have to become an investment banker in a number of industries to reorganize them. At lunch, we discussed the need to address the auto industry and the plan to enlist Steve Rattner, whom I had hired at Lehman in 1981. I had met Steve when he was a reporter covering the Treasury for the *New York Times*. In February 2009, Steve was under investigation for his role in getting pension advisory business. The White House either seemed not to care about the impending scandal or was unaware of it. In either case, Steve was appointed and did a good job helping GM right itself.

Meanwhile, Congress addressed the issues of regulation. Tim Zagat was a classmate of Congressman Barney Frank. I pushed Tim to ask Barney if I could talk to him, because he had no background in finance. As chair of the House Financial Services Committee, he had to be involved in legislation. Barney told Tim that he didn't think he would be involved. The final legislation is called Dodd-Frank.

A word about Chris Dodd is also appropriate. Chris is an acquaintance of many years, and I had supported him in his campaigns. In 2007 and early 2008, Chris, who was chairman of the Senate Banking Committee with oversight over the financial system, was living and campaigning for president in Iowa. Yes, with Wall Street burning, he was in Davenport.

Congress passed the Dodd-Frank Act to regulate the banking business. It runs 2,200 pages with 1,500 sections. Its central authority is the Federal Stability Oversight Council, a council of regulators unlikely to agree.

Complexity notwithstanding, in the ten years since its passage, we have had no catastrophic financial failures. A clearinghouse for derivatives finally exists, and capital ratios for banks have improved.

Despite the efforts of the Trump administration and persistent outcries from the industry over excessive regulation, to Congress's credit, it has modified, not repealed, Dodd-Frank. Its essential elements remain.

Dodd-Frank established the Bureau of Consumer Financial Protection. I favored such an agency, given the dismal record of financial institutions in dealing with consumers. Years ago, for example, I had written Sandy Weil, then head of Citibank, to ask for an explanation of a foreign exchange charge described on my monthly statement. Sandy, who would have been my boss at Amex, never responded. If I couldn't get help from a friend, how could the average consumer?

At the same time, I opposed the appointment of Elizabeth Warren, who was the advocate of the bureau. Warren, now a national figure, was too hard-edged and divisive. I likened her to Ralph Nader, whose book *Unsafe at Any Speed* had helped create the political push for the National Highway and Vehicle Safety Act in 1966. Because President Johnson appointed a noncontroversial executive director, the safety bureau was more effective. Effectiveness and relevance depends on how a leader leads and the manner by which they effect change.

Trump is intent on eviscerating the bureau. Hopefully, the bureaucracy will, as always, outlast his political appointee.

In late 2009, Phil Angelides, the former treasurer of California, was named chairman of a Financial Crisis Inquiry Commission impaneled by Congress to investigate the collapse and the roles of the various participants. On January 13, 2010, the first day of the commission's hearings, I appeared on a panel of three immediately after the testimony of those I called the perpetrators: the CEOs of Goldman Sachs, JPMorgan, Bank of America, and Morgan Stanley.

I don't know why the chairman asked me to testify, but I was honored. Susan and I spent the night at the Hay Adams across from the White House. I flew in from a business trip in Memphis and met her at the hotel. I asked her to bring my blue suit; as I unpacked, I realized she had packed my blue suit jacket, but the trousers were my tuxedo bottoms. When I graduated from Harvard, I had kidded with my friend John Gross about which of us would be the first to appear before a congressional committee. It was fifty years later. It had been a long wait, and I was to about to win a college bet in a maître d's outfit. I could only hope that no one noticed the banker criticizing other bankers and government regulatory agencies wearing formal pants.

The esteemed panel met in the enormous House Appropriations Committee Room chamber. The temperature was so low that my teeth chattered as we listened to the questioning of the four bankers. Frankly, they performed below expectations. Lloyd Blankfein of Goldman had been briefed so thoroughly to admit nothing that when asked by the chairman what the firm's exposure was to credit default swaps, he answered he did not know. If this was true, he should have been fired immediately. Jamie Dimon was cool, as always, but not substantive. Nor was John Mackey, who provided the bluster for which he was well known. The only chief executive who came off well was Brian Moynihan of Bank of America, who had the advantage of recently becoming CEO.

My points that day were simple. I said that the debacle was the failure of both the regulators and the banks. They shared responsibility because the structure of regulation did not keep pace with changes in the financial industry.

While much has been written about the changes in regulation of the industry and their effect on the crisis, I did not think that any one change created the climate for failure. What the debacle did underscore, though, was that regulations and the agencies that administer them do not change quickly. Government bureaucrats will always lag behind the more dynamic and ever-changing financial markets. Additionally—while I do not demean the intelligence of regulators—the capitalist system rewards and attracts smarter, more agile people than government.

Michael Lewis wrote that the commission's report was one of the best he had ever read, but the report was not issued until February 2011, too late to have any impact. Its conclusions were on target. Corporate governance failed. Regulatory agencies failed. Systems didn't keep up with volumes. Ethics had declined. And, most important, nothing had changed to prevent it all from happening again. While these conclusions seemed indisputable, four Republican members voted against the report. By the time of release, its conclusions were lost in the blur of Dodd-Frank legislative negotiations and partisan bickering.

CHAPTER 36 ⎯⎯⎯⎯⎯⎯⎯⎯⎯⎯⎯⎯⎯⎯⎯⎯⎯⎯⎯⎯⎯⎯

New York State Government 2010–2013

In December 2010, newly elected New York State Governor Andrew Cuomo invited me to serve on the Council of Economic and Fiscal Advisors. I had served on Mario Cuomo's Advisory Economic Board, which rarely met. I had met Andrew only once, when he came to my office to solicit a campaign contribution. In that meeting, Diane Coffey and I showed him the New York City Tax Guide that Marilyn Rubin and I had produced the previous year. He asked if we could produce a similar guide for the state by the time of his inauguration in January 2011. We did.

At the first meeting of his economic advisers, including prominent New Yorkers such as Felix Rohatyn, Pete Peterson, and Denis Hughes of the AFL-CIO, the governor said he had two economic priorities: infrastructure and tax reform. He was going to establish an infrastructure bank and a tax commission. I didn't realize it at the time, but Cuomo was "commission happy." Fifteen members volunteered to be associated with the infrastructure bank. I chose the tax commission. After the meeting, the governor asked Peterson whether his foundation would underwrite the tax commission. Pete agreed, "Only if Peter Solomon chairs it."

Tax policy had interested me since my time in the Treasury Department. No one else cared about President Carter's 1980 tax proposals, so I had carried the deflated ball. The experience led me to

Senator Russell Long and to a realization that my smartest Treasury colleagues were in tax policy.

As taxes increased sharply after 2002, and I realized how little my fellow New Yorkers knew about their own tax realities, I decided it would be an interesting exercise to produce an analysis of New York City taxes.

Obviously, before I began, I tried to find existing analyses. Certainly, I thought, the Citizens' Budget Commission, urban research centers at NYU or Columbia, or other good government groups would have produced a summary and explanation. But none existed. Even the city's own website on taxes was inadequate.

In 2009, I had called Marilyn Rubin, a professor at City University who had done excellent work when I was in City Hall. I asked her how difficult it would be to create a guide to New York City taxes, one that detailed the history of each tax, subsequent legislation modifications, how much revenue it generates, and who pays it.

A year later, we produced a sixty-eight-page "Guide to New York City Taxes." Our family foundation underwrote the cost. We distributed a bound version to business, labor and civic leaders, and to city, state, and federal elected officials. Fewer than ten recipients sent an acknowledgment.

Ironically, David M. Frankel, Mayor Bloomberg's commissioner of taxation and finance, was the most enthusiastic recipient of our guide. The commissioner hailed it as the best summary of New York City taxes. He asked to put it on the city's website, but we refused because he would not commit to displaying the entire guide, including areas critical of the city.

After the meeting of economic advisers, I heard nothing from the governor about the tax commission. However, in January 2011, Larry Schwartz, the secretary to Cuomo, asked me to serve on a commission with a different mission, the SAGE Commission, established by executive order to restructure the state's government. No restructuring had been done since Governor Al Smith in 1928.

The twenty-six SAGE commissioners included state elected officials, political donors, and interested citizens such as Kevin Ryan,

Bob Zimmerman, and Neil Cole. The chairman was Antonio Perez, the CEO of Kodak, an unfortunate choice since Kodak declared bankruptcy a few months later. Perez resigned, and Lt. Governor Robert Duffy became chairman.

The SAGE Commission had an initial plenary meeting in Albany, which the governor failed to attend, a lead indicator of his involvement. I became chair of the environmental and transportation task forces.

The best that can be said about my involvement was that it was educational. Aided by Ben Lilienthal and the able staff director Derek Utter, I spent hours making sense of the state's bureaucracy. Our task force met with the commissioners of environmental protection and transportation, and with other interested groups, including the unions. We studied the extensive material. It became clear that unless the political leadership vested in the governor pushed for major improvements, the commission would be left tinkering with modest improvements.

Let me illustrate what I mean. Transportation in New York State is organized into eleven geographically defined districts. Our analysis concluded that five districts would be sufficient and could still provide locally needed services such as snowplowing and culvert maintenance. The state could consolidate the eleven separate staff jobs, such as real estate and legal, into a single district. Obviously, consolidating a bureaucracy means jobs and power moving from one locally elected official to another. This isn't going to happen unless there is an overall plan for the entire bureaucracy based on what in the merger business is called a "has-gets" analysis. If Syracuse or Rochester loses a transportation office, for example, what jobs can be shifted to them?

A restructuring also requires management talent and political clout, neither of which was available in transportation.

The commission's research uncovered endless redundancies and out-of-date bureaucracies. The Erie Canal, for example, was a magnificent public works project of Governor DeWitt Clinton in 1843. It opened the port of New York to the west. Today, the 550 miles of recreational water cost the state $80 to $100 million annually. Worse, there is an Erie Canal Commission that oversees the expenditure. The

Erie Canal advocates claim there is valuable developable land along the canal. Our analysis, however, concluded that few parcels had any economic development potential except for recreational purposes. The canal's sole benefit was a source of water for agriculture and industry along its length. The commission doesn't charge for the use of this resource.

It is obvious that the Erie Canal Commission should be combined with the New York Turnpike Authority so that, among other productivity gains, the canal workers, when idle in the winter, might help clear the roads of snow. Despite the fact that the canal and turnpike workers are represented by two different unions, bringing these agencies together seemed possible. No one in the governor's office, however, was willing to focus on negotiating an agreement. So the Erie Canal flows on, costing the citizens money that New York doesn't have.

Bureaucratic conundrums abound. The state's primary protector of the environment is the Department of Environmental Protection. Yet, for reasons no one in government understands or remembers, responsibility for coastal management resides with the state's Department of State, an agency located far inland and lacking the practical knowledge of conditions that you'll find in individual towns and cities along the Atlantic shoreline. I knew from firsthand experience the difficulties this illogical situation can cause. Our house on Swan Cove on Hook Pond in East Hampton had a wooden dock built in 1937 when the house was constructed, and a forty-foot bulkhead. Both were badly deteriorated. In my efforts to rebuild these structures, I found myself in a bureaucratic game of ping-pong, made more amusing because I was at that time on a commission charged with recommending how to structure the environmental functions of the state.

I challenged the Department of State to define its responsibilities and to rationalize why it should continue to supervise coastal management. It had no answer. I then asked specifically why it thought it had responsibility for Hook Pond, clearly not a coastal site. The department head told me that it was the fiduciary for the federal government's corps of engineers, which was responsible for the pond.

I called the corps of engineers' New York office. The office denied it had any connection to Hook Pond, which it had trouble identifying. "Why would we ever have anything to do with an inland pond?" the corps official asked me.

"Would you put that in writing?" I asked.

"No," he answered. He couldn't do that.

Sometime during this period, as I spent money on environmental advisers who tried to fathom the state's objections to lowering our dock two feet so it was nearer the current water level and restoring a bulkhead, John McCarter stayed at our home. John had spent over a decade as the president of the Field Museum in Chicago, a major environmental organization. He was amazed that Albany bureaucrats would be nitpicking these modifications when East Hampton Village had no hesitation.

Eventually, I won the battle to restore the bulkhead.

In February 2013, after two years, the SAGE Commission issued a glossy report claiming credit for annual savings of $1.6 billion. The largest dollar savings were closing excess jails and a change in state employees' health care plans. It accomplished goals, such as modernizing licensing procedures, eliminating a few of the hundreds of supervisory boards and commissions, and creating a consolidated financial service agency. Derek Utter is still at work implementing recommendations. But the heralded reorganization of state government never happened. The governor never met with the commission in person, nor did he even have the courtesy to write a thank-you letter to those who served on it.

Meanwhile, months had passed since 2010. Then one Thursday, Larry Schwartz called to ask if I would be available the following Tuesday for an announcement of the tax commission. I said yes. More months passed. In October 2012, Schwartz called again. Would I be available the following Tuesday? Yes, I would. But again nothing happened.

My experience with the SAGE Commission should have alerted

me to the governor's lack of genuine interest in commissions, and if that wasn't enough, the months of delay certainly indicated tax reform was not a high priority.

Finally, in December 2012, Schwartz called with a third alert. Apparently, the governor was now under pressure to deliver on his promise in his January 2012 State of the State speech to appoint a tax commission. This time, there was no press conference. The governor merely issued a press release—not even an executive order—appointing the New York State Tax Reform and Fairness Commission. The commission's mandate was, on a revenue-neutral basis, to propose administrative and legislative reforms to the complex tax system.

The casual announcement was another ignored red flag. Schwartz named eight commissioners. I knew the commission's co-chair, Carl McCall, who was SUNY's chairman and had run for governor. The list oddly excluded Bob Wilmers, CEO of the M&T Bank, a major upstate employer whom I added.

The commissioners were the following:

- Thomas H. Maddox, the state commissioner of the Department of Taxation and Finance
- Dall W. Forsythe, former budget director, whom I knew when he worked for Carol Bellamy
- Alan D. Schwartz, executive chairman of Guggenheim Partners and former CEO of Bear Stearns
- James W. Wetzler, a former state tax commissioner
- James Parrott, chief economist for the Fiscal Policy Institute
- Deborah Wright, chairman, president, and CEO of Carver Bank Group
- J. Pat Barrett, an upstate Republican and chairman of the Olympic Regional Development Authority
- Robert G. Wilmers, chairman and CEO of M&T Bank

Subsequently, I asked Mayor Bloomberg to allow his Tax Commissioner David M. Frankel to join the commission. Discussing state tax policy without input from the city would limit the commission's effectiveness. I didn't clear the Frankel appointment with Schwartz.

Schwartz asked if we could deliver our report by March. When I said three months wasn't possible, he insisted. I told him that if he insisted, he should find another chairman. He told me that the governor knew he couldn't credibly do the commission without me.

We agreed that we would have short-term proposals by March and longer-term recommendations by late fall 2013.

We needed to examine administration of the tax code, particularly the property tax, and then each category of state taxation. Commissioner Mattox assigned Deputy Commissioner of Tax Policy and Analysis Robert D. Plattner as our staff director. Plattner, however, would not allow us to call him executive director, another tipoff to the administration's commitment. Despite Plattner's initial reluctance, he and his staff completed comprehensive analyses of each of the tax categories, except the one analyzing business incentives. The analyses are appended to the commission's final report and might be the most important and lasting impact of the commission.

Envision this bizarre situation: a commission established by press release with no budget and with a staff wanting to keep its distance. We were set up to fail. I had experienced the limp results of the SAGE Commission, and I was not going to be co-chairman of a failed tax commission.

In the merger business, process determines result. We set a rigid schedule of meetings, featuring monthly full commission meetings for two hours in our offices at 1345 Avenue of the Americas. Every Monday morning at eleven o'clock, we had a conference call, including Andrew Sugrue of my office, Plattner, Michael Hyman, the New York City tax commissioner, sometimes Co-chair McCall, and Marilyn Rubin.

The state code is incomprehensible, opaque, and unfair, partially because of its exemptions and its antiquated definitions.

Personal income taxpayers have to make up to eighty modifications to their adjusted gross income (AGI). There are 154 exemptions to the state's sales/use tax. There are close to $2 billion of tax incentives and tax credits to businesses annually. Definitions of banking, communications, and utilities ignore regulatory changes, market forces, and technological advancements. The sales tax uses such antiquated terms as "soda fountains" and "grocery stores." The same product is taxed or exempt, depending on where it is bought or consumed. The iconic New York bagel is exempt from sales tax—unless it is sliced, in which case it is taxed. Different counties have sales taxes on different goods and services.

New York State ranks as the worst business environment, and its citizens are among the most heavily taxed. In the state fiscal year of 2012–2013, the state and local government levied about $146 billion in taxes. The code taxes every aspect of personal and business life, including personal and business income, the purchase of goods and services, estates, taxes aimed at specific transactions, and taxes disguised as fees. The state also oversees property taxes imposed by counties and localities. Separate entities, such as New York City and Yonkers, have their own taxes and taxing authorities.

By March, our analysis was too premature to make a substantive proposal. The sole substantive proposal was elimination of a tax return filing for about three hundred thousand low-income residents. Unpredictably, Parrott and other progressives objected, worrying that the taxpayers would be lost in the system and would not receive their earned income tax credit (EITC).

Carl McCall and I insisted on an extensive outreach effort in Buffalo, Long Island, Westchester, and the city. We solicited letters from public officials. Despite our frequent extra meetings, our commission had no leaks and, partly as a result, no press coverage. We felt like a stealth commission. The press was either incredibly lazy and uninterested, or they viewed the commission as irrelevant.

The commission did not address the state's spending. New York State's high taxes are driven by the high level of spending. It is worth noting that to reduce taxes beyond a certain point requires tighter controls on spending.

Property taxes represent about $50 billion or 40 percent of the total taxes paid to the state and local tax authorities. New York State is one of three states that lack a standard for property assessment. Most states reassess every three or five years. New York reassessments are random. Citizens regularly and successfully contest their assessment because of ambiguity, and corporations are infuriated by being assessed at different amounts for the same class of property. The commission recommended that the state adopt the most common standard, namely 100 percent of market value.

The business community had worked for years with the state's Department of Taxation to modernize New York's corporate tax. Initially, I thought reaching agreement in this area was beyond our ability. Fortunately, I was wrong. Given the passage of Gramm-Leach-Bliley, we proposed the elimination of the distinction between banks and corporations and even got agreement on lowering the corporate tax rate. Today, that change in the business tax is the commission's most substantive accomplishment.

James Parrott initially opposed this apparent tax break for the banks and argued for revenue neutrality within corporate tax reform. An obvious trade was eliminating or curbing the state's business incentive programs.

Business incentives turned out to be a major bone of contention with the governor and to a lesser degree within the commission. New York State grants business incentives generously and with no accountability in terms of whether they created or retained jobs. There is no postgrant accounting.

Tax credits favor a few at the expense of most. The state has $2 billion of business incentives annually weighted toward the brownfields credit and $420 million of refundable tax credits for the film industry. About 5,500 corporations and twenty-four thousand individual taxpayers benefit from these incentives. By comparison, there are almost nine million individual taxpayers and six hundred thousand corporate taxpayers in New York State. The arithmetic is simple. If one eliminated corporate incentives used by fewer than 1 percent of tax filers, the state could lower all corporate taxes for 100 percent of the filers by 30 percent.

The credits are so abused that, until a modification, the Ritz Carlton in White Plains was the largest beneficiary of the brownfield credits.

Another large user in New York City was an Ikea furniture store in Brooklyn. In neither case was the remediation of groundwater or soil remediation a major part of the cost. Outrageous examples are endless. Comcast received $25 million in cash for moving Jimmy Fallon's talk show to New York City. It is unlikely he was going to Indiana.

Worse, these credits are refundable, meaning the state writes a check. I told the governor in one of our few meetings that refundability makes the tax credit program a spending program, and they should be included in the executive budget. Bob Megna, the budget director, told the governor I was correct.

From the start, I forewarned Larry Schwartz that the commission would inevitably conclude that credits were too numerous, complicated, and costly. Our final proposals didn't, in fact, eliminate credits but curbed them and recommended ways to audit their value by creating and retaining employment. The commission asked the Tax Department's staff under Plattner to do analyses of each tax. Under instructions from Tax Commissioner Maddox and, obviously, the governor's office, the Tax Department refused to do a study of tax credits.

With the lukewarm approval of my fellow commissioners, I hired Marilyn Rubin and Dan Boyd, a well-respected economist from Rockefeller Institute, to do a study of incentives. No foundation—even the Rockefeller Foundation—would underwrite the $100,000 cost, afraid as they were of bucking the headwinds coming from the second floor of the Capitol. Ultimately, Pete Peterson and our family foundation paid for the study.

The report confirmed our worst suspicions. When it came time to print the commission's final report, the state refused to include the Rubin-Boyd study. I warned Schwartz and Megna that they were laying the groundwork for an unnecessary controversy, but they insisted. I also told them that I would publish it on my firm's website, which I did. Sure enough, when the commission's final report was issued, the principal focus was on why the Rubin-Boyd Report was not included.

Nowhere is the state's tax code more capricious than in the area of sales tax. New York State collects $11.3 billion from its sales tax of

4 percent. This tax is, of course, in addition to local taxes. The sales tax has not kept pace with consumer spending. In 1960, the New York State sales tax was equal to 45 percent of personal income. By 2004, the amount was reduced to 33 percent, and by 2011, it was 28 percent. There are many good reasons to broaden the sales tax and to eliminate a number of ridiculous exemptions. The tax receipts of the state are more volatile because of the overweighting of the personal income tax versus the sales tax. The sales tax contributes 18 percent of the total tax revenues, as opposed to most states, where it is 25 and 35 percent.

Traditionally, sales taxes are generally viewed as regressive, taxing the poor disproportionately. But taxing services is not as regressive. And as incomes grow, the tax on higher-end goods means the wealthier are carrying a greater share. The commission's proposals to extend the sales tax to more services would increase the state's tax revenues by an estimated $1.5 billion from consumers and $300 million from businesses.

Underscoring the sales tax issue, research showed that of the total $3.2 billion the state annually forgoes in revenues as a result of these tax exemptions, only $900 million—less than one-third—benefits households earning under $50,000, while households earning in excess of $100,000 reap $1 billion in tax savings. Thus, contrary to common opinion, exemptions and exceptions subsidize higher-earning taxpayers. It is also easy to credit lower-income taxpayers for any increases in sales tax.

The largest exemption to the sales tax is food, but even we didn't have the nerve to suggest taxing food. We did, however, recommend the elimination of the clothing exemption arbitrarily pegged at $110. This exemption started in 1997 in response to competition from New Jersey. Over the years, it has been raised and lowered and occasionally replaced by sales tax–free days. There is no data to verify its effect. I questioned Karen Hoguet, a senior executive at Macy's, and other retail friends, asking how much they valued the exemption. While they all preferred the status quo, none could justify it. Meanwhile, the clothing exemption alone reduces state revenues by $800 million annually.

We offered a simple solution to offset any additional burdens on lower-income residents by proposing that a portion of the additional taxes raised fund an expanded household credit to make whole all taxpayers below $100,000 in taxable income. But the legislature ignored the sales/use tax proposals, as has the governor. They are afraid that it will be viewed as a simple tax increase. It isn't, though, and the additional revenue could be offset by a reduction in other taxes such as the personal income tax.

The exodus of New York State wealthier citizens is a widely discussed phenomenon. Prior to the enactment of the Trump tax legislation in 2017, there did not appear to be a single reason for the flight. In fact, the data did not support an exodus to any single state, including Florida. On the contrary, there is data contesting the idea of a net migration. Witness the growth of New York City over the past decade. Still, even before the Trump tax law, New York State's relatively high personal income tax (PIT) and an estate tax (combined with cold weather) are undoubtedly two catalysts for flight.

The Tax Cuts and Jobs Act of 2017 exacerbates New York State's problems. Its principal sections as they apply to individuals, among other items, limit the deductibility of state and local taxes and cap property tax deductions at $10,000. The legislation, which clearly was aimed at more urban states and politically blue states, effectively and materially increases the tax burden of middle-class and wealthier taxpayers.

Over the course of time, the added burden, combined with embedded taxes and spending, will undoubtedly lower real estate values and increase the likelihood of richer taxpayers fleeing to less heavily taxed regions.

Our commission did not address the PIT because it was scheduled to be reduced. Given subsequent federal action, our conclusions would have been less relevant.

We did address the estate tax. The estate tax raises less than $1 billion annually from about ten thousand estates. The curious fact is that few taxpayers know their state tax rate, but everyone knows that New York State has an estate tax. It is one of only fifteen states with some sort of inheritance levy. We were able to convince progressives to recommend raising the exempt limit from $1 million to $3.5 million, which would exempt about 73 percent of the estates. Many middle-class estates are revalued at more than $1 million because of increases in home real estate values and the value of small businesses.

Governor Cuomo and the legislature jumped unexpectedly on this recommendation. Cuomo, in one of my two private meetings with him, Schwartz, and Megna, remarked that as he went around the state, he heard people more concerned about estate taxes. The legislature raised the estate tax exemption to $5 million but added a gift tax and left in a nonsensical "cliff" provision providing for only a $1 million exemption once an estate exceeds $5 million.

The Trump tax bill, however, enhances the federal estate and gift tax exclusions until 2025. As a result, New York is even more isolated, and the fact that it retains any tax will encourage residents to leave.

Our goal was to deliver the report in early November 2013, and we were on schedule to do that. Without notice, on October 2, the governor announced a second tax commission, the Tax Relief Commission, co-chaired by my co-chair Carl McCall and former New York governor Republican George Pataki. This commission was charged with recommending ways to reduce the state's property and business taxes, with its report due by December 6, 2013. Governor Cuomo established the new commission at a press conference without acknowledging the existence of our commission.

He appointed Dall Forsythe and Jim Wetzler from our commission, as well as my friend Billy Rudin. These commissioners told me that they were not forewarned of their appointment.

My first reaction was to dissolve our commission. I read the following statement to our commissioners:

> When we scheduled this meeting, I had expected
> to resign as co-chair of this commission. I believe and
> have conveyed to the governor personally, his associates
> and to many of you, that the establishment of the new
> commission demeaned this commission and its excellent
> work. I told the governor he had "thrown us under

the bus" in favor of a new commission that is clearly political in nature. The governor, in his announcement and press info kit that I have given you, redefined our mandate from his broad charge when he announced our commission in December to the narrow Simplification Commission.

Over the past three days, the governor has apologized to me for his clumsy handling of the announcement of the new commission. James, Alan, and others not on this new commission have been helpful in pointing out to the governor that, as I noted

to him, he had "stepped all over his own lead" and not helped himself.

Let me be clear. The governor appointed me and each of you. He can do whatever he wants with the commission but not with us or our reputations.

I am now convinced that the governor understands these issues. By demeaning our work and truncating our mandate with its objective and serious analyses and recommendations, he has hurt his own credibility. The governor is serious about tax simplification and a more equitable system which will create jobs.

I told him, as our commission has frequently discussed, that our goal is to provide a menu of ideas, demonstrating good tax policy free from folklore and mythology, to the State's political leaders and give them choices. By not waiting for the menu, the governor and the legislature will end up with the traditional smorgasbord of half-baked ideas.

The governor has recognized this issue. He has asked me to remain as co-chair as have other interested people, people who want to see our ideas, have them vetted publicly, and who want to see a product with all the excellent analyses the staff and you my fellow commissioners have done. They are afraid that without such a final report, our excellent work will vanish. According to the governor, this is his wish as well.

The governor and I have agreed that I will continue as co-chair. He asked that we deliver our report in mid-November in the Red Room in Albany to a public meeting. We will not deliver it at the same time as the second commission because we are not the step child of that commission. We are the parent. Separation is important for our credibility and for his.

The governor will further figure out how to redress the public relations aspects of his announcements.

We have done serious work. You have been excellent colleagues to me and Co-Chair McCall. The staff has worked well and diligently. While my instincts involving the integrity of this process initially pushed me in one direction, my discussions with the governor give me some assurance that, for whatever his reasons, he now is engaged and understands. To that end, he has told me that he plans to meet with our full commission to reassure you and me.

Thank you.

A number of people in the state government called me, underscoring that the governor had no interest in independence, and he was worried about our recommendations. I pointed out that if he was so worried, maybe he would have met with the commission, and furthermore, except for our criticism of the business incentive programs, there was nothing controversial about our consensus.

Once again, the commission members were supportive, and Kathy Wylde, president of the Partnership, begged me to continue. She argued that our modernization of corporate taxes, the proposals to simplify and eliminate antiquated definitions, broadening the sales tax, the estate tax reforms, and, perhaps most importantly, the tax research work, would all be lost if we disbanded the commission.

One reason we had been successful is that I strove diligently to listen to the views of all parties. I spoke frequently to E. J. McMahon, a conservative economist with deep experience in state issues. While we disagreed on certain things, his insights were important. Equally, James Parrott, the progressive commission member, helped me understand a number of practical issues that a lower-income resident would confront.

E. J. McMahon suggested that George Pataki visit me. He did, and it was one of the most bizarre meetings of my career. Pataki was shocked that a tax commission already existed, never mind that we'd been working for nine months. I also learned that the former governor had accepted the co-chairmanship with Carl without ever talking directly to Andrew Cuomo. Finally, Pataki said that he had a commitment from Cuomo that in this legislative session, he would recommend reducing the tax rate to 6.75 percent, the level when he left office in 2006.

That last revelation really got my attention. I told Pataki that the reduction of the PIT to that level would reduce tax revenues by up to $3.2 billion and that there was no way Cuomo would recommend this reduction. I said he must have misunderstood the governor.

Pataki said he was grateful for the meeting. He apparently was not the only one who didn't know there was already a commission. The esteemed *New York Times* carried the news of the McCall/Pataki commission without noting our work. In the end, this slapdash, politically motivated venture accomplished nothing more than obscuring our commission and most of its work. It made me wonder what possible motive Governor Cuomo could have had for his ridiculous behavior.

The final weeks of our commission were a nightmare. Bob Megna, who should have had better things to do, kept insisting that we employ glowing verbiage to describe Andrew Cuomo's heroic changes in the business environment and use other language irrelevant and inappropriate in the report of an independent commission. Ultimately, I told him that if the Cuomo administration did not approve the text as the commission members had written it, I would release the report myself on the internet. That threat worked, and he backed off.

Except for noting that the Rubin-Boyd study of business incentives had been excluded, the press mostly ignored our report. It had been an exhausting eleven months, during which about 40 percent of my time had been given to the commission. My commissioners and co-chair praised me for the process, the depth of research, outreach, and the consensus we reached. Rob Plattner tells me periodically that we made great contributions and more will happen. All commissioners signed our report, unlike that of the McCall/Pataki commission, which Pataki himself refused to sign because Cuomo double-crossed him on the promise to recommend the tax reduction.

Andrew Cuomo remains a mystery to me, his staff, and, perhaps, to himself. He genuinely believes that taxes are too high and regulations too complex. He wants to simplify and restructure government. He wants to appoint commissions to examine important issues. But he has no follow-through. He has little ability to relate to his staff or to people he asks for help. He is alone. He has no interest in other people's opinions. He establishes dozens of commissions, then turns his back on them. His mind is quick, but his look is fierce. His mouth may smile, but his eyes don't. He wants to be president, but he can't say thank you.

CHAPTER 37

2008: Did We Learn Anything?

How far have we come since 2008 in terms of fixing the problems that caused the financial crisis? Sadly, not very. For all that has been written and said about Wall Street and despite more restrictive legislation and supposedly rejuvenated regulators, finance remains an industry that challenges control.

The incident of the London Whale illustrates what I meant in 1989 when I said, "I didn't want my reputation or net worth dependent on people I scarcely knew trading securities I barely understood in times zones I rarely visited." Simply put, Jamie Dimon, the chief executive of JPMorgan Chase, acknowledged as an outstanding executive, in the spring of 2011–12 was not aware that his employees in London were violating his bank's procedures and rules. That lapse caused a loss of $6.2 billion.

The facts revealed by the Senate Permanent Subcommittee on Investigations, chaired by Carl Levin with John McCain as ranking minority member, are appalling. In 2006, JPMorgan—the world's largest financial holding company and derivative dealer—established what it called its synthetic credit portfolio (SCP). The initial purpose was to invest the bank's $350 billion of excess deposits. In 2011 alone, the notional value of its derivative holdings grew from $4 billion to $51 billion. In the first quarter of 2012, the notional value exploded to $157 billion.

Testifying before the subcommittee, Dimon said that the role of the SCP portfolio "morphed into something that rather than protect the firm, created new and potentially larger risks." That "morphing," it should be noted, took place under the direct supervision of the bank's chief investment officer as well as its chief financial officer, both of whom were vice chairmen. All trading firms have risk parameters, one measure of which is risk-weighted assets (RWA). In December 2011, senior management instructed the chief investment officer to reduce its RWA to enable the bank to meet its regulatory capital requirements.

But as the report of the subcommittee revealed, rather than dispose of the high-risk assets in SCP, the chief investment officer launched a trading strategy that "called for purchasing additional long-term derivatives to offset its short derivatives and lower the chief investment officer's RWA in that fashion." In other words, this person charged with holding down the bank's risk level was doubling down—with Morgan's money—like one of those extreme high rollers that casinos call a "whale." The trading strategy "eliminated the hedging protections that the SCP was originally supposed to provide."

Wall Street by then had developed techniques for valuing risk that gave the illusion of solidity but in reality were neither absolute nor entirely accurate. The so-called VaR, or value at risk, measured risk with 95 percent accuracy. The bank used VaR and four other metrics; even if they were in combination accurate, the SCP breached its limits 330 times in the first four months of 2012.

As the portfolio increasingly lost value in 2012, the chief investment officer "deviated from the valuation practices it had used in the past to price credit derivatives." One of the problems with derivatives is accurate pricing. Typically the bank and other financial institutions used the midpoint in daily prices in the marketplace. But starting in the first quarter of 2012, JPMorgan's chief investment officer began "to assign more favorable prices." To illustrate the lack of controls, it wasn't until April when the press began to report on the huge trades in London that the bank caught the change in pricing. Management also noticed that the chief investment officer and the bank's investment bank assigned "different values to identical derivative holdings."

JPMorgan noted the favorable pricing policies in an internal memorandum in May, but it took a month to review internal communications and determine that the employees had not acted in "good faith." Due to this discovery, JPMorgan restated its earnings in July, but not because it now realized the losses were much higher. In fact, in this enormous financial institution, a loss of an additional $660 million wasn't "material," JPMorgan said in a July 2012 press release. It noted that the actions taken by the chief investment officer didn't violate bank policy or generally accepted accounting rules; rather, the bank made the change because of the lack of "good faith" shown by the traders. What a ridiculous statement.

During this period, CEO Jamie Dimon continued to call the Whale's actions a "tempest in a teapot." It took months for him to acknowledge management failures.

The conclusions of the subcommittee summarized the situation but should alert the world at large that there is little doubt these large, complex institutions will continue to be plagued by unexpected losses because of size, geographic dispersion, and management inadequacy. The story of the Whale may be a story of rogue traders. But the system creates and rewards executives who take risks with other people's money.

In the case of the Whale, the office of comptroller of the currency was in the dark until most of the damage was done and exposed by others. It claimed it was supplied with inadequate and opaque information, but the subcommittee charged it with a lack of oversight. In conclusion, the subcommittee wrote the following:

> The Morgan Whale trades provide a startling and instructive case history of how synthetic credit derivatives have become a multi-billion dollar source of risk with the U.S. banking system. They demonstrate how inadequate derivative valuation practices enabled traders to hide substantial losses for months at a time; lax hedging practices obscured whether derivatives were being used to offset risk or take risk; risk limit breaches were routinely disregarded; risk evaluation

models were manipulated to downplay risk; inadequate regulatory oversight too easily dodged or stonewalled; and derivative trading and financial results were misrepresented to investors, regulators, policy makers; and the tax-paying public, who when the banks lose big, may be required to finance multi-billion-dollar bailouts.

JPMorgan Chase was fined $1 billion. In response, the board fired members of senior management, including a vice chairman, and reduced Jamie's bonus.

The dance continues. In 2013, a number of banks were fined for their rigging of the London Interbank Offered Rate (Libor), the rate at which banks settle among themselves on a daily basis. Apparently, for years a number of banks had been fixing the rate to the advantage of banks and to the disadvantage of investors. Despite all the increased regulation and heightened security, both in the US and abroad, traders manipulated a basic instrument of finance, one with supposedly little complexity and much transparency.

More fraud ensued. In late 2014, banks, led by Citi and JPMorgan Chase, were fined for fixing currencies. Another day, another several billion dollars. Neither the CFTC nor the OCC noticed these violations.

In 2016, it was revealed that at Wells Fargo, viewed as a conservative, well-run bank with Warren Buffet as a shareholder, thousands of employees had created 2.1 million unauthorized retail accounts to meet aggressive quotas. A year later, documents indicated that Wells Fargo had charged more than eight hundred thousand customers with interest on auto loans they neither needed nor agreed to purchase. The SEC failed to catch these abuses.

Goldman Sachs, in 2019, is facing criminal charges both in Malaysia and the US in connection with a scandal known as 1MDB.

What lessons did I learn from the 2008 crisis and from nearly six decades of advising and investing during multiple crises?

First, paraphrasing President Kennedy's comments about a rising tide raising all boats, in the case of an ebb tide, they all get stranded.

Every company got hurt in 2008. The difference between more and less important crises is extent and duration. A big crisis such as 2008 and a big crisis in a company or in a city takes longer than anticipated until recovery. I think in terms of a minimum of seven years, although more recent studies point to ten years.

In terms of private investing, the Great Recession differed from normal crises in that diversification of investments provided limited protection against loss. One reason is the increased linking of assets and investments in the global economy. The values of investments are now affected by investment decisions made by investors in other asset categories. For example, we know today that actions such as equity and debt hedges, inclusion in baskets of securities, and the syndication of loans to unregulated hedge funds will affect the value of a single investment.

One notable example of an exogenous action affecting value occurred in the 1987 crash, when the Harvard endowment and a small number of other institutions sold so-called insurance. The uncoordinated but simultaneous actions are chronicled in the Brady Commission report written by Bob Glauber.

Second, financial crises are endemic to the financial system. In my career, we have had a number, starting with a massive sell-off in the equity markets in 1962. By experiencing these traumas, I have learned that it is better to remain calm and make no quick investment decisions. While it may sound Pollyannaish, if you have faith in the US economy, neither the economic threats of OPEC nor the collapse of Lehman Brothers will, in the longer term, disrupt growth in the value of assets.

Third, there are few consistently good stock pickers. Without one of those advising you, you are better in index funds.

Marvin Schwartz is a famous investment adviser at Neuberger Berman. In 2004, I invested with him, and as the financial crisis deepened, I asked him to take me out of all financial investments, one being AIG. Marvin assured me he knew everything about AIG. So the fourth moral is that even the best stock pickers fall in love.

Fifth, I have a rule about investing. If you can't explain an investment to an eleven-year-old girl, don't invest. I say girls because anyone with daughters knows they question everything. Sons just shrug. Susan suggested a number of times that I invest with Bernie Madoff, as many of her friends had done. After I met with an investor with Madoff in the early 2000s, I told Susan I hadn't the foggiest idea how Madoff made money. It took a decade for Susan to stop thinking I was a bit slow.

The same need for clarity and steadiness; the ability to question your knowledge and logic; and the need to acknowledge and act on facts, not opinion or preconceived biases—all these are relevant as well to our business of advising corporate clients.

Crises in business, government, and philanthropy test your mettle. Experience gives you the courage to understand the dangers but remain as calm as possible and create positive responses.

The collapse of Lehman and disruption at other investment banks in 2008, and the success of smaller, independent investment banks combined to spawn more than three hundred new boutiques. I said, only half-joking, that many people must have said, "If Peter Solomon can do that, I can too!" A number of independent firms became publicly owned and have grown, using financial engineering to convert annual banker compensation into capital gains. It is an attractive recruiting vehicle as long as the firm grows.

The financial crisis did not change the ethos or culture of PJSC. PJSC remains client-centric. We have always been unambiguous and straightforward about whom we work for and what we feel comfortable doing. This has served us and our clients well, while the conflicts and self-interest of our larger competitors remain on front pages weekly.

CHAPTER 38

Moving On

Management succession is critical to sustained vitality. In 1989, I thought I would continue for a decade and then, in my early sixties, leave for another career. As it turned out, after thirty years, I was still working and enjoying the business. But tempus fugit, and I worried about the competitive strength of our firm.

Like many founders, I didn't want to retire. Pete Peterson, at eighty-nine, warned me about retirement. I enjoy the intellectual challenges of the business. I still liked taking business trips, although age changed the nature of my business travel; where once I had visited a city for several days, calling on companies and clients and otherwise seeking new business, I now make targeted calls. Fewer of my contemporaries are working. Prospects wonder why a presumably successful senior banker is calling on them as if he had nothing better to do.

For at least fifteen years, I had worked on a succession plan. A founder owes his colleagues a successor. The social contract stipulates that they give you their loyalty, and for that, you owe them careers. My hopes for a longer-term relationship with Credit Lyonnais had come to naught. I realized that my partners would neither have the money nor the gumption to buy my interests at a fair market value. Ironically, while our business requires the ability to determine value, when bankers become principals, their sense of fair value deserts them.

In 2015, I approached BNP Paribas, suggesting it buy a minority interest in PJSC. The conversations morphed into the proposal that

BNP merge its US and South American advisory businesses into PJSC and we own 51 percent of the combined operations. BNP was under regulatory pressure from the state of New York and the Federal Reserve and would eventually pay a $9 billion penalty, the largest in US history.

These discussions proceeded to the point where we had a negotiated transaction, but I had made a serious mistake. I had assumed that Alain Papiasse, one of the top four senior officers, had cleared the idea with the three other top officers of the bank. I had ignored my own experience—nothing is more bureaucratic than a French institution. French history celebrates revolts against institutions, but once a Frenchman gets into one of those institutions he railed against, he becomes the defender of the status quo. The deal collapsed.

During this period, our business continued. The fourth incarnation of the merger between Office Depot and Staples. Ken Berliner had taken over managing the account after I left the board. He had done a good job, and as a result of the proposed merger, he negotiated a $34 million success fee. Ken had been president of PJSC for thirteen years and had been with the firm for twenty-two years at that time. He was my presumptive heir and had made several attempts to buy control from me, but each attempt had failed when he balked at minor dollar amounts. I admired his tenacity as a banker and his commitment to the firm, but his harsh demeanor was not consistent with my view of our firm's culture. Despite my reservations, in the negotiations with BNP, I had insisted that Ken become CEO after the merger.

Often in life, circumstances resolve one's indecision. Ken insisted in an unfortunate manner on an amount of compensation stemming from the Office Depot proposed merger.

As a result, I made a decision that he wouldn't succeed me. He was welcome to remain at our firm, but he left in 2015.

∾

In May 2015, Susan and I were in Paris for our annual weekend on behalf of AFMO. Guy de Panafieu asked if I would meet with Laurent Mignon, the CEO of Natixis, a large French financial institution. Over the course of the next year, I negotiated a transaction that sold 51 percent ownership to Natixis and sold most but not all of my ownership and gave me a ten-year contract as chairman of the firm. From a strategic perspective, the transaction allowed our firm to expand its international reach, extend its financial services to financing for clients and particularly private equity firms, eliminate the issues of succession, create an attractive platform for new talent, and offer a large capital gains payout for my younger partners (with no cash investment).

The negotiation of the transaction was one of my most trying professional experiences. I didn't realize how hard it is to sell a business when one is the founder. Pete Peterson told me in 1989 to name the business Peter J. Solomon, saying my name is the "only thing going for me." (I think he meant it nicely.) It is a cliché that when one represents oneself, he has a fool for a client. I did represent myself but with able help from Bob Glauber, distinguished finance professor, senior adviser to our firm, and lifelong friend. The difficulty derived from the situation that I was simultaneously negotiating with Natixis and with my partners, represented by Marc Cooper and Ken Baronoff.

The Natixis negotiation centered on price and control. I had proposed to sell 25 percent of the firm for a certain amount. After initially agreeing to the price and the 25 percent, Laurent Mignon, Natixis CEO, changed course three months later, saying his accountants insisted he buy 51 percent immediately or, alternatively, have a three-year option to acquire another 26 percent to get to 51 percent. I dismissed the accounting dilemma and understood he wanted to hedge his investment. Frankly, while it complicated the deal, the two-stage purchase price was high, and I knew that once Natixis bought 25 percent, we would be in the driver's seat.

Nevertheless, my partners had legitimate worries about the ambiguity of the option and were sensitive to the fact that they and their colleagues wouldn't receive any proceeds from the initial sale.

I had retained nominal ownership of about 75 percent of PJSC. I had, over the years, expressed the thought—but not the commitment—that if we sold the business, I would take 50 percent of the proceeds. It was a thought I should never have expressed. The 50 percent was particularly irrelevant because Berliner had left the firm. He had always told me and his colleagues that his rightful proceeds would be 25 percent. Thus, the remaining partners should own no more than 25 percent.

On January 3, 2016, Cooper, Baronoff, and I flew to Paris to meet with Mignon and his head of banking, Marc Vincent. Fortunately, they had taken a liking to Cooper and, by that time, had done enough reference checks on me to feel comfortable with the firm.

I met with Laurent Mignon alone and told him that my partners were not comfortable with the option, but I preferred it. As he knew, I did not want to sell control of the firm in 2016, but I told him my colleagues would not agree to the option.

I asked how much value he ascribed to the option. He gave me an amount. Prior to the meeting, I reminded myself that I had contemplated a sale for fifteen years and the last dollar was less important than getting the deal done.

Planning helps define options and opportunities. At that moment, events had coalesced, and it was essential to capitalize on the timing. Berliner's departure removed a roadblock. The French would have been uncomfortable, and he would have limited my ability to give adequate ownership to our other partners.

It was the moment to act. I told Laurent I would lower my price by an amount larger than the amount he mentioned if he could not convince my partners to do this option alternative. In essence, I would give up my control premium to secure the support of my partners.

The final transaction seemed to please my partners and Natixis. I retained 46.5 percent of PJSC before selling 36.5 percent to Natixis for cash. My partners received 54.5 percent and sold 16 percent for cash. The total of 49 percent we collectively retained would be contractually acquired by Natixis in years six through ten at ten times earnings before taxes.

Equally important, we established a governance that has limits on Natixis' ability to operate PJSC for eight years. Laurent realized that most transatlantic acquisitions fail because the foreign bureaucracy eventually strangles the entrepreneurial spirit.

Pete Peterson emailed me that at no time had he ever seen a

deal where everyone said something nice and no one criticized the transaction.

The immediate question is, did I feel differently at the office having given up absolute control? Of course, but the positive side of different. My successors, Marc and Ken, are doing an excellent job. They have the qualities of leadership. I have relieved myself of the curse of the founder, that unmistakable dread that you are ultimately responsible for your colleagues and, particularly, for the staff that has put their trust in you. I have paid my last bonuses. But like a trained athlete, I cannot rid myself of the competitive urge to see which adviser represented the merged companies.

The partnership with Natixis is working well. Laurent Mignon and Marc Vincent are good partners. The combination is beginning to capitalize on opportunities to expand the reach of both firms. In addition, Laurent was promoted to chief executive of Natixis' parent company and has asked me to join its supervisory board.

಄

Byron Wien, a longtime friend, once said that I always had a punch list, and I did what was on the list. That was true. In my twenties, I, like many others influenced by visions of the Kennedy family, had dreamed of a successful business career, positions in government, maybe a political career, philanthropic impact, and a large and happy family.

The Solomons-Rabbs certainly had a similar clan with the three boisterous Rabb brothers in Boston. Mother had the same confidence, optimism, and humor. Two months before she died, Jim Solomon was reading to her as she lay almost comatose in her bedroom at 834 Fifth Avenue. The bands marching in the Columbus Day Parade blared. Jim said, "Ga (her nickname), can you hear the bands?"

She sat up, said, "You have to be dead not to hear that!" and lay down. Mother never said another word.

Mother made it especially clear that our strength emanated from the family. Until she died in 2006 at ninety-seven, she made sure family celebrations such as Susan's and my wedding and bar mitzvah celebrations were held in her apartment. My older brother, Richard, and I had always been close, sharing a bedroom growing up; I followed him to Camp Kennebec and every academic institution. When he and Ann moved to New York City with their sons, John and Jim, in 1969, our families melded as his sons became like older brothers to Joshua, Abigail, and Kate. They had stayed out of most trouble, avoiding drugs and other pitfalls plaguing middle-class New York kids. They went to good colleges and were hardworking. Despite two starter marriages, the five are responsible parents, and our families are enjoying a gaggle of grandchildren. When Susan and I married, her daughter, Laura, became Kate's best friend, and her son, Josh, blended into our family.

A highlight of family celebrations was Abigail's wedding. She was the last of the five siblings to get married. Having spent so much of her life on Martha's Vineyard, she had always envisioned a wedding in a Chilmark field on a bright sunny day. She was a beaming bride at Beetlebung Corner. We all have dreams, and as Laura said at her wedding in Vero Beach, a girl only starts planning her wedding at age four. We have few lasting goals in life, and to see a child fulfill one of their wishes is a parent's dream. My observation on parenting is the objective to get your children to age thirty alive. We accomplished that goal.

But life is fragile. In November 2010, I invited John Solomon to a panel discussion with the secretary of Homeland Security at the Council of Foreign Relations. John wrote a blog called "In Case of Emergency," a guide to what citizens should do to prepare for and survive emergencies of all sorts. John's blog was widely followed, particularly by professionals in his area of expertise. It surprised me that John was so well-known. While we were close and I consulted him on every article I wrote, he had a quiet life and career working from his home.

When John arrived at the panel discussion that evening, he looked wan, weak, and was sweating profusely. After the meeting, I drove him home and insisted that he see a doctor by the next day.

Saturday morning, Richard called with the shocking news that John had been diagnosed with acute myeloid leukemia (AML), a usually fatal disease. Where did this disease come from? It isn't hereditary. John was a strapping forty-five-year-old father of two girls. How could it be? Mother used to say that into every life a little rain must fall, but AML is a devastating monsoon.

John decided to be treated at Memorial Sloan Kettering, whose board I had joined several years earlier. He spoke to Laura Landro, who had survived CML leukemia and written of her experiences, and to our cousin Dr. David Livingston, a world-renowned cancer expert and former president of Dana Farber Cancer Institute.

AML is initially treated by chemotherapy with the hope of getting the cancer into remission. If the cancer returns, the modern practice is to perform a bone marrow transplant. Hopefully, the patient can find a donor with a bone marrow match. In John's case, none of our family could give John a perfect match. The risk of a bone marrow transplant is the body's rejection of the marrow and a subsequent condition, "graft versus host" disease, which destroys the body from within. John's transplant was in May 2011. He died that November.

His death was a devastating loss. Temple Emanuel was filled with mourners, including almost every member of his class at Collegiate where he'd been head boy. As I told the family at one point in John's treatment, this was a nightmare from which we will not awaken.

Did we make the right decisions about John's care? Ann felt with justification that the doctor who assured her and John of her devotion was not available for much of that critical summer after the diagnosis. A review of the medical attention concluded that everything possible had been tried. But I know from my business career that whenever you take a responsibility, you must be present. If you are not and something goes wrong, it is your fault. When people put their trust in you, you have to be there for them.

John's death changed our family forever. His widow, Abby, and two daughters, Sara and Rebecca, have rebuilt their lives. John would be proud of them. Ann and Dick don't go a day without thinking of their lost son. And I, too, rue my inability to save his life in an institution where I was and still am involved. What good is influence if it cannot be wielded in a life-and-death situation?

Getting older makes you reflect. My fiftieth Harvard reunion in 2010 had been a mixed experience. We went with my college roommate Marty Gross and sat with college friends. Three of those friends, including Marty, died in 2015 and 2016.

I often think about Ed Koch's determination to remain relevant. After he left public office, he kept reinventing himself with television shows, movie criticism, articles sent every other week to scores of friends and critics, and political agitation. A few years before his death, he began the New York Insurgency to provoke the state legislature and governor into better ethics laws and redistricting of the state's election districts. I helped finance the effort. Assembly Speaker Shelly Silver was blocking our efforts. Frustrated, Ed called me and said he needed $25,000 to purchase billboards, proclaiming, "Shelly Silver is a schmuck." For one of the few times, I said, "No!" I should have let him do it.

Ed had achieved his goal of staying in the conversation, even to the point that the movie *Koch* premiered several days before his death and was publicly released the day he died. What a wonderful way to go. At Ed's funeral at Temple Emanuel, I said to Diane Coffey that while Ed hated funerals because they weren't about him, he would have loved this one. It was *all* about him.

My determination to continue in business turned on the issue of relevance. While I have any number of interests, New York is ultimately a city of business. Once you give up a business position, you run the risk of being, as I once said, just another guy with money.

CHAPTER 39

Hannah and Her Cousins

When our oldest granddaughter, Hannah, was eleven, she picked up the manuscript of this book, flipped through to see if she could find her name, then declared there should be a chapter titled "Hannah."

Hannah is right. The legacy of a life well spent lies in the people and works they leave behind. As a grandfather having lived long enough to get his children to maturity, I wonder what my grandchildren will remember about me. And, of course, I wonder what they will become. What will their lives look like? What influence will I have had on them?

Victor Borge, the Danish comedian, said he had three children, one of each kind. With twelve grandchildren, we have personalities reflecting more than just the influences of Susan, me, or their other grandparents. And, surely, nature will dominate nurture.

When Monet painted his water lilies series at the end of his life, the edges of some of the paintings were left unpainted, revealing the canvas. In 1970, Mother had bought one of this series painted in 1919 near the end of Monet's life. It was her prized possession. Mother had been told by her dealer, Mr. Jennings at Knoedlers Gallery on Fifty-Seventh Street, that Monet had never finished the painting. Forty-two years later during a visit to a Monet exhibition in Paris at the Grand Palais, the audio guide explained that the water lily paintings with unpainted edges had, in fact, been left looking unfinished because

460

Monet wanted to give a sense of a life not finished. The curator of the exhibition explained that Jackson Pollack, in his drip paintings, was influenced by Monet. Jackson's paintings are denser in the center of the canvas, becoming sparse as they reach the canvas's edge. Both artists give a sense of possibilities spilling beyond the confines of these particular works.

At eighty, I am not in this memoir writing a postscript to a life. I have tried to sketch a fresco of a life in process, like the creations of Monet and Pollack (but without their genius). It is a purposely incomplete canvas.

Because I was secure about my roots, my journey has been easier. While I have never known the specifics of where I was going, I have never had any doubts from whence I came. Sense of family gave me the security to be optimistic and confident. I never felt that life owed me a living, because my parents and grandparents never assumed life owed them anything. Equally, I never felt guilty about what material wealth or positions I was able to achieve, which may have been facilitated, but not assured, by birth or material possessions. I could see as my life transpired that many contemporaries with the same advantages, materially or socially, did not seem to have similarly progressed. I reconciled myself to the reality that others might attribute anything I achieved to my advantages, as Ed Koch did when he hissed at me, "I don't care if you say you are poor and Polish. To me, you will always be rich and German."

My legacy to Hannah and her eleven younger sisters and cousins (Julia, Madeline, Rush, Seka, Solzy, Rachel, Benji, Jake, Jasper, Oliver, and Becky) and their parents (Joshua, Abigail, and Kate Solomon, Josh Rebell and Laura Gross and their spouses), then, is simple. It is a sense of their roots, family solidarity, and the knowledge of where they have come from, so they, too, will have the security to choose wisely where they go.

Retiring is not taking the step of not working at a job full-time or not going to an office. Retiring is the loss of curiosity. It is distancing oneself from the challenges of society and, by that distance, becoming less relevant. If Eric Erickson says the last stage of life is the tension between despair and generativity, relevancy is a key to vitality in my last decades.

Fortunately, the fabric of my life has left untidy threads. In retailing, the industry is in a seminal moment where disruption may be without precedent. Too much selling square footage, multichannel distribution, a more informed and mobile customer, rising costs of health care, and the need to invest in technology systems are just four of the factors coalescing in the second decade of the twenty-first century.

For me intellectually, the turmoil in the distribution industries is exciting. What services and formats will emerge? How long will the preferences of the millennium generation continue to be the predominant influence? What will be the values of the next generation?

For PJSC, turmoil is a boon. If we maintain our standards and competitive position, the opportunities to advise managements on strategic decisions will abound.

❧

Spencer Hays was a smooth-talking salesman from Garrison, Texas. Ken Baronoff had cultivated him as a PJSC client. Spencer owned four private enterprises, each built around personal selling. The businesses probably had an aggregate value of $750 million. Ken asked me to meet Spencer, and, over several years, he learned of our apartment in Paris and our interest in art. Spencer and his wife of sixty years had accumulated the largest collection of Nabis art, the period in French painting from 1890 to 1905 represented by painters Bonnard, Vuillard, Redon, Sérusier, and Gaugin.

Spencer had ambitions for the American Friends of the Musée d'Orsay (AFMO) and its related institution, Musée de l'Orangerie. Oddly, unlike the Louvre, Pompidou, and nearly every institution in Paris, the Orsay had no "Friends" group even though it is the most popular museum for American tourists.

Given our apartment in Paris and the fact that, at the time, I didn't have a business connection with a French bank, I thought chairing a Paris charity might give more purpose to our time in Paris. I agreed to lead the group but only if Susan would enjoy it and become co-chair. I also hoped, in gratitude, Spencer would give PJSC his businesses to sell.

It may be harder to build a not-for-profit than a business, particularly one based on another continent. We had to define our mission and provide the raison d'être for Americans to support a foreign charity. Potential supporters would most likely own a home in France, have a French spouse, or have an interest in art, hopefully French.

It took five years for us to overcome the indifference of the museum's administration on whose behalf we were working, but eventually we were able to create an active American Friends' organization supporting acquisitions at the Orsay.

Concurrently, Spencer Hays was contemplating donating his collection of three hundred Nabis paintings to the Orsay. It would be one of the most important collections given to the French nation. Spencer insisted that the Orsay commit to hanging the bulk of the collection permanently, and, at my urging, the museum acquired a building, freeing space within its existing galleries.

American tax law allows a living American to get a tax deduction for a gift to a foreign entity only if the item is first given to a US 501 (C) (3) not-for-profit organization. An estate donation, on the other hand, can be given directly and receive tax benefits. Spencer planned to use both methods.

Negotiations became sticky. Spencer wanted to use AFMO as the donation conduit, but AFMO could not take possession even for a short period of time. It couldn't afford to insure the art or curate it, as required by the IRS. France, before announcing the gift, insisted that Spencer and Marlene sign an unequivocal pledge that, regrettably, would trigger a US tax. Obviously, Spencer would not sign such a pledge.

With two weeks to go before the October 22 signing, the French government had not budged. Spencer called me in despair. I told him that we would involve Jennifer Franklin, a skilled not-for-profit lawyer at Simpson Thacher & Bartlett, who had represented Leonard Lauder on his gift of Cubists to the Met. Jennifer devised an acceptable agreement, and the signing occurred with pomp and circumstance before Ambassador Jane Hartley and 250 AFMO supporters in the Elysee Palace. President Francois Hollande awarded Spencer and Marlene the Commandeur of the Legion d'Honeur.

Susan and I had achieved AFMO's goals, and we turned the chair over to Spencer and Liz Kehler. We had gotten close to raising $1 million annually, had almost three hundred members, completed ten projects, and created a closer relationship between AFMO and its museums.

Spencer died suddenly from an aneurism in March the following year at his New York City apartment at age eighty-two. Fortunately, he lived to see his and Marlene's gift hailed in France and the US. As Susan commented, his obituary reflected his philanthropy and not just his business success.

❧

Giving away money thoughtfully can take a lot of time.

In 1993, I established the Solomon Family Scholarship Fund at Harvard College. Over twenty-five years, ninety undergraduates have received three years of financial aid from this fund. The recipients have achieved prominence in science, medicine, academia, public policy, business, and law in the US and abroad.

For Susan and me, an important aspect of the program is our interaction with current undergraduates and graduates. We host an annual dinner in Cambridge with past and present Solomon Scholars, smaller events in New York, and maintain contact with graduates throughout the world, helping them with their personal and professional issues.

We plan to expand our interaction, and to this end, at the request of the scholars, we established an exclusive Facebook page so they can network with one another. It appears that at Harvard, as elsewhere, there is tension between the loneliness of the digital world and the need to connect. We hope to bridge this gap.

I had been reluctant to join a hospital board since Mt. Sinai and my stint as chairman of Health and Hospitals. But science and issues surrounding cancer have intrigued me. When Dick Beattie suggested I join the board of Memorial Sloan Kettering, I accepted.

John's illness and subsequent death intensified my commitment to cancer research. When I learned that blood cancers were underfunded relative to breast, lung, and other more well-known cancers, Susan and I decided, in connection with MSKCC's resources, to fund a genomics program to look for genetic mutations in patients with different blood cancers. In the short term, our funding led to rapid, cost-effective mutational studies for MSKCC patients with AML and other forms of leukemia. In fact, not only did the studies increase the speed and accuracy of diagnosis, they reduced the cost.

Under the direction of Dr. Marcel van den Brink, head, Division of Hematologic Oncology, and Dr. Ross Levine, a protégé of our cousin, Dr. David Livingston, MSKCC has invested in innovative technologies that have led to discovery and translational research in blood malignancies.

We cannot get John back, but the research and clinical work we are funding is helping others stricken.

For 35 years, I have been a trustee of the American Museum of Natural History. During that period, President Ellen Futter's vision has propelled the museum into new areas of science, education and exhibition.

My dream had always been for the museum to create an insectarium, an exhibition space devoted exclusively to 80 percent of known species. In 2016, the museum embarked on a major expansion. Earlier, we had established the Solomon curator in entomology. Susan and I agreed to fund a new insectarium located at the entrance of the new building.

I had hoped that David Rockefeller, a beetle collector, might endow the insectarium. But David never forgave the museum that, forty years earlier, had lost his childhood beetle collection by idiotically returning it to him by mail. I sent David a handwritten letter in 2017 inviting him to the opening three years hence. He died before responding.

We are involved in the content of the insectarium, pushing the designers to include live bugs, food composed of insects, connections with the museum's collections, research, and expeditions, and using virtual reality to put visitors inside hives and nests.

Beyond our philanthropy, our children have pursued their interests, from education and social welfare to the environment and religious organizations. Their commitments are a legacy as meaningful as our own projects.

❧

I had not given up on my ambition to increase my involvement in political life. I had hoped that the New York State Tax Commission and the Sage Commission would lead to more involvement. For reasons I explained earlier, this did not happen.

While I deplored the impact of money in political campaigns, I had decided to test effectiveness of targeting support.

In 2008, with John Eastman, we evolved a plan to focus on electing US senators from states where two hundred thousand votes won. Because of my relationship with Rock Ringling, executive director of the Montana Land Reliance, and my ownership of a ranch in McLeod, Montana, our first candidate was Jon Tester, a Montana State senator.

Jon won and has been reelected twice. In 2018, he won despite repeated campaign visits by Trump to Montana. We also supported Mark Begich, the mayor of Anchorage, Alaska, who beat incumbent Ted Stevens but lost in 2014.

The issue of partisan politics is a central issue in our political discourse. The Far Left and Right backed by extreme groups are terrifying congressmen, threatening incumbents with well-financed primaries.

In the House of Representatives, because of gerrymandering, only about thirty seats are open to either Republicans or Democrats. Thus, to change the composition of the House and eliminate extremists, we need to focus on the primaries, which, in most districts, are tantamount to election.

I analyzed the spending of all 435 primary and general election races in 2012 and decided that with approximately $300,000 per race, one could change the outcome of many primaries.

During a speech at John's Island Club in 2014, I mentioned my plan to fund moderate candidates in primaries. Unexpectedly, a member in the audience suggested that I contact No Labels, a then new political group formed to foster bipartisan behavior in Congress.

I have been working with No Labels since that time. In 2016, together, we supported moderate Republican and Democrat primary candidates in Kansas and Florida who won and went on to be elected. In 2018, we intervened in a number of primaries with more successes than failures.

During the 115th Congress, we encouraged the formation of the bipartisan caucus "Problem Solvers" of forty-eight representatives equally divided between the parties. The caucus had limited results translating its bipartisan agreements into law because of the power of the Speaker to control the legislative calendar and to discipline members who do not toe the party line. Partially in desperation, No Labels began a campaign to change the rules of the House.

In the 116th Congress, the election for Speaker was contested because of the emergence of a revitalized Left Wing of the Democratic Party. Josh Gottheimer, the Democrat co-chairman of the Problem Solvers, delivered nine crucial votes to Pelosi and was able to obtain her agreement to support critical parts of the No Labels' agenda. The most important change, known now as the consensus calendar, states that if there are 290 co-sponsors of a bill, it must go to the floor and be voted on.

Hopefully, the unprecedented achievement by the caucus will enable more bipartisan and moderate behavior. We need, as Senator Susan Collins told me, moderates to be more outraged than extremists.

The Trump presidency has agitated me more than I would have anticipated or wanted. I had interacted with Donald Trump frequently over the course of our lives in New York. For decades, I said that Donald lied as a matter of course, but he didn't lie to deceive; his lies were always easy to disprove. He lied to distract and confuse. His lies were a tactic. Golfers often commented that he cheated in tournaments. And it was common knowledge in New York that, if you dealt with him, there was a likelihood that you might not get paid or might be sued. According to USA Today and Jim Zirin, before he took office, Trump sued or was sued 3,500 times. But Donald had a seductive flamboyance and always seemed to be in on the joke. He was good company if not a good partner.

When he ran for president, I dismissed him, but I also realized that voters might think his antics, insults, and out-of-the-usual political discourse statements were just campaign stunts and rhetoric and did not reflect the real Donald. But it was the real persona of Le Donald.

The Trump presidency is troubling and not principally because of domestic policies or his antagonism toward our Western Alliance. His embrace of the imperial presidency, his incivility, and the incessant barrage toward anyone or any institution who opposes him may have a lasting destructive impact on American society.

At lunch with Vernon Jordan in 2018, we reflected that we had seen worse times: 1968–1973, for example, during Vietnam, cities burned, leaders were assassinated, and two presidents quit. It took four well-meaning presidents—namely, Ford, Carter, Reagan, and Bush forty-one—to overcome the damage wrought. How long will it take this time?

❧

Every day remains an adventure. On my way to Monro's annual meeting in Rochester, I reflected with the taxi driver, a month to the day older than I, on the changes in that city over our lifetimes, encapsulating a number of trends common to our generation. The list included the flight of companies such as Eastman Kodak, Gannett, Bausch and Lomb, and Xerox, all of which I had called on at one point in my career. He remembered B. Foreman Company, the upscale department store where Dad had started his career in 1930. The driver hoped Rochester could replace the loss of manufacturing and arrest urban decay and drug use, issues I had dealt with in New York City three decades earlier. Despite the observations, he was optimistic, mentioning emerging employers Monro, Wegmans Supermarkets, and Paychex, each of which was thriving.

Successes and setbacks, setbacks and successes. One is an excuse for celebration, the other a chance for education. Months before he died at 106, Eric Newman whispered in my ear, "Keep going." The tale continues.

INDEX

Miranda Warning 370
Miron, Ken 335
Monet, Claude 460
Monro Muffler 210, 270-274, 293, 330,
   345, 376, 393, 406, 468
Moody's 159, 266, 366
Morgan Stanley 3, 34, 71, 239, 254, 255,
   259, 276, 295, 364, 385, 427
Moynihan, Brian 195, 427
Moynihan, Pat 18, 124, 191, 193,
   195, 198
Mr. Coffee 109, 110, 111
   Black & Decker 49, 110, 366
   Boston Consulting Group 110
   DiMaggio, Joe 110, 111
   Glazer, Sam 109
   Marotta, Vince 109, 110
Mt. Sinai Hospital 59, 114, 383
Murdoch, Rupert 225, 226
Murphy, Steve 101

N

Natixis 453-456
Neiman Marcus Group Inc. 395
Nelson, Bruce 342
Neuberger Berman 450
Newman, Andrew 345, 374
Newman, Eric 373, 468
Newman, Evelyn 373
New York Public Radio 411
New York State Tax Reform and
   Fairness Commission 434
   Barrett, J. Pat 434
   Boyd, Dan 438
   Business Incentives 435, 437,
   443, 445
   Corporate Tax 437, 443
   Estate Tax 440, 441, 443
   Forsythe, Dall W. 434
   Frankel, David M. 430, 434
   Hyman, Michael 435

Maddox, Thomas H. 434
McCall, Carl 434, 436, 441
Megna, Bob 438, 441, 444
Parrott, James 434, 437, 444
Plattner, Robert D. 435
Property Tax 134, 435, 436, 440
Rubin-Boyd Study 438, 445
Sales Tax 436, 438, 439, 443
Sugrue, Andrew 435
Schwartz, Alan D. 434
Tax Credits 81, 136, 435, 436,
   437, 438
Tax Cuts and Jobs Act of 2017 440
Wetzler, James W. 434
Wilmers, Robert 434
Wright, Deborah 434
New York Stock Exchange 15, 287,
   362, 376
New York Tax Relief Commission 441
New York Times 3, 123, 137, 147, 155,
   156, 157, 178, 187, 192, 201, 221,
   223, 414, 425, 444
New York Yankees' Fantasy Camp 298
   Blanchard, Johnny 299
   Ford, Whitey 298, 299, 300
   Guidry, Ron 139, 299, 300
   Mantle, Mickey 298, 299, 306
   Rivers, Mickey 299
Nicklaus, Jack 307
Nike, Inc. 396
Niven, Jamie 34
Nixon, President | Richard 73, 81
   Khrushchev, Nikita 5
No Labels 467

O

O'Brien, Bob 297
Ocean Beach Club 20, 23
Office Club, Inc. 337
Office Depot, Inc. 336-343, 359, 409, 453
OfficeMax 337, 339-341, 343

Z

www.ingramcontent.com/pod-product-compliance
Lightning Source LLC
Chambersburg PA
CBHW030411100426
42812CB00028B/2922/J